ON BEING UNFINISHED

ON BEING UNFINISHED

COLLECTED WRITINGS

Anne E. Patrick

Susan Perry, editor

ORBIS BOOKS
Maryknoll, New York 10545

ORBIS BOOKS
Maryknoll, New York 10545

Fathers and Brothers
MARYKNOLL™

Founded in 1970, Orbis Books endeavors to publish works that enlighten the mind, nourish the spirit, and challenge the conscience. The publishing arm of the Maryknoll Fathers and Brothers, Orbis seeks to explore the global dimensions of the Christian faith and mission, to invite dialogue with diverse cultures and religious traditions, and to serve the cause of reconciliation and peace. The books published reflect the views of their authors and do not represent the official position of the Maryknoll Society. To learn more about Maryknoll and Orbis Books, please visit our website at www.maryknollsociety.org.

Library of Congress Cataloging-in-Publication Data

Names: Patrick, Anne E., author. | Perry, Susan (Editor at Orbis Books), editor.
Title: On being unfinished : collected writings / Anne E. Patrick ; Susan Perry, editor.
Description: Maryknoll : Orbis Books, 2017. | Includes bibliographical references and index.
Identifiers: LCCN 2017018495 (print) | LCCN 2017040415 (ebook) | ISBN 9781608337200 (e-book) | ISBN 9781626982550 (pbk.)
Subjects: LCSH: Catholic Church—United States—Doctrines—History—20th century. | Christian ethics—Catholic authors.
Classification: LCC BX1751.3 (ebook) | LCC BX1751.3 .P38 2017 (print) | DDC 230/.2—dc23
LC record available at https://lccn.loc.gov/2017018495

CONTENTS

Foreword

Anne E. Patrick was a significant figure in Catholic moral theology. She was a Sister of the Holy Names of Jesus and Mary who taught theology at Carleton College in Minnesota for twenty-nine years. Patrick was the first feminist to be elected president of the Catholic Theological Society of America. Two other women had served as president before her, but they did not identify themselves primarily as feminists. The Catholic Theological Society also conferred on her its highest award—the John Courtney Murray Award. She also helped to organize the first meeting of the Woman's Ordination Conference in Detroit in 1975 and in that same year wrote an early article supporting the ordination of women in the Catholic Church. She continued to address this issue in later years.

An interesting story lies behind her election as president of the CTSA in 1989–90. On the surface she was an unlikely candidate. She had received her doctorate from the University of Chicago in 1982 less than ten years before she served as president of the organization that describes itself as "the principal association of Catholic theologians in North American and the largest professional society of theologians in the world." In addition, at that time there were a number of feminist theologians who had been writing in this field for a much longer time. She was actually elected vice-president at the 1987 convention and automatically became president later on. An important factor in her election was the brilliant plenary address she gave to the Society at the 1987 convention on the topic "The Linguistic Turn in Moral Theology." Here she showed a deep knowledge of philosophy and its consequences for moral theology. Her in-depth, well-written, and well-delivered address captivated her audience. In the subsequent election, the other candidate did not stand a chance. A number of us agreed, afterward, that it was unfair to have one candidate for president give a plenary address. If the candidate gave a brilliant talk, as Anne Patrick did, there was no doubt who would win the election!

A colleague at Carleton College described Anne as having a quiet but confident demeanor. In my judgment, she was truly a gentle woman but with a steel spine and a determined willingness to speak the truth to power. My description of Anne as gentle with a spine of steel brought back to me my dislike of the hymn entitled "Hail Mary, Gentle Woman." The description of Mary as a gentle woman seems to indicate that she was quiet and passive, but her Magnificat recounts the story of the one who did great things for her and put down the mighty from their thrones and raised up the lowly. In the light of my description and appreciation of Anne Patrick, if I were writing the words to a hymn like that, I would have to add to the word gentle the other adjective strong. Anne Patrick was both strong and gentle. She was not flamboyant; her rhetoric was never sensational; her disagreements were never personal; but she was a woman of strong opinions as she worked for change in the church and the development of moral theology.

In many ways, Anne Patrick's personal story well illustrates the developments in the Catholic Church from the pre–Vatican II times through Vatican II to the present. After graduating in 1958 from the Academy of the Holy Names (a college preparatory high school in Silver Spring, Maryland, run by the Sisters of the Holy Names of Jesus and Mary), she entered that religious community. At nineteen she found herself teaching grammar school in Florida like so many other religious sisters in those days. She had to work part time and in summers to get her BA degree in 1969 from Medaille College and her MA in English in 1972 from the University of Maryland. In the 1960s, she had no thought of being a professor of moral theology. At that time moral theology for all practical purposes existed only in Catholic seminaries and was taught by Catholic priests. She could never even have dreamed that she would teach theology at the very prestigious Carleton College in Minnesota founded by the Congregational Church and that she would retire from Carleton in 2009 as the William H. Laird Professor of Religion and Liberal Arts. She had to assume that her later vocation would continue to be a high school teacher in the schools run by her order.

Things, however, were changing. In this book she recalls a jolt in her own thinking when she read the *Pastoral Constitution on the Church and the Modern World* of Vatican II, which insisted on the full equality and equal dignity of women and men. This jolt opened up the way for her to embrace feminist thought. She had been teaching religion and literature in high school, and her Master's thesis at the University of Maryland in 1972 showed these interests—"Eschatological Perspectives in the Major Novels of Graham Greene." In that same year she entered the Divinity School of the University of Chicago in the program on religion and literature. However, during her time as a doctoral student at the University of Chicago she was also heavily involved in the work of church reform and the reform of religious life. In 1975, for example, she wrote an article calling for the ordination of women while still a graduate student at Chicago. During this time, she was also heavily involved in the reform of her own religious community—the Sisters of the Holy Names of Jesus and Mary. She received her Ph.D. from the University of Chicago Divinity School in 1982 with a dissertation on "H. Richard Niebuhr's 'Ethics of Responsibility': A Resource for Literary Criticism."

There is no doubt that her interest in English literature that developed while she was teaching in the 1960s had a great influence on her future academic interests. But a question arises. What more could she have done teaching and researching in moral theology if she had not taught in grammar and high schools for twelve years? In those days a patriarchal and sexist church did not think that religious women could teach theology.

Four essays in this book well illustrate her use of literature in support of moral theology. Many of the other essays in this book also frequently appeal to literary illustrations. Her literary interest also comes through in her own writing style. Moral theologians, myself included, usually have a very turgid writing style, but Anne Patrick wrote gracefully and in a clear, captivating manner. She worked hard on her manuscripts, constantly polishing them until she was satisfied. The quantity of her writing is not extensive. She wrote only three books, but the quality of her writing in these books and her many other essays is outstanding. In the final fourteen years of her life, Anne Patrick struggled with breast cancer, but in the last years she was determined to edit and polish the essays that appear in this book. With the help of her sister Mary and others she was able to finish this project shortly before she died in July 2016.

The profundity of her thought, the captivating writing style, and her creative imagination are present throughout the book. I was particularly taken by her essay "On Being Unfinished: *De Imperfectione*," which was originally an address to the graduates at the Carleton College Honors Convocation in 2009—after she herself had been diagnosed with breast cancer. These graduates had to be thinking of their goals for the future as they were leaving college. Most of us as Americans in the twenty-first century are constantly striving to reach our goals. Patrick recognized the importance of finishing our projects, but she also insisted that we should learn to appreciate beauty in the process itself. Her starting point for this poignant reflection is a painting that was hanging in her office: "Navajo Weavers" by Harrison Begay. The picture portrays two Navajo women weavers not quite half finished with a rug, which probably needed 180 more hours of work before it was completed. What captivated her in this picture is that the artist shows beauty in a project less than half finished. The artist wants us to appreciate that there is beauty even in the process of weaving. This expresses the Navajo spiritual ideal of walking and even working in beauty. In our world today we all need to learn to appreciate the beauty in the process of our walking and working and living and not only in our end products.

A good number of these essays deal with feminism, a topic she first addressed in the early 1970s even before she received her doctorate. Patrick has proposed a broad definition of feminism to indicate a position that involves a solid conviction of the equality of women and men and a commitment to reform society and the church so that the full equality of women is respected. Such an approach also involves reforming the thought systems that legitimate the existing unjust social order. The problem here is sexism, which manifests itself in patriarchy and androcentrism. Patriarchy involves social patterns of domination and superiority, while androcentrism sees women as so different from men that their roles are circumscribed or special.

Such an androcentrism is found especially in the Catholic Church. Pope John Paul II insisted on different gender roles for female and male and emphasized a special genius of women. Probably he meant this as a positive comment about the role of women, but such a position restricts women from certain roles such as priesthood. John Paul II accepted an approach that sees the role of women and men as complementary, but complementarity ultimately involves subordination for women. Feminists like Patrick describe this as "an essentialist" approach. How would men like it if all the leadership roles in the church were reserved to women!

Pope Francis at times definitely adopts an androcentric approach, and he has maintained that the restriction of the priesthood to males is not open to discussion. However, Patrick hopes that is not the last word. Francis has insisted on the need in the church for dialogue and set in motion reforms in the church calling for such dialogue. He has referred to preaching as "a mother's conversation." Patrick concludes that there still can, should, and will be change with regard to the ordination of women—a position she has maintained since 1975.

Anne Patrick's major contribution to moral theology is in the area of conscience as indicated by the titles of her three books—*Liberating Conscience: Feminist Explorations in Moral Theology* (1997), *Women, Conscience, and the Creative Process* (2009), and *Conscience as Calling* (2013). Many of the essays in this book also deal with conscience. Conscience before Vatican II was seen in terms of obedience to law. Patrick has insisted on the creative aspect of conscience.

In my judgment there are three roots in Vatican II that ground this move from obedience to creativity. First, Vatican II insisted on the vocation of all Christians to holiness. The story of the rich young man in the Gospel of Matthew well illustrates this change from obedience to creativity. The rich young man claimed that he had obeyed all these laws from his youth, but he could not accept Jesus' invitation to holiness and perfection. Those called to holiness must strive to grow in holiness, which calls for an active and creative response to the signs of the times in one's life and in all aspects of social life. In this book Patrick acknowledges the clear connection between morality and spirituality. The second root in Vatican II is the eschatological understanding that every Christian has the vocation to creatively make God's reign more present in our world. The third root in Vatican II is the shift from a classicist to an historically conscious understanding and method. Historical consciousness recognizes that the human subject as knower and actor is embedded in changing history and culture that affect the way in which the human person thinks and acts. These three aspects from Vatican II clearly ground the emphasis on the creativity aspect of conscience.

Yes, creativity is very significant, but Patrick also insists on responsibility. Creativity must be responsible; responsibility gives guidance and direction to creativity. Patrick's approach here is similar to Bernard Häring's insistence that conscience must be free and faithful. I think Patrick's understanding of conscience as a creatively responsible self is a more helpful understanding than that of Häring.

Closely related to the understanding of conscience as a creative responsible self is the understanding of prophecy and the prophet's role in the church in general and in the life of individual Christians. Anne Patrick has insisted on the prophetic role of theologians and of vowed religious in the church. Patrick, both as a theologian and a member of a religious community, has carried on in her own life the role of the prophet. Her insistence on the equality and equal dignity of all women has been a prophetic voice in both church and society. Often in this book she raises up the prophetic voices of women who have gone before in history as well as some contemporary women. In her own work she has strongly criticized the understanding and reality of the role of women in the church. Patrick has strongly disagreed with the Vatican's attitude and approach to women religious in this country. For forty years she has advocated in theory and in practice for the ordination of women in the church. She has disagreed with aspects of the hierarchical church's teaching on sexuality and abortion.

Just as she does not absolutize the role of creativity in conscience, she likewise has a nuanced view of the role of prophets and prophecy.

She has discussed the roles and different positions of the two groups of religious women in the United States—the Leadership Conference of Women Religious (LCWR), which has about 80 percent of religious women belonging to it, and the Council of Major Superiors of Women Religious (CMSWR). She has strongly supported the LCWR because of its understanding of the role of women and the role of religious life today. But she recognizes that both groups have roots in Vatican II's understanding of the church. She quotes with approval the words of another feminist theologian who says that both groups serve the gospel. Yes, she strongly disagrees with the approach of the CMSWR, but she recognizes that this is a legitimate approach in the life of the contemporary church.

Patrick has also explained the theory behind her approach to not absolutizing the prophetic role. Her Christian realism recognizes that there can be prophets on both sides of the same issue. Likewise, trying to be prophetic can at times result in a moralism that brings discouragement and disunity. She agrees with the concept of prophetic obedience proposed by Sandra Schneiders. In her own words, Patrick recognizes that three virtues are necessary to guide the role of feminist women religious aspiring to prophecy. Humility is not a false sense of unworthiness but rather is grounded in our human sinfulness and finitude. In other words, all of us might be wrong. Creative responsibility involves the disposition to step back from a situation of difficulty, look at options imaginatively, and take reasonable risks for the sake of new and better possibilities. This creative responsibility likewise requires the third virtue, namely the virtue of courage.

In conclusion, this book well illustrates the many contributions Anne Patrick has made to Catholic moral theology—her dialogue with literature, a creative imagination and graceful writing style, a strong feminist commitment and method, a deeper understanding of conscience as both creative and responsible, a nuanced understanding of the important role of prophets in the church.

Charles E. Curran
Elizabeth Scurlock University Professor of Human Values
Southern Methodist University

Acknowledgments

When Anne E. Patrick approached me in January 2016 about any interest I might have in editing a collection of her essays for Orbis Books, I felt very honored and gladly accepted. I had known Anne for at least two decades, seeing her regularly at meetings of the Society of Christian Ethics, the College Theology Society, and the Catholic Theological Society of America. In addition, we discovered our shared and treasured Minnesota roots. Anne was highly respected within the theological community for her work on the formation of conscience and as a wise and helpful colleague. As this project unfolded, Anne, first diagnosed with cancer in 2002, faced new medical challenges but was able nonetheless to choose the material she wished to include and to suggest a method of organization. Anne also chose the title and the cover art.

As Anne's health continued to deteriorate, members of her family, and especially Anne's sister Mary Patrick Garate, stepped in to help. Even as Anne entered hospice care, she continued to work on the project, dictating notes to Mary, before her death on July 21, 2016. Mary and I then gave Anne's notes on each essay to Heather Dubrow, a close friend and former colleague of Anne's at Carleton College in Northfield, Minnesota, and currently the John D. Boyd, SJ, Chair in Poetic Imagination in the English Department at Fordham University. We are most grateful to Professor Dubrow for the introductions she wrote that highlight—as Anne wished to do herself—the reasons for including each essay in this collection. We are also grateful to Charles Curran, Anne's close friend and colleague, for his Foreword. Thanks go as well to Jim Keane of Orbis who has overseen the project from its beginnings.

The many publications and texts of lectures of Anne E. Patrick are available in the archives of Loyola University in Chicago.

Susan Perry

INTRODUCTION

Theological Writing as an Art of Ministry

Artists were other people, I always knew, until someone asked me to look at my life from this angle. And there it was, evidence lined up on a shelf and in sheaves of accumulated articles. The internal evidence is also convincing. For one thing, there's the knowledge that composing a chapter feels to me like composing an opera. An article can't just plod through a logical path of data, but needs somehow to sing, to create subtle harmonies and disclose truth by its beauty as well as its facts. For another, there's the joy that comes when a work is going well, and when it feels complete, the best that can be done within the limits of any creative endeavor.

The sense of gratitude and completion was probably greatest when I was ready to publish my first book, *Liberating Conscience*, in 1996.[1] After six years of effort, I found the chapters sufficiently good, true, and beautiful, to give them to the world of readers. As a writer, I had rejoiced like this before, but never so much as when I finally shipped off hundreds of pages and an incongruously small computer disk to an office in New York.

Simone Weil once confided to her notebook, "The work of art which I do not make, none other will ever make it."[2] Such a feeling has been urging me along for quite a few years now. While working on the book, I wasn't always sure the effort was worth it, but I *knew* that something like what I was attempting was needed, and this belief kept me going. Belief, and a small photo, taped to a cabinet beside my computer. When the words weren't coming, when the research seemed pointless, I would glance up at the photo and remember why I was doing this work. The snapshot was of a Brazilian two-year-old, smiling in the arms of his teenage stepsister. From birth he had been destined to die

---

Adapted from an article of the same title in Sisters Today *72:3 (May 2000): 162–72.*

early from starvation or violence, but something had interrupted the bleak chain of causality set in motion by his unlucky birth. What rescued him was the compassion of an ordinary Catholic family in a Sao Paulo *favela* who actually *saw* their neighbors and found their needs for survival more pressing than their own desires to have "the best of everything" for themselves. I wrote *Liberating Conscience* in the hope that Catholics everywhere would come to see the moral life in such a manner.

What I envisioned was a dream well worth my efforts, and I was confident enough of its source to write it down:

> A mysterious and transforming hope for the future has taken hold among the world's peoples, and energies formerly devoted to militarism are now focused on the earth and its creatures. The ozone layer is replenished, the rain forests are replacing themselves, and air quality in Mexico City is as fine today as it was two centuries ago. Drinking water is as pure in Sao Paulo and Lagos as it is in Stockholm and Palm Springs.[3]

I believed that serious rethinking of moral theology was needed if Catholics were going to help turn this futuristic vision into a new reality, and this is why I had written my book. It was that simple. But what led me to think I could take on such a task is a longer story.

The great stress on tradition, silence, and obedience during my first years in religious life (1958–1965) hardly fostered the notion that my ministry should be devoted to an art of self-expression. Someone looking at my retreat notes on obedience would not have surmised that pieces like "'What Never?' 'Well, Hardly Ever': A Report on Surveys of Women's Involvement in the Church" or "Sex-Role Stereotyping and Catholic Education" would flow from the pen of this docile young sister who was busy enough arranging flowers for chapel and giving piano lessons. Much less, "A Conservative Case for the Ordination of Women," for heaven's sake. I would not have guessed it myself. Yet such titles, and more besides, were published within a decade after my final profession of vows in 1965. How did this happen, and why am I so sure now that the art of writing is central to my ministry, and thus to my life?

Undoubtedly the fact that literary gifts ran in my family had much to do with it. School writing assignments came easily enough, though these rarely invited independent thought. Indeed, the crowded classrooms of my postwar youth were not conducive to the sort of divergent

-productive thinking I would later learn is crucial to creativity. My writing skills were well honed in English and journalism classes, but trust in the value of my original ideas was dormant. When I left home at seventeen to "become a sister," I wanted to bring the good news of salvation, as I understood it in 1958, to the multitudes, but this gospel had long been written and explained by others. My job was to learn their works and convey their wisdom to others.

The teaching I aimed to do should have required a college degree by 1960, when I completed my novitiate training and began full-time ministry, but it did not in my case, for reasons few readers of *Sisters Today* need to be told. I did, however, take plenty of courses before accumulating enough credits for a bachelor's degree in 1969. I had stitched together an English major from classes taken mainly during weekends and summers, but did not feel well educated. I sought to remedy this by obtaining a master's degree in English from the University of Maryland, which I believed would help me achieve the *new* ambition for my life as well. This goal had been set soon after the Second Vatican Council: "becoming a theologian." News reports during council sessions had shown me what theologians could do for the church, and a lecture by Monika Hellwig in Albany, New York, around 1967 made the impossible seem likely. Women, too, could contribute in this way. My task was to figure out how and get started.

The Vatican II documents had also inspired me, especially the words on rights to culture, education, and non-discrimination. These passages spoke to my life, for I saw all too clearly the ways gender had impeded my apostolic work. It had been difficult to enter full-time ministry at age nineteen with only two college credits in music, the field I was assigned to teach, in some cases to students my own age. I realized that men who gave their lives to church service would have received both college and graduate training before being sent to the harvest at twenty-four. Thus from a matrix of post-conciliar reflections was born a feminist theologian, who lacked only the specialized training and credentials before she could express what she was coming to understand.

I had already become a writer, though I did not put things that way yet. It had happened without my noticing it, as I was elected to chapters of renewal and found myself composing resolutions and position papers and even an updated rule for the congregation, which was widely appreciated although not adopted for use. I was eager to begin theological studies in 1969, but full-time study was out of the question then, for I had just been named chair of the theology department at my alma mater, the Academy of the Holy Names in Silver Spring, Maryland. At the time I had six credits in theology, earned from novitiate classes in Gregorian chant, Mariology, and Catholic social teaching. I felt the only way I could parlay those credits into an admission ticket to graduate theological studies would be on the strength of my literary background. The master's program in English would become my ticket to divinity school, for I had learned that an excellent school existed at the University of Chicago, and it had a program in Religion and Literature.

The assignment to Silver Spring had been accompanied by a provincial mandate to do what I could to help start a Sisters' Council in the Archdiocese of Washington, DC, since I had previous experience with the one in Albany, New York. I was soon involved with a steering committee, and then served as the founding president of the Council of Women Religious during 1971–1973. These were years of many activities and considerable intellectual stimulation. I read theology out of interest and for my teaching, studied literature for evening classes at the university, and discovered the early writings of Mary Daly and other feminists. I also became active in the fledgling National Assembly of Women Religious (NAWR). Meanwhile current events made me ponder ethical controversies over how to dismantle institutional racism, how to end the war in Vietnam, how to deal with the *Humanae Vitae* crisis, and how to reform the welfare system.

As the graduate literature courses began to add up I discovered the fiction of Graham Greene and became intrigued by the way theological preoccupations figured so effectively in works such as *The Power and the Glory* and *The Heart of the Matter*. I proposed a thesis on "Eschatological Perspective in the Major Works of Graham Greene," which would explore how his fiction set an agenda for theology by challenging simplistic understandings of the mysteries of death, judgment, heaven, and hell. I was soon digging into works by Paul Tillich and Karl Rahner to find ways to express what I was seeing in the novels. I studied Greene's autobiography as well, and came to adapt his practice of writing 500 words a day to my own circumstances, sometimes tallying as many as 2,000 or 2,500 as I rushed to finish the thesis.

By the summer of 1972 my master's degree was earned, the Sisters' Council was on its feet, my ambition to study theology was stronger than ever, and the proposal to do this full-time had long been voiced to community officers. It did not take much to turn me into a writer as well. The catalyst was a *Reader's Digest* piece by Alan Lakein, a time-management expert, with this message: to achieve your life-goals, get your plans in focus, define small tasks, and take action now. It dawned on me that I was a grown-up with a master's degree. What was keeping me *now* from putting my thoughts in print? I decided to publish an article every month. Opportunities soon tested that resolve.

In May of 1972 I had delivered a keynote address for the School Sisters of Notre Dame, meeting in Baltimore to consider new developments in ministry. When the invitation first came, I assumed there was confusion on the caller's part, for I had never before given a major talk outside my own community. Did she perhaps mean to call Sister Ann Patrick Ware, SL, who was a nationally known writer?[4] To my amazement, they actually wanted the president of the Washington, DC, Sisters' Council. So I prepared a talk on "Creative Ministry: Apostolic Women Today," which combined insights from my chapter renewal work and studies in creativity theory and feminism. Soon afterward, I heard from Jacqueline Rumley, IHM, who wanted the text for what became the final issue of *Sister Formation Bulletin*.[5] My article called for a change in church law to permit the "possibility of women participating in full Christian sacramental ministry" and probed the connections between women's religious vocations and the broader issues of women's liberation.[6] Meanwhile Carl Balcerak, editor of the NCEA journal *Momentum*, requested an article discussing the implications of tensions over "avant garde nuns" for Catholic education. I replied that in my experience women religious in various sorts of dress collaborated very well, and proposed to write on "Sex-Role Stereotyping and Catholic Education" instead.[7]

Thus it happened that my first articles since the *Silver Quill* in high school both appeared in December 1972. Preparing them taught me that the quota of one article a month was too ambitious for a full-time teacher, but clearly I *could* write for publication. I who had simply wanted to become a "teaching sister" had turned into an artist—not the pianist I might have been, but a keyboard artist of a different sort. I now knew that 500 words a day was possible, and sooner or later some of what piled up was worth sharing.

I continued to accept invitations to write during the years I studied and taught part-time at the University of Chicago Divinity School (1973–1980). My primary work then was "to become a theologian," but in the process I found time to write a column for *Liturgy* and prepare various essays for publication. For example, during the International Women's Year (1975), I wrote for two periodicals devoting issues to this theme. For *New Catholic World* I developed an argument that still makes sense to me, "A Conservative Case for the Ordination of Women."[8] The piece claims that in a world recognizing the full human dignity of women, there is risk to the values of sacraments and church order if women's gifts for sacramental ministry and liturgical leadership are not affirmed and celebrated officially. A much longer essay on "Women and Religion: A Survey of Significant Literature, 1965–1974" analyzed works in the emerging field of women's studies in religion.[9]

The writing project that occupied me during 1978–1982 was a doctoral dissertation, *H. Richard Niebuhr's "Ethics of Responsibility": A Resource for Literary Criticism.* I was also busy as a teacher, conducting five graduate courses at the University of Chicago Divinity School before coming to the Religion Department at Carleton College in 1980. The practices that had supported my writing before I began teaching at this level were soon supplemented by a new technique for staying with long, complex projects. On days when I was not ready to write 1,000, or even 250 words, I could at least spend time doing research and sketching plans, and so I began logging my hours of work as a writer. I would note the date, the focus of each hour's efforts, and the time and place. The ritual helped me re-enter the process I had left behind, and the record showed me that every "trough" of a few seemingly fruitless hours would eventually be followed by something that felt more productive. I was learning to trust the creative process, to recognize that my task was to be faithful to the effort. If I showed up at the job like a diligent factory worker, the insights and ways of phrasing them would be given. That approach to the art of writing resulted in a 500–page dissertation by September 1982. Finally I had earned the credential that would allow me combine the art of writing with the expertise of a theologian.

The writings most important to my ministry since then have been in the area of moral theology, which the Second Vatican Council identified as especially in need of renewal. In the "Decree on Priestly Formation," *Optatam Totius,* the bishops declared: "Special attention needs to be given to the development of moral theology...It should show the nobility of the Christian vocation of the faithful, and their obligation to bring forth fruit in charity for the life of the world" (#16).[10]

As soon as I was qualified, I joined scholarly organizations that would foster my contributing to this renewal effort, the Society of Christian Ethics (SCE) and the Catholic Theological Society of America (CTSA). After sharing some ideas informally at the CTSA moral theology seminar in 1982, I was invited to publish reflections on "Ethics for Church Professionals?" and to serve on a steering committee for the seminar for three years.[11] The contacts made in these societies led to more opportunities to publish my writings as well as to invite others to reflect on important questions during CTSA conventions.

In 1985 the CTSA elected me to a two-year position on the board of directors. The board soon faced the question of how to respond to the 1986 dismissal of a former CTSA president, moral theologian Charles E. Curran, from the Catholic University of America because he was not willing to retract the conclusions of his research in sexual ethics. It was in the immediate wake of that controversy that the president-elect Michael Scanlon asked me to prepare an address for the 1987 convention, with the assigned title "The Linguistic Turn and Moral Theology."[12] Although linguistic philosophy had never been my special interest, the opportunity to speak in this forum was an important one, and I knew the church deserved my best efforts in view of the current crisis. I gave something like 200 hours to the project during a busy school year (my first as department chair), and was able to offer insights that were well appreciated. In fact, after the lecture I was elected to the presidential office, which extended my years on the board until 1991.

The CTSA gives special power to its president-elect to set the theme and invite the main speakers for its annual meeting. Hoping to use this power well, I was grateful when it came to me that underlying the moral theology debates was the problem of how to balance Divine Providence and human freedom. I soon proposed a convention on "Providence and Responsibility: The Divine and Human in History," and began orchestrating a work that called on the creativity of many other theologians.

It was important to bring new voices into the discussion, especially those of persons whose experiences of history were not typical for the average seminary and university professor of theology. As the third woman elected to presidential office in CTSA history, following Agnes Cunningham, SSCM (1977–78) and Monika Hellwig (1986–87), I knew that the efforts of men who sought justice for women had played a major role in my rapid advancement in the organization. It became my concern to extend this welcome also to women and men of color.

Because experiences of Providence are affected by the specifics of a group's history, I invited speakers who would bring cultural and racial-ethnic diversity to CTSA plenary sessions. Who better to open the convention than a panel comprised of a Sister of Providence scholar of religion, and theologians from Native American, Hispanic, and Black Catholic backgrounds? Who better to draw it to a conclusion than a team of Latino systematic theologians?[13] The results of everyone's reflections were published in the 1989 *CTSA Proceedings*, and although this is not catalogued as a book under my authorship, I have rarely known such artistic fulfillment as when the whole of that convention was gathered as a resource for future study. My belief that such art can contribute to social change was confirmed within two years of the convention, when the CTSA elected its first "minority" board members, Jamie T. Phelps, OP, in 1990 and Orlando O. Espín in 1991, both of whom had given papers in 1989.

My responsibilities as religion department chair at Carleton College and a CTSA officer occupied me for most of 1986–1991. During the spring of 1989, however, I was a visiting professor at the University of Tulsa. There I gave a lecture on the moral theology crisis, which eventually became the first chapter of *Liberating Conscience*.[14] I also learned much about writing from two prolific theologians, Denise and John Carmody. Denise chaired the religion department, and John was a full-time writer. John, who died of cancer in 1994, gave me the encouragement and advice I most needed to hear when he shared the fact that even someone who wrote all day for a living found it difficult to re-enter a writing project after being away on a trip. He said that resuming work after a hiatus is just as hard for a writer as starting to run again feels to an athlete who has been away from the track. Thanks to John, I finally understood my main frustration as a writer over the years. The problem wasn't with my abilities, but with my unrealistic expectations, and the fact that my job in the Midwest and my community and family commitments in the East had required so much time, energy, and travel. I resolved to start a book, and soon signed a contract for the volume that would appear as *Liberating Conscience* in 1996.

During the year I was CTSA president, 1989–1990, I spent a sabbatical leave at the Institute for Ecumenical and Cultural Research in Collegeville, Minnesota. With support from Carleton College, I carried out research on George Eliot and prepared several essays for publication. I also conducted business for the CTSA and worked on my presidential address, initially by contacting sisters of my community from Africa, Brazil, and rural Mississippi for information on the status of women in their cultural situations. After further study of the emerging theology of inculturation and various topics in ethics and feminism, I wrote "Inculturation, Catholicity, and Social Justice."[15]

The time away from my usual teaching responsibilities had deepened both my commitment to writing and my sense of need for social support for the solitary tasks of study, reflection, and composition that theological writing requires. There had long been such support—especially from a friend in Chicago, Anne E. Carr, BVM, who had read and critiqued drafts of my articles for a dozen years—but after 1990 I became more intent on finding support also among writers where I lived. I joined a Minneapolis writers' organization, The Loft, and participated in a faculty prose writers' group at Carleton College. In 1994–95 a Faculty Development Grant provided another opportunity for full-time writing, and in September I began intense work on the fourth chapter of *Liberating Conscience* during a week at Norcroft, a writers' colony for women overlooking Lake Superior. Writer-friends in St. Paul, and at the Studium of St. Benedict's Monastery in St. Joseph, Minnesota, were especially helpful that year, and I have continued to meet regularly ever since with two college teachers there, Mara Faulkner, OSB, and Nancy Hynes, OSB. All three of us have published the books that were unfinished when we began meeting in 1995, and we are helping each other now with new projects.[16]

Perhaps because of this collegial circle at the Studium, I find myself writing more often on ethical matters related to the experiences of sisters; in 1999 I published two such essays. For a volume on virtue ethics and ministry, I compared cases from the history of my own New York Province of the Sisters of the Holy Names, one involving the Diocese of Brooklyn in 1939 and the other the Archdiocese of Miami fifty years later. The chapter's title, "'His Dogs More Than Us': Virtue in Situations of Conflict between Women Religious and Their Ecclesiastical Employers," was suggested when one sister summed up her years in a very difficult mission by observing, "Father cared more about his dogs than about us."[17] A very different article, "A Ministry of Justice," examines the brief history of the National Assembly of Women Religious (called after 1982 the National Assembly of Religious Women to signify the full inclusion of lay members), as a case study of the strengths and weaknesses of post–Vatican II idealism.[18]

Neither a ministry of writing nor a vocation in the arts had been in my thoughts when I set out to "become a sister" in 1958, nor did I dream then of my subsequent calling to theology. A century ago my ideas might have made it into some letters and class presentations, but not likely into print under my own name. My development as a writer has been helped by the example and encouragement of many authors, and by the availability of forums such as *Sister Formation Bulletin* and *Sisters Today*.

"Becoming a theologian," I have come to understand, requires becoming an artist as well. My genres may differ, but my aspirations resemble those of novelists I have admired. Joseph Conrad once characterized art as "a single-minded attempt to render the highest kind of justice to the visible universe, by bringing to light the truth, manifold and one, under-lying its every aspect." He knew also that the artist "speaks to our capac-ity for delight and wonder, to the sense of mystery surrounding our lives and to the subtle but invincible conviction of solidarity that binds to-gether all humanity."[19] Such ideals do very well for a moral theologian on the cusp of a new millennium.

Notes

1. Anne E. Patrick, *Liberating Conscience: Feminist Explorations in Catholic Moral Theology* (New York: Continuum, 1996).

2. Quoted here from Rosalie Maggio, comp., *The Beacon Book of Quotations by Women* (Boston: Beacon, 1992), 21.

3. Ibid., ix–x.

4. In 1985 I was a guest at a birthday celebration for Ann Patrick Ware in New York, and since that time we have enjoyed sharing various instances of being mistaken for each other.

5. Anne E. Patrick, SNJM, "Creative Ministry: Apostolic Women Today," *Sister Formation Bulletin* 19, no. 1 (Fall 1972): 8–14.

6. Ibid., 12.

7. Anne E. Patrick, "Sex Role Stereotyping and Catholic Education," *Momentum* 3, no. 4 (December 1972): 6–13. Balcerak took his own photos for the magazine, and placed one of myself standing behind a theological dictionary opposite the first page of an article by a canon lawyer, Clara Maria Henning, "Are Women Theologians Being Taken Seriously?" (15–19).

8. *New Catholic World* (May/June 1975): 108–11.

9. *Theological Studies* 36 (1975): 737–66; reprinted in *Woman: New Dimensions*, ed. Walter Burghardt (New York: Paulist, 1977), 161–89.

10. Quoted here from Walter M. Abbott, ed., *The Documents of Vatican II* (New York: The America Press, 1966).

11. *New Catholic World* (January-February 1983): 21–24.

12. *CTSA Proceedings* 42 (1987), 38–59. A revision of this essay became the second chapter of *Liberating Conscience*, "Conscience at the Crossroads: Invita-tion to Radical Conversion," 40–71.

13. The panelists on "Providence and Histories: Some American Views" were Barbara Doherty, SP, P. Michael Galvan, Marina Herrera, and Jamie T. Phelps, OP. Plenary addresses were given by Anne E. Carr, BVM, Charles E. Curran, and Orlando O. Espín with Sixto J. Garcia.

14. "Conscience and Community: Catholic Moral Theology Today" was de-livered February 13, 1989 and published by the University of Tulsa in the War-ren Lectures Series in Catholic Studies.

15. *CTSA Proceedings* 45 (1990), 41–55.

16. Nancy Hynes, OSB, edited the essays of Mariella Gable, OSB, as *The Literature of Spiritual Values and Catholic Fiction* (Lanham, MD: University Press of America, 1996), and told the story of Gable's persecution by the local bishop in a biographical introduction. She then completed a biography of J. F. Powers. Mara Faulkner, OSB (with photographer Annette Brophy, OSB) published *Born of Common Hungers: Benedictine Women in Search of Connections* (Notre Dame: University of Notre Dame Press, 1997) and at the time was seeking a publisher for a book of poetry and also working on a memoir.

17. In James F. Keenan, SJ, and Joseph Kotva, Jr., *Practice What You Preach* (Franklin, WI: Sheed & Ward, 1999), 293–313.

18. "A Ministry of Justice: The 25-Year Pilgrimage of the National Assembly of Religious Women," in Mary Jo Weaver, ed., *What's Left: Liberal American Catholics* (Bloomington: Indiana University Press, 1999), 176–89.

19. Joseph Conrad, *Tales of Land and Sea* (Garden City, NY: Hanover House, 1953), 106.

I

HISTORY IN THE MAKING

1

THE APOSTOLATE

Crisis and Coresponsibility

*At a workshop in 1969, when she was only twenty-eight years old
and only four years after her final vows as a religious, Anne Patrick
delivered this extraordinary address. Anticipating positions that she
would develop and refine later in her career, she characteristically describes authority as not dictating answers but encouraging the coresponsibility of institutions and individuals. Thus this first essay
exemplifies her judicious and balanced participation in issues central
to the church. — Heather Dubrow (hereafter HD)*

Sisters, your presence here today is cogent testimony to the importance
of the topic of the apostolate. Despite immediate pressures from busy
apostolic lives, you have chosen to give a day to consider this apostolate in deeper perspective, to ask what we are doing and why, and
what we will be doing in the future. You evidently neither take the
apostolate for granted nor fail to assume personal responsibility for the
apostolic activity of our community.

When the Apostolic Life Commission met during the weekend of
February 15 and 16 [1969], we felt a sense of urgency in two regards. We
were concerned both with the work of our commission and the problem
of communication. We knew that nearly every chapter delegate had
asked to be on this commission as her first choice. Last year the choices
of the delegates had been rather evenly distributed among the three
commissions, but this year's first choices showed an overwhelming interest in the apostolate, and seemed to mark our area as one of prime

*Address presented at a 1969 meeting of the Apostolic Life Commission, from the New
York Province Records, Archives of the Sisters of the Holy Names of Jesus and Mary,
U.S.-Ontario Province.*

concern. In addition, we felt a special need to improve communications within our province between all the sisters and all the comission members. In an area as vital as that of the apostolate, it seems essential that all views be heard and shared before action is taken to the chapter. We know that many of you find ditto papers and bulletin board communiqués inadequate, to say the least, and we are also aware that many sisters find local discussions, especially in smaller missions, useful, but very limited. Thus we drew up our program with the special objective of stressing personal communication and sharing.

As you know so well, the first phase of our program did involve local discussions. These we will hear about later in the day. Today's regional workshop, Phase II of the program, has been planned as a sharing session concerning concepts of the apostolate, our present status in this region and the province, and trends and possibilities for the future. Phase III we view as especially important. Often when we leave a community gathering such as this, we go away inspired, but without any practical outlet for our inspirations. This outlet we hope we have provided in the form of the Apostolic Life Commission's long worked on questionnaire. We hope that by the end of the day you will understand why we have asked each question, and will know that we sincerely hope to work toward practical results from the data we gather. Thus your individual work on Phase III should have practical bearing on the immediate and long-range decisions of this province regarding the apostolate.

CRISIS

We do seem to be at a crisis point as far as the apostolate is concerned. Before developing this further I would like to quote the observation made by Sister Paulina Mary at a workshop she gave last fall in Albany. Sister noted that the Chinese character for "crisis" is a composite of two other characters—one character signifying "danger," and another signifying "opportunity." It is in this twofold perspective that I would like to consider the current apostolic crisis—it is a dangerous moment, but also one full of opportunity.

What are the dangers of the present apostolic situation? Only brief mention needs to be made of the danger of complacency. There may be some temptation to glory in past accomplishments and maintain that our present goodwill and efforts are indeed fulfilling all that God could possibly be asking of us. But this is a relatively insignificant danger when contrasted with the possible dangers of answering current challenges with half-measures, or, still more serious, of yielding to pessimism, discouragement, and apathy in the face of the many problems that confront us.

Our problems are complex, and stop gap measures will not solve them. Last year's Apostolic Life Commission survey brought out a number of these problems. They include serious financial needs and needs concerning the quantity and quality of the staffs of the various schools we serve. Uneven distribution of workloads and too heavy workloads are seen as problems also. Communications problems and problems with relationships are found on various levels—with administration and staff, between religious and lay teachers, among religious, with clients, and with the larger community. Budgetary constraints bring problems concerning space and equipment. There is the ever-present time-pressure problem, and there are various personal items that deserve mention also. Such include job dissatisfaction, feelings of inadequacy in a professional position, lack of training or professional opportunities, and, in some cases, the conservative-liberal tension. Let me interject here a view of this tension—a tension which, though its effects are indeed real, may be more a semantics or communications problem than a conflict of values. John Gardner, the former secretary of Health, Education and Welfare, has asserted that the concepts of conservatism and liberalism are really old-fashioned. In his book *Self-Renewal*, which is about institutional as well as personal renewal, he quotes Peter Drucker: "In a world buffeted by change, faced daily with new threats to its safety, the only way to conserve is by innovating. The only stability possible is stability in motion."[1]

Not only are our problems many and complex—they tend to interact and multiply, A plus B interacting with A plus B in a relationship of multiplication becomes far more complex than either factor was originally.

It seems that the problems we are experiencing are not unique to this community. They appear time and again on surveys conducted by various religious communities and by dioceses throughout the country. In one sense they constitute a danger, for they threaten our continued existence, or at least the continued existence of the apostolate as we now engage in it. It is a common place that unless outside financial aid comes soon our Catholic educational system will take on a different and reduced picture.

But such a crisis has always spelled out opportunity for those who trust in God, and who view the events of history as one of the ways God reveals himself to us. Precisely because of the many apostolic questions facing us, we have begun to re-examine our apostolic lives, and are, individually and as a community, asking serious questions of ourselves. And in the process, we find that we are talking more with each other about the things that concern us most vitally, and are thus deepening our sense of community. From this questioning we find that our concept of the apostolate has shifted, almost imperceptibly, from one that was concerned with works done, and that viewed the apostolate *almost* as something that worked *ex opera operato* the moment a sister undertook any charge given under obedience, to one that, to quote last year's Apostolic Life Commission's chapter proposal, considers the apostolate as "dynamically person-oriented" and "transcending things done and focusing on personal witness." The apostolate is seen as ecclesial-linked, and as involving a Christian response to a human need. Finally, our apostolate in education is now viewed in the broad sense of the word education, and is seen as integrated with, not separate from, other aspects of our life. The publications that resulted from last year's provincial and general chapters contain such concepts of the apostolate as personal witness and ecclesial-linked mission, and emphasize the importance of the individual apostolic woman, whose membership in our community should facilitate her fullest participation in the church's heritage of Christian response, as well as immeasurable wealth in the generosity and zeal of our sisters. Thus our apostolic situation is indeed one of promise and opportunity. Realistic optimism, not complacency or pessimism, should be what characterizes our spirit as we work for the so needed renewal of our apostolic lives.

Before proceeding to the second part of this talk, coresponsibility, I feel it is essential that we consider for a moment the fact that our heritage should give us grounds for optimism. I am speaking here not only of our heritage from the 1840s, but wish to stress particularly that of the 1950s and 1960s. Too often, in a time of historical change, those caught up in the present are concerned only with criticizing the immediate past, and fail to recognize that present advancements are rooted in this immediate past. For example, there are those who laud Vatican II as inaugurating a "second spring" in the church, and who do not see that the climate that made the recent ecumenical council possible had its basis in such forgotten items as Pius XII's encouragement of modern scripture scholarship. And in our own province, as we prepare to assume more and more coresponsibility in the apostolate as well as in other areas of our lives, we should not view this as a radical departure from the recent past, but as a natural outgrowth of steps that have been initiated by provincial leaders in the last decade. To be sure, we cannot remain at the status quo. But we can appreciate what we have achieved at the same time as we look for ways of improving it.

CORESPONSIBILITY

The term "coresponsibility" has been popularized recently by Cardinal Suenens in his book *Coresponsibility in the Church*, and his words on apostolic coresponsibility seem especially fitting in the context of today's workshop. The cardinal writes:

> It is too easily said that every consecrated life is apostolic life by definition, and that whatever activity is engaged in is apostolic because of the intention which animates it. Even supposing that this is so, it still remains true that human activities, whether they be nursing, teaching or anything else, do not all possess the same apostolic quality, concentration or urgency. It is still true that the Christianization of the world which is confided to all in coresponsibility is not furthered in the same way by any action whatever; there is a hierarchy of values.[2]

Earlier, Sister Angelica Seng, a Franciscan, had written that "unless the sisters actively engaged in apostolic work are dreaming, planning, and initiating, the type of continual, creative adaptation which is necessary to respond to the needs of our time cannot take place."[3]

Coresponsibility is not simply a governmental form; it is an apostolic attitude. Response to needs is basic to Christian mission, and in the Christian community, it is fundamental that such response be shared. I believe that we will see not only a revitalized apostolic spirit, but also an increase in vocations, as more and more we assume the responsibilities that follow from our baptism. Each of us should be able to read something like *Pacem in Terris* or *Progressio Populorum* and realize that this is more than ecclesiastical rhetoric or inspiring "spiritual reading"—that it is a message that should prompt *us* to respond.

As an individual Christian, I cannot wait for such a message to filter through the hierarchy of a religious community structure before I am to take it seriously. Rather, each one of us, on the "hier-" or the "lower-" "archy," must be tuned to all frequencies, for the Spirit breathes where he wills. The current theology of religious authority seems to view authority as a means of coordinating the various responses made by the members, not as a system for dictating responses. This evolution in our philosophy of structure is providentially occurring at the same time as more active apostolic interest is growing, as sisters become more and more aware of contemporary needs.

Let me make myself clear on this point. I do not intend at all to imply that present authority, or past authority, for that matter, actually desired that we should be passive, that we should not think seriously and seek to exercise initiative and take action on the issues that confront our Christian consciences. Authority has inherited the same structure that non-authority did, and I am sure would be more than glad if we all became more *actively* responsible, not *to* authority, but *with* authority.

Practical problems will of necessity arise as we move toward more collegial frameworks, especially in the area of individual and community goals. As a person, I am a purposive being, and so is everyone else in the community a purposive being. In order for me to exercise my rights and responsibilities as a person and as a Christian, I must set goals for myself. And these goals may not always coincide, or may not immediately coincide, with what are known as "community goals." This is a normal occurrence in any society, and a socially oriented person will resolve the conflict in favor of the society, the greater good, the "common good," if her belief in the community is strong, and if she identifies with the community's goals. And this is easier the more that this "common good" is known and clearly recognized as a *good*. Here the challenge to a religious community is staggering. Given the sacredness of the person, the value of each individual sister—and people *are* our prime resource—and, in our case, given persons of unusual dedication, who have for years demonstrated their willingness to sacrifice valuable personal goods for the church and the community of mankind—confronted with such persons, the religious community must be very sure of what goals it holds as a community. It should have Christian goals, known goals, and goals that are shared by the members. We cannot think of our community as an abstraction. We are the Sisters of the Holy Names, for all practical purposes.

I am not speaking here of transcendental goals, for we have no difficulty with these. Who would say she did not desire the glory of God, the sanctification of souls, or participation in the church's mission of education? But can such goals be measured? Can they be defined in concrete terms? Has not our problem been that we have attempted to define something that transcends the present reality to a great extent, that we have tried to measure something that is not quantitative? The interpretation of these transcendental goals that we all share will vary from decade to decade, from region to region, and thus it is necessary that we have a framework that will support the interpretations that we as a community agree upon. These interpretations will take the form of concrete, measurable, and at least somewhat realizable goals. These will be both long- and short-range goals, and will be more or less temporary. They will very likely take the form of priorities that we must establish as a province. They will be based on our transcendental goals, but will not be taken for final, immutable goals. I think this distinction between transcendental and non-transcendental goals is the answer to the dilemma of, "Are we being true to the spirit of our foundress if we make sweeping changes in the form of our apostolate?" If we distinguish the goals that Mother Marie Rose and her companions had, we will surely see that her founding of Catholic schools was not a final, transcendental goal, but rather a non-transcendental, possibly temporary goal set up because she and her companions, and the church in her situation, felt that this concrete goal was the best means of realizing the transcendental goals of glorifying God and spreading the message of the gospel.

Such a distinction should enable us to retool our apostolic efforts with a minimum of trauma. With a minimum of trauma, not with a minimum of effort. There is much to be done in coresponsibility if we are to renew our apostolate so that we can meet the needs of the last decades of the twentieth century as effectively as possible. We cannot predict the changes that will come in the next few years. Technological advances are progressing at an incredible pace, so any concrete adaptations that we make will be obsolete within a few years of their implementation. What will insure our continued effectiveness is not any concrete program—be it one that we already have in existence, or one that we might like to adopt in the near future; rather it will be our lack of attachment, our real return to the gospel injunction to "travel light."

It is quite interesting to me that the Sisters of St. Joseph of Buffalo were told by an agnostic research expert whom they paid thousands of dollars to evaluate their apostolic works that "you've got to stay loose."[4] Of course, we will work in buildings and institutions, though the tendency toward coresponsibility will probably mean that we will more and more share responsibility for the institutions we serve with various dioceses or other organizations. But our commitments to various institutions cannot be *per omnia saecula saeculorum*. If others can do what we once did, and if something else needs to be done, then as sisters we should be ready to move to the frontiers of new apostolic needs, always allowing for individual differences. Not everyone will want to do this, and our apostolic structures should be flexible to allow for various responses. Many of us, no doubt most of us, would like to continue our present form of apostolate, and our apostolic aspirations call for continual improvement of our present situations. Others of us feel called to one of the present, or foreseeable frontiers. Our apostolic structure will be stronger if both types of responses are possible.

The situation might be compared to the problem of a very old house. You can't tear down the present one before the new one is built. We are now in the process of planning the new one. We have an opportunity now to see what features we like about the present one. These we will definitely want to incorporate into our new plans. At the same time, we are in a perfect position to eliminate the annoying features of the present dwelling. And as we realize that the process has begun, there will not be the same "will it ever end?" feeling as we patch the roof again or once more try to repair the faulty plumbing. We really believe that it *is almost* the last time, as we look at the bulldozers across the street. Moving away from metaphor, if we can establish our concrete apostolic goals and directions, and make them known, we will not have the "will it ever end?" feeling when a new, untrained principal is named over the summer, or when Sister X, with a degree in math, or perhaps just 97 credits toward a B.A., has to fill in in junior high social studies somewhere next fall, for we know it *is almost* the last time, and that provisions are being made for the very prompt training of the principal and for proper placement of the teacher. Or it *will* be almost the last time, if we take this as our responsibility, not solely that of provincial administration.

Actually, many of our concrete apostolic decisions will be made for us in the near future as the dioceses we serve undertake scientific studies of their educational programs and move toward consolidation of schools, shared resources, phasing out of some works, and phasing in or development of others. There will be opportunities for diversity of works and unity of purpose.

I spoke earlier of a need for checking out our concrete, non-transcendental goals. These may not all be written goals. If we find that we have two goals that are mutually non-realizable, as we may have now due to overextension, we must establish priorities. To do this we must study ourselves, our aspirations, our needs, and our present commitments. We must listen to each other and co-respond. We must think long about what it means to have a person-centered rather than an institution-centered apostolate. And we must love each other enough to wish for each other honestly and effectively the good that we all wish for ourselves—namely that I can say, "I am, as far as I can see, as apostolically effective as I could hope to be; definitely more effective as a sister in this community than I could ever be by myself."

And as we work now today and in the weeks to come to examine our present situation and to plan our goals and priorities for the future, let us with St. Paul "entrust our future to God who called us as we leave behind the things that are past and with hands outstretched to whatever lies ahead we go straight for the goal, our reward, the honor of our high calling by God in Christ Jesus (Phil. 3:14).

Notes

1. John Gardner, *Self-Renewal: The Individual and the Innovative Society* (New York: Harper & Row, 1963), 7.

2. Leon Joseph Cardinal Suenens, *Coresponsibility in the Church* (New York: Herder & Herder, 1968), 173.

3. Sister M. Angelica Seng, OSF, "The Sister in the New City," in *The Changing Sister*, ed. Sr. M. Charles Borromeo Muckenhirn, CSC (Notre Dame, IN: Fides Publishers, 1965), 260.

4. Michael McKenna, "Report of Research," December 21, 1968, Buffalo, New York.

2

SEXIST LANGUAGE AND SYMBOLISM

Unjust and Idolatrous

Exemplifying the concern with gender manifest in many essays in this volume, Anne Patrick skillfully dovetails telling personal anecdotes with more general reflections. If language can fetter us, Anne Patrick also believed that used appropriately it could contribute to the goal movingly expressed in her essay on the apostolate: "As Christians and as religious, we should be the freest of all people." —HD

Following a model the National Conference of Catholic Bishops used for the pastoral letters *The Challenge of Peace* (1983) and *Economic Justice for All* (1986), in the mid-1980s a committee of bishops launched a series of hearings around the country as part of a process of preparing a pastoral letter on "Women's Concerns." Some Catholic women felt closed off from this process because the official hearings were limited to participants invited by the committee. Several Catholic feminists in Washington, DC, therefore took the initiative of inviting people to "open" hearings, and arranged for four hours of testimony to be presented on March 4, 1985. Among them was Sister Maureen Fiedler, SL, then active at the Quixote Center, a social justice organization, and later host of the National Public Radio program "Faith Matters." Each hour of testimony involved several speakers and some questions from audience members on the announced topic. I came to Washington from Union Theological Seminary in New York, where I was on a research sabbatical from Carleton College, and spoke on the panel "Women in Church Structures." The full text of my testimony on "Sexist Language and Symbolism: Unjust and Idolatrous" is provided here. —Anne E. Patrick

---

A testimony given March 4, 1985, at a session convened to influence the U.S. bishops who were attempting to prepare a pastoral letter on "Women's Concerns."

From childhood I have been bombarded by messages from my culture that as a female I am a member of an inferior caste. I recall my first grade teacher announcing that the girls would be jealous, but she wanted to tell the whole class that the boys were invited to a special "father and son" dinner. There was nothing similar for mothers and daughters, which was hardly surprising to me because already at six I was on to the fact that our genetic handicap put females at a disadvantage in the world. The fact that my male classmates could be altar servers and safety patrols while the best we girls could aspire to was cleaning the blackboards simply reinforced the message of inferiority that was conveyed by our textbooks, the authority patterns around us, the grammatical rules we were taught, and even the language of our prayers.

Even the language of our prayers. In 1985 the textbooks are better than they were in the forties and fifties, the safety patrol is integrated, and so is the Little League. But the symbols of religion—the words and images that go with our deepest spiritual experience—what about them? The sad fact I must testify to tonight is that my Roman Catholic religious culture continues to use verbal and nonverbal symbols in ways that reinforce a bias against women. And the sadder fact is that so many Catholics and church leaders do not even see the problem. When I try to understand why it is that people do not recognize the evil done by sexist language for persons and sexist imagery for God, when I try to understand why this concern is regarded as no problem at all or a trivial one at most, I am helped by thinking of sexist language and symbols as a barely visible pollutant in the atmosphere that keeps the members of the church and society unhealthy in various ways. Feminists have suffered enough to detect its levels easily. We are not having attacks of asthma and emphysema for no reason. Some of us feel about ready to keel over dead from the oppressive atmosphere, but the fact that our sensitivity is heightened does not mean there is no danger for the rest of the population. Like the canary in the coal mine, the feminist who shows the symptoms of justice deprivation should be taken with utmost seriousness by the rest of society, for the fact is that the sexist symbol system is killing us all.

Not all by itself and not all at once of course, but slowly and surely sexist symbolism increases our morbidity because it shores up an ideology of domination, indeed of domination that expresses itself violently when those who are supposed to be subordinate show signs of "not knowing their place," which happens to be at the bottom of an unjust power relationship, an oppressive system.

And what does it mean to be oppressed? Most basically, I am oppressed when someone else tries to play God over me by defining the meaning of my life without respect for the mystery that is essential to my human personhood. And this oppression becomes set in concrete when I internalize the oppressor's assessment of my purpose and worth. In other words, there are both objective and subjective dimensions to oppression—factors outside myself, and factors within. Psychological oppression is harder to document than the grosser forms of physical oppression such as slavery, but in both the mystery and worth of a person are violated by an oppressor's attempting to define what someone else is good for, and not good for. There does not even have to be a conscious oppressor to enact the oppression if the social and mental structures of domination and subordination are already in place. For the terrible thing about oppression is that once it is internalized it perpetuates itself without need of deliberate decision or physical force.

And this is where language and other symbolic forms come into play. It is an established principle of modern linguistics that the limits of my language are the limits of my thought. Language and symbol, in other words, are powerful tools for shaping reality. And sad to say, the language and nonverbal symbols Catholics usually experience in church tend to shape a reality where God is thought of as male and where men and boys are valued as superior to women and girls. These two things go together, of course. The arrangement is a combination of idolatry and injustice, for by imaging the Deity overwhelmingly in male terms we confuse a transcendent Divine Reality with what even the Book of Genesis would recognize as a truncated image, since we read in Genesis 1:27 that the image of God is "male and female." And the idolatrous construction of a God whose masculinity is an overwhelming attribute and of a Christ whose maleness is thought to count for more than his humanity functions to sacralize a social order that proclaims that male dominance is the order of reality and female inferiority the way things really are.

No theologian could put it better than the child named Sylvia who wrote the following letter to God: "Dear God, Are boys better than girls? I know you are one, but try to be fair." Sylvia has learned that God is male and that even God has a hard time appreciating her full human worth. She could well have learned this in a Catholic church, where females have minor roles on the altar at best, and where the hymns, prayers, sermons, and overall structure of the liturgy continually reinforce her sense that being a girl is second-rate.

Why does the church continue to inflict on Sylvia a hymn that implies the "faith of our mothers" doesn't deserve mention, doesn't quite cut it in comparison with that of our fathers? Will her generation of women, like mine, be trained to think of themselves as among the "lesser things" that men must leave behind when they go off to do the great work of the world, and that clergymen must leave behind when they go off to do the great work of God? You know the lines:

> Rise up, O men of God!
> Have done with lesser things,
> Give heart, and soul, and mind, and strength
> To serve the King of kings.

This is only one of countless hymns and prayers I can no longer utter. Even when I hear a less militaristic hymn such as "Yahweh is the God of my salvation," the second line tends to stick in my throat: "I trust in him and have no fear." Why must we always speak of God as "he" or "him"? asks an automatic sexism detector in my consciousness. I gasp as the "justice quality index" plummets. And yet I do want and need to worship the God of my salvation. It is simply that I cannot do it in words that legitimate idolatry and injustice, which means that less and less can I do it in most Catholic churches.

Last Sunday I worshipped with some Christians who appreciate the moral and religious seriousness of this issue. Ours was a Lenten ritual, with emphasis on the mystery of repentance and conversion. As part of the ritual we changed the following words to an ancient Gregorian melody: "Jerusalem, Jerusalem, be converted to our gracious God." Jerusalem is a metaphor for the church. Our gracious God, whose care for us is well symbolized in the terms Mother and Father, continues to call us to live more justly. How long, O Jerusalem, how long?

My niece Jane Varner Malhotra, then sixteen, also spoke on this 1985 panel about her frustrations as a fourth-grader who had wanted to be an altar server in the 1970s. She gave up this ambition after the bishop of Fort Wayne, Indiana answered her letter by saying that he would like to allow this but the Vatican policy prevented it. (Jane, by then the mother of four, did serve on the altar at my golden jubilee liturgy in 2010, and in 2015 she greeted Pope Francis on the Washington, DC mall with a sign "Ordain women.") I believe all four hours of the testimony were videotaped in 1985, and then edited into a 45-minute summary that was sent to all the members of the bishops' committee. As I observe in *Liberating Conscience*, "[T]he U.S. bishops concluded in 1992 that a decade-long effort to compose a pastoral letter on 'women's concerns' was best abandoned. After four drafts and sig-nificant Vatican intervention, they were unable to reach a consensus on the proposed document and instead agreed to publish the fourth draft as simply a committee report."[1]

Note

1. Anne E. Patrick, *Liberating Conscience: Feminist Explorations in Catholic Moral Theology* (New York: Bloomsbury Academic, 1997), 21.

3

TOWARD RENEWING
"THE LIFE AND CULTURE OF FALLEN MAN"

Gaudium et Spes *as Catalyst for*
Catholic Feminist Theology

*In this essay Anne Patrick argues that certain limitations in the oth-
erwise impressive document* Gaudium et Spes *were in fact poised
to spur subsequent feminist critique. Her recognition of that possibility
anticipates not only the balance of optimism and clear-eyed realism
in much of her writing but also her approach to the treatments for
cancer that she endured for over a decade; she characteristically cast
the onerous side effects of some of the chemotherapy as "challenges."*
—HD

In discussing "The Proper Development of Culture," *Gaudium et Spes*
(hereafter cited as *GS*) ranges widely over theological, ethical, and educational matters pertaining to "the cultivation of the goods and values
of nature" (no. 53).[1] The tone of this section of the conciliar document is
largely positive, conveying an openness to new possibilities and a hope
that proper development of culture will lead to "a world that is more
human" (57). Twenty years later, the church continues to grapple with
the items this text identified as sufficiently novel to warrant our times
being called "a new age of human history" (54), items that include cultural and religious pluralism, new developments in the physical and
human sciences and in technology, and increasing aspirations toward
autonomy and responsibility on the part of women and men across the
globe. But when one surveys the section, "The Proper Development of

Adapted from a chapter of the same title in Feminist Ethics and the Catholic Moral
Tradition, *ed. Charles E. Curran, Margaret A. Farley, and Richard A. McCormick
(New York: Paulist, 1986), 483–510.*

Culture," in light of the entire document of *GS*, and in light of subsequent developments in the church, there is a change in the scene since 1965 that stands out for its significance and impact, a change that seems not to have been anticipated by the document and yet is arguably, at least in part, a result of *GS*. This development is the enhanced sense of full personhood and moral and social responsibility now articulated by Catholic women, a number of whom are solidly established as professional theologians.

How did it happen that women, once presumed to be silent and acquiescent, docile and supportive of male ecclesiastical authority, came to take positions in opposition to "official" Catholic teachings on questions ranging from God-language and women's ordination to conception control, homosexuality, and even abortion?[2] An extraordinary development has taken place in Roman Catholicism since the appearance of *GS*, and this chapter indicates the connection I see between the words of this document and the emerging feminist critique of the tradition by Catholics who regard themselves as loyal members of the church. It is my impression that the rhetoric of *GS* struck forcefully on a female population that was ripe for implementing its ideas and carrying them beyond anything anticipated by the Fathers of the Council.[3] My claim here is that the limited vision of social justice articulated by this document paved the way for a more adequate Christian feminist vision of justice among Catholics who might otherwise have felt it necessary to choose between either a traditionally Catholic or a secular feminist philosophy of life and view of justice. What made the difference was the opening of theological education and research to women, which lessened the insularity of male theologians and at the same time gave women the tools to argue our case for justice in the forum that was responsible for legitimating our subordination.

GAUDIUM ET SPES: PRODUCT OF ANDROCENTRIC CULTURE

There is no reason to suppose that the Council Fathers ever anticipated the sort of contributions Rosemary Radford Ruether, Elisabeth Schüssler Fiorenza, or Margaret A. Farley would make to Catholic theology. It is true that no. 55 recognizes that in general women as well as men are eager to mold the culture of the societies to which they belong:

> In each nation and social group there is a growing number of men and women [*virorum ac mulierum*] who are conscious that they themselves are the craftsmen [*culturae artifices*] and mold-

ers of their community's culture. All over the world the sense of autonomy and responsibility increases with effects of the greatest importance for the spiritual and moral maturity of mankind. This will become clearer to us if we place before our eyes the unification of the world and the duty imposed on us to build up a better world in truth and justice.

However, the egalitarian reference to women and men together here is highly unusual; although *GS* does employ *mulier* alone in various contexts, it generally avoids *vir*, using instead forms of the ambiguous term *homo*, which are nearly always rendered in the generic masculine ("man" or "men") in English."[4] Thus women are not specified in the crucial paragraph that voices the hope that "more of the laity [*plures laici*] will receive adequate theological formation and that some among them will dedicate themselves professionally to these studies and contribute to their advancement," in which the Fathers also declare that "Those involved in theological studies in seminaries and universities should be eager to cooperate with men [*hominibus*] versed in other fields of learning by pooling their resources and their points of view" (62). There is every likelihood that readers of this paragraph would infer a presumption on the part of its authors that intellectual circles were overwhelmingly, if not exclusively, male. For this they could hardly be blamed, given that women were excluded from the early sessions of Vatican II and were admitted only as silent observers during the final two sessions. Indeed, as Albertus Magnus McGrath recalls in her study "Women and the Church," the noted British economist Barbara Ward was not allowed to address the Council Fathers, her paper instead being delivered at the third session by a man.[5]

During the Council there were, of course, a number of significant statements made concerning justice for women, and Archbishop Paul Hallinan of Atlanta filed a proposal during the final session that women be encouraged to become "teachers and consultants" in theology.[6] But although Hallinan's proposal was widely noted by the press, it never reached the assembly floor, and the text of *GS* does not specifically promote the involvement of women in theology.

Thus, although the document does represent some progress on the question of justice for women, its tone and contents (especially when rendered in English) betray a decidedly androcentric bias, indeed a blindness to the sexism in its understanding of human rights and dignity. Nonetheless, the language of the document at least leaves open the possibility that women might interpret in their favor statements the text left ambiguous, for there are no passages specifically ruling out the participation of women in theology. Furthermore, by affirming intellectual freedom in theology, the highly significant final sentence of the section on culture states a principle that contributed both to male support of women's involvement in the discipline and also to the development of feminist positions by both male and female theologians:

> But for the proper exercise of this role [of theologian], the faithful, both clerical and lay [*sive clericis sive laicis*], should be accorded a lawful freedom of inquiry, of thought, and of expression, tempered by humility and courage in whatever branch of study they have specialized. (62)

Later in this essay, I probe in some detail the document's limitations where justice for women is concerned, but what needs to be stressed first are two factors that offset these limitations and enabled *GS* to be the groundbreaking document it was. These are essentially theological affirmations that permeate the document and that make it possible for Catholics who read it to carry its spirit beyond the literal sense of the text.

KEY THEOLOGICAL AFFIRMATIONS

In the first place, it is impossible to exaggerate the import of the document's stress on the essential equality of all persons (*homines*) and of its recognition that "forms of social or cultural discrimination in basic personal rights on the grounds of sex...must be curbed and eradicated as incompatible with God's design" (29). Here the Fathers incorporate into their own text a critical principle that continues to be seized upon by their readers as a basis for carrying the spirit of *GS* beyond the implementation envisioned by most of its episcopal authors.

In the second place, along with this important affirmation that God intends a society in which the essential equality of woman is recognized, the Fathers also affirm a more dynamic, historically conscious understanding of God's will for humanity than had previously held sway in post-Reformation Catholicism, with all that this implies in terms of openness to the genuinely new. The tone of confidence with which this document speaks of the abiding presence of God's Spirit in history, with the accompanying recognition that even ideals may develop and improve, had the potential to counter a spirituality that feared to transgress static divine orders. Indeed, in contrast to this negative spirituality, *GS* invited believers to look beyond the forms that symbolized past understandings of God's will and concentrate instead on the essential divine values of truth, justice, and love that pulse at the heart of the tradition.

Early in *GS*, the words of section 11 establish a new sort of piety, one far different from the passive, defensive piety associated with the period following the "modernist crisis," which had sought to protect itself from worldly influences, retreating to the safety of prescribed and seemingly immutable patterns of Christian life:

> The people of God believes that it is led by the Spirit of the Lord who fills the whole world. Moved by that faith it tries to discern in the events, the needs, and the longings which it shares with other men of our time, what may be genuine signs of the presence or of the purpose of God. For faith throws a new light on all things and makes known the full ideals which God has set for man, thus guiding the mind toward solutions that are fully human.

These two theological affirmations—that God wills for society to reflect the essential equality of the sexes and that history is the locus of the activity of God's Spirit—gave expression to a perspective that was already experienced, if not articulated, by many Catholics, especially women and men in societies where God's liberating intent with respect to women had already been felt in "secular" feminist movements for women's educational and political rights. For these women and men, to read *GS* (especially no. 29) was to discover a powerful rebuttal to the old arguments against women's advancement in society. It was to hear at last a belated disavowal on the part of the international hierarchy of such prejudiced episcopal interventions against social equality as Cardinal Gibbons's 1911 words against women's suffrage in the United States: "When a woman enters the political arena, she goes outside the sphere for which she was intended. She gains nothing by that journey. On the other hand, she loses the exclusiveness, respect and dignity to which she is entitled in her home."[7]

WOMEN AND THEOLOGY

But beyond this, to read *GS* was to be invited to make connections that even its authors had not made, to move by a logic implicit in the text from affirmation of women's rights in society to affirmation of women's rights in the church, beginning with the right to theological education and to participation in the advancement of theology itself. In the two brief but eventful decades since this document appeared, a profound change in the theological scene has occurred, a change that can be summed up by saying that the nouns "woman" and "theologian" are no longer mutually exclusive terms. This fact that women are now teaching and writing theology as professionals in the Catholic Church testifies to tremendous efforts on the part of justice-minded women and men. Risk, sacrifice, suffering, and unflagging labor have been required for women to earn the necessary academic credentials, enter the theological forum, and begin to influence the discussion. These accomplishments, which I briefly review, represent a creative application of the injunctions of *GS* 62 to extend participation in theology beyond the ranks of the clergy and to promote "lawful freedom of inquiry, of thought, and of expression" among theologians.

In 1985, when women could study theology in virtually all the American doctoral programs open to men, it was easy to forget what things were like a generation before. But relatively equal access to theological education is a very new item indeed for women. All the female members of the Catholic Theological Society of America (CTSA) whose doctorates in theology date from the 1950s were graduates of a single far-sighted program at Saint Mary's College, Notre Dame. These women earned Ph.D.s rather than the traditional canonical degree for Catholic theologians, the S.T.D., and at least one American Catholic woman in the 1950s wanted that traditional ecclesiastical degree enough to go abroad in pursuit of it. Mary Daly recalls her experience in the autobiographical preface to the 1975 edition of *The Church and the Second Sex*:

> There was no place in the United States where a female was allowed to study for the "highest degree" in this field, the "canonical" Doctorate in Sacred Theology. Since I would settle for nothing less than the "highest degree," I applied to study in Fribourg, where the theological faculty was state-controlled and therefore could not legally exclude women...[M]y classmates were nearly all priests and male seminarians...in the crowded classrooms there frequently were empty places on each side of me...[8]

Another American woman also earned an S.T.D. abroad in the 1960s, namely, Sister Agnes Cunningham, S.S.C.M., who in 1968 completed a dissertation for the theology faculty at Lyons entitled "Toward a Theology of Christian Humanism."[9] Daly, a laywoman, had supported herself in Switzerland by teaching philosophy to American students who were in Fribourg for "junior year abroad" programs. Cunningham's education had been financed by an anonymous lay benefactor who had approached her religious superiors with the idea of backing the preparation of a sister theologian as an experiment. Daly's financial struggle was certainly the more typical experience for women, both religious and lay, who earned doctoral degrees in Europe, Canada, and the United States in subsequent years.

It is also noteworthy that when women were first admitted to doctoral studies in theology at The Catholic University of America, they were confined to the Ph.D. program and were not eligible for the S.T.D., an inequity that·was repaired by the early 1970s. Meanwhile, Ph.D. programs had become available to women at Marquette, Boston College, and a number of other Catholic universities by the late 1960s. By that time a handful of Catholic women had also entered doctoral programs in some of the traditionally Protestant schools, including Chicago, Yale, and Union/Columbia, among others. Rosemary Radford Ruether, the most influential Catholic woman theologian of the time, earned her Ph.D. from Claremont in 1965. In large part this development was an outgrowth of the new ecumenical movement launched by Vatican II, and in many cases it was the result of foresight on the part of leaders of women's religious communities, as well as of initiative on the part of the individual women who undertook to study theology in an ecumenical context. For these women to finance their educations and succeed in situations where most of the students and all the faculty were male was a major accomplishment, whether they studied in Catholic universities or in other institutions of higher learning; the fact that the situation is better for women studying theology today is due in great measure to their pioneering efforts.

Once the degrees were earned, women who wanted to contribute as theologians had to find employment and make their way into the professional organizations. There are now [1984] 349 women (approximately 25 percent of whom are Catholic) listed at doctoral or professional levels in the most recent directory published by the Women's Caucus of the American Academy of Religion.[10] In 1980, this figure stood at 168. Not all these women are employed, but many have found good positions and have contributed to the profession through various publications and through involvement in the College Theology Society, the American Academy of Religion, the Catholic Theological Society of America (CTSA), and in professional groups specializing in such areas as biblical studies, church history, liturgy, and Christian ethics. Jill Raitt, a Catholic theologian who earned a Ph.D. from The University of Chicago in 1970, served as president of the American Academy of Religion during 1981.

Anne E. Carr, a 1971 University of Chicago graduate, was the first woman tenured in that university's Divinity School. Monika Hellwig, who obtained a Ph.D. from The Catholic University of America in 1968, became the first woman to receive the John Courtney Murray Award for Distinguished Achievement in Theology in June, 1984. Mary Collins, a 1967 Ph.D. graduate from The Catholic University of America, began her term as the first woman president of the North American Academy of Liturgy in January, 1985.

Women's progress in the CTSA has been relatively rapid, given its unpromising beginnings. In *The Church and the Second Sex*, Mary Daly describes in the third person her own disillusioning experience of nineteen years ago:

> In 1966 an American woman who holds a doctorate in theology traveled to Providence, Rhode Island, to attend the annual meeting of the Catholic Theological Society of America, of which she is a member...When she attempted to enter the ballroom of the hotel in which the meeting was being held in order to attend a buffet for members of the society, she was prevented from doing so by one of the officers, a priest. When she insisted upon her right to enter, the priest threatened to call the police. She replied that in this case it would unfortunately be necessary for her to call the newspapers. After a long and humiliating scene, she was finally permitted to enter. This was the debut of the female sex in the Catholic Theological Society of America.[11]

Surely this experience contributed to Daly's decision, formalized by the early 1970s, to leave the Catholic Church and proclaim herself a post-Christian feminist. Some justice-minded men of the CTSA, however, were resolved to open things up, for by 1969 Agnes Cunningham had been elected to the board of directors of the society, and one or two women have served on the board every year since 1975. Cunningham, in fact, progressed during the 1970s through the offices of secretary, vice-president, and finally president of the society, giving the first presidential address by a woman in 1978. Monika Hellwig, elected vice-president in 1984, became the second female president of the CTSA in June, 1986. About 10 percent of those attending the meeting when Hellwig was elected were female, and admissions statistics show an increasing percentage of women entering the society. In 1983, for example, more than one-third of the forty-five new members accepted were female.

There is no question that the rapid entry of women into the profession influenced the discussion, for the topics being treated by theologians generally reflect in some measure the agenda that many women carried into the theological forum. A notable instance is the justice issue of sacramental sex discrimination, often termed the women's ordination issue. The gathering of twelve hundred women in Detroit at the first Woman's Ordination Conference in 1975 was enormously significant, for it was the first time a sizable number of theologically trained female scholars and ministers convened to do theological reflection on the status of women in the Roman Catholic Church. Speakers for that occasion included Rosemary Radford Ruether, Margaret A. Farley, Anne E. Carr, and Elisabeth Schüssler Fiorenza, as well as Richard McBrien, Carroll Stuhlmueller, and George Tavard.

It is likely that the caliber of the theological papers given at the meeting had something to do with the Vatican's 1977 reiteration of the traditional position against women's ordination.[12] It is also significant that American Catholic theologians responded to the Vatican declaration by publishing a closely reasoned analysis and refutation of its arguments against ordaining women. Forty-four women and men contributed to this project, which was edited by Leonard Swidler and Arlene Swidler and published as *Women Priests: A Catholic Commentary on the Vatican Declaration*.[13] The work bears testimony to the fact that matters were far from settled by the Sacred Congregation for the Doctrine of the Faith, and that American theologians had taken to heart the words of *GS* 62 acknowledging that the "proper exercise" of their role requires "a lawful freedom of inquiry, of thought, and of expression, tempered by humility and courage in whatever branch of study they have specialized."

The influence of the women's agenda on the theological discussion is also apparent in the fact that the CTSA commissioned a study of women in church and society, published in 1978, as well as in the fact that many male and female scholars now take care to avoid sexist language in their ordinary discourse and in their references to Divine Reality as well. Other examples of the influence of women's concerns on theology abound. Special issues of journals such as *Liturgy*, *Theological Studies*, and *New Catholic World* have been devoted to these matters. Raymond E. Brown's Hoover Lecture of January 1975, advertised as an address on New Testament studies and ministry, surprised its ecumenical audience by its content: a discussion of the question of women's ordination.[14] Bernard Cooke's article on "Non-Patriarchical Salvation," which appeared in the tenth anniversary issue of *Horizons* in 1983,[15] and Daniel Maguire's 1982 presidential address to the Society of Christian

Ethics, entitled "The Feminization of God and Ethics,"[16] also reflect the influence of feminist theology, as does the fact that when the moral theology seminar of the CTSA took stock of matters it needed to concern itself with during the 1980s, the first item on an agenda proposed by Richard A. McCormick in 1982 was "Feminism in the Church."[17]

It should be clear from the above that the labors of women have had considerable impact on contemporary theological discussions. It should also be apparent that the trend is for this influence to increase, judging from such items as the recent establishment of the Women's Theological Center in Boston, the opening in 1984 of an M.A. program in Feminist Spirituality at Immaculate Heart College in Los Angeles, and the inauguration in 1985 of the *Journal of Feminist Religious Studies*.

Anne E. Carr observes in a 1983 article that the emergence of organized feminist groups of ministers and scholars within the Protestant and Catholic churches over the last two decades has led to a distinctive form of the "theology of liberation":

> Like its Black and Latin American counterparts, feminist theology begins with the concrete experience of women (consciousness-raising), understands itself as a collective struggle for justice (sisterhood), and aims toward a transformation of Church and societal structures consistent with the practical implications of the Gospel.[18]

The literature of Christian feminism, she adds, involves three tasks: critiquing the past, recovering "the lost history of women" in the tradition, and "revisioning Christian categories in ways which take seriously the equality and the experience of women."[19] Carr observes further that the Christian feminist movement is decidedly ecumenical, with Protestant and Catholic theologians alike involved in various aspects of a common project:

> They use the central and liberating Gospel message of equality, mutuality, and service and their own experience to criticize those elements in the tradition which capitulate to take-for-granted patriarchal norms. And they use the central biblical tradition of justice and equality to criticize sexist patterns and practices in culture and society.[20]

Another Catholic feminist, Janet Kalven of the Grail movement, describes the project in even more basic terms. What religious feminists are about, according to Kalven, is "simply drawing out the implications of affirming that women are full human beings made in the image of God."[21]

A FEMINIST READING OF *GAUDIUM ET SPES*

To illustrate what feminist theology can involve, I conclude this chapter with a feminist analysis of *GS*, concentrating on Part One and on the chapter from Part Two dealing with "Culture." As I have indicated, there is no question that this document conveyed Good News to the faithful, and particularly to women. Its insistence on the full humanity of woman—fully equal to man and created with him in the divine image—represents a decisive break with a long tradition of misogynist Christian anthropology, which had taught that woman is ontologically inferior to man and less reflective of the divine image. The import of this new understanding of woman's full humanity cannot be overstated, and its articulation by Vatican II in 1965 is to be celebrated.

Nevertheless, the context in which this new teaching is affirmed—the document *GS* and other conciliar and post-conciliar documents—makes clear that the *implications* of this new affirmation of woman's full humanity have yet to be recognized and carried out to their logical conclusions in the church. This was not, of course, a task for Vatican II; rather it is an ongoing charge for the faithful who have benefited from the legacy of *GS*, *Lumen Gentium*, *Dignitatis Humanae*, and other momentous conciliar documents. To critique *GS* in light of its crucial insight of woman's full humanity, then, is to affirm as well its other central theological insight, namely, its recognition that it is God's Spirit who moves in the historical quest for fuller solutions to the mystery of ideal human existence on earth (11). In what follows here, then, I draw out some implications of the document's affirmation of woman's equality by describing five limitations of *GS* that a feminist perspective judges in need of rectifying. These concern the areas of language, nature and culture, social analysis, ethical norms, and theological affirmations.

Language

The first thing that strikes a feminist reader of the English translations of *GS* is their use of "generic" masculine nouns in countless instances where a more felicitous rendering of the Latin would have allowed the language of the document to affirm woman's full humanity by including her unambiguously in the words about humanity. In view of the fact that as early as 1974 the *Journal of Ecumenical Studies* adopted an editorial policy proscribing the generic use of "man," it can only be regretted that there is not yet available an English translation of *GS* that employs "men and women" or "persons" in contexts where the Latin uses plural forms of *homo.*

To be sure, not everyone recognizes the moral seriousness of the feminist complaint about language. It requires a good deal of empathy and no small amount of moral imagination to appreciate the harm that is done so subtly to the psyches of males and females alike when the very structures of speech imply that one form of human being sufficiently encompasses all that is essential to humanity, that it can stand in place of the other form, apparently without significant remainder. Without getting into the question of whether in fact forms of *homo* functioned as generic masculine forms in Latin culture, one can recognize that today nothing would be lost and much would be gained had the opening line of *GS* been translated so as to make it unambiguously evident that the Fathers cared about "The joy and hope, the grief and anguish" of the women as well as the "men of our time."

The issue of language in this document is not merely a matter of translation, however, for the Latin text itself is replete with usages that have the effect of rendering females invisible. Of particular significance is the frequent use of forms of *frater* and *filius* in contexts where the full inclusion of women in the Christian community would require *soror* and *filia* as well. Again, the point is not trivial, though it is not yet universally acknowledged. In a culture where the superiority of males has been assumed, it is taken for granted that "brotherhood" encompasses an ideal for human community and that "God's sons" is an adequate way of speaking of God's children. However, from the perspective of those who appreciate the power that language has over thought and who recognize the injustice perpetuated by sexist language, the words employed in *GS* 55 to express the Fathers' interpretation of the duty "to build up a better world in truth and justice" can only be understood as ironic: "We are witnessing, then, the birth of a new humanism, where man [*homo*] is defined before all else by his responsibility to his brothers [*fratres*] and at the court of history."

These words are ironic, albeit unintentionally so, because until people recognize that the ideal of "brotherhood"—which excludes half of the world's population from consideration—is part of the problem of global injustice, there can only be very limited progress toward the better world for which the authors of *GS* hoped. The wisdom of certain strains of popular Catholicism, which finds it proper to specify both sexes in such classic texts as the Easter hymn "O filii et filiae" and the

Litany of the Saints, has something to teach official Catholicism in this regard.

Nature and Culture

A second problematic area concerns the views on nature and culture that undergird *GS*. Here the difficulty is perhaps best described as one involving a "root metaphor" that governs the conciliar understanding of these realities. The metaphor derives from Genesis1:28 ("And God blessed them, and God said to them, 'Be fruitful and multiply, and fill the earth and subdue it; and have dominion over the fish of the sea and over the birds of the air and over every living thing that moves upon the earth'") and is essentially a metaphor of domination of nature. Section 9 of *GS* speaks approvingly of "a growing conviction of mankind's ability and duty to strengthen its mastery over nature," and section 57 refers to a divine design whereby "mankind's" task is "to subdue the earth and perfect the work of creation." The metaphor implies that humanity is superior to "nature" and is divinely authorized to be violent in its regard. What such a concept of culture as "mastery over nature" fails to provide is the sense of humanity's *continuity* with the rest of nature and, indeed, of our interdependence with the earth and the rest of the physical universe. There is an unresolved tension in the document between its several approving references to "conquering," "subduing," and "mastery" in relation to Earth and nature (all implying a degree of violence)—see nos. 9, 34, 38, 53, 57, and 63—and the ideal it proclaims at the close of 92: "[W]e ought to work together without violence and without deceit to build up the world in a spirit of genuine peace."[22]

Not unrelated to this is the tendency of the document to regard woman's "nature" rather differently from the way it treats the "nature" of "man."[23] When the document speaks of human nature in general, it stresses the element of mystery, the sense that God alone can supply the full answer to the question which each person is to oneself. When *GS* speaks of woman's nature, however, it conveys a sense of fixity that contrasts with an earlier reference to a "dynamic and more evolutionary concept of nature" in general (5). Thus one reads in the chapter on culture (60): "At present women are involved in nearly all spheres of life: they ought to be permitted to play their part fully according to their own particular nature. It is up to everyone to see to it that woman's specific and necessary participation in cultural life be acknowledged and fostered."

The passage is ambiguous, for were a truly evolutionary view of woman's "nature" intended, it could indeed be a summons to women's liberation. But the term "specific" with respect to woman's participation in cultural life suggests that this is not the case, and subsequent church documents have made it clear that official Catholicism has not applied teachings about the dynamic and mysterious quality of "human nature" so fully to female forms of that nature as to male. Indeed, this became apparent the day following the promulgation of *GS*, when the Fathers of the Council addressed several closing letters to various constituencies. Their message to women indicates that past attitudes were still very much in the ascendency. Even the existence of this message itself is telling, since there is no document addressed simply "to men," although there are messages addressed to "rulers," "men of thought and science," "artists," and "workers." This very arrangement of categories carries the implication that women are thought of primarily in terms of sexual roles, while men are regarded in terms of diversified vocational contributions. Indeed, this is made clear in the opening sentence of the message to women: "And now it is to you that we address ourselves, women of all states—girls, wives, mothers, and widows, to you also, consecrated virgins and women living alone—you constitute half of the immense human family."[24] The message goes on to mention that "the vocation of woman" is in the present era "being achieved in its fullness," a statement whose tone of assurance that the church already knows what this vocation is stands in marked contrast to what is said in the message to workers ("very loved sons"): "The Church is ever seeking to understand you better."[25]

Social Analysis

A third area of concern regarding *GS* involves the social analysis it provides, which for all its acuity in so many respects is regrettably limited on two points of importance, especially to women. In the first place, there is a sense in which women are only partly visible to this analysis. While it is good that women's progress toward our rights is generally affirmed by the document, it is cause for regret that the limited nature of this progress, especially in the developed countries, is not acknowledged. Blindness to the real situation of women is particularly evident in the line from *GS* 9 that "women claim parity with men in fact as well as of rights, where they have not already obtained it." Leaving aside for the moment the question of whether "parity," with its weaker connotation of "equivalence" rather than "equality," is an adequate norm for progress toward justice, what amazes a feminist reader of this sentence is the implicit claim that women have achieved a fair situation in some parts of the world. The claim is not documented, and indeed it would be impossible to defend, given the actual status of women worldwide. As the sociologist Constantina Safilios-Rothschild observed ten years after the promulgation of *GS*:

> [D]espite some progress in some areas, the status of women is still quite low…If we accept that a society is modern when it "is successful in removing social and structural constraints and in establishing appropriate compensatory mechanisms so that all individuals, regardless of their categorical membership such as age, sex, race, religion, ethnic origin, or social class, can have equal access to a wide range of options in all life sectors," no society can claim to have achieved modernity…[Even in Western, developed] societies…sex discrimination has not been eliminated and probably it has not even decreased. It has only changed form: from open, direct discrimination to subtle, sophisticated sex discrimination, which tends to be more effective and difficult to fight.
>
> The status of the majority of women who live in the Third World is still low and ongoing social changes either do not affect their status or tend to even further deprive them of options and opportunities.[26]

The factors examined by Safilios-Rothschild in the cross-cultural study that resulted in the conclusion quoted above were educational and vocational training, employment and other economic roles, marriage and the family, power and political participation, and health and nutrition. Today most analysts of women's status worldwide would support her conclusion that it generally remains lower than man's status.[27]

Given that the text was approved with such a notable misconception about women's actual status left to stand in *GS* 9, it is not surprising that other suggestions of the "invisibility" of women occasionally appear, such as the failure of the document to mention rape or domestic violence, both of which are suffered frequently by women worldwide, in its list of crimes against life and human integrity and dignity (27).

A second problematic aspect of the social analysis in the document is its tendency to press the valid distinction between the church and the rest of society so far that the religious institution escapes the criticism that is leveled against the broader society.[28] Whereas *GS* 26 affirms in general that "the social order requires constant improvement," the more specific sociological reference to the church in 44 is considerably weaker:

The Church has a visible social structure, which is a sign of its unity in Christ: as such it can be enriched, and it is being enriched, by the evolution of social life—not as if something were missing in the constitution which Christ gave the Church, but in order to understand this constitution more deeply, express it better, and adapt it more successfully to our times.

A feminist social analysis, of course, would claim that the church order ought to be a model of justice and equality for society in general, rather than simply a gradually enhanced reflection of "the evolution of social life," and would provide detailed practical suggestions toward achieving this goal.

Ethical Norms

Paragraph 26 also articulates a social ideal that includes ethical norms —particularly justice and love, which are solidly endorsed by feminists. The key passage reads: "The social order requires constant improvement: it must be founded in truth, built on justice, and enlivened by love: it should grow in freedom towards a more humane equilibrium." What *GS* fails to acknowledge, however, is the way in which norms of justice and love can themselves paradoxically function to legitimate oppression if they are not subject to criticism from a perspective that appreciates the full humanity of women. In an article supplying just such a critique, Margaret A. Farley demonstrates the need for theology to draw out the implications of the change from "past assumptions regarding fundamentally hierarchical patterns for relationship between men and women and today's growing acceptance of egalitarian patterns of relationship." She points out that "the 'old order' was clearly one in which women were considered inferior to men and in which women's roles were subordinate, carefully circumscribed, and supplementary." And this "old order" resulted in *theories of justice* that "systematically excluded the possibility of criticizing sexism." By contrast, the "new order" that Farley and other feminists applaud "is based upon a view of women as autonomous human persons, as claimants of the rights which belong to all persons, as capable of filling roles of leadership in both the public and private spheres, as called to equality and full mutuality in relation to both men and women."[29]

What Farley then suggests is that theological ethics needs to develop new interpretations of the traditional principles of love and justice, interpretations that will give impetus to rather than impede progress toward a society that recognizes women as full persons. Whereas *GS* evinces no sense that Christian ideals of love and justice have been in any way problematic for women, Farley's feminist perspective allows her both to critique inadequacies in traditional understandings of these ideals and to offer constructive alternatives in their stead. Thus, with respect to "Christian love" she proposes that its component of "equal regard" is empty if it does not include real equality of opportunity, that its dimension of "self-sacrifice" is false if tied in with misconceptions about female "passivity," and that its aspect of "mutuality" is inadequate if based on analogues found "in the mutuality of relationships between parent and child, ruler and subject, master and servant" rather than on a full recognition of the equality of women and men."[30]

With respect to justice she argues that adequate understandings of both individual and common good require a shift from strict hierarchical models of social organization to more egalitarian ones, noting that "in fact the good of the family, church, etc. is better served by a model of leadership which includes collaboration between [male and female] equals" than one which places a single male leader at the head of the community.[31] In the end, new understandings of justice and love are found to be mutually reinforcing norms for this Christian feminist ethic:

> That is to say, interpersonal communion characterized by equality, mutuality, and reciprocity may serve not only as a norm against which every pattern of relationship may be measured but as a goal to which every pattern of relationship is ordered. Minimal justice, then, may have equality as its norm and full mutuality as its goal. Justice will be maximal as it approaches the ultimate goal of communion of each person with all persons and with God.[32]

Such a perspective would find the ideal of parity expressed in *GS* 9 inadequate insofar as this concept, usually associated with agricultural economics, implies that less-than-equal shares are just ones. "Parity" is not analyzed in the document, but it is the sort of norm that, when applied to human society, tends to accept unequal distribution of literacy, income, and food on grounds that needs for schooling, remuneration, and nourishment differ according to gender roles, men and boys "naturally" requiring more of all because of their actual or prospective positions of dominance.

A feminist perspective also finds inadequate the ideal of "brotherhood," which is articulated so often in *GS*, precisely because the word reinforces patterns of vision that select out the sisters from our midst (who, across the globe, are less educated, poorer, and hungrier than their brothers in every major society) and thus undermines the very laudable traditional norm articulated in 27, the injunction to look upon the neighbor "as another self." As long as one does not see the specifics of female neighbors, so will one's neighbor-love remain inadequate in their regard.

Theological Affirmations

Finally, a feminist analysis of *GS* must attend to what is said and, perhaps more important, what is implied about Divine Reality in this text. Here again, the problem can best be approached by the avenue of metaphor. It is an accepted theological principle that all language about God involves analogy, which means that no human expressions about Divine Reality are ever adequate to the Mystery to which they refer. In the Western religious traditions the metaphor of human fatherhood, which carries, unfortunately, the weight of longstanding patriarchal associations, has traditionally been emphasized in descriptions of Divine Reality and in the language of worship. Many scholars have pointed out, however, that even ancient biblical texts do not limit their language about God to male images such as father, warrior, and lord (although indeed these predominate), but also employ on occasion female metaphors to describe divine qualities and activities.[33]

What is problematic about the language used in *GS* to refer to God is that it relies so heavily on male imagery that it risks reinforcing a naive but widespread tendency to take the metaphor of God as "father" too literally, with the resultant reinforcement of the patriarchal values such language has long legitimated. There are resources within the tradition for countering this tendency, but the Council Fathers, like most Christians two decades ago, were evidently unaware of the connections between societal injustice toward various oppressed groups and patriarchal religious language. Their treatment of atheism can hardly be faulted for not recognizing what was only beginning to be apparent in Western culture, namely, that patriarchal God-language is one of the ways in which "believers" can be said, in the words of *GS* 19, "to conceal rather than to reveal the true nature of God." Twenty years later, however, it has become clear that the rejection of Christianity lamented by the Council Fathers is sometimes due to the idolatrous use of religious language that continues to support the "father-rule" so many associate with values and behavior they see as harmful to humanity and threatening to the rest of creation as well.[34]

Thus, were a council to address the issue of alienation from Christianity today, it would be essential to build on the insights of feminist theologians such as Rosemary Radford Ruether, Elisabeth Schüssler Fiorenza, and Bernard Cooke, who claim that the tradition was originally distinguished by a nonpatriarchal understanding of Divine Reality, which can be expressed in terms of the "Abba" experience of Jesus[35] as well as in terms of the "Sophia-God" experience of Jesus. As Schüssler Fiorenza concludes from her study of early Christian sources:

> To sum up, the Palestinian Jesus movement understands the ministry and mission of Jesus as that of the prophet and child of Sophia sent to announce that God is the God of the poor and heavy laden, of the outcasts and those who suffer injustice. As child of Sophia he stands in a long line and succession of prophets sent to gather the children of Israel to their gracious Sophia-God. Jesus' execution, like John's, results from his mission and commitment as prophet and emissary of the Sophia-God who holds open a future for the poor and outcast and offers God's gracious goodness to *all* children of Israel without exception. The Sophia-God of Jesus does not need atonement or sacrifices. Jesus' death is not willed by God but is the result of his all-inclusive praxis as Sophia's prophet. This understanding of the suffering and execution of Jesus in terms of prophetic sophialogy is expressed in the difficult saying which integrates the wisdom and *basileia* traditions of the Jesus movement: "The *basileia* of God suffers violence from the days of John the Baptist until now and is hindered by men of violence" (Mt 11:12). The suffering and death of Jesus, like that of John and other prophets sent to Israel before him, are not required in order to atone for the sins of the people in the face of an absolute God, but are the results of violence against the envoys of Sophia who proclaim God's unlimited goodness and the equality and election of *all* her children in Israel.[36]

It is indeed good that Vatican Council II, particularly in *Gaudium et Spes*, began a process of restoring to a central place in Catholic piety an appreciation of God's power and presence that stresses the metaphor of the gentle, inviting, and guiding Spirit, who affirms creation and inspires and sustains human hope and community (11, 93). Surely the fruits of Catholic feminist theology, which the episcopal authors did not anticipate from their work, bear witness today to the truth of the affirmation from Ephesians 3:20–21 with which they conclude the document *GS* (93). In sisterly solidarity with these brothers, then, I also conclude: To this Sophia-God, who by the "power at work within us is able to do far more abundantly than all we ask or think...be glory in the Church and in Christ Jesus, to all generations, for ever and ever. Amen."

Notes

1. My title cites the *Pastoral Constitution on the Church in the Modern World* (*GS*), no. 58. This and subsequent citations of the English translation of this text are from Austin Flannery, O.P., ed., *Vatican Council II: The Conciliar and Post Conciliar Documents* (Northport, NY: Costello Publishing Co., 1975). Citations of the Latin text are from *Sacro sanctum Oecumenicum Concilium Vaticanum II: Constitutiones Decreta Declarationes*, vol. 1 (Vaticanum Typographium, 1967). As to the meaning of "feminist," I employ the term here in a broad sense to indicate a position that involves (a) a solid conviction of the equality of women and men, and (b) a commitment to reform society, including religious society, so that the full equality of women is respected, which requires also reforming the thought systems that legitimate the present unjust social order. Both women and men can thus be "feminist," and within this broad category there is enormous variety in levels of commitment, degrees of explicitness of commitment, and, of course, in opinions regarding specific problems and their solutions. Feminism is a concept that is best understood in dialectical relationship to the concept of sexism. For an insightful analysis of these concepts, see Patricia Beattie Jung, "Give Her Justice," *America* 150 (April 14, 1984): 276–78. In focusing on the Catholic feminist theology that has developed in part as the result of *GS*, I am conscious of the limits of my work. Clearly, many other dimensions of what the document said about "culture" could have been discussed, and clearly, my own perspective is limited by my status as an educated white woman from the United States. There remains a great need for the voices of women of color and of women from less privileged backgrounds to be heard in the theological forum. As long as the voices of nonwhite experience are out of the mainstream of theological inquiry, so long will this discipline risk being skewed and out of line with life. It simply will not do if the justice won by women in theology is shared only by white women from the upper and middle classes of Western society.

2. For examples of positions recently articulated by women that challenge certain Catholic teachings while remaining solidly grounded in the Catholic tradition, see Rosemary Radford Ruether, *Sexism and God Talk: Toward a Feminist Theology* (Boston: Beacon, 1983); Joan Timmerman, *The Mardi Gras Syndrome: Re-*

thinking Christian Sexuality (New York: Crossroad, 1984); as well as essays by women contributors to Robert Nugent, ed., *A Challenge to Love: Gay and Lesbian Catholics in the Church* (New York: Crossroad, 1984); Leonard Swidler and Arlene Swidler, eds., *Women Priests: A Catholic Commentary on the Vatican Declaration* (New York: Paulist, 1977); and the periodical *Conscience*.

Catholic women writers, not all of whom are theologians, are by no means unanimous in their analyses, programs, and degrees of dissent from official teachings. In this, of course, they resemble male writers on religious subjects. The above examples are but a sampling from a vast and growing body of feminist literature bearing on Catholic life and thought. I have treated these developments at some length in two articles, from which I occasionally borrow in the present essay, with the permission of Paulist Press. These are: "Women and Religion: A Survey of Significant Literature, 1965–1974," in Walter Burghardt, ed., *Woman: New Dimensions* (New York: Paulist, 1977), 161–89, and "Coming of Age: Women's Contribution to Contemporary Theology," *New Catholic World* 228 (March/April 1985): 61–69. I also want to acknowledge here the assistance given me by two feminist thinkers, Anne E. Carr and Janet Walton, who read an earlier version of this chapter and made valuable suggestions for revisions.

3. Perhaps my own case will help to illustrate the phenomenon of the extraordinary existential impact of *GS* upon some women. I first read the document in the edition edited by Walter M. Abbott, S.J. (New York: America Press, 1966) during a thirty-day Ignatian retreat in the summer of 1967. Schooled in a strict interpretation of the vow of poverty, I had not since 1958 possessed a book like this that spoke so directly to my life and aspirations, and for some reason I felt entitled to take the then remarkable step of underlining and marking this ninety-five-cent paperback so that I could easily find key passages again. Passages that struck home particularly were those dealing with the rights of all, including women, to educational and cultural development. In 1967, I had been teaching high school students for seven years, but despite assiduous application to college extension courses during summers and weekends, I was far from completing my B.A. degree. The words of the document gave expression to my own basic sense of the wrongness of this situation, which I realized even then was tied in with the status of women religious in the church, and they offered a spirituality to counter the prevalent one that legitimated injustice and waste of talents. These words inspired me to take initiatives I would not have considered earlier. I arranged with my religious superiors to be released from classroom duties for three months during the 1968–69 school year, and that spring I completed my B.A. at age twenty-eight, two years earlier than I would otherwise have done and eleven years after I had entered church service. That summer of 1969, I began to study German, the first step in a long program of further study that would finally allow me to become active in the Catholic Theological Society of America in 1978. By 1972, I was heavily involved in organizing Catholic women religious and beginning to publish my developing feminist views. As I reflect on these developments, I feel that had the breakthroughs of *Pacem in Terris* and *Gaudium et Spes* not

taken place, it is quite likely that my talents and energy would long since have left the world of institutional Catholicism and been invested instead in "secular" pursuits, a course taken by countless women ahead of me. For another account of the impact of Vatican II and *GS*, see Mary Daly, *The Church and the Second Sex*, both the original and the revised "feminist post-Christian" editions (New York: Harper and Row, 1968 and 1975).

4. Indeed, the term *vir* is not indexed in the Vatican edition of the conciliar documents, although the parallel term *mulier* is included in the index. It is also interesting to note certain other distinctions the index draws or fails to draw: *Fratemaas, Fratres et Sorores Religiosae,* and *Fratres separati* are all listed. The last of these terms, heard often at the Council, inspired Gertrud Heinzelmann to entitle her collection of interventions regarding women made during Vatican II *Die getrennten Schwestern: Frauen nach dem Konzil* (Zurich, 1967).

5. (Garden City, NY: Image Books, 1976), 8.This volume appeared earlier under the title *What a Modern Catholic Believes about Women* (Chicago: Thomas More Press, 1972), where the incident is described on p. 5. Mary Daly discusses the place women and women's concerns were given at Vatican II in *The Church and the Second Sex* (1975), 118–31.

6. Daly, *The Church and the Second Sex* (1975), 131. Hallinan's statement appears in George Tavard's *Woman in Christian Tradition* (Notre Dame, IN: University of Notre Dame Press, 1973), 127–28.

7. Quoted by Rosemary Radford Ruether in "Home and Work: Women's Roles and the Transformations of Values," in *Woman: New Dimensions*, ed. Walter Burghardt (New York: Paulist Press, 1977), 77.

8. Daly, *The Church and the Second Sex* (1975), 8. As Daly indicates in this post-Christian feminist introduction to her earlier work, she completed doctorates in both philosophy and theology at Fribourg. Had Vatican Council II not taken place, she declares in the same introduction, she might never have written *The Church and the Second Sex*.

9. Mary I. Buckley, now of St. John's University (NY), earned the Th.D. in 1969 from the University of Münster, as did Elisabeth Schüssler Fiorenza in 1970.

10. See Lorine M. Getz and Marjorie L. Roberson, compilers, *A Registry of Women in Religious Studies* (New York: The Edwin Mellen Press, 1984).

11. Daly, *The Church and the Second Sex* (1975), 141–42.

12. For the proceedings of the Detroit Conference, see Anne Marie Gardiner, ed., *Women and Catholic Priesthood* (New York: Paulist, 1976).

13. (New York: Paulist, 1977).

14. This lecture was later published under the title, "The Meaning of Modern New Testament Studies for the Possibility of Ordaining Women to the Priesthood," in Raymond E. Brown, *Biblical Reflections on Crises Facing the Church* (New York: Paulist, 1975), 45–62.

15. *Horizons* 101 (Spring 1983): 22–31. This journal is published by the College Theology Society, an organization that developed to meet the needs of growing numbers of Catholic theologians, many of them laypersons, who were not teaching in seminaries. Its membership is not limited to Catholics, and the

organization continues to focus on the concerns of those teaching in colleges and universities.

16. This address is published in the 1982 edition of *The Annual of the Society of Christian Ethics.*

17. "Moral Theological Agenda: An Overview," *New Catholic World* 226 (January–February 1983): 4–7.

18. "Coming of Age in Christianity: Women and the Churches," *The Furrow* 34 (June 1983): 347.

19. Ibid., 348.

20. Ibid., 351.

21. Janet Kalven, "Women's Voices Began to Challenge after Negative Vatican Council Events," *National Catholic Reporter* (April 13, 1984), 20.

22. I suggest that the biblical metaphor should be recognized as suffering from the limitations of the patriarchal culture from which it emerged and the text should be reinterpreted so as to emphasize a different metaphor, one of caring or stewardship. The import of biblical attitudes toward the Earth and nature has been amply discussed by Christian theologians since the appearance of Lynn White's famous article, "The Historical Roots of Our Ecologic Crisis," in *Science* 155 (1967): 1203–7. See, for example, Ian G. Barbour, *Technology, Environment, and Human Values* (New York: Praeger, 1980) and Roger Lincoln Shinn, *Forced Options: Social Decisions for the 21st Century* (New York: Harper and Row, 1982), and various works by Ruether.

23. The theme of "nature" is an important and much debated one in feminist writing. For theological contributions to this discussion, see Valerie Salving's essay of 1960, "The Human Situation: A Feminine View," reprinted in *Womanspirit Rising*, ed. Carol P. Christ and Judith Plaskow (New York: Harper and Row, 1979), 25–42; and Ruether's *Sexism and God-Talk*, especially 72–92. For instances of the secular feminist discussion, see Sherry B. Ortner, "Is Female to Male as Nature Is to Culture?" in *Woman, Culture and Society*, ed. M. Z. Zimbalist and L. Lamphere (Stanford, CA: Stanford University Press, 1974), 67–87; and Penelope Brown and L. J. Jordanova, "Oppressive Dichotomies: The Nature/Culture Debate" in The Cambridge Women's Studies Group, *Women in Society: Interdisciplinary Essays* (London: Virago Press, 1981), 224–41.

24. Walter M. Abbott, S.J., ed., *The Documents of Vatican II* (New York: America Press, 1966), 732–33.

25. Ibid., 735–36.

26. "The Current Status of Women Cross-Culturally: Changes and Persisting Barriers," an article first published in *Theological Studies* 36 (December 1975) and reprinted in Walter Burghardt, *Woman: New Dimensions*, 27. Safilios-Rothschild is quoting her own earlier research in the above passage.

27. For example, Lucille Mathurin-Mair, a Jamaican who is Secretary General of the World Conference of the UN Decade for Women, has recently observed that today, "Women stand in the wings, as political expediency gives lowest priority to those social and economic sectors which serve society's vulnerable groups, of whom Third World women and their families constitute the most

numerous and the most vulnerable. Not surprisingly, the current United Nations review of the Decade [1975–85] concludes that 'the condition of the majority of women in the developing world has changed, at most, marginally...'" See her article, "The Quest for Solidarity," in *New World Outlook* (January 1985): 56. This entire issue of the magazine, a monthly published by the General Board of Global Ministries of the United Methodist Church, is devoted to the theme of "Women Challenging the World."

28. The implications of this tendency are evident in such observations as the following passage from the 1977 Vatican Declaration, reaffirming a traditional position against women's ordination: "Thus one must note the extent to which the Church is a society different from other societies, original in her nature and in her structures." Here the distinction between the church and other societies is used to counter arguments that modern social developments indicate the need to alter a longstanding tradition. See "Declaration on the Admission of Women to the Ministerial Priesthood," in *Vatican Council II: More Postconciliar Documents*, ed. Austin Flannery (Grand Rapids, MI: Wm. B. Eerdmans, 1982), 342. The tendency also accounts for the discrepancy sometimes noted between official church concern for violations of human rights in various extra-ecclesial political entities and unconcern for violations of human rights within the institutional church. For a discussion of this problem, see Leonardo Boff, *Church: Charism and Power* (New York: Crossroad, 1985), 32–46.

29. "New Patterns of Relationship: Beginnings of a Moral Revolution," in *Woman: New Dimensions*, ed. Burghardt, 53–54.

30. Ibid., 56–57.

31. Ibid., 69.

32. Ibid., 69–70.

33. For a rich discussion of this dimension of the Old Testament, see Phyllis Trible, *God and the Rhetoric of Sexuality* (Philadelphia: Fortress, 1978).

34. In *Sexism and God-Talk*, Ruether describes an understanding of patriarchy widely shared by other religious feminists: "By patriarchy we mean not only the subordination of females to males, but the whole structure of Father-ruled society: aristocracy over serfs, masters over slaves, king over subjects, racial overlords over colonized people" (61). Thus, the patriarchal system is understood most fundamentally to be a system in which some dominate others, and besides being associated with sexism, it is also linked with racism, classism, militarism, violence, and ecological irresponsibility.

35. The significance of the New Testament references to Abba and Pater remains at issue among scholars. Besides the above-cited works of Cooke and Ruether, see Robert Hamerton-Kelly, *God the Father* (Philadelphia: Fortress, 1979), and Phyllis Trible's critical review of this book in *Theology Today* 37 (1980): 116–19. More recently, Madeleine I. Boucher has provided detailed exegetical evidence to counter the positions of Joachim Jeremias and Hamerton-Kelly regarding the alleged "centrality" of the "father symbol" for God in the religious understanding of Jesus. In a paper presented to the Catholic Biblical Association of America meeting in New Orleans August 12, 1984, "The Image

of God as Father in the Gospels: Toward a Reassessment," Boucher suggests that "the increasing frequency of the father image for God (much more common in Matthew and John than in earlier materials) may have been not so much a theological as a christological development. It is the understanding of Jesus as 'the Son' that leads to language about God as 'the Father.'"

36. Elisabeth Schüssler Fiorenza, *In Memory of Her: A Feminist Theological Reconstruction of Christian Origins* (New York: Crossroad, 1983), 135.

4

FEMINIST ETHICS IN THE NEW MILLENNIUM

The Dream of a Common Moral Language

In detailing the work of several of her fellow feminist ethicists, Anne Patrick demonstrates their extensive contributions, realized and potential, to the development of moral theology. She connects these often divergent voices by tracing their shared goal of building solidarity, thoughtfully described here as engaging with sources ranging from Catholic theologians to the Polish labor movement. —HD

When the bishops of the Second Vatican Council spoke of "signs of the times" and "questions of special urgency," few of them were thinking of the women's movement for justice, and probably none anticipated that something called feminist ethics would soon appear on the Catholic theological scene. But arguably the council itself catalyzed this development in ways that are worth recalling today, in this context of millennial musings on what ethics should be like in the next century. The document that gives us the phrase, "Questions of Special Urgency," *Gaudium et Spes*, the "Pastoral Constitution on the Church in the Modern World," stated that God intends a society in which the essential equality of women and men is recognized, and declared that where the "fundamental rights of the person" are concerned, discrimination based on sex "is to be overcome and eradicated as contrary to God's intent" (#29).[1] The same document also affirmed that history is the locus of the activity of God's Spirit, and God's people are led by this Spirit in their efforts to "build up a better world in truth and justice" (11, 55): As we read in paragraph 55:

Adapted from a presentation given at the conference "Questions of Special Urgency: Ethical Dilemmas in the New Millennium (I)" on June 24, 1999 at the Theology Institute at Villanova University.

In each nation and social group there is a growing number of men and women who are conscious that they themselves are the craftsmen and molders of their community's culture. All over the world the sense of autonomy and responsibility increases with effects of the greatest importance for the spiritual and moral maturity of mankind.

In addition to affirming women's dignity and equality, and commending historical efforts on behalf of justice, *Gaudium et Spes* contributed directly to the development of feminist ethics, at least of the Catholic sort, by voicing in paragraph 62 the hope that "more of the laity will receive adequate theological formation and that some among them will dedicate themselves professionally to these studies and contribute to their advancement." By thus welcoming formerly excluded Catholics to the guild of theology, the council opened itself to ideas that would soon transform the enterprise in ways that no one could anticipate in 1965. Furthermore, by articulating the value of freedom of intellectual inquiry, *Gaudium et Spes* implicitly deepened its endorsement of the possibility of significant change. As paragraph 62 concludes, "In order that such persons [those trained in the sacred sciences] may fulfill their proper function, let it be recognized that all the faithful, clerical and lay, possess a lawful freedom of inquiry and thought, and the freedom to express their minds humbly and courageously about those matters in which they enjoy competence."

Finally, in another document promulgated on that busy December 7, 1965, the Council singled out moral theology as especially in need of development. In their "Decree on Priestly Formation," *Optatem Totius*, the bishops declared that:

Special attention needs to be given to the development of moral theology. Its scientific exposition should be more thoroughly nourished by scriptural teaching. It should show the nobility of the Christian vocation of the faithful, and their obligation to bring forth fruit in charity for the life of the world. (16)

The effect of this statement is to establish norms for the practice of moral theology. It should be accountable to science, nourished by scripture, inspiring in its articulation of the ideals of Christian living, and of practical benefit to the world. We may discern a fifth norm in the passage from *Gaudium et Spes* about freedom of inquiry and expression, for with such freedom comes the responsibility to pursue truth rigorously and to express one's findings appropriately, in the words of the council, with humility and courage.

The fact that these bishops called for the *development* of moral theology indicates their recognition that our ethical tradition had not been living up to its potential, and the world has been the poorer as a result. The Council's insistence that moral theology "bring forth fruit in charity for the life of the world" suggests that past emphasis had been too individualistic and too otherworldly, too preoccupied with the future state of believers' souls, to take sufficient notice of its effects on the worldly welfare of persons within and beyond the Catholic community. Today, decades after the council, this call for the development of moral theology still stands in need of fulfillment. Progress has been made, but the discipline is not yet sufficiently integrated with biblical spirituality, nor is it fully adequate to the needs of our world.[2]

I believe the challenges to moral theology are deeply religious and moral ones. We are being called on the one hand to foster a more radical trust in God, and on the other to develop a more thoroughgoing ethic of justice. To me the situation calls for change greater than anything we have yet seen; we need no less than a revolution of Catholic consciousness. A profound conversion is called for, a shift of attention, a turning from certain preoccupations to new topics and new ways of seeing old ones.[3]

My thesis here is that Catholic feminist ethics is contributing to this process of conversion and is fostering the development of moral theology called for by the Council. I also think that we may hope for the "planned obsolescence" of feminist ethics to be underway at some point in the next millennium, ideally within the next century. Although I do not expect this to happen in my lifetime, I believe feminist ethics should have a limited life span, and should make a graceful exit once its goals have been achieved. We will be ready for its departure when women are recognized as fully human and fully capable of moral decision-making, sacramental leadership, and church governance; we will be ready when women's moral experience is routinely incorporated into moral reflection at every level of the church and the academy. We are far from ready now, but we have come some distance in the twentieth century, and there is reason to hope for a future that is better than the past we have known. This future is the dream of my title, adapted from the poet Adrienne Rich, "The Dream of a Common Moral Language."[4] Rich gave her original title, *The Dream of a Common Language*, to a volume of love poetry, something not at all removed from theology, if one shares Gustavo Gutiérrez's notion that theology can be "a love letter" to God and the church.[5] In any case, the "dream of a common moral language" is certainly one that fits well with the natural law tradition of Catholic moral theology, which aspires to communicate and collaborate with all persons who strive to know and do what is right and good.

For the present essay I have narrowed the topic of feminist ethics to that practiced in the Catholic context, not only because this is my own tradition but also because Catholics have been leading contributors to feminist religious thought. If the hopes of the Second Vatican Council are to be realized, it will be up to Catholics to bring this about, and the more of us who see feminism as central to the reform of our tradition, the sooner this reform will be likely to happen. Of course, Catholics who do feminist ethics are often in conversation with Jewish, Protestant and secular feminist thinkers, and sometimes with those from other traditions as well. My focus here, however, will be on how feminist ethics contributes to the conciliar mandate to make moral theology, and by extension the ethical lives of Catholics, more fruitful for the common good of all the earth's inhabitants, both now and in the future. I have reviewed conciliar influences on the development of feminist approaches to Catholic moral theology because it is crucial to situate this enterprise solidly in the tradition that gave it impetus. Certainly there remain tensions between Catholicism as we have known it and feminism, but we have found considerable common ground already. My discussion that follows is divided into in three sections:

1. Feminist Ethics: Vision and Voices

2. Harbingers of Hope: Feminist Ethicists as Theorists and Practitioners of Solidarity

3. Living in the Meantime

Finally, I conclude by returning to the ideal of my subtitle, "the dream of a common moral language." This is the situation toward which feminist ethics is working, when sufficient attention to particularities of difference will have transformed ethical discourse to a point of full inclusivity. At this point, feminist ethics itself can leave the platform because its goals will have been reached. Women will no longer be perceived or treated as a lesser form of humanity, but will view ourselves and be recognized by men as fully human and fully capable of moral decision-making, sacramental leadership, and church governance; our moral experience will routinely be incorporated into moral reflection at every level of the church and the academy. In view of this long-term goal, then, I begin by offering some

definitions of terms and historical background, preliminary information that provides a basis for thinking about the future. Here I address
the questions, "What is feminism?" and "What led to the emergence
of feminist ethics in Catholicism?"

FEMINIST ETHICS: VISION AND VOICES

Just as maps are not actual territory but representations that orient and
guide us, so verbal definitions are not full depictions of "reality" but resources that aid our understanding of complex movements and enter-
prises such as "feminist ethics."

Feminism. There are many definitions and types of feminism, with
considerable controversy about the meanings and implications of the
various types. Feminists all agree that there has been a historic bias
against women, and they seek to overcome the problems known as sexism, androcentrism, and patriarchy. Where definitions of feminism are
concerned, one crucial distinction should be noted. Some definitions
emphasize the participation of women as *subjects* of their own liberative
process against sexism, stressing the fact that women, not men, must
liberate themselves from injustice. Other definitions emphasize the fact
that human beings of both sexes are capable of recognizing and seeking
to remedy sexism. These two types, designated respectively as "woman-
centered feminism" and "inclusive feminism," are different, but each
captures true aspects of the movement and has useful applications.

Historian Gerda Lerner provides an example of a "woman-centered" approach when she describes feminist consciousness as:

> the awareness of women that they belong to a subordinate
> group; that they have suffered wrongs as a group; that their
> condition of subordination is not natural, but is societally de-
> termined; that they must join with other women to remedy
> these wrongs; and finally, that they must and can provide an
> alternate vision of social organization in which women as well
> as men will enjoy autonomy and self-determination.[6]

I do not believe Lerner means by this definition to exclude men
from sharing in the alternate vision or working toward its social realization, but her definition recognizes that there is indeed a difference
between being the subject of a liberative process and participating em-
pathetically in such a movement when one does not suffer the precise
injustice oneself.

While accepting the value of Lerner's approach, I have also found it useful to employ an "inclusive" definition of feminism, and have suggested that feminism is a position that involves two elements: (1) a solid conviction of the equality of women and men, and (2) a commitment to reform society so that the full equality of women is respected, which requires also reforming the thought systems that legitimate the present unjust social order.[7] This implies that men and boys can be feminists, and indeed do well to assume this moral stance. Finally, however one defines the term, it needs to be said that feminists differ widely in their analyses of injustice, levels of commitment to liberating action, degrees of explicitness of commitment, and opinions regarding specific problems and their solutions.

Sexism, patriarchy, androcentrism. Various thinkers distinguish "patriarchy" and other key terms of feminist thought in slightly different ways, but there is basic agreement that bias against females has both social-systemic and intellectual-attitudinal components. Theologian Elizabeth A. Johnson provides a helpful analysis in her groundbreaking volume *She Who Is*. Johnson regards sexism as a "social sin that has debilitating effects on women both socially and psychologically, and interlocks with other forms of oppression to shape a violent and dehumanized world." She names the "twin faces" of sexism as "patriarchy" and "androcentrism."[8] In a later volume Johnson stresses that sexism is "a pattern of thinking and acting that subordinates women on the basis of their sex." Sexism expresses itself *structurally* as *patriarchy*, "the social arrangement where power is exercised of necessity by the dominant males, with others ranked in descending orders of dominance," and *intellectually* as *androcentrism*, "the thought pattern that takes the human characteristics of the adult male as normative for the whole of humanity, consigning whatever deviates from this to the outer realms of otherness or deficiency." Whether social or ideological in expression, Johnson argues, sexism has the effect of "making women mostly invisible, inaudible, and marginal, except for the supportive services they provide."[9]

Patricia Beattie Jung has developed a cogent ethical analysis of the relationship between sexism and feminism in a 1984 *America* article entitled, "Give Her Justice." Jung's argument is elegant in its simplicity: sexism involves an unjust distribution of the benefits and burdens society has to offer, and feminism is the commitment to right that imbalance. Not to be committed to feminism, in other words, is to be complicit in sexism.[10]

I find Jung persuasive on this point—that feminism is a moral position highly to be commended, since it is the name for the willingness to overcome the injustice of sexism—and I have long been comfortable describing my own work as theologian and ethicist in these terms. I am aware, however, that ambiguities of definition, and especially of connotation, have colored the meaning of feminism for many persons, and there are some good reasons why others are less comfortable accepting or proclaiming that their efforts are "feminist." In the first place, there is the basic concern of men not to claim themselves as subjects of a liberative process that is not actually their own. Secondly, there is the strategic choice of women and men not to complicate what may already be difficult rhetorical challenges when they are seeking to influence an audience that cannot hear them further if the term "feminism" is dropped within fifty feet of their paragraphs. Finally, and most importantly, from the vantage point of women of color there has been the need to dissent from the racism and false generalizations long associated with white feminism in this country, which has too often spoken about women as if the experiences of European-American females were the only ones that mattered. Thus a number of African American and Latina scholars have claimed more precise designations for their own efforts, employing the novelist Alice Walker's term "womanist" in the former case, and theologian Ada María Isasi-Díaz's parallel term "*mujerista*" in the latter. At the same time these scholars usually acknowledge, explicitly or implicitly, that their work on behalf of justice for women is a dimension of feminism when it is properly understood and functioning in a genuinely pluralistic way.[11] Two representative contributors to Catholic feminist ethics from these groups are discussed in more detail later on—M. Shawn Copeland and Ada María Isasi-Díaz—but for now I want to address the nervousness about claiming feminism that affects European-Americans who believe in women's equal dignity but are reluctant to use the designation "feminist."

Ironically, "feminism" is the moral position that dare not speak its name in certain circles. Catharine R. Stimpson notes that feminism has become an "F-word" of sorts, and ethicists may sometimes prefer not to employ it in a climate in which the concept has been trivialized, demonized, or otherwise burdened beyond recognition. Nevertheless, I believe Stimpson is right to assert that feminism brings several gifts to society: "a moral vision of women in all their diversity, and of social justice; political and cultural organizations (like battered women's shelters); and psychological processes that enable men and women to re-experience and re-form themselves."[12] Stimpson acknowledges, however, that "[e]ven feminists fear feminism." They may feel conflicted about gender and social change, and may be inclined to whisper that they are feminists while adding under their breaths that they regret having to be. Nevertheless, the moral vision and programs of feminism are "too compelling to ignore," and I agree with Stimpson's conclusion that only the appropriate and frequent use of the term is likely to restore its ethical meaning and reasonableness to the public at large.[13]

For this reason, I believe theologians and ethicists do well to claim their commitment to feminism explicitly whenever it is relevant to their efforts, for by doing so they keep the essential meaning of feminism as a commitment to justice before the church, which is historically so implicated in sexism. To women, who have inherited the opportunities to teach and publish as the result of long struggles by foresisters who entered these professions in times much less favorable to females than our own, I say it is important to claim the moral vision of feminism explicitly. This forthrightness will keep us from being what Stimpson has called "languid heiresses," who are "living on a trust fund from history," spending the money but failing to add to the principal. It will also bring more positive connotations to the minds of others, who will grow to understand the value and complexity of feminism more readily as more of us claim and clarify the designation.

To men, whose feminism is different from women's, I say that their commitment will be most edifying when they speak well of the moral vision of feminism and act in ways that clearly manifest their desire to remedy past injustices. I commend the example of theologians such as Walter Burghardt, Charles Curran, and Richard McCormick, who have served Catholic feminism in ways that make their opposition to sexism quite clear. As editor of *Theological Studies*, Burghardt devoted an entire issue during the 1975 International Women's Year to the subject of "Woman: New Dimensions," providing a forum for the thought of scholars including Rosemary Radford Ruether, Elisabeth Schüssler Fiorenza, Mary Aquin O'Neill, and Margaret A. Farley to reach a wide and influential audience of Catholic theologians. The fact that Raymond Brown and George Tavard also contributed to that December 1975 issue of *Theological Studies* was important too, for their presence in the volume on women encouraged the collaboration necessary for significant change to occur.

A few years earlier, a regular contributor to *Theological Studies*, Richard A. McCormick, had advanced the cause of feminism by including a discussion of the women's liberation movement in his "Notes on Moral Theology" for March 1972. McCormick's notes, which appeared annually in *Theological Studies* for two critical decades following the Second Vatican Council, from 1965–84, have been influential for the church internationally. Moreover, by the time McCormick wrote about women's liberation in late 1971, he had received the highest honor from the Catholic Theological Society of America (CTSA; then known as the Cardinal Spellman Award, 1969) and had just completed his year as president of the CTSA (1970–71). He thus brought considerable stature to the discussion of women's liberation, and would have been more likely heard by theological colleagues than a less powerful figure. It is worth quoting McCormick here, and recalling or imagining a situation quite different from our own, a time when very few women were teaching in graduate programs in moral theology or Christian ethics. Margaret Farley may have been the only Catholic woman doing so; in March 1972 she was in her first year as professor at Yale Divinity School, with her dissertation not quite complete. McCormick begins his 1972 reflections on women's liberation by citing a thinker associated with the Grail Movement:

> As Janet Kalven points out, women's liberation has come into existence against the background of the black movement, student movements, and the third-world emergence and has adopted very often their heady rhetoric, guerilla tactics, and shrill anticapitalist ideology. But surely it would be a pity if these sometimes bizarre tactics and the violent rhetoric blinded us to the genuine moral dimension cast up by the new feminism.[14]

He concludes by declaring that theology's task concerning women's liberation is threefold. It must critique unjust models of women's humanity and replace them with just ones, shaped from the "richness of the Christian tradition." Secondly, theology must "put its own house in order by encouraging the emergence of women theologians of competence and influence in far greater numbers." And finally, theology must

> insist that the Church...must teach what it is to be human by her own inner life. If her own structures and ministry continue to speak of humanity in terms of but one sex, must we not think that the Church is seriously compromising her mission in the contemporary world? I believe so. Granted, there are hosts of practical pastoral problems to work out; but here is a chance for genuine leadership. Too often in the past the Catholic community has almost reluctantly accommodated after everybody else has shown the way.[15]

Perhaps McCormick had in mind here the hierarchy's opposition to women's suffrage, which had been voiced by many American bishops in the first two decades of this century, perhaps most eloquently by Cardinal James Gibbons in a 1911 interview with the *New York Globe*:

> "Women's suffrage," questioned the Cardinal?..."I am surprised that one should ask the question. I have but one answer to such a question, and that is that I am unalterably opposed to woman's suffrage, always have been and always will be... Why should a woman lower herself to sordid politics? Why should a woman leave her home and go into the streets to play the game of politics?...When a woman enters the political arena, she goes outside the sphere for which she was intended...[and] loses the exclusiveness, respect and dignity to which she is entitled in her home."[16]

Cardinal Gibbons, who is rightly remembered as a progressive leader where the rights of working men were concerned, certainly spoke for the old order when it came to women's suffrage. His confidence that the nature, scope, and purpose of women's lives should be determined by men is something he shares with certain church officials alive today who have progressive views on many other questions but are unwilling even to allow discussion of change on matters such as tubal ligation or women's ordination. In 1972, when McCormick published his appreciative discussion of the women's movement in *Theological Studies*, it is likely that the hierarchy's belated endorsement of women's political rights was among the items he had in mind in lamenting that "[t]oo often in the past the Catholic community has almost reluctantly accommodated after everybody else has shown the way." He voiced the hope that this pattern would change, that there might be some "fresh...bold move," but recognized that there was not much precedent for the kind of boldness he envisioned. Nevertheless, McCormick concludes his groundbreaking discussion by insisting that women's liberation confronts the church with a "serious moral problem and, it would seem, an idea whose time has come."[17]

McCormick's leadership on this matter did not end in 1972. A decade later he discussed "the most important areas within the field of moral theology in need of exploration and research over the next five to ten years" at the moral theology seminar of the Catholic Theology Society of America. The list he presented to a roomful of mostly male colleagues at this June 1982 gathering in New York began with "moral issues related to feminism."[18] He urged attention to the question of women's ministry and declared that although "no individual can claim an unqualified right to ordination as a priest," still "a class of persons could argue that, if there is no solid theological justification, this exclusion is a denial of a right—a right not to be *unfairly* interfered with in the *pursuit* of a possession or a goal." He also pointed out that one might claim that the faithful in general "have a right to the *fullness* of priestly ministry as they work out their salvation," and because theological justifications for the current exclusion of women have not been convincing, "the matter must be viewed as unfinished and open to further development."[19]

On this subject it is worth adding that Bishop Raymond Lucker of New Ulm, Minnesota, is also among clerics long on record as pointing to the need for the church to overcome sexism. Indeed, in 1991 Lucker observed that the fact that women's ordination cannot be discussed is "a sign of injustice."[20] He published this opinion in 1991, three years prior to Pope John Paul II's apostolic letter "*Ordinatio Sacerdotalis*," which sought to close the question by declaring "that the church has no authority whatsoever to confer priestly ordination on women, and that this judgment is to be definitively held by all the church's faithful."[21] The Catholic Church is for the time being in a period of official silence on the question of women's ordination, but works published earlier can hardly be taken off the shelves, and new reflections will find their way into print, albeit through independent publishing houses. For example, when the Benedictine monks who sponsor the Liturgical Press obeyed an injunction not to distribute Lavinia Byrne's study, *Woman at the Altar: The Ordination of Women in the Roman Catholic Church*, although it had already been advertised in their 1996–97 catalog, the independent publishing house Continuum brought it out promptly in New York.[22]

Returning to Richard McCormick, a recent and important instance of his support of feminism involves the publication, in collaboration with Charles Curran and Margaret Farley, of the ninth volume in a series of "Readings in Moral Theology" he had previously co-edited with Curran. The publication of this work in 1997 keeps the importance of feminist ethics before the guild of Catholic moral theology and also makes it easier for students to have access to otherwise fugitive contributions by leading contributors to feminist ethics. Among the twenty-five essays in this anthology, several are by scholars in related disciplines such as historical theology or biblical studies, but most are by women (and one man) who are well-established in the field of Christian ethics.

This background information from the last three decades amounts to a story with a moral. Christian ethics, including the feminist variety, is at its best when it is judiciously proactive about where it puts its efforts, and when it tackles difficult topics in a way gauged to help change the world for the better. Richard McCormick is an outstanding example of such proactivity, demonstrating an effective solidarity with a marginalized group. Whether or not he is appropriately called a feminist can be argued either way, but this is not nearly so important as what he has done with his power as a leading practitioner in the guild of Christian ethics. His decision to write appreciatively on women's liberation in 1972 helped create a climate in which Rosemary Radford Ruether's volume of *Liberation Theology*, also published in 1972, could be received more favorably and by a wider Catholic audience than might otherwise have been the case.[23] It also seems likely that many of the women whose feminist essays were published in the anthology *Readings in Moral Theology No. 9* benefited from the climate to which Burghart and McCormick contributed in the seventies, especially those who were in graduate school or seeking employment at that time, when very few women were tenured as theologians.[24]

Consider the mandate McCormick set in 1972, that male theology must "put its own house in order by encouraging the emergence of women theologians of competence and influence in far greater numbers." This has happened, and it has not happened by accident. The participation of women in the Catholic Theological Society of America is a case in point. The first women to be admitted as active members of this formerly male and clerical organization were Elizabeth Jane Farians and Cathleen M. Going, who joined in 1965. By 1977 female membership had reached 5 percent and by 1992 it stood at 17 percent; presently [1995] I would estimate that it is about 20 percent.[25] But today women are perceived as much more numerous than we actually are because we have been elected to leadership in this society disproportionately to our numbers, and I have to infer that other male theologians have been sharing the moral vision articulated by McCormick a quarter century ago, for we women would not have had the votes to bring this off by ourselves. Agnes Cunningham was the first woman elected to presidential office, in 1977, and since then two women were elected in the 1980s and four in the 1990s. The current president is Margaret Farley, who designed a convention that took place in Miami in June 1999, on the theme of "Development of Doctrine." The papers and conversations that resulted from her efforts are helping to nudge the tradition into the next millennium with appropriate verve, faith, and commitment.[26] The emergence of women in the field of theology is change that can be measured, and the case suggests to me that ethicists will also do well to think even more practically about how feminist values can become realized in the next century.

Of course, women's own efforts and commitments were the primary factor in our entering the guild and developing a new approach to ethics, and that is a story too complex to tell in any detail here. Suffice it to say that the first generation of women scholars in this field set an impressive example by their commitment to a methodology that gave priority attention to women's experience in its diversity and complexity as they reflected on various theoretical and practical questions in ethics. Margaret Farley notes in her entry on "Ethics and Moral Theologies" for the *Dictionary of Feminist Theologies* that there are two factors that make Christian feminist ethics "feminist": In the first place, "it is opposed to the subordination of women to men on the basis of gender," and in the second, "it incorporates a central methodological focus on the experience of women."[27] The reasons for this methodological commitment are well stated in the introduction to the first volume of religious feminist ethics published in this country, a 1985 collection entitled *Women's Consciousness, Women's Conscience: A Reader in Feminist Ethics*, co-edited by the Catholic scholars Barbara Hilkert Andolsen and Christine E. Gudorf, and a Lutheran, Mary D. Pellauer. They write:

> The patriarchal legacy of the West has hidden women's experience from ethical view... Too often, society creates a vision of "feminine" experience which keeps women subservient to men, alienated from our own human wholeness, and isolated from other women.[28]

These pioneering editors sound a theme that will be plumbed often by subsequent authors, namely the diversity of female experience:

> There is no homogeneous woman's experience. Women's lives are very different. Among the differences which seem the most significant are the following: Some women are mothers; others are not. Some women come from upper class backgrounds; others, from the middle class; still others, from the working class or from poverty. Some are lesbian; some heterosexual. Women are black, native American, Asian American, or Latina... Women have very different work experiences as homemakers, clerical workers, service workers, factory operatives, managers, or professionals. If feminist ethics is to be based upon the experience of *all* women, then such differences in experience must be acknowledged and incorporated into feminist theory.[29]

Although this diversity entails that one cannot generalize uncritically about something called "women's experience," and especially that women from more powerful groups cannot presume to speak for all women, feminist ethics should not for this reason drift into a skeptical relativism. Indeed it has not usually done so, certainly not in the case of the Catholic authors included in the volume mentioned above. Along with recognizing diversity among women, these thinkers are also conscious that all women share female embodiment and suffer some injustice on account of gender. Therefore, many claims about what is harmful and beneficial to women do have validity—for instance, claims about the evils of malnutrition, rape, and battering.

Lisa Sowle Cahill used the occasion of her 1993 presidential address to the Catholic Theological Society of America to argue this point cogently in a lecture entitled, "Feminist Ethics and the Challenge of Cultures." Notwithstanding the insights of postmodern philosophers such as Foucault and Habermas about the limits of reason, our common humanity inspires Cahill to affirm the basic insight of the Aristotelian-Thomistic natural law tradition, namely "a commitment to an objective moral order, knowable by reasonable reflection on human experience itself, especially on the purposes and values all societies share."[30] There can, in other words, be "intercultural ethics," and given the "crying injustices worldwide of poverty, war, hunger, and oppression of whole peoples, and of women among all peoples," there must be sustained efforts to reach agreement on matters of justice and human well-being.[31] This position is widely shared by other Catholics who do feminist ethics.

Besides its commitment to justice for women and its methodological focus on women's experience, Catholic feminist ethics is a highly theological enterprise. It shares the liberationist perspective of feminist theology in general, whose aim has been well described by systematic theologian Elizabeth Johnson: "By Christian feminist theology I mean a reflection on God and all things in the light of God that stands consciously in the company of all the world's women, explicitly prizing their genuine humanity while uncovering and criticizing its persistent violation in sexism, itself an omnipresent paradigm of unjust relationships."[32]

The principle of the "preferential option for the poor," so central to liberation theology and important also to recent Vatican teaching, leads Johnson to state as the aim of feminist religious discourse a goal that is widely shared by Catholic feminist ethicists, namely "the flourishing of poor women of color in violent situations."[33] When women from the most oppressed situations flourish, it seems clear, we can safely assume that life is better for everyone.

The vision of feminist ethics, in sum, is one of justice, mutuality, and inclusivity. The last three decades of the twentieth century have seen the emergence of women into the field of moral theology, thanks to their own efforts and the proactive welcome extended by men who shared this vision. Now that women's voices have come into the discussion, what new things are stirring? What harbingers of a hopeful future are with us as we face the next millennium?

HARBINGERS OF HOPE

FEMINIST ETHICISTS AS THEORISTS AND PRACTITIONERS OF SOLIDARITY

The most crucial thing that needs to happen as we enter the next century involves a refocusing of moral energy, which I have called the "turn to the oppressed." If moral theology is to fulfill the mandate of Vatican II and inspire the faithful to "bring forth fruit in charity for the life of the world," somehow Catholics' moral energy must burst through the casing of legalism and dutiful individualism that was stressed in their moral formation. Only then can it blossom into an effective responsibility that will bear fruit for the life of the world. When I survey the many contributions of Catholic feminist ethicists since the 1970s, one especially encouraging theme is solidarity, a newly emphasized virtue and practice, which is necessary for realizing the ideals of justice central to feminism and Christianity alike. Without solidarity, moral theology is at risk of lapsing into "gourmet ethics," a preoccupation with individual moral righteousness, especially among those whose affluence allows them to worry about choices that are beyond the realm of possibility for most human beings, particularly the poor.

Solidarity can also help feminist ethics avoid the theoretical paralysis that may otherwise happen as a result of the rapid proliferation of subfields in ethics, whether those of "identity groups" such as Latinas and African Americans, or those of topical fields such as bioethics, ecology, sexual ethics, and so on. Obviously these subdivisions have purpose and value, but the insights from each need to be brought together for everyone's practical benefit. A spirit of solidarity can inspire those with particular interests to gather the gleanings from specialized work and make these available for wider discussions of the common good. It is surely a sign of hope that reflections on solidarity and an ethical methodology that expresses solidarity are prominent in the writings of many Catholic feminists who do ethics.

According to Matthew Lamb's discussion of "solidarity" in the *New Dictionary of Catholic Social Thought*, the term was first employed in papal teachings in the early twentieth century in an effort to shape a social theory that avoided both the individualism of liberal capitalism and the various problems of authoritarian communism. "Solidarity" is the English translation of a modern German word, *Solidarismus*, originally linked with the labor movement, and its first magisterial use seems to have been in Pope Pius XI's encyclical of 1931, *Quadragesimo Anno*, which had been written by the social theorist Otto von Nell-Breuning. As Lamb indicates, "Catholic solidarism aimed at transposing pre-modern understandings of natural law, of human being as essentially social, and of society itself as organic and cooperative, into the modern contexts of industrialized societies with complex exchange commodities."[34] The term "solidarity" was later used in the encyclicals of Pope John XXIII, *Mater et Magistra* and *Pacem in Terris*, as well as in the conciliar document *Gaudium et Spes* and Pope Paul VI's encyclical *Populorum progressio*. It has been especially prominent in the writings of Pope John Paul II, and its association with the Polish labor movement that played such a key role in dismantling the communist bloc in eastern Europe is well known.

Lamb notes that Pope John Paul II was the first to employ the term solidarity to denote a virtue, which he characterizes in his 1987 encyclical *Sollicitudo Rei Socialis* ("On Social Concern") as more than mere feelings of compassion, but rather "a firm and persevering determination to commit oneself to the common good," which is to be practiced not only between individuals and socio-political entities but between human beings and the natural environment.[35] Solidarity, moreover, goes beyond simple "interdependence," and is very close to classical understandings of charity. According to Pope John Paul II, solidarity "helps us to see the 'other'—whether a person, people or nation—not just as some kind of instrument, with a work capacity and physical strength to be exploited at low cost and then discarded when no longer useful, but as our 'neighbor,' a 'helper,' to be made a sharer on a par with ourselves, in the banquet of life to which all are equally invited by God."[36]

Liberation theologians such as Jon Sobrino have also emphasized solidarity, but it is especially prominent in the writings of Catholic feminist theologians, perhaps because they have reason to think that the magisterium itself needs to be more consistent in practicing solidarity with regard to women.

The virtue and practice of solidarity begins with the commitment to the oppressed, which in liberation theology has been called the "option for the poor." Solidarity above all requires a disposition to give priority to those who are voiceless, marginalized, or oppressed in any situation about which we do moral reflection. Its first moment must be one of attention, and especially of listening. Such listening requires more than mere politeness; rather it presumes a real openness and a willingness to be affected and to change as a result of what has been heard.

The importance of such listening is illustrated in the examples I discussed earlier, the decisions of Walter Burghardt and Richard McCormick to use the power of their social location in a field that had traditionally marginalized women, namely Catholic theology, to create a space where women's voices could be heard and eventually transform the field. Now that women are established in the theological community, they have not only enriched the theoretical meaning of solidarity but have also exemplified the virtue in much of their own practice. These Catholic women ethicists are harbingers of hope for a better future, helping to span the gap between a century that has known too much violence and injustice and a new millennium that can be considerably more peaceful, compassionate, and just if we, with God's help, make it so.

There are many Catholic feminist thinkers whose work is relevant here, although for reasons of space I have selected six for discussion below: Ada María Isasi-Díaz, Margaret A. Farley, Patricia Beattie Jung, Barbara Hilkert Andolsen, M. Shawn Copeland, and Rosemary Radford Ruether. These scholars have all set new directions, and their very practice of ethics exemplifies what solidarity entails and thereby deepens our understanding of its meaning and requirements. These thinkers are building a bridge to the next millennium, and we will do well to cross it in their company. If we do, we shall also encounter many others who have valuable things to teach us along the way.

Ada María Isasi-Díaz is a Latina born in Cuba who has lived in the United States for nearly forty years. A leader of the Women's Ordination Conference in the late 1970s, she later studied theology and ethics at Union Theological Seminary. She now teaches in the Theological School at Drew University and publishes works that demonstrate a distinct emphasis on solidarity. In 1988 she co-authored a volume with a Mexican-American colleague, Yolanda Tarango, which was largely built from interviews with women from diverse Latina backgrounds, including Mexican, Puerto Rican, and Cuban. Entitled *Hispanic Women: Prophetic Voice in the Church*, this work emphasizes the actual words of the women interviewed, thereby affirming with unprecedented immediacy the experiences of those previously marginalized from theological scholarship.[37] This book also provides summaries of each chapter in Spanish, a practical way of broadening the circle of those who have access to the work and a subtle reminder to Anglo readers of the importance of the language spoken by the fastest-growing segment of the U.S. Catholic population. In 1993 Isasi-Díaz published a work elaborating her *mujerista* theology, *En la Lucha: A Hispanic Women's Liberation Theology*. This book is more theoretical than the one she wrote with Tarango, but it still draws from an organic process of listening to women from a broad range of Latina cultural and economic backgrounds.[38]

In her most recent book, *Mujerista Theology* (1996), Isasi-Díaz devotes an entire chapter to "Solidarity: Love of Neighbor in the Twenty-first Century." There she describes solidarity as "the appropriate present-day expression of the gospel demand that we love our neighbor."[39] She indicates that solidarity is a matter of effective, cohesive struggle governed by an understanding of interconnected issues; it goes well beyond mere agreement with and support of a people's cause. Solidarity requires mutuality as well as praxis, she insists, and its "goal is not the participation of the oppressed in present social structures but rather the replacement of those structures by ones in which full participation of the oppressed is possible."[40]

Although she has an academic position, Isasi-Díaz continues to work with grassroots Latinas and endeavors to bring their experiences into her reflections on theological and ethical topics. I have never forgotten the powerful words she quoted from a Puerto Rican woman in her early sixties in her first book. This mother of twelve said about her decision to have a tubal ligation despite the objections of doctors, husband, and priest: "I would have had twenty-four children if I had listened to them."[41] I hope that magisterial authorities will listen more attentively to such women, something that Isasi-Díaz's books certainly facilitate. If they listen, they will have to discover a way of allowing for reasonable exceptions to current policies that absolutely prohibit sterilization, even under conditions where pregnancy poses a serious threat to a woman's health.

Margaret A. Farley—A similar methodological interest in the diverse experiences of those who have not made the ethical rules is evident in Margaret Farley's important study from 1986, *Personal Commitments*. Her opening chapter describes instances where a commitment vowed in marriage or religious life has meant joy, growth, and fulfillment—not without struggle, to be sure, but on the whole a positive experience. But she also describes instances where such commitments have brought largely negative results, including pain, tragedy, and despair. Keeping this mix of experience in mind, Farley reflects on the meaning and obligatory force of personal commitments in a context where people "find [them]selves faced with an ever-widening range of options...and a confusing rate of change that never lets [them] rest from making decisions."[42] Her conclusion is balanced, and well grounded theologically. Because only God is to be loved absolutely, our human commitments to love within such finite frameworks as marriage or a religious community will appropriately be assessed in light of whether they actually allow for the focused love that was promised to endure and flourish, or whether for some reason they have become inimical to this flourishing of love, and perhaps even harmful to the well-being of persons. Human loves and the frameworks designed to serve them must be assessed in light of the norm of justice, Farley believes. In some cases this norm will require that the framework should be maintained until death, whereas in others justice may oblige a person to change the framework of a commitment, for example by obtaining a divorce or a dispensation from religious vows. Nevertheless, she concludes that the original commitment to love does continue to bind the one who made it:

> Should we be justified in changing the framework of a commitment, the special claim we have given to our love still obligates in some way. Even when we must end a marriage or leave a community or withdraw from a project, the special right of the other at least obligates us, to the extent we are able, to change the commitment with care, without violence on our part, with some form of fidelity to the love we originally promised...
> [T]he commitment-obligation to a fundamental love does hold even through the changing of the instrumental commitment that was meant to serve it.[43]

In subsequent writing Farley lives up to her commitment to attend to the experiences of those who have been on the margins when the tradition was shaped. Her work in progress on sexual ethics, to be published soon under the title *Just Love*, has been informed by the voices of persons whose experiences have much to teach the tradition, especially women and sexual minorities.[44] At the same time, her knowledge of and esteem for the classical tradition is evident in her writings, and praised by her scholarly colleagues. In 1992 Farley became the second woman in the history of the Catholic Theological Society of America (CTSA) to receive its John Courtney Murray Award for achievement in theology. (Systematic theologian Monkia Hellwig had been so honored in 1984). The following excerpt from the citation read by CTSA President Michael J. Buckley on that occasion conveys the balance and solidarity that characterize Farley's work:

> With the 1992 John Courtney Murray Award, the Society honors a scholar who bears out Murray's own commitment to public responsibility and social justice. Like Murray, our recipient draws on St. Thomas' concern for reasonable moral discourse and the integration of love and justice. Reinterpreting Aquinas and Murray for the post–Vatican II world, this theologian makes a special commitment to justice and equality for those excluded from power—especially for women—in family, society, and Church.[45]

With Lisa Sowle Cahill, Farley is one of only two Catholic women who have been elected president of both the Society of Christian Ethics, where she served in 1993, and the Catholic Theological Society of America, where she assumed the presidency in 1999. In stating her goals for the latter office, Farley stressed her intent to make the organization an even more welcoming forum for the full range of theological voices, so that minorities—whether of gender, racial-ethnic background, or place along the conservative-progressive spectrum—can enjoy full access to the give and take of theological conversations.[46]

Patricia Beattie Jung, who teaches at Loyola University in Chicago, is a third feminist ethicist whose writings exemplify the sort of proactive solidarity that is requisite for the development of moral theology. Two books of hers are especially notable. In preparing them she worked collaboratively with male scholars, one Catholic, the other Protestant. It took courage and generosity for her and Thomas A. Shannon to publish in 1988 an anthology of essays entitled *The Catholic Abortion Debate* in order to make widely available a range of arguments about the moral, political, and ecclesial dimensions of this topic. Jung and Shannon sought "to present the middle ground of the abortion debates," because they believed that "on both sides of the debate it is possible to develop reasonable arguments based on commonly held principles." These editors deliberately omitted perspectives from the "radical right and left," but included contributions by cardinals of the church and by a diverse group of Catholic feminists, among various others chosen because their arguments seemed "responsible," "complex," and "often not that far apart."[47] In the heated and often disrespectful context of late twentieth-century abortion politics, Jung and Shannon knew they risked trouble by undertaking this publishing project, and they might well have gathered essays on a controversy with a lower decibel rating. But they resisted the temptation to self-censorship and undertook a task they anticipated might be thankless, in a spirit of solidarity with many Catholics of conscience who have been endeavoring to discern a reasonable and responsible position on a public policy question that is more complex than it has been portrayed.

More recently Jung has published a work on another topic that will be engaging reflection in the churches well into the next century. This is a study from 1993 entitled *Heterosexism: An Ethical Challenge*, which she authored jointly with the late Ralph F. Smith, then a professor of liturgy and colleague of Jung's at Wartburg Theological Seminary, a Lutheran institution in Dubuque, Iowa. In this book Jung and Smith conduct an ethical analysis of their topic that involves careful attention to the biblical and natural law traditions as well as to the human costs of maintaining the "reasoned system of prejudice" they designate as "heterosexism."[48] Their study serves an ecumenical community that is currently struggling with many questions on this issue, and predictably will continue to do so well into the twenty-first century. It exemplifies one of the aspects of solidarity that I have mentioned above, namely the willingness to listen to marginalized others to the point of being affected by what they say, and possibly changing as a result. Jung and Smith, who characterize themselves as "heterosexual persons of different genders, each married [to other partners] with children," were transformed by sustained listening to their students from the gay community. In the "Introduction" they voice their realization that publishing this work on behalf of justice for sexual minorities would entail some risks:

> Speaking publicly on homosexuality in the present climate means facing on occasion the kind of condemnation and ostracism that gay men and lesbian women face daily. The personal and professional risks borne by others who have taken this path before us are plain to see…With this book we acknowledge that the life stories of gays and lesbians, like the life stories of women and people of color, have helped to persuade our hearts and minds that we cannot stand by while injustice reigns.[49]

Barbara Hilkert Andolsen—A fourth Catholic feminist whose ethical writings are notable for their solidarity with persons who live at some remove from the centers of power, is Barbara Hilkert Andolsen, who teaches social ethics at Monmouth University in New Jersey. Her doctoral dissertation, published in 1986, was a study of racism in the nine-teenth-century white women's movement, entitled *Daughters of Jefferson, Daughters of Bootblacks,* and in subsequent books she has continued to focus on issues of gender, race, and class.[50]

In 1989 she wrote *Good Work at the Video Display Terminal: An Ethical Analysis of the Effects of Office Automation on Clerical Workers.* There she called attention to the various health and economic justice concerns that computers and other technologies have raised for the largely fe-male clerical work force.[51] In her most recent book, *The New Job Contract: Economic Justice in an Age of Insecurity* (1998), Andolsen reaches an interesting insight about solidarity with respect to the employment pat-terns now practiced in the United States. She notes that there has been a transition from a traditional employment paradigm in which a dili-gent and skilled worker could often expect long-term employment with the same company, to what is now a much less secure labor situa-tion, even for middle-class, white-collar workers. This new paradigm, known as the "employability" model, "does offer workers a chance to develop skills that will make them 'employable' in the external labor market," but does not provide the security typical before corporations adopted the tactic of "downsizing" to remain competitive in a rapidly changing global economy.[52]

Corporations today are also turning more and more to "contingent workers," that is, "part-timers, temporary workers, and ·contract work-ers," who typically lack health and retirement benefits, and who face considerable economic insecurity. Women comprise the majority of these contingent workers, and Andolsen is "disturbed that contingent work continues a pattern of insecure work for many persons of color and for some white women." But her research shows that the new "em-ployability" paradigm also means that "many men, including many white men, are losing ground in this economy, while some economically privileged (primarily white) women are doing much better."[53] Her nu-anced conclusion voices an important challenge where solidarity is con-cerned: "Women as a group have not achieved economic parity with their male peers. Nevertheless the substantial economic progress made by some women raises... sharp questions about the moral responsibility of economically 'successful' women. What are the possibilities of a soli-darity that will bind those privileged women to the women and men who are excluded or marginalized in the labor markets of the informa-tion age?"[54]

Andolsen believes there are important resources for answering this question within Catholicism, both in its tradition of social thought that calls for "a conversion to solidarity with the socially disadvantaged" and especially in the "eucharist as a source of motivation to act in solidarity with the many workers and their dependents whose employment security has been seriously diminished as a result of the shift to the new employability contract."[55] Sadly, however, Andolsen acknowledges that the eucharist itself is burdened by sexism and sometimes by racism as well, and is presently an ambiguous sacrament for feminists of both sexes. Nevertheless she values the eucharist as a celebration between our present "brokenness" and our hoped-for "wholeness," which is eminently capable of nourishing "solidarity with economic 'outcasts' in the global labor market." Thus Andolsen commends eucharistic spirituality as a way of growing in awareness of the problematic aspects of the seemingly thriving U.S. economy: "Regular participation in the eucharist—with an openness to the values that it embodies—should create and strengthen in worshipers a sense of the connectedness among human beings, with the whole created world, and with the Creator/Redeemer."[56]

The last two thinkers I shall discuss, M. Shawn Copeland and Rosemary Radford Ruether, are not active in the specialized guild of ethics or moral theology, but rather are identified with liberationist and political approaches to historical and systematic theology. Each is centrally concerned with matters of justice, however, and has published works that are appropriately called "feminist ethics."

M. Shawn Copeland, whose contributions to black theology and liberationist political theology more generally date from the 1970s, even prior to her doctoral studies, now teaches at Marquette University. Like Andolsen, she has a particular interest in the situation of workers, especially factory and domestic workers, and the links between solidarity and eucharistic practice. In an important essay published in 1995, she argues that "the Eucharist with its precise denotation of the meaning of the Incarnation of the Second Person of the Trinity as Jesus of Nazareth and his sacrifice for us illustrates in a most striking and accessible way the meaning of solidarity for Christians."[57] But the Eucharist will be an "empty gesture," she maintains, "if we have not confessed our sins; repented of our participation and/or collusion in the marginalization of others.

Copeland continues:

> The Eucharist is at the heart of the Christian community...Eating the bread and drinking the cup involve something much deeper and more extensive than consuming the elements of this ritual meal...there are social as well as sacramental conse-

quences to the Eucharist. For to be one in Christ Jesus is to reject those systems of living that deprive women and men of human and political rights, that oppress the poor, that suppress women, that authorize racism, that promote discrimination against men and women because of fear of their sexual orientation, that obstruct the self-determination of the peoples of the world.[58]

In a 1987 essay on "The Interaction of Racism, Sexism, and Classism in Women's Exploitation," Copeland called for a "critical feminist theology" of global dimensions, "which refuses to rank or order oppression; which takes up the standpoint of the masses, the marginated and those beyond the margins; and which is committed to justice in the concrete." Overcoming the collusion of Christianity in the oppression of women and people of color, Copeland points out, requires the collaboration of theologians with other analysts within and beyond the tradition, especially those trained in critical understandings of economics, sociology, and politics.[59]

In recent years Copeland has bridged the discussion between womanists and other feminists, most explicitly in a ground-breaking 1994 address to the College Theology Society, which was quoted above for its insights on the eucharist and solidarity. Entitled "Toward a Critical Christian Feminist Theology of Solidarity," this lecture challenges Christian feminist theologians of all backgrounds to go beyond the *rhetoric* of solidarity and commit themselves to the *critical practice* of solidarity. Speaking at St. Mary's College, Notre Dame, on the occasion of the fiftieth anniversary of the first Catholic graduate program in theology open to women in this country, Copeland argues that

> focus on solidarity not only problematizes the practice of theology for Celtic, Anglo, European-American feminist theologians, but also for indigenous North American and Asian American women theologians, for mujerista and womanist theologians. Focus on solidarity calls for an end to facile adoption of the rhetoric of solidarity by Celtic-, Anglo-, European-American feminists, while they ignore and, sometimes, consume the experiences and voices of the marginalized and oppressed, while, ever adroitly, dodging the penitential call to conversion—to authenticity in word and deed.[60]

Authentic solidarity, she observes, means recognizing that common problems do not automatically lead to sisterhood and that differences must be respected but not absolutized. Her suggestions for getting beyond "naive, 'politically correct,' clichéd rhetoric of solidarity" to authentic Christian praxis are twofold. In the first place she calls for "active and attentive listening" to differentiated voices within and beyond one's own community. Such listening demands different virtues of those who are relatively more implicated in systems of oppression than of those who are less so. Thus she enjoins white women to practice humility, resolve, and relinquishment in an ongoing effort to balance attentive listening with appropriate speaking. She urges red, brown, yellow, and black women to forego manipulative stances in favor of honesty, courage, and appropriate self-criticism. And she invites everyone to practice patience and restraint, "an ethics of respectful listening and an ethics of thinking before speaking," which is grounded theologically in the experience of God's liberating Word.[61]

In addition to this disciplined process of hearing and speaking, Copeland insists that a complex form of social analysis is also needed for the praxis of solidarity. This analysis involves critiquing one's own horizons, developing general descriptions of the factors at play in oppressive situations, probing the patterns that emerge from such descriptions, judging the incongruities thus uncovered in the light of the Gospel, and coming to specific decisions and commitments for action. The process is a continual one, and it is possible only in community and through the gift of God's Spirit.[62]

The implications of Copeland's critical perspective may be seen in a volume she co-edited in 1994 with New Testament scholar Elisabeth Schüssler Fiorenza, *Violence Against Women*. This book is a Christian theological and ethical analogue to such secular feminist works as the volume *Transforming a Rape Culture*, published in 1993.[63] It gathers essays by women from Europe, Asia, and the Americas that explore the sociocultural factors, particularly gender construction and religious ideology, associated with violence against women in systems of patriarchal power. In a concluding essay Copeland makes several proactive suggestions for change on the basis of her critical analysis of the material in this anthology. First, the church must repent its historic misogyny as well as its ambivalence, complicity, and direct engagement in violence against women: "...the blood of raped, battered, abused and murdered women summons the church to its own *kenosis*," or self-emptying in effective acts of penance that contribute to real change. Second, the church must develop a new model of pastoral care that values women's experience and replaces the "aesthetic of submission" associated with so much religious imagery and ritual in favor of an "aesthetic of liberation" that will inspire a "non-oppressive, non-sexist truly human and Christian future." Third, the church must adopt a renewed theological anthropology and challenge media and religious influences that reinforce unjust patterns in domestic relations, distort understandings of sexual desire and pleasure, and promote dualist or reductively "essentialist" views of women. Finally, the church must develop a pastoral ministry that heals the effects of clergy sexual misconduct against women and children, thereby restoring their bodies to "erotic and spiritual integrity" and the Body of Christ to "ontological and sacramental integrity."[64]

Rosemary Radford Ruether—The sixth feminist ethicist is the most prolific, and I emphasize here only one dimension of her many contributions, namely her recent work on ecofeminism, a topic that undoubtedly will increase in importance in the next century. What is now called ecofeminism is not a new interest for Ruether, however, for one of her earliest books, *Liberation Theology* (1972), deals with the connections between gender injustice and mistreatment of the earth.[65] Her analysis has deepened in subsequent years, and in 1992 she published a wide-ranging and scientifically informed work, *Gaia and God: An Ecofeminist Theology of Earth Healing*. There Ruether argues that we must respect the interdependence of human and non-human living creatures and take action "in defense of the global commons of forests, oceans, and atmosphere." Major changes are needed, including the willingness to acknowledge that "life is not made whole 'once and for all,' in some static millennium of the future. It is made whole again and again, in the renewed day born from night and in the new spring that rises from each winter."[66]

Her 1998 book, *Women and Redemption: A Theological History*, takes the argument from there and probes how different interpretations of this central religious mystery have developed in Christian history, culminating in the new possibilities emerging from contemporary feminist theologies. Drawing on her training in classics and historical theology, Ruether traces the connections between ideas of gender and redemption in the New Testament, and in the patristic, medieval, and reformation periods of church history. The theme is then pursued in several chapters dealing with particular regions: one discussing North American Shakers and feminist abolitionists of the nineteenth century, and three that survey recent feminist theologies in Europe, North America, and the vast territories of Latin America, Africa, and Asia. She looks especially to these last approaches for insight toward building "a more authentic basis for solidarity among women, and between men and women, to rebuild more life-sustaining societies in their own lands and between nations on a threatened Earth."[67]

Ruether's commitment to solidarity with marginalized groups is longstanding. She took part as a Delta ministries volunteer in Mississippi in 1965 and spent her first years of seminary teaching (1965–1976) at the Divinity School of Howard University, an historically black institution in Washington, DC.[68] In a groundbreaking 1974 study, *Faith and Fratricide,* she challenged Christians to rethink their attitudes toward Jews, and more recently she has also lifted up the concerns of the Palestinians and drawn attention to the sufferings brought upon the people of Iraq by U.S. airstrikes and economic sanctions.[69] Her interests in ecology and in justice for women everywhere led her to edit an anthology entitled, *Women Healing Earth: Third World Women on Ecology, Feminism, and Religion* (1996), where she brings voices from Africa, Asia, and Latin America to a wide readership in North America and Europe.[70]

There is a prophetic urgency to Ruether's introduction to this collection, in which she surveys North American feminisms and finds some lacking, especially when they fail to make the connections between "their actual social context as heirs and beneficiaries of [patriarchal] conquest as First World affluent people." Merely to deal with the psycho-spiritual level by reconnecting with nature and celebrating embodiment, she maintains,

> can become a recreational self-indulgence for a privileged counter-cultural Northern elite if these are the only ideas and practices of ecofeminism; if the healing of our bodies and our imaginations as Euro-Americans is not connected concretely with the following realities of over-consumerism and waste: the top 20 percent of the world's human population enjoys 82 percent of the wealth while the . . . poorest 20 percent of the world's people, over a *billion* people—disproportionately women and children—starve and die early from poisoned waters, soil, and air.[71]

Ruether discerns two notable differences between the Northern ecofeminists and those writing from Asian, African, and Latin American contexts. In the first place, the latter group is much more vividly aware of the human and economic factors involved in ecological devastation, for these women know on a daily basis how drought and deforestation cause hardship and death. Secondly, they are more likely to be realistic in recognizing the ambiguities both of Christian and tribal traditions, instead of tending, as many Northern women do, rigidly to condemn their own Western Christian heritage while romantically idealizing tribal cultures. Ruether believes that studying the analyses from

African, Asian, and Latin American women's perspectives can inspire European and North American feminists to keep more focused on the connections between their own economic privileges, the impoverishment of the world's majority, and the diminishing quality of earth's soil, air, and water. She also hopes that the examples of "third world" women will encourage Northern ecofeminists to be "less dogmatic and more creative about what is good and bad, usable and problematic, in our own cultural legacies," drawing out the good from traditions that range from Hebrew, Greek, and Christian, to Nordic, Celtic, Slavic, and modern.[72]

Additional examples of solidarity—As I indicated at the outset of this section, the above list is limited to six authors simply for reasons of space. Among many other Catholic feminist ethicists whose work exhibits the quality of solidarity with those who are "other," three deserve special mention because of their stature in the field. Christine E. Gudorf is the author of important books on victimization and sexual ethics.[73] She has also worked with others to prepare volumes of case studies for discussion by students, most recently a forward-looking collection co-edited with Regina Wentzel Wolfe, *Ethics and World Religions: Cross Cultural Case Studies*.[74] Lisa Sowle Cahill, whose books deal with a range of topics including bioethics, sexual ethics, and issues of war and peace, has also written on feminism with particular attention to cross-cultural concerns.[75] Cahill used the occasion of her 1993 presidential address to the Catholic Theological Society of America to probe "Feminist Ethics and the Challenge of Cultures," concluding with a challenge to her colleagues: "How can the Catholic theological academy both account for theoretically and underwrite practically the struggle of women worldwide to live their lives for themselves and for others with human dignity?"[76] Finally, Mary E. Hunt, who, like Ruether, is an activist as well as a theologian, has not only written an important study on friendship, but has also encouraged networking among feminists of various backgrounds and callings, especially through the organization she founded in 1983 with Diann L. Neu, the Women's Alliance for Theology, Ethics, and Ritual (W.A.T.E.R.).[77] Of particular interest here is Hunt's leadership in promoting conversations among ecofeminists in the Americas through a series of gatherings in 1997 and 1998 called "A Shared Garden." Graciela Pujol, a Uruguayan who participated in these meetings—held first in Santiago, Chile, next in Washington, DC, and then in Recife, Brazil—observes that they have been "irreplaceably rich experience[s]," especially for "women who had never before left their homeland or their city." She comments thus on what participants concluded after visiting several poor neighborhoods in northeast Brazil: "Change was not viewed among these women as anything in the near future...But they did have a stubborn trust in solidarity, as the one way to survival."[78]

A commitment to solidarity characterizes the work of a number of other Catholic feminists who are working in the field of ethics in addition to those who have been mentioned above. Their efforts, as well as the efforts of those who labor in other theological disciplines and in various practical ministries, are helping to shape a future that will be more just, less violent, and friendlier to the earth than the past we have known in the twentieth century.[79]

LIVING IN THE MEANTIME

I find it daunting to imagine what challenges the next millennium will bring to feminist ethics, and I am not enough of a futurist to feel confident in listing priorities even where the twenty-first century is concerned. Certainly such political and economic developments as new forms of warfare (for instance, air campaigns that minimize risk to the military personnel of the powerful, democratic nations while tolerating "collateral damage" to civilians in the enemy countries) and the globalization of banking, industry, and commerce will call for creative responses from ethics. Certainly concerns about the environment, health care, and technologies of all sorts will mount, especially those that affect the genetic makeup and reproduction of our species. Feminist ethics will, I hope, bring its commitment to the well-being of women and its attention to women's experience in all its complexity to these issues. I believe it will contribute much to the discussions, since women's well-being is constitutive of the wider common good that all ethics must seek.

My emphasis in terms of future recommendations will be more general here, however. Ethics has grown very specialized in the twentieth century, and although the complexity of new problems warrants this development, I would like to see Catholic feminist ethics contribute a balancing emphasis on some matters that cut across the various subfields that have developed within ethics, not only those organized around practical topics such as bioethics and sexual ethics, but also those designated as "feminist," "womanist," "*mujerista*," and so on into the increasingly diverse future. Of course these specialities are important, and it has been important to name and describe them, but whatever else feminist/womanist/and *mujerista* ethicists are doing,

I hope that we will feel sufficiently established as we enter the next millennium to give our energies to matters that transcend these projects. I also hope that feminist ethics in the future will rise to four challenges that it faces at the end of this millennium.

1. *Staying ecclesial,* despite discouraging signals from the hierarchical magisterium where certain topics of great concern to women are involved. I agree with Barbara H. Andolsen and M. Shawn Copeland that the eucharistic community is important for fostering the practical solidarity that the feminist ethical agenda requires, and I also think that we need this community to sustain our faith, hope, and love on a long-term basis. Eucharist done in memory of Jesus and the divine gift of salvation can be an occasion of grace and solidarity for all. Where else is it likely that the poor, middle class, and wealthy members of society will encounter each other as persons? Where else can those blinded by greed and paralyzed by fear learn to let go of what blocks their human flourishing and set out with new energy to live justly and walk humbly with their God? Surely God's grace is not confined to the rituals of any tradition, and surely a principled absence from services that are noninclusive and alienating can be justified as a survival strategy. But Christian feminists who do observe this contempory version of "Eucharistic fast" will need to find satisfying answers to the "where else" questions I have raised, for a spirituality cut off from communion with the poor and disenfranchised members of society, who tend to show up in church more often than in spas and conference centers, is at risk of becoming one more consumer item. Moreover, the ongoing reform of the church requires the presence of members who claim to have the vision of what God is calling the church to become.

2. *Gaining a public voice,* now that the academic one seems reasonably secure in view of so many women having gained tenure and recognition in professional circles. I hope the twenty-first century will see more women trained in moral theology who write regularly for the Catholic and secular press and who appear as experts on radio and television. Such thinkers have much to bring to public debates on matters such as genetic research, the use of fetal tissue in developing medical treatments, the problem of gun violence, and other issues that will emerge in the future. Rosemary Radford Ruether writes often on current issues in the *National Catholic Reporter*, Lisa Sowle Cahill contributes occasionally to *America,* and Carol A. Tauer brings insight to bioethics discussions on *Almanac,* a local public affairs program produced by the PBS affiliate in

St. Paul-Minneapolis (KTCA), but for the most part Catholic feminist ethicists have not broken into the national secular media. We should challenge ourselves and encourage each other to send essays to journals such as *The Atlantic Monthly* and *The New Yorker* and op-ed pieces to newspapers such as *The Washington Post, The New York Times,* and *The Los Angeles Times.*

3. *Contributing more directly not only to virtue theory but also to the education of persons, especially the young, to virtue* as it is coming to be newly understood. This will mean collaborating with other fields beyond ethics, notably with experts in education and the helping professions.[80] These fields are less prestigious and well-heeled than medicine, a prominent conversation-partner with ethics in the twentieth century, but they are nonetheless crucial for changing a society that now promotes greed and consumerism as if they were social goods. Besides solidarity, my wish-list of virtues to be emphasized includes newly interpreted versions of justice, patience, chastity, sobriety, and hope.

4. Giving thought to the practical details of *shaping a new order* that avoids the injustices of patriarchy while carrying on the necessary functions that this problematic form of social organization has, despite its faults, accomplished in the past. In other words, now that the feminist critique of patriarchy has gained a solid footing, we should give more attention to constructing and sustaining alternative social patterns.

CONCLUSION: THE DREAM OF A COMMON MORAL LANGUAGE

The present essay has argued that Catholic feminist ethics is contributing to the renewal of moral theology called for by the council, and that it is poised to do much in the next millennium toward realizing the conciliar goal of "bearing fruit for the life of the world." I have indicated that the practice of solidarity by men of justice was instrumental in women's gaining access to the guild of theological ethics, and that since gaining access these women have enriched our understanding of what solidarity entails not only by their theoretical reflections but also by their own practice. I have articulated several challenges now facing the field, and I conclude by observing that the labors of these feminists are helping the wider human community to implement four principles that were agreed to in 1993 by representatives of various traditions as part of a "Declaration toward a Global Ethic." These principles are:

1. Commitment to a culture of non-violence and respect for life.
2. Commitment to a culture of solidarity and a just economic order.
3. Commitment to a culture of tolerance and a life of truthfulness.
4. Commitment to a culture of equal rights and partnership between men and women.[81]

Signatories to this 1993 declaration included persons from many faith traditions: Bahais, Brahma Kumaris, Buddhists, Christians, Hindus, Jains, Jews, Muslims, Neo-pagans, Sikhs, Taoists, Theosophists, Zoroastrians, and representatives of several indigenous religions (including Akuapi, Yoruba, and Native American) as well as a few interreligious organizations. Catholics contributed much to this declaration, and our moral tradition has a great deal of wisdom to bring to the task its signatories identified as incumbent on all religions today, namely to convert the world's peoples to "a common global ethic, to better mutual understanding, as well as to socially beneficial, peace-fostering, and Earth-friendly ways of life."[82]

It has been my contention here that Catholic feminist ethics is playing a crucial role in helping to bring about this conversion to a common global ethic. For the first part of the next millennium it will continue to have a distinct identity and to play this role. But eventually its goals will have been reached, and feminist ethics can then make a graceful exit from the scene. Thanks to the divine Spirit, who works mysteriously in our ambiguous lives and history to renew the face of the earth, Catholics will eventually succeed in clearing the impediments of patriarchy from the stream of moral wisdom that is our heritage. We will then begin to realize the dream of a "common moral language," through which insights and questions can be shared among ourselves and with others in ways that are both intelligible and beneficial.

Notes

1. Quoted here from Walter M. Abbott, ed., *The Documents of Vatican II* (New York: America Press, 1966), 227–28. Subsequent references to conciliar documents are from this widely studied edition. For a new, inclusive-language translation, see Austin Flannery, OP, ed., *Vatican Council II: Basic Edition* (Collegeville: Liturgical Press, 1996). For a fuller discussion of the impact of *Gaudium et Spes*, see Anne E. Patrick, "Toward Renewing 'The Life and Culture of Fallen Man': '*Gaudium et Spes*' as Catalyst for Catholic Feminist Theology," in

Judith A. Dwyer, ed., *"Questions of Special Urgency: The Church in the Modern World Two Decades after Vatican II* (Washington, DC: Georgetown University Press, 1986), 55–78.

2. My own volume, *Liberating Conscience: Feminist Explorations in Catholic Moral Theology* (New York: Continuum, 1996), from which I draw occasionally in the present essay, aims to contribute to this task of developing moral theology.

3. Patrick, *Liberating Conscience*, 12–13.

4. Adrienne Rich, *The Dream of a Common Language: Poems 1974–1977* (New York: W. W. Norton & Company, 1978).

5. See Gustavo Gutiérrez, *A Theology of Liberation*, rev. ed. (Maryknoll, NY: Orbis Books, 1988), xlvi.

6. Gerda Lerner, *The Creation of Feminist Consciousness* (New York: Oxford University Press, 1993), 14. She believes that patriarchy depends on mistaken assumptions about gender, which "constructed the male as the norm and the female as deviant; the male as whole and powerful; the female as unfinished, physically mutilated and emotionally dependent" (p. 3).

7. This definition is discussed in Patrick, *Liberating Conscience*, 7–8.

8. Elizabeth A. Johnson, *She Who Is: The Mystery of God in Feminist Theological Discourse* (New York: Crossroad, 1992), 22.

9. Elizabeth A. Johnson, *Women, Earth, and Creator Spirit* (New York: Paulist, 1993), 24.

10. Patricia Beattie Jung, "Give Her Justice," *America* 150 (April 14, 1984), 276–78.

11. For influential examples of these approaches, see Delores S. Williams, *Sisters in the Wilderness: The Challenge of Womanist God-Talk* (Maryknoll, NY: Orbis Books, 1993) and Ada María Isasi-Díaz, *Mujerista Theology* (Maryknoll, NY: Orbis Books, 1996). Alice Walker's original description of "womanist" opens her volume *In Search of Our Mothers' Gardens: Womanist Prose* (San Diego: Harcourt Brace Jovanovich, 1983), xi–xii.

12. Catharine R. Stimpson, "The 'F' Word," *Ms.* (July/August 1987), 80.

13. Ibid., 196.

14. Richard A. McCormick, *Notes on Moral Theology 1965 Through 1980* (Washington, DC: University Press of America, 1981), 385.

15. Ibid., 392.

16. *N.Y. Globe*, June 22, 1911 (Documents of the Catholic Bishops against Women's Suffrage, 1910–1920; Sophia Smith Collection, Smith College. Quoted here from Rosemary Radford Ruether, "Home and Work: Women's Roles and the Transformation of Values," *Theological Studies* 36 (1975): 653.

17. McCormick, *Notes on Moral Theology 1965 Through* 1980, 392.

18. David Hollenbach, "Seminar on Moral Theology: The Future Agenda of Catholic Moral Theology in America," *CTSA Proceedings* 37 (1982): 176. Hollenbach summarized several panelists on this topic, including McCormick, whose reflections were revised and published elsewhere; see note no. 19, below.

19. Richard A. McCormick, "Moral Theological Agenda: An Overview," *New Catholic World* 226 (Jan./Feb. 1983): 4–5.

20. Raymond A. Lucker, "Justice in the Church: The Church as an Example," in *One Hundred Years of Social Thought*, ed. John A. Coleman (Maryknoll, NY: Orbis Books, 1991), 100. The late auxiliary bishop of Baltimore, P. Francis Murphy, was also outspoken on this topic. Indeed, in an editorial published shortly after his funeral, the *National Catholic Reporter* noted that "Murphy was unyielding in his support for women's ordination, even in an era when many bishops refrain from making any favorable comment on the issue in public for fear of reaction from the far right and discipline by the Vatican" ("For the Bishop, a Fittingly Provocative Sendoff," September 24, 1999, 32).

21. Pope John Paul II, "Ordinatio Sacerdotalis," #4 (Apostolic Letter on Ordination and Women), *Origins* 24 (June 9, 1994): 51.

22. Lavinia Byrne, *Woman at the Altar: The Ordination of Women in the Roman Catholic Church* (New York: Continuum, 1998). The work was originally published by Cassell in Great Britain in 1994.

23. Rosemary Radford Ruether, *Liberation Theology: Human Hope Confronts Christian History and American Power* (New York: Paulist, 1972).

24. For example, one of my own early articles, "Women and Religion: A Survey of Significant Literature, 1965–1974," was written at Burgardt's invitation during my second year of studies at the University of Chicago Divinity School and published in *Theological Studies* 36 (December 1975): 737–66.

25. *CTSA Proceedings* 50 (1995): 302. Current statistics will be available when the next directory is published by CTSA in late 1999 or 2000.

26. *Proceedings of the Catholic Theological Society of America* 54 (1999). General information about the CTSA is available at: http://carver.holycross.edu/organizations/ctsa.html.

27. Margaret A. Farley, "Ethics and Moral Theologies," in Letty M. Russell and J. Shannon Clarkson, eds., *Dictionary of Feminist Theologies* (Louisville: Westminster John Knox Press, 1996), 89.

28. Barbara Hilkert Andolsen, Christine E. Gudorf, Mary D. Pellauer, eds., "Introduction," *Women's Consciousness, Women's Conscience* (Minneapolis: Winston Press, 1985), xii–xiii.

29. Ibid., xv.

30. Lisa Sowle Cahill, "Presidential Address: Feminist Ethics and the Challenge of Cultures," *CTSA Proceedings* 48 (1993): 73.

31. Ibid., 77.

32. Johnson, *She Who Is*, 8.

33. Ibid., 11.

34. Matthew L. Lamb, "Solidarity," in Judith A. Dwyer, ed., *The New Dictionary of Catholic Social Thought* (Collegeville, MN: Liturgical Press, 1994), 908.

35. Pope John Paul II, quoted in ibid., 909.

36. Pope John Paull II, *Sollicitudo rei socialis*, #39, quoted here from Jean-Yves Calvez, "Sollicitudo rei socialis," *The New Dictionary of Catholic Social Thought*, ed. Matthew L. Lamb (Collegeville, MN: Liturgical Press, 1994), 915.

37. Ada María Isasi-Díaz and Yolanda Tarango, *Hispanic Women: Prophetic Voice in the Church* (San Francisco: Harper & Row, 1988).

38. Ada María Isasi-Díaz, *En La Lucha: A Hispanic Women's Liberation Theology* (Minneapolis: Fortress Press, 1993).

39. Ada María Isasi-Díaz, *Mujerista Theology: A Theology for the Twenty-first Century* (Maryknoll, NY: Orbis Books, 1996), 32.

40. Ibid., 35.

41. Isasi-Díaz and Tarango, *Hispanic Women*, 53.

42. Margaret A. Farley, *Personal Commitments: Beginning, Keeping, Changing* (San Francisco: Harper & Row, 1986), 7.

43. Ibid., 99.

44. Margaret A. Farley, *Just Love: A Framework for Christian Sexual Ethics* (New York: Continuum, 2006). Earlier works include the articles, "Sexual Ethics," in Warren T. Reich, ed., *The Encyclopedia of Bioethics*, and "An Ethic for Same-Sex Relations," in Robert Nugent, ed., *A Challenge to Love* (New York: Crossroad, 1983), 93–106.

45. "Secretary's Report: John Courtney Murray Award," *CTSA Proceedings* 47(1992): 185.

46. *CTSA Proceedings* 54 (1999).

47. Patricia Beattie Jung and Thomas A. Shannon, eds., *Abortion and Catholicism: The Catholic Debate* (New York: Crossroad, 1988), 4.

48. Patricia Beattie Jung and Ralph F. Smith, *Heterosexism: An Ethical Challenge* (Albany: State University of New York Press, 1993), 13.

49. Ibid., 10.

50. Barbara Hilkert Andolsen, *Daughters of Jefferson, Daughters of Bootblacks: Racism and American Feminism* (Macon, GA: Mercer University Press, 1986). Recently Andolsen edited the professional resources section of *The Annual of the Society of Christian Ethics* on "Selected Topics in Feminist and Womanist Ethics" (Washington, DC: Georgetown University Press, 1994): 257–305.

51. Barbara Hilkert Andolsen, *Good Work at the Video Display Terminal: An Ethical Analysis of the Effects of Office Automation on Clerical Workers* (Knoxville: University of Tennessee Press, 1989).

52. Barbara Hilkert Andolsen, *The New Job Contract: Economic Justice in an Age of Insecurity* (Cleveland: Pilgrim Press, 1998), vii.

53. Ibid., 4–5.

54. Ibid., ix.

55. Ibid., 119.

56. Ibid., 137.

57. M. Shawn Copeland, "Toward a Critical Christian Feminist Theology of Solidarity," in Mary Ann Hinsdale and Phyllis H. Kaminski, eds., *Women and Theology* (Maryknoll, NY: Orbis Books, 1995), 27.

58. Ibid., 30–31.

59. M. Shawn Copeland, "The Interaction of Racism, Sexism and Classism in Women's Exploitation," in Elisabeth Schüssler Fiorenza and Anne E. Carr , eds., *Women, Work and Poverty* (Edinburgh: T & T Clark, 1987), 25–26.

60. Copeland, "Toward a Critical Christian Feminist Theology of Solidarity," 3.

61. Ibid., 25–26.

62. Ibid., 28–29.

63. Emilie Buchwald, Pamela R. Fletcher, and Martha Roth, eds., *Transforming a Rape Culture* (Minneapolis: Milkweed Editions, 1993). The editors define a "rape culture" as "a complex of beliefs that encourages male sexual aggression and supports violence against women" (vii).

64. M. Shawn Copeland, "Editorial Reflections," in Elisabeth Schüssler Fiorenza and Copeland, eds., *Violence Against Women* (Maryknoll, NY: Orbis Books, 1994), 121–22.

65. Rosemary Radford Ruether, *Liberation Theology: Human Hope Confronts Christian History and American Power* (New York: Paulist, 1972). The chapter "Mother Earth and the Megamachine: A Theology of Liberation in a Feminine, Somatic and Ecological Perspective" is especially relevant (115–26).

66. Rosemary Radford Ruether, *Gaia and God: An Ecofeminist Theology of Earth Healing* (San Francisco: HarperSanFrancisco, 1992), 272–73.

67. Rosemary Radford Ruether, *Women and Redemption: A Theological History* (Minneapolis: Fortress Press, 1998).

68. Rosemary Radford Ruether, "The Development of My Theology," *Religious Studies Review* 15 (January 1989): 1.

69. See Rosemary Radford Ruether, *Faith and Fratricide: The Theological Roots of Anti-Semitism* (New York: Seabury, 1974); Rosemary Radford Ruether and Herman J. Ruether, *The Wrath of Jonah: The Crisis of Religious Nationalism in the Israeli-Palestinian Conflict* (New York: Harper & Row, 1989); and Rosemary Radford Ruether's dedication to *Gaia and God*: " . . . to Adiba Hkader and her four daughters, Ghada (twenty-one), Abir (seventeen), Ghalda (fourteen), and Ghana (twelve), and all the other mothers and children who died in the early morning of February 13, 1991, in a bomb shelter in Baghdad that was shattered by two American 'smart bombs.'"

70. Ruether, *Women Healing Earth: Third-World Women on Ecology, Feminism and Religion* (Maryknoll, NY: Orbis Books, 1996).

71. Ibid., 5.

72. Ibid., 7.

73. Christine E. Gudorf, *Victimization: Examining Christian Complicity* (Philadelphia: Trinity Press International, 1992); and *Body, Sex, and Pleasure: Reconstructing Christian Sexual Ethics* (Cleveland: The Pilgrim Press, 1994).

74. Regina Wentzel Wolfe and Christine E. Gudorf, eds., *Ethics and World Religions: Cross-Cultural Case Studies* (Maryknoll, NY: Orbis Books, 1999); see also Robert L. Stivers, Christine E. Gudorf et al., eds., *Christian Ethics: A Case Method Approach*, 2nd ed. rev. (Maryknoll, NY: Orbis Books, 1994).

75. Lisa Sowle Cahill's recent books include a volume co-edited with Margaret A. Farley, *Embodiment, Morality, and Medicine* (Dordrecht: Kluwer Academic Publishers, 1995) as well as two studies she authored, *Sex, Gender, and Christian Ethics* (Cambridge: Cambridge University Press, 1996); and, *Love Your Enemies: Discipleship, Pacifism, and Just War Theory* (Minneapolis: Fortress Press, 1994).

76. Lisa Sowle Cahill, "Feminist Ethics and the Challenge of Cultures," *CTSA Proceedings* 48 (1993): 83. A revised version of this paper is published under the title "Feminist Ethics, Differences, and Common Ground: A Catholic Perspective," in Curran, Farley, and McCormick, eds., *Feminist Ethics and the Catholic Moral Tradition*, 184–99. See also Cahill, "Moral Theology and the World Church," *CTSA Proceedings* 39 (1984): 35–51, and "Feminist Ethics," *Theological Studies* 51 (March 1990): 49–64.

77. Mary E. Hunt, *Fierce Tenderness: A Feminist Theology of Friendship* (New York: Crossroad, 1991). Besides publishing *WATERwheel*, a newsletter containing brief essays and lists of resources, Hunt and Neu maintain a website of information on feminist issues in religion at www.hers.com/water.

78. Graciela Pujol, "Miracles from Shared Gardens," trans. Sally Hanlon, *WATERwheel* 11 (Winter 1998–99), 6.

79. In addition to the thinkers discussed above, several other Catholics who have contributed substantially to ethics are also represented in the anthology *Feminist Ethics and the Catholic Moral Tradition*, including Sidney Callahan, Toinette Eugene, Christine Firer Hinze, Susan A. Ross, and Maura A. Ryan.

80. The Minnesota author Carol Bly has shown leadership here by publishing *Changing the Bully Who Rules the World: Reading and Thinking About Ethics* (Minneapolis: Milkweed Editions, 1996).

81. Hans Küng and Karl-Josef Kuschel, eds., *A Global Ethic: The Declaration of the Parliament of the World's Religions* (New York: Continuum, 1993), 24–26.

82. Ibid., 36.

II

INSIGHTS FROM IMAGINATIVE LITERATURE

5

MASS MEDIA AND THE
ENLARGEMENT OF MORAL SENSIBILITY

Insights from Theology and Literary History

Anne Patrick analyzes the reasons why mass media generally skirt certain crucial social issues, notably racism, sexism, and anti-Semitism. Characteristically balancing a call to action and a recognition of impediments to it, she recommends that her fellow teachers avoid the trap of merely relying on films to present social issues rather than "provid[ing] our students with analytical tools and avenues for taking action, not to mention some grounds for hope." In identifying bigotry toward Islam as an area for future action—a recommendation especially timely in the year this volume is published—the essay reminds us that Anne Patrick's legacy includes not only advocacy but also effective models for such action. —HD

The theme "Mass Media and the Enlargement of Moral Sensibility" invokes a metaphor of size, asking us to think about moral development in terms of a widening scope of ethical concern. We might have spoken instead of a "heightened moral awareness" or, in a context emphasizing electronic communications technology, of a more "finely tuned" conscience. But the metaphor of size does serve well, and it suggests that the influence of the American theologian H. Richard Niebuhr (1894–1962) in setting the task for this section of essays is not insignificant. For Niebuhr has shown in a much-studied book from 1960, *Radical Monotheism and Western Culture*, that where the ethical obligation to love our neighbor is concerned, the boundaries we draw separating those who really count as neighbors from those who are more or less

---

Adapted from a chapter of the same title in Mass Media and the Moral Imagination, *ed. Paul A. Soukup and Philip J. Rossi (Kansas City: Sheed & Ward, 1994), 249–58.*

irrelevant or expendable when we make decisions are of utmost moral and religious importance.[1]

Niebuhr recognized that despite professing faith in one God, most Christians tend to slip from the ideal of radical monotheism. We center our lives not on the "One beyond the many" but on such finite values as success, knowledge, wealth, or what he termed "social gods." Niebuhr believed that the chief obstacle to authentic faith is our tendency to put boundless trust and loyalty in finite objects, groups, and causes instead of in the principle of Being-itself. Placing the family, the nation-state, or even the church at the center of life is a subtle form of idolatry, he emphasized, for only God is worthy of absolute trust and loyalty. Niebuhr affirmed that there is value in family and country, in science and technology, and in organized religion, but he insisted that such value is relative to the ultimate Source of value. What this entails for ethics is that the perspective of universal love and justice must supersede narrow self-interest or group-interest.

These theological points are fundamental to the topic of this essay, for moral sensibility in need of enlargement is sized according to our basic stance toward ultimate reality. Because none is God but God, moral sensibility must be enlarged to include concern for the entire community of being. The lectures that became *Radical Monotheism and Western Culture* were delivered at the University of Nebraska in 1957, but Niebuhr's critique of the morality of religious and secular persons in America remains valid today. The commercialism, consumerism, and idolatry toward the nation-state are very much related to Niebuhr's point about social gods. So also are such evils as racism, sexism, and anti-Semitism, which have long marked American society despite our protestations of belief in human dignity and equality. Affirm as we might that all persons have rights, we still operate much of the time according to a mentality that does not consistently regard those outside the tribe—whether of family, gender, nation, race, religion, or other category—as neighbors in an ethically meaningful sense. Some might find Niebuhr too harsh a critic of Western culture. After all, Western culture has given us the notion of universal human rights, not to mention considerable insight into universal human dignity, a recurring theme in modern Catholic social teaching. Nonetheless we do not need to look far to find instances where racism, sexism, and anti-Semitism affect our society today; we continue to be guilty of exactly the sort of tribalism Niebuhr described.

I have begun with a theological foundation for ethical universalism because the enlargement of moral sensibility is connected with deep religious matters, including the mysterious phenomenon we term conversion. For this reason it would be naive to suppose that sophisticated new media formats can package the gospel in a way that makes enlargement of moral sensibility automatic. Classical notions of sin and grace have bearing on the question of how the media influence our consciences, and the long history of Christian reflection on the theological and psychological ramifications of these doctrines is relevant here.

If we have learned anything from centuries of debates about Pelagianism, for example, we should be aware that we are never in full control of such phenomena as conversion. That having been said, it still seems reasonable to think that media can sometimes influence the human mind and heart in such a way that conversion to more authentic forms of faith and morality becomes more likely than would otherwise be the case. Grace can surely operate in cultural forms as well as in natural ones—indeed, culture itself is an aspect of human nature. And whether or not they would express it in Christian language, many artists have worked with media in the hope of casting a critical light upon excessive self-interest and group-interest, seeking by whatever tricks are up their sleeves to enlarge our moral sensibilities.

The tribalistic attitudes selected for attention here—racism, sexism, and anti-Semitism—support relationships of injustice because they presume, often beneath the level of awareness, that some people are more fully human, have greater dignity, and have interests that count more than others. Moreover, our very theories of ethics have at times reinforced these skewed perceptions, for example, by stressing property rights in a slavery-based economy, or to take a current example, by teaching about woman's so-called "special nature" and thereby legitimating sexism.[2] Certain individuals have been aware of these problems for quite some time, but more generalized awareness, with the behavior changes that flow from such awareness, has been mighty slow in coming. What we are asking, then, is whether the judicious use of mass media can hasten this growth in awareness and thus contribute to moral progress in our society.

INSIGHTS FROM LITERARY HISTORY

Before turning to the question of television's possibilities in this regard, it is good to recall that cultural elites have been worrying and wondering about the moral influence of mass media ever since the printing press made it possible to spread ideas and attitudes through appealing narratives that could be widely distributed at little cost. The questions we ask today about mass media and enlarged moral sensibility, as well as the question folks are always pursuing about how media damage moral sensibility, are direct descendants of questions posed in the eighteenth and nineteenth centuries about the positive and harmful effects of reading novels.[3] We might remember that novels became high culture only in the twentieth century, about the time network radio began to reach large audiences, and that movies began to be studied as a serious art form only when television had become the dominant popular expression of culture. Some of the best minds of the last century were occupied with using novels, the mass media of their day, to exert moral influence, and we can learn from what happened to their efforts.

Harriet Beecher Stowe's *Uncle Tom's Cabin* (1852) was the biggest media event of the nineteenth century in this country, with arguably the greatest influence on the moral sensibilities of white Americans. As Jane P. Tompkins has remarked, "Uncle Tom's Cabin was, in almost any terms one can think of, the most important book of the century."[4] Thanks to Stowe's skilled use of sentimental conventions involving the symbolism of religion and the family, the consciences of thousands of white readers were substantially enlarged, at least for a while. Bonds of sympathy were created between white readers and fictional Black characters, who were seen, perhaps for the first time, to have human qualities and human needs. We can learn much from the Stowe example. We should note in the first place that although the book put in question some aspects of racism, it hardly eliminated it. Victims were romanticized, and the story's "happy ending" involved not the incorporation of Blacks as full citizens of the United States, but rather their return to a mythically idealized Africa. Today many readers find Stowe's handling of racism flawed; indeed, there are grounds for calling the novel itself racist. But also to be borne in mind is the fact that this powerful story is absent from the standard lists of American classics. The prevailing excuse for this omission is that *Uncle Tom's Cabin* lacks whatever "great art" requires, as defined, of course, by those whose social location of power and privilege allows them to control definitions of what art should and should not involve.

Fortunately critics are now reevaluating *Uncle Tom's Cabin* and other "sentimental novels" of the last century, and offering good reasons to include some of them in the American literary canon. Tompkins, for example, argues convincingly that modernist assumptions of the literary establishment are to blame for the neglect of this important book:

In modernist thinking, literature is by definition a form of discourse that has no designs on the world. It does not attempt to change things, but merely to represent them, and it does so in a specifically literary language whose claim to value lies in its uniqueness. Consequently, works whose stated purpose is to influence the course of history, and which therefore employ a language that is not only not unique but common and accessible to everyone, do not qualify as works of art. Literary texts such as the sentimental novel, which make continual and obvious appeals to the reader's emotions and use technical devices that are distinguished by their utter conventionality, epitomize the opposite of everything that good literature is supposed to be.[5]

Of the many nineteenth-century readers affected by Stowe's book, there is one I want to single out for attention here because *Uncle Tom's Cabin* was among the factors that led her eventually to choose popular fiction as the medium for communicating her own religious and moral vision. Mary Ann Evans read the novel in September 1852, and four years later began to write fiction herself, which she published under the name "George Eliot." Her letters leave no doubt that Stowe's books influenced her decision to write novels designed to enlarge the moral sensibilities of literate citizens of England. Her last two novels, *Middlemarch* (1871–72) and *Daniel Deronda* (1876), in fact, challenge sexist and anti-Semitic attitudes directly. Writing to Stowe shortly after the latter book was published, George Eliot put her hope thus: "There is nothing I should care more to do, if it were possible, than to rouse the imagination of men and women to a vision of human claims in those races of their fellow-men who most differ from them in customs and beliefs."[6]

Middlemarch has been regarded as a classic for half a century, but the seriousness of its critique of sexism is only recently beginning to be recognized; *Daniel Deronda* is a rarely read effort of nearly nine hundred pages that influential critics have dismissed as too moralistic in tone on the Jewish question, with art thereby suffering.[7] The extent to which these texts enlarged the moral sensibilities of Victorian readers is difficult to gauge, and neither was a "media event" comparable to *Uncle Tom's Cabin.* My own informed guess is that sexist and anti-Semitic assumptions did suffer erosion in the minds of some readers, though the process was generally subtler than what went on with the Stowe novel.[8] In any event, the author's recognition of the limits of her own highly intelligent work, crafted in a medium that addressed the most thoughtful of readers, tells us something about how hard it is to enlarge moral sensibilities. For one thing, it is clear that few efforts will escape criticism, either on ethical or artistic grounds. For another, there is reason to suspect that ideological factors affect judgments about art as well as about morals.[9] And for a third, even relatively good efforts to enlarge moral sensibility succeed only in a slow and incomplete fashion. Even assuming that popular art can have some influence for enlarging moral sensibility, the words George Eliot wrote to the author of *Uncle Tom's Cabin* in 1869 remain true today:

> I dare say you have long seen, as I am beginning to see with new clearness, that if a book which has any sort of exquisiteness happens also to be a popular widely circulated book, its power over the social mind, for any good, is after all due to its reception by a few appreciative natures, and is the slow result of radiation from that narrow circle...[O]ne must continually feel how slowly the centuries work toward the moral good of men [*sic*].[10]

PRIME-TIME TELEVISION

As we leave this popular author of the last century, who functioned as both Sybil and Dear Abby of her day, and consider contemporary efforts to deal with racism, sexism, and anti-Semitism on television, we can only ask: If George Eliot is describing what happens to the green wood, what can we hope for in the dry? Turning to prime-time TV, let us bear in mind something implied in George Eliot's rather discouraging—she would say, realistic—observation, namely that it is a mistake to assume that change for good or ill is a monocausal phenomenon. The factors that influence human beings are complex, and images on a screen or words on a page are only some of the factors that affect moral sensibility. This insight has practical implications for parents and educators. What people see on TV does exert influence, no doubt about that. But far more powerful are the real persons who sit around the living room with the viewer, or who use or lose the chance to bring social analysis and ethical wisdom to bear on classroom discussions of what has been seen and heard.

Certainly there are many differences between prime-time TV and the media situation one hundred years ago, one of the most important of which concerns authorship. Whatever distinctions literary critics may want to draw about authors, implied authors, or intentional fallacies, we are in a different ballpark altogether when we start to talk about who is responsible for programs that succeed or fail in treating social issues on television. These programs are not the work of individual authors, but rather are "committee products," developed by teams who work with a constant sense that producers, sponsors, and network executives are looking over their shoulders.

Media expert Todd Gitlin provides an informative and fascinating account of what goes on behind the scenes of commercial television in the 1985 volume *Inside Prime Time*. The most disconcerting fact he points out is that the whole television production system practices a more or less automatic self-censorship, refusing even to get near questions that would make sponsors nervous. After describing how pressure from the Kimberly-Clark Corporation led in 1982 to the cancelling of the Lou Grant show (which had featured Ed Asner, an actor known for his political activism), Gitlin observes that this case was unusual because it involved direct pressure from a program's sponsor: "Normally there is not even the suggestion of overt political concern at the networks, and normally advertisers do not intervene so directly in network affairs. Their interests form the context that decision-makers take for granted."[11]

To put matters another way, it is usually unnecessary for a sponsor to intervene because the production team anticipates the concerns of those who finance their efforts; the "normal network mentality" involves indifference to anything but ratings, and so the aim becomes to displease as few viewers as possible in order to keep them all watching.

If what Gitlin says about automatic preconscious self-censorship is true, then the shows that come to mind as efforts to enlarge moral sensibilities, and, in particular, to challenge racist, sexist, or anti-Semitic attitudes, are just flukes. They do not come along very often, and when they do they are certainly limited, one might well say flawed. But rarities like *Roots* or *Holocaust* and successful series like *The Cosby Show* or *Murder, She Wrote* are about as good as it had gotten. During the conservative 1980s, networks did not hope for the audience shares that *Roots* and *Holocaust* surprised them with in the preceding decade, and for all the good *The Cosby Show* accomplished by providing images of a successful African-American family, can anyone recall an episode where a Huxtable child (or adult, for that matter) had to wrestle with racism?

There needs to be more ethical analysis of the issues involved in the shows that do deal with the areas of moral growth singled out for attention here. Recall, for instance, the debates that went on around the *Holocaust* mini-series in 1978. Many Jews and others argued that it was essential to portray something of the event, and tolerable to use melodrama for the sake of holding a mass audience that needed to know, at a minimum, that the Holocaust occurred. On the other side

Elie Wiesel was insisting that, of course the Holocaust must be remembered, but for goodness sake, not as a TV show.[12] The question of what means are capable of holding audiences at the same time as viewers are challenged or informed on difficult topics is by no means an easy one to settle.

Another area for investigation concerns the advantages and limits of the programs that try out newer approaches to representing female characters (such as *Cagney and Lacey*) or that make tentative forays into disputed areas such as sex-roles or surrogate motherhood. It also is worth pondering why prime-time shows seem oblivious to Christian anti-Semitism in America, as well as to the now prevalent bigotry toward Arabs and matters Islamic. I cannot address such questions here, but simply put them on the agenda for future consideration. Clearly we are only beginning to do the work that can lead to more effective use of the media in enhancing ethical awareness. To conclude, I would stress three points to bear in mind as this work proceeds, two based on Gitlin's research and the last on my own experience as an educator.

In the first place, we should recognize that network paranoia about audience ratings and advertising contracts sharply reduces the likelihood that challenging social material will make it to prime-time viewers. Gitlin reports that one network executive told him that "the networks are always mistaking real social issues for little human-condition stories." The tendency to ignore the sociopolitical dimension of problems is so well-entrenched, Gitlin notes, that "for weeks, whenever I told executives I was trying to understand how television dealt with social issues, they proceeded to tell me about movies dealing with alcoholism, cancer, drugs, crippling illness, death and dying." Personal stories are "routinely depoliticized," he emphasizes, and "stories about racial conflict get sidetracked or bleached."[13] There is an especially great reluctance to treat material involving racism or anti-Semitism, for sponsors are very nervous about anything that puts in question the myth of a united America. According to Gitlin, the airing of the film *Masada* was unusual, and his comment on its success is telling: "*Masada*—about 'Jews and history,' two 'downer' 'subjects in industry terms—could nonetheless be a hit because, despite rising anti-Semitism, there was no national constituency for the Romans."[14]

A second and more subtle finding from Gitlin is that in those cases when social issues do get an airing, they tend to be psychologized rather than analyzed in social and political terms. His discussion of the ABC drama, *Inside the Third Reich*, which is influenced by writings of T. S. Adorno objecting to "the spurious personalization of objective issues," illustrates the problem well. Observes Gitlin:

The high-rated May 1982 *Inside the Third Reich* was based, of course, on the memoirs of Hitler's architect and minister for war production, Albert Speer, supplemented by hundreds of hours the writer-producer spent interviewing Speer. The movie's vision retained the blinders that led Speer into the Nazi movement and kept him there. Speer's motives were pared down to the television-sized staple of Faustian ambition, revealing nothing of Nazism's historical mainsprings: inflation, nationalist panic, anti-Semitism. For the sake of balance, Speer was issued an anti-Nazi wife, but by Part II she had degenerated into the familiar nagging *Hausfrau* whose principal objection was that political meetings were pulling her husband away from his family nest... *Inside the Third Reich* did open with newsreel footage including the dread images of heaped corpses found in the death camps at the end of the war. The movie proper included some valuable reminders that Hitler's rants and Goering's bluster were responsible for mass murder. But the bulk of the movie was family angst, petty palace intrigues, and pageantry passing for historical understanding. ABC's expensive European locales simulated authenticity without challenging Speer's worldview, which was that he was mysteriously trapped by Hitler's charisma.[15]

These two problems identified by Gitlin, the avoidance of controversial social topics and their reduction to personal-psychological problems instead of socio-political ones, deserve thoughtful probing by all who are interested in media and the enlargement of moral sensibility.

A third matter concerns not so much the decisions of those who produce prime-time shows or educational videos, but rather the educators who make use of filmed material as aids to teaching about social issues in the classroom. Educators who care about overcoming social injustice must beware of what I call the "displaced guilt flick syndrome." Otherwise we who are bothered by injustice may fall into the trap of dealing with our own feelings of guilt and powerlessness by using documentaries or half-way decent TV programs simply to tell our students how bad things are. It is a kind of lazy way out. We suppose that since we can't be Martin Luther King or Oscar Romero, maybe this video will inspire one of these young persons to go out and change the world. I am not saying we should never show films like *Hunger in America* or *Bitter Harvest*, or video clips reporting the latest atrocity in some war-torn part of the globe, but unless we provide our students with analytical tools and avenues for taking action, not to mention some grounds for hope, our socially relevant films may be more paralyzing than empowering. We may, in other words, be using media more for our own comfort than for changing anything in the world, which I take to be the point of enlarging moral sensibility in the first place.

Notes

1. H. Richard Niebuhr, *Radical Monotheism and Western Culture* (New York: Harper & Row, 1960).

2. For discussions of this anthropological question, see Dorothy L. Sayers, *Are Women Human?* (Grand Rapids: Eerdmans, 1971); Mary Aquin O'Neill, "Toward a Renewed Anthropology," *Theological Studies* 36 (1975): 725–36; Sara Butler, ed., *Research Report: Women in Church and Society* (Bronx, NY: Catholic Theological Society of America, 1978): 32–40; and Mary Aquin O'Neill, "Imagine Being Human: An Anthropology of Mutuality," in *Miriam's Song II* (West Hyattsville, MD: Priests for Equality, 1988) 11–14.

3. For a discussion of evangelical perspectives on fiction, see Samuel Pickering, Jr., *The Moral Tradition in English Fiction, 1785–1850* (Hanover, NH: University Press of New England, 1976).

4. Jane P. Tompkins, "Sentimental Power: *Uncle Tom's Cabin* and the Politics of Literary History," in *The New Feminist Criticism: Essays on Women, Literature, and Theory*, ed. Elaine Showalter (New York: Pantheon Books, 1985) 83.

5. Ibid., 84.

6. M. E. Lewes to Mrs. Harriet Beecher Stowe, 29 October 1876, in *The George Eliot Letters*, vol. 6, ed. Gordon S. Haight (New Haven: Yale University Press, 1955), 301.

7. In a December 1876 review for *The Atlantic Monthly*, Henry James dismissed the Jewish section of *Daniel Deronda* as "cold," and in the highly influential study *The Great Tradition* (1948; Garden City, NY: Doubleday, 1954), F. R. Leavis went so far as to suggest that this Jewish half (which he found "fervid" rather than "cold") be excised and the remaining novel entitled *Gwendolen Harleth* (150). The James review, "*Daniel Deronda*: A Conversation," is published as an Appendix to this edition of the Leavis book (300–19). Some years later Leavis withdrew his suggestion about cutting away the "bad part" of *Daniel Deronda* in the essay, "George Eliot's Zionist Novel," which appeared first in *Commentary* 30 (October 1960): 317–25, and subsequently as an introduction to a 1961 edition of *Daniel Deronda* published by Harper Torchbooks. But this late acknowledgment that the "flawed" sections of the novel were too tightly bound up with its "greatness" to be removed did little to offset the influence of the original suggestion, which was much more widely circulated than the retraction.

8. The ethical dimensions of these novels are discussed in Anne E. Patrick, "Rosamond Rescued: George Eliot's Critique of Sexism in *Middlemarch*," *Journal*

of Religion 67 (1987) 220–38; and in "George Eliot's Final Experiment: Power and Responsibility in *Daniel Deronda*," in *Morphologies of Faith*, ed. Mary Gerhart and Anthony C. Yu (Atlanta: Scholars Press, 1990) 319–42.

9. Although the James-Leavis objections to *Daniel Deronda* have to some extent been accepted by many Christian and secular interpreters, Jews have from the first tended to read the novel in a much more favorable light. In *George Eliot: The Jewish Connection* (Jerusalem: Massada, Ltd., 1975), Ruth Levitt traces the influence of this text on figures including the influential Zionist, Henrietta Szold; the first president of the Jewish Theological Seminary, Solomon Schechter; and, the American poet Emma Lazarus. Levitt asks, "Did George Eliot . . . not influence Zionism in [Theodore] Herzl's time by preparing the very air which Herzl breathed in England, by planting the seeds of his acceptance with her idealistic hero and her unforgettable and prophetic words?" (74). More recently, Irving Howe describes the character Deronda as "abundantly virtuous but only intermittently alive" in his "Introduction to *Daniel Deronda*" (New York: New American Library, 1979). Howe insists, however, citing the opinion of Lionel Trilling, that the idealization needs to be understood in light of the need to oppose the Fagin-stereotype of the Jewish villain with a "counter-myth," a necessary step toward allowing a "fully shaded humanity to characterization of Jews" (xiii).

10. M. E. Lewes to Mrs. Harriet Beecher Stowe, 8 May 1869, in *The George Eliot Letters*, vol. 5, 30–31.

11. Todd Gitlin, *Inside Prime Time* (New York: Pantheon Books, 1985), 11.

12. In an essay that appeared in the *Chicago Tribune* for April 19, 1978 under the headline "Trivializing the Holocaust: Semifact and Semifiction," Wiesel called the film, "untrue, offensive, cheap," and maintained that "the witness does not recognize himself in this film." He concluded: "The Holocaust must be remembered. But not as a show."

13. Ibid.,179–80.

14. Ibid., 198.

15. Ibid., 190–91.

6

ROSAMOND RESCUED

George Eliot's Critique of Sexism in Middlemarch

*This essay on the nineteenth-century novelist George Eliot is related
to Anne Patrick's doctoral dissertation—completed after her arrival
at Carleton College while carrying demanding teaching and administrative responsibilities. Eliot was among the authors discussed in
relation to Niebuhr. Like the essay that follows in this collection,
"Imaginative Literature and the Renewal of Moral Theology," it expresses one of her characteristic credos: we need to replace simplistic
teleological models of progress with a recognition of what we can
learn from earlier people and situations that are too often submerged
in or ignored by those models. —HD*

To the student of modern religious thought surveying the curricula of
most seminaries and universities, the philosophy and religion shelves
in most libraries, or the footnotes of works by Tillich, Barth, Rahner,
and other much-studied male thinkers, it might appear that the involvement of women in theological and ethical debates is a recent
thing, dating perhaps from Simone de Beauvoir's 1949 study *Le deuxième sexe* or Mary Daly's 1968 application of de Beauvoir's thought to a
believer's concerns, *The Church and the Second Sex*.[1] Revisionist scholarship has of course been proving that appearance is deceptive on this
matter, for women have been actively engaged with religious and
moral questions at least since the first century, and particularly so since
the nineteenth century.[2]

The absence of their names from typical booklists and curricula,
however, does suggest that retrieving the insights of women thinkers of

---

Adapted from "Rosamond Rescued: George Eliot's Critique of Sexism in Middlemarch," The Journal of Religion *67, no. 2 (April 1987), 220–38. Copyright © The
University of Chicago.*

the past will involve different methods and materials than have usually been employed. After all, women of the nineteenth and early twentieth centuries encountered great obstacles in their efforts to influence the public discussion of religious and moral questions, and this fact affected the way they went about their work. Denied until quite recently the university education and ecclesiastical ordination that would have enabled them to gain the pulpit and the professorship—the arenas where men typically enjoyed the opportunity to influence thought—women of necessity resorted to the pen.[3] Most female writers, however, eschewed the formal language of scholarship and expressed their views in fiction, autobiography, letters, and essays rather than in systematic works of constructive theology or moral philosophy.[4]

A paradigm case from the last century is Mary Anne Evans (1819–1880), who was certainly as knowledgeable about scientific, philosophical, and religious matters as many of her male contemporaries long recognized as productive theologians. She translated some of the most influential religious scholarship of her day, and displayed remarkable knowledge and insight on religious matters in essays published in the *Westminster Review*.[5] But the form her work took when she came into her own as a constructive thinker was fiction, a *metier* she considered utterly demanding of intellectual rigor on the artist's part. Indeed, "George Eliot" regarded her novels as a form of empirical research into the deepest religious and moral questions. "My writing," she wrote in 1876,

> is simply a set of experiments in life—an endeavor to see what our thought and emotion may be capable of—what stores of motive . . . give promise of a better after which we may strive—what gains from past revelations and discipline we must strive to keep hold of as something more sure than shifting theory.[6]

No less than William James was George Eliot investigating the nature and varieties of religious experience, was she probing the "cash value" of the creeds and commitments of believers of various sorts.

To illustrate the significance of this woman's contribution to modern thought I shall work in the pages to follow a single vein of the rich lode of theological and moral insight left by George Eliot. The vein I have selected—her ethical critique of sexist attitudes and social arrangements in the novel *Middlemarch* (1871–72)—is not so apparently theological as some of her other insights, but it is nonetheless related to her recognition of the negative consequences for women and men of a problematic form of "social faith," something a contemporary analyst influenced by the thought of H. Richard Niebuhr would identify as the idolatrous "henotheism" of patriarchy.[7]

One reason for selecting this vein rather than, say, her views on eschatology or revelation, is the contribution it can make to contemporary theological reflection on the sinful structures of sexism, with all that this implies for religious life and teaching. A second reason is that this subject touches on a debate among literary critics concerning whether or not George Eliot can be regarded as a "feminist" author.

In a recent article Ellen Ringler observes that George Eliot "occupies a profoundly uneasy position among feminist literary critics," and reports that of fifteen representative analyses published during 1972–78, only two considered *Middlemarch* to be a "profoundly feminist" novel.[8] Ringler basically sides with this minority, maintaining that *Middlemarch* displays the "impressive personal dominance" of several strong female characters (despite their "apparent social submission" to men) and at the same time criticizes the educational and social limitations imposed upon these women. She adds, however, that feminist "uneasiness" concerning the text remains justified because George Eliot's narrator stops short of expressing the "healthy anger" warranted by the obvious social injustice, ending the tale instead with "sad resignation or phrases about the 'incalculably diffusive' effects" of the life of the female protagonist, Dorothea Brooke.[9]

Since the period surveyed in Ringler's article a number of other critics have added evidence in favor of George Eliot's proto-feminism, but none has argued so complete a case for the centrality of such concern to the action of the novel as I shall propose below.[10] While the analyses of Ringler, the feminist authors she cites, and most of the subsequent discussion stress the female character Dorothea, they pay comparatively little attention to the male protagonist Tertius Lydgate. What I shall claim is that *Middlemarch* contains a systematic critique of gender stereotyping, one which is integral to the action of the novel and central to its chief thematic concern. I shall argue that Lydgate's tragedy is much more closely linked with his flawed perspective on women than most readers recognize, and that the narrator does not share the common opinion that the failure of this idealistic young doctor is due chiefly to the selfishness of his wife Rosamond Vincy.

Whether the result of sexist biases on the part of readers, artistic choices on the part of George Eliot, or some combination of both factors, Rosamond gets more than her share of opprobrium from most readers of *Middlemarch*. They do not consider that the banker Bulstrode's crimes are much greater than anything she has done; that it is the connection with Bulstrode, not Rosamond, that strains an already tenuous relationship between the doctor and the town community to the breaking point; or that the egoism of Dorothea's first husband Casaubon is more ingrained and more vicious than that of the spoiled young woman first discovering that the world was not created solely to satisfy her desires. Nor do most readers dwell much on the fact that Rosamond's decision to inform Dorothea that Will Ladislaw has not been unfaithful is the action upon which the happiness of Dorothea and Will directly depends. Instead they tend to take at face value Lydgate's bitter remark, mentioned in the novel's Finale, that Rosamond was his "basil plant," that is, "a plant which had flourished wonderfully on a murdered man's brains."[11] The judgment of critic Ellen Moers is not unusual: "Lydgate's career in science [was] destroyed by the terrible Rosamond Vincy."[12] Rosamond is by no means an admirable character, but she tends to receive more blame for her husband's failure than she deserves. It is from this degree of readerly injustice that my analysis would "rescue" her, an operation I undertake not so much for Rosamond's sake as for the sake of retrieving insights of great significance for ethics that George Eliot achieved in this text and that have yet to be fully appreciated.

CENTRALITY OF THE CRITIQUE OF SEXISM

The fictional experiment that is *Middlemarch* is designed primarily to investigate the causes of a character's success or failure to live a good and beneficial life, thereby contributing to the "growing good of the world" (p. 896). Not surprisingly, the experiment shows that causes are *multiple*; various character traits and external realities combine to "determine" the outcome of the lives we see depicted in this story.[13] What may surprise a contemporary reader, however, is the originality and perceptiveness displayed by George Eliot in recognizing just how significant as determinants are the sexist attitudes and social arrangements that influence the people of Middlemarch. Although terms current today such as "sexism," "pedestalism," and "gender stereotyping" were not part of the author's vocabulary, there is no doubt she was aware of the psychological and moral realities they denote.[14]

George Eliot's assessment of the problematic status of women includes two main factors: a recognition of the wrongness of certain attitudes toward women, especially assumptions of intellectual inferiority; and, a concern about the moral effects of the limited social roles of women, particularly women of the middle and upper-middle classes. These related factors are of central thematic importance to *Middlemarch*, for they limit the human possibilities of women and inhibit true mutuality between women and men, thereby increasing for both sexes the difficulty of leading good and effective lives. The critique is apparent in the novel's Prelude, which contrasts the accomplishments of Theresa of Avila with the situation of "later-born Theresas . . . helped by no coherent social faith and order" (p. 25), and which specifically raises the issue of women's "natures" and social lot.[15] This theme is immediately reinforced in the motto for the first chapter, the following lines from Beaumont and Fletcher's *The Maid's Tragedy*: "Since I can do no good because a woman, / Reach constantly at something that is near it" (p. 29).

Evidently for George Eliot the attitudes toward women prevalent in her day were matters for moral criticism. But did her readers share this concern? It is likely that most did not, and consequently, an important part of her agenda involved providing her audience with a reading experience that would prompt rethinking about these matters. In other words, the author seems to have here an educational aim structurally similar to that of her last novel, *Daniel Deronda* (1876). In both works she is combating social prejudice: in *Middlemarch* the focus is on sexual prejudice, and in *Deronda* it is on ethnic and religious prejudice, particularly anti-Jewish attitudes.

Given the disparity between George Eliot's own views on women and those of her readers, as artist-educator she faced a substantial challenge if she hoped to trigger rethinking on these matters. In meeting this challenge she is flexible in the way she resorts to her well-stocked rhetorical arsenal, sometimes employing direct statements, sometimes humor or ironic commentary, and sometimes dramatic evidence. Having established the thematic importance of this topic in serious fashion in the Prelude and first chapter motto, she subsequently lightens her approach for a time by having one of the most ridiculous characters in the novel, Dorothea's uncle Mr. Brooke, utter clichés about the alleged intellectual inferiority of women. Voiced as they are in the course of Brooke's own incoherent speeches, these prejudicial statements are neatly undermined by their contexts. For example, Brooke declares in chapter 2, "'Young ladies don't understand political economy, you know'" (p. 39), and immediately shows his own inability to discuss Adam Smith.

In these early chapters George Eliot reinforces her point occasionally by means of ironic narrative commentary. "Women were expected to have weak opinions," the narrator observes in chapter 1, "but the great safeguard of society and of domestic life was, that opinions were not acted on" (p. 31). And, in the next chapter, she offers the following memorable comment when describing Sir James Chettham's thoughts about himself and Dorothea: "A man's mind—what there is of it—has always the advantage of being masculine—as the smallest birch tree is of a higher kind than the most soaring palm—and even his ignorance is of a sounder quality" (p. 44).[16]

Given George Eliot's own intellectual preeminence, it is hardly surprising to see her poking fun at assumptions about feminine mental inferiority. But although criticism in the early pages of *Middlemarch* is offered in a largely humorous vein, the seriousness of her complaint becomes apparent when the moral effects of stereotypical attitudes toward women begin to show up in the human relationships that form the dramatic core of the novel. For the practical results of regarding women as intellectually inferior to men include limiting their educational opportunities and their involvement in public life, and lessening the possibility of truly mutual relationships between men and women. These factors contribute directly to the marital difficulties of the two most important characters in Middlemarch, Dorothea and Lydgate.

Notwithstanding the independence she shows toward her family and Sir James Chettham, at seventeen Dorothea Brooke is very much a product of her culture. Her idealizing of marriage with the forty-five year-old pedant Edmund Casaubon is a direct result of the limitations that have been placed on her as a woman: "Here was something beyond the shallows of ladies-school literature: here was a living Bossuet, whose work would reconcile complete knowledge with devoted piety; here was a modern Augustine who united the glories of doctor and saint" (p. 47). Not satisfied with traditional feminine roles, Dorothea yearns "to make her life greatly effective," and the idea of marrying Casaubon appeals to her as a mode of transcending the limitations of her present state: "the union that attracted her was one that would deliver her from her girlish subjection to her own ignorance, and give her the freedom of voluntary submission to a guide who would take her along the grandest path" (p. 51).

Dorothea's notions of life with Casaubon are entirely unrealistic: "'There would be nothing trivial about our lives...It would be like marrying Pascal. I should learn to see the truth by the same light as great men have seen it by'" (p. 51). These notions, of course, are challenged as soon as she enters the new state, and the recounting of this process of disillusionment contributes much to the pleasure of reading *Middlemarch*.[17] But if Dorothea comes eventually to question Casaubon's intellectual stature, he remains rigidly entrenched in traditional views of feminine inadequacy. Or to be more precise: sensing his own inadequacy, and fearing the challenges that Dorothea's inquisitive nature innocently levels at his façade of greatness, Casaubon retreats to stereotypical views to protect his threatened ego. Thus when Dorothea suggests that he compensate Will Ladislaw for the wrong that had been done his mother, Casaubon responds, with "biting emphasis": "'Dorothea, my love, this is not the first occasion, but it were well that it should be the last, on which you have assumed a judgment on subjects beyond your scope . . . [Y]ou are not qualified here to discriminate'" (p. 410).

SEXISM AND LYDGATE'S TRAGEDY

The critique of popular attitudes toward women is even more developed in George Eliot's handling of the relationship between Lydgate and his wife Rosamond Vincy. Indeed, Lydgate's tragedy can be directly traced to his prejudices toward women, which caused him first to marry the sort of woman he did and then to relate to her in a manner that inhibited mutual love. To be sure, Rosamond herself bears much responsibility for the failure of their relationship, but this fact only brings out another facet of George Eliot's basic critique of sexual prejudice. For Rosamond fits a stereotypical feminine "ideal": she combines physical beauty with disinterest in "masculine" concerns (such as Lydgate's interest in medical reforms), and she focuses all of her energies on the domestic sphere. True, her greatest concern is with the central figure of the domestic sphere—herself—and it is clear that George Eliot deplores Rosamond's egoism. But she also understands how much Rosamond's character has been shaped by a prejudicial process of socialization whereby she blindly accepted the "feminine" role of cultivating the qualities that would make her admired, especially perfection of appearance and demeanor. This prepared Rosamond nicely for getting a husband, but not for relating to one.

Because Rosamond is so selfish and Lydgate so well-intentioned, and because his tragedy is such a disappointment to narrator and reader alike, there is danger that the latter will uncritically adopt Lydgate's own perspective on the reasons for his difficulties. Thus, as I have indicated, his description of Rosamond as a destructive "basil plant" is likely to be taken at face value. Yes, one is inclined to agree, Rosamond is entirely to blame. Her own response to this indictment is made in characteristically self-justifying fashion, which only adds to the reader's dislike for her: "Rosamond had a placid but strong answer to such speeches. Why then had he chosen her? It was a pity he had not had Mrs. Ladislaw [Dorothea], whom he was always praising and placing above her." It is, however, important to observe that the narrator credits Rosamond's analysis somewhat, and stresses the matter of "justice" in her regard: "And thus the conversation ended with the advantage on Rosamond's side. But it would be unjust not to tell that she never uttered a word in depreciation of Dorothea, keeping in religious remembrance the generosity which had come to her aid in the sharpest crisis of her life" (p. 893).

It is not clear here whether the narrator intends Rosamond's conversational "advantage" to be understood as due to the cogency of her point, or to the fact that Lydgate simply had no words with which to answer her. In either case, her mention of Lydgate's attitude toward Dorothea is significant, for it is arguably a factor in his domestic problems, and thus in his overall failure to do the socially beneficial medical work that had once been his ambition.

How is this so? Lydgate's attitude toward Dorothea can be summed up thus: she is for him a "special case" of femininity, a cut well above ordinary womankind. A contemporary feminist would recognize her as a "woman on a pedestal." Lydgate himself says as much in chapter 76 when reflecting on the conversation in which Dorothea had expressed her confidence in him and her willingness to come to his aid:

> "This young creature has a heart large enough for the Virgin Mary. She evidently thinks nothing of her own future, and would pledge away half her income at once, as if she wanted nothing for herself but a chair to sit in from which she can look down with those clear eyes at the poor mortals who pray to her. She seems to have what I never saw in any woman before —a fountain of friendship towards men—a man can make a friend of her." (p. 826)

There is no doubt that Dorothea has behaved admirably and has truly helped Lydgate by responding so sympathetically to his plight. But she is a limited creature, something of which the narrator, if not Lydgate, is aware. It is surely significant that the narrator stresses Dorothea's limitations at precisely those points where she is most praised by Lydgate.

Twice within a few pages of chapter 76 the narrator tells us that besides being noble and generous, Dorothea is also childlike and unrealistic.

Evidently George Eliot wants to buck the tide of her characters' enthusiasms, to introduce into the reader's consciousness a corrective principle that allows for criticism of both Dorothea and Lydgate. It is of course a delicate matter to criticize characters who are idealistic and generous, and who have suffered unjustly. But George Eliot's scientific and educational aims require such criticism, for it is her view that these characters might have done better, and her hope that others may learn from an analysis of the factors contributing to their relative failures. Thus by narrative criticism she invites the reader to speculate about what alternatives each might profitably have pursued.

The critique of Dorothea is summed up in the word "childlike." She is naive, inexperienced, and lacking in critical powers of the imagination. This seems largely the result of the narrow education and range of experience that were her lot, and thus Dorothea's responsibility for her lack of insight is greatly diminished. But still George Eliot seems to want her readers to consider how Dorothea might have done better. It is significant that so close on the heels of the observation that "Of lower experience such as plays a great part in the world, poor Mrs. Casaubon had a very blurred shortsighted knowledge, little helped by her imagination," Dorothea speaks confidently about the possibility of "making [Lydgate's] life quite whole and well again..." (p. 822), and seems to assume that his marital problems can be solved as easily as his monetary ones. This mistake is apparently the result of her interpreting his situation simply as if it were her own. She identifies uncritically with Lydgate, and projects her own experience too literally onto his situation.

What she does not recognize is that Lydgate's attitude toward Rosamond is a major part of the problem—that Lydgate, in fact, echoes Casaubon in his attitudes toward women. Nor does she appreciate the importance of Lydgate's admission of some responsibility for Rosamond's lack of understanding. "'I ought to be more open,'" he says at one point, and a bit later, "'I know very well that I ought not to have left anything to be told her by others, but—'" (pp. 823–24). These remarks show the beginnings of an awareness that Rosamond's lack of sympathy for him is not entirely due to her being a creature of a different species. Had Lydgate been able to deepen this awareness and act on it, perhaps his life would have ended more successfully than it did. But Lydgate's stereotypical thinking prevents him from cultivating this awareness. Condescension toward his wife and idealization of his female rescuer combine to support his conviction that Rosamond will make life intolerable for him if they remain in Middlemarch.

WOMAN AS A SPECIES APART:
STEREOTYPING, ALIENATION AND MORAL BLINDNESS

The stereotypical thinking that contributes to Lydgate's downfall in-volves three prejudicial ideas about women, which culminate in the conclusion that women are essentially members of a different species from men. In the first place, Lydgate regards women as less intelligent than men, a mistaken opinion he shares with Brooke, Chettham, and Casaubon. In chapter 16 the narrator combines ironic foreshadowing with criticism of the young doctor's view of female intelligence:

> Certainly, if falling in love had been at all in question, it would have been quite safe with a creature like this Miss Vincy, who had just the kind of intelligence one would desire in a woman —polished, refined, docile, lending itself to finish in all the del-icacies of life, and enshrined in a body which expressed this with a force of demonstration that excluded the need for other evidence. (p. 193)

There is no doubt that Lydgate considers this "decorative" femi-nine intelligence to be inferior to masculine judgment on practical questions, as becomes apparent in conversations with Rosamond after they are married. When, for example, she questions the necessity of having the furniture inventory made, Lydgate declares "angrily": "'This is idle, Rosamond. You must learn to take my judgment on ques-tions you don't understand'" (p. 642). These words are a terser echo of Casaubon's admonition to Dorothea in chapter 37: "'Dorothea, my love, this is not the first occasion, but it were well that it should be the last, on which you have assumed a judgment on subjects beyond your scope...[Y]ou are not here qualified to discriminate" (p. 410).

On the immediate questions, the narrator tends to agree with Lyd-gate's view that the furniture needs to be inventoried and with Dorothea's opinion that Will deserves recompense, but at a deeper level she is critical of both Lydgate and Casaubon for assuming that masculine judgment is superior to feminine. Among the clues to this interpretation is the imagery of "biting" associated with the admoni-tions of both husbands, a detail that helps to reinforce in the reader's mind a sense that although the two men are very different, they share a common failing. Thus the "biting emphasis" of the above-cited words of Casaubon is balanced by the biting quality of Lydgate's reaction in chapter 64 to Rosamond's having taken their house off the market without his knowledge:

> "It was of no consequence then that I had told you imperative reasons of another kind; of no consequence that I had come to a different conclusion, and given an order accordingly?" said Lydgate, *bitingly*, the thunder and lightning gathering about his brow and eyes. (p. 709; emphasis added)

Although the narrator sympathizes with Lydgate here, she recognizes that his anger and insistence on superior judgment are counterproductive: "The effect of any one's anger on Rosamond had always been to make her shrink in cold dislike, and to become all the more calmly correct, in the conviction that she was not the person to misbehave, whatever others might do" (p. 709).

There are many strands of causality leading to such an impasse, a number of which are beyond Lydgate's control. But one contributing factor *is* at least partly his responsibility, namely his condescending attitude toward women, an attitude about which the reader has been reminded earlier in chapter 64. There, George Eliot notes Lydgate's growing concern over his indebtedness, and describes his efforts to persuade Rosamond to cooperate in lowering their household expenses. In depicting the developing sense of alienation between them the narrator is especially critical of Rosamond's egoism, but she also implies that Lydgate's problems stem in part from a failure to appreciate women as persons: "this rather abrupt man had much tenderness in his manners towards women, seeming to have always present in his imagination the weakness of their frames and the delicate poise of their health both in body and mind" (p. 699).

In the ensuing conversation, Rosamond makes, albeit in an insensitive manner, some observations about Lydgate's professional practices that he would do well to consider. He, however, stubbornly insists that these matters are not her province. Thus in response to her admonition, "'You should be more careful not to offend people, and you should send out medicines as the others do . . . [Y]ou should think what will be generally liked'" (pp. 699–700), Lydgate betrays his inability to benefit from criticism as well as his fundamental feelings of superiority over women. The narrator observes:

> Lydgate's anger rose; he was prepared to be indulgent towards feminine weakness, but not towards feminine dictation. The shallowness of a waternixie's soul may have a charm until she

becomes didactic. But he controlled himself, and only said, with a touch of despotic firmness—"What I am to do in my practice, Rosy, it is for me to judge." (p. 700)

Again, when Rosamond makes the quite reasonable observation that Bulstrode ought to give him a salary for the work he does at the hospital, Lydgate refuses to consider her opinion: "'It was understood from the beginning that my services would be gratuitous. That, again, need not enter into our discussion'" (p. 700). Other instances of Lydgate's insistence on his superior powers of judgment could be adduced, but the above are sufficient to demonstrate how his prejudice about female intelligence contributed to his downfall.

A second, related sexual prejudice is Lydgate's tendency to view woman as designed chiefly to minister to man's needs for consolation and adornment, to regard her as an object rather than an equal companion. Evidence of this prejudice is contained in some of the above-cited commentary, and it is especially pronounced in chapter 58, where the narrator describes how far Lydgate "had traveled from his old dreamland, in which Rosamond Vincy appeared to be that perfect piece of womanhood who would reverence her husband's mind after the fashion of an accomplished mermaid, using her comb and looking-glass and singing her song for the relaxation of his adored wisdom alone" (p. 628).[18]

Finally, there is the assumption that this lesser being is weak and in need of masculine support. Again, there is evidence of this prejudice in the commentary already cited; to the above I shall simply add the narrator's poignant analysis of Lydgate's perception of his marital relationship after Dorothea had assisted both him and Rosamond: "Lydgate had accepted his narrowed lot with sad resignation. He had chosen this fragile creature, and had taken the burthen of her life upon his arms. He must walk as he could, carrying that burthen pitifully" (p. 858).

All of these notions contribute to the basic problem in Lydgate's view of women, the tendency to regard them as belonging to a different species. This problem is subtly anticipated during the narrator's portrayal of the first encounter between Lydgate and Rosamond, which takes place in chapter 16. During that first conversation he flatters her thus:

"An accomplished woman almost always knows more than we men, though her knowledge is of a different sort. I am sure you could teach me a thousand things—as an exquisite bird could teach a bear if there were any common language between them. Happily, there is a common language between women and men, and so the bears can get taught." (p. 189)

The fact is, however, that Lydgate does not expect Rosamond's "different sort" of knowledge ever to challenge his own. Moreover, the two-species imagery he employs to describe men and women undermines the possibility of genuine communication and mutuality between the sexes. To think of Rosamond as an "exquisite bird" and of himself as a "bear" is symbolically to deny the possibility of a common language. With such a perspective, this "bear" cannot get taught. Given Lydgate's own use of different-species imagery, it is ironic that he is later troubled to discover that Rosamond sees things this way also. After an argument about the furniture inventory he reflects despondently: "It seemed that she had no more identified herself with him than if they had been creatures of different species and opposing interests" (pp. 642–43). And later, when Lydgate is striving to maintain some affection in the wake of another instance of domestic tension, the same imagery recurs: "He wished to excuse everything in her if he could—but it was inevitable that in that excusing mood he should think of her as if she were an animal of another and feebler species. Nevertheless she had mastered him" (p. 719).

The theme is sounded again at the close of chapter 75, where the narrator depicts a crucial exchange between Rosamond and Lydgate. The doctor had not been able to tell his wife about the cloud of suspicion hanging over him after the death of Raffles, but she has finally learned of it from her family. The narrator is both sympathetic toward Lydgate as he shrinks from the pain of the unfeeling response he anticipates from his wife and critical of his failure to keep trying to communicate:

We must remember that he was in a morbid state of mind, in which almost all contact was pain. Certainly Rosamond in this case had equal reason to complain of reserve and want of confidence on his part, but in the bitterness of his soul he excused himself;—was he not justified in shrinking from the task of telling her, since now she knew the truth she had no impulse to speak to him? But a deeper-lying consciousness that he was in fault made him restless, and the silence between them became intolerable...(pp. 813–14)

Following this deeper impulse, Lydgate attempts to discuss the problem, but he is immediately discouraged by the fact that Rosamond says so little in response to his questions.

He had begun to question her with the intent that their conversation should disperse the chill fog which had gathered between them, but he felt his resolution checked by despairing resentment. Even this trouble, like the rest, she seemed to regard as if it were hers alone. He was always to her a being apart, doing what she objected to. (p. 814)

And once he capitulates to this judgment that "he was always to her a being apart," (which is in fact but the corollary of his own view that she is a weaker, less intelligent being), his tragedy is sealed. He cannot surmount the feelings of discouragement and bitterness that are stirred by her lack of concern for him. Thus, when Rosamond returns to her proposal that they leave Middlemarch and go to London, Lydgate yields to despair and a sense of permanent alienation from his wife. As a result, "They lived on from day to day with their thoughts still apart, Lydgate going about what work he had in a mood of despair, and Rosamond feeling, with some justification, that he was behaving cruelly" (p. 816).

The phrase "with some justification" is important. Obviously there is much about Rosamond Vincy the narrator does not endorse. But implied in this phrase is a recognition that Rosamond experienced some unfairness in her married life, particularly as a result of Lydgate's moodiness and angry remarks. Moreover, related to these difficulties in communicating is a prejudicial arrangement of roles within the marriage whereby Rosamond is expected to yield her judgment entirely to her husband's and to do nothing without his approval, while he can make decisions that concern them both without consulting her. On more than one occasion Lydgate peremptorily insists that his judgment is to be respected in both professional and domestic matters, whereas her opinion carries no weight in either sphere. And, whatever one may think about Rosamond's reluctance to have the house put up for sale, it is at least worth noting that Lydgate would not consider any modification in his professional life, but insists on a radical change in the only life Rosamond has known.

Again, it is not to excuse the actions Rosamond takes behind his back (such as taking the house off the market and writing for help to Sir Goodwin Lydgate without her husband's knowledge) to point out that Lydgate himself tends to proceed without consulting his wife. He arranges for the furniture inventory before telling her about it, and he resolves to go to Quallingham to request help from Goodwin himself, a decision "he had never mentioned to Rosamond" because "he did not want to admit what would appear to her a concession to her wishes after indignant refusal" (p. 714). Before he can proceed, of course, Goodwin's curt letter of refusal (which is addressed to him, though written in response to Rosamond's letter) arrives, and Lydgate angrily declares: "'It will be impossible to endure life with you, if you will be always acting secretly—acting in opposition to me and hiding your actions'" (p. 715). The fact that Rosamond could make a similar statement does not occur to him. Even when Lydgate tries to soften his words, he does not realize that he expects a degree of openness and confidence from her that he is unwilling to extend himself: "'Can you not see, Rosamond, that nothing can be so fatal as a want of openness and confidence between us?'" (p. 717).

The narrator, however, is aware of this lack of mutuality, and points to the problem again in chapter 75, while describing their situation after Rosamond has learned from her father about the "infamous suspicions" concerning Lydgate: "Certainly Rosamond in this case had equal reason to complain of reserve and want of confidence on his part; but in the bitterness of his soul he excused himself..." (p. 814). This conversation, in fact, is the climax of Lydgate's tragedy, for the mindset he adopts during it—"despairing resentment" and a conviction that "he was always to her a being apart"—leads him to take her statement, "I cannot go on living here. Let us go to London" (p. 815) as an inevitable prediction. As a result, he is unable to respond with hope when Dorothea later offers him a salary for his work at the hospital.

RELIGIOUS AND MORAL IMPLICATIONS:
GENDER STEREOTYPING AS INIMICAL TO THE INTUITION OF RELATEDNESS

The causal link between Lydgate's prejudices concerning women and the despairing attitude that leads to his downfall can be summarized as follows. To begin, he is convinced that Rosamond is of a lower and weaker species, and that communication with her is impossible. Then, as if in reaction, he mistakenly assumes that his good experience with Dorothea is simply due to her splendid, saintly qualities. He idealizes her so much that he does not see that his own openness and dropping of "proud reserve"[19] are factors in the "friendliness" of their exchange. Thus instead of allowing his positive experience with Dorothea to lead to some questioning of his preconceptions about women in general (which might have resulted in a different attitude toward Rosamond), Lydgate simply thinks of Dorothea as a rare exception: "'She seems to have what I never saw in any woman before—a fountain of friendship towards men—a man can make a friend of her'" (p. 826).

This idealizing keeps him from taking stock of the factors in himself that contributed to his personal and professional failures, notably his proud reserve and need to be independent of others. In fact, it is his insistence on being as independent as possible that prevents him from accepting any more than the minimum necessary aid from Dorothea. If he had been willing to accept her offer of a salary for his work at the hospital (which would have involved recognizing the validity of her judgment as well as Rosamond's), perhaps Lydgate might have been able eventually to achieve some of his professional goals. Instead, he remains hardened in his judgment of what is possible, and uses Rosamond's weakness as an excuse for not dealing with his own limitations. By telling himself that Rosamond must have her way, he can blame his professional failure on her and still save face by maintaining that he has upheld the masculine duty of providing financially for his weak and frivolous wife. But he remains angry at her and at himself for this despairing compromise with his ideals, as is evident in the caustic remarks he occasionally lets slip in the ensuing years.

All told, George Eliot's assessment of Lydgate's tragedy recognizes the contributing factors of fate and personal failings, with emphasis on the latter. As the narrator observes in chapter 58, "It always remains true that if we had been greater, circumstances would have been less strong against us" (p. 632). What I have attempted to show is that certain social realities nourished the pride that led to his downfall. These realities had to do especially with prejudicial attitudes about the nature and role of women, attitudes that Lydgate adopted uncritically and then suffered from without ever learning from his suffering.

However, George Eliot's critique of Lydgate is designed to enable her readers to benefit from his experience. It is a subtle critique, whose most basic point is that Lydgate never achieved the insight that would have enabled him to transcend his injured pride and despair. Whereas Dorothea comes to recognize the unity of life and her part in it and thus is able to surmount her feelings of grief and despair, Lydgate never stops seeing himself as an alienated victim of the otherness around him—especially the female otherness he chose to marry. The part his views on Rosamond play in his tragedy are summed up in a passage several pages after the climactic chapter 80, in which George Eliot had described Dorothea's mystical sense of unity and her transcendence of personal suffering. The two passages thus seem calculated to encourage readers to reflect on the different worldviews and on their outcomes for each character.

In chapter 80, we learn how Dorothea, following her night of disillusionment and grief over Will Ladislaw's apparent faithlessness, observes on the road "a man with a bundle on his back and a woman carrying her baby"—she sees, that is, others, male and female, carrying burdens. She also senses the "largeness of the world" and realizes that "she was a part of that involuntary, palpitating life, and could neither look out on it from her luxurious shelter as a mere spectator, nor hide her eyes in selfish complaining" (p. 846).

By contrast, at the end of chapter 81, we read how Lydgate views life after Dorothea's second visit to Rosamond: "Lydgate had accepted his narrowed lot with sad resignation. He had chosen this fragile creature, and had taken the burthen of her life upon his arms. He must walk as he could, carrying that burthen pitifully" (p. 858).

George Eliot, I am convinced, thinks there is something wrong with that picture. Whereas Dorothea has a vision of "largeness" and sees others carrying appropriate burdens, Lydgate has a vision of narrowness, and sees himself carrying an inappropriate burden, "this fragile creature," his wife. Instead of growing toward real sympathy, a disposition based on a sense of unity with other beings, Lydgate is arrested at a point of pitiful self-pity, a disposition linked with his sense of being superior to and separate from the other with whom he must share life. Indeed, the connection between Lydgate's sexual prejudice and his final despair is well captured in these lines, whose imagery is the negative counterpart of the climactic lines concerning Dorothea.

Of course, Rosamond herself is hardly faultless in all of this, but George Eliot's objections to her egoism are so apparent that the matter needs no elaboration here. Indeed, the critique of Rosamond is so sharp and relentless that the seriousness of Lydgate's own failings can easily escape notice. I have therefore concentrated on the latter, though both partners share responsibility for the failure of their marriage and thus for Lydgate's failure "to do good small work for Middlemarch, and great work for the world" (p. 178). (That Rosamond had no parallel ambition is both a symptom and a cause of her problems.) But it is also clear that "society" shares much of the blame for their failures, insofar as each has been socialized to view the world in a way that inhibits mutuality. Thus George Eliot has supplied dramatic evidence of her recognition of the moral implications of gender stereotyping. The sort of thinking that regards men and women as creatures of different species is shown to inhibit the growth and effectiveness of both sexes; it is inimical to the ideal of George Eliot's "ethic of sympathy," namely the "deep-seated habit of direct fellow-feeling with individual fellow-men" (p. 668).

There remains the intriguing question as to why George Eliot, usually so compassionate an author and such an advocate of compassion, treats Rosamond Vincy so unsympathetically in this novel—far less sympathetically than she treats the male egoists Casaubon and Bulstrode. My tentative answer is that the reason has something to do with the limits of fiction—one cannot draw every character in a complex novel in the depth that does full justice to each one's life-struggle. But the important thing to observe is that the author herself seems to have felt that much more could and should be said about the "type" of the beautiful, self-centered young woman. Indeed, George Eliot's next novel, *Daniel Deronda*, can well be regarded as an attempt to do justice to a character who had been given rather short shrift in *Middlemarch*. Gwendolen Harleth, its female protagonist, embodies Rosamond's unfinished ethical agenda, and the action of the narrative culminates in her transcendence of the egoism that was so pronounced in the novel's early chapters. To be sure, *Deronda* involves much more than the story of "Rosamond's Rescue," but that is clearly central to the last novel written by George Eliot.

Notes

1. Simone de Beauvoir, *Le deuxième sexe* (Paris: Gallimard, 1949); Mary Daly, *The Church and the Second Sex* (New York: Harper & Row, 1968).

2. For examples of recent works that document women's leadership in Christian life and thought over the centuries, see Rosemary Ruether and Eleanor McLaughlin, eds., *Women of Spirit: Female Leadership in the Jewish and Christian Traditions* (New York: Simon & Schuster, 1979); Elizabeth Alvilda Petroff, ed., *Medieval Women's Visionary Literature* (New York: Oxford University Press, 1986); and Rosemary Ruether and Rosemary S. Keller, eds., *Women and Religion in America: A Documentary History*, 3 vols. (New York: Harper & Row, 1981–86).

3. This in itself was no small accomplishment, as Sandra M. Gilbert and Susan Gubar have shown in their study of women writers of the nineteenth century, *The Madwoman in the Attic* (New Haven, Conn: Yale University Press, 1979).

4. In *A Literature of Their Own: British Women Authors from Brontë to Lessing* (Princeton, NJ: Princeton University Press, 1977), 144, Elaine Showalter observes that "the religious novel was the essential instrument of female participation in the male monopoly on the theological debate." The same sort of participation was going on across the Atlantic, according to historian of American-religion religious Ann D. Braude, who notes: "The daughters of New England Divines expressed their rejection of their fathers' harsh theology in sentimental novels which became the best-selling books of the nineteenth century" ("Spirits Defend the Rights of Women," in *Women, Religion, and Social*

Change, ed. Yvonne Yazbeck Haddad and Ellison Banks Findly [Albany: State University of New York Press, 1985], 426).

5. Two of her translations have remained the standard English versions of the German originals: *The Life of Jesus Critically Examined* (1846; reprint, Philadelphia: Fortress Press, 1972) by David Friedrich Strauss, and *The Essence of Christianity* (1854; reprint, New York: Harper & Row, 1957) by Ludwig Feuerbach. Her nonfiction articles are published in *The Essays of George Eliot*, ed. Thomas Pinney (New York: Columbia University Press, 1963).

6. These words, taken from George Eliot's letter of January 25, 1876, to Joseph Frank Payne, have provided Bernard J. Paris with a title for his valuable study of the intellectual background of her fiction, *Experiments in Life: George Eliot's Quest for Values* (Detroit: Wayne State University Press, 1965); Paris quotes from the letter on p. vi of his study. Eliot has long been recognized as a great intellectual, but because she is classified as a novelist, her ideas have been studied in literature departments and have had little influence on theology and religious ethics. For an illuminating treatment of her place in nineteenth-century thought, see Diane Postlethwaite, *Making it Whole: A Victorian Circle and the Shape of Their World* (Columbus: Ohio State University Press, 1985).

7. See H. Richard Niebuhr's *Radical Monotheism and Western Culture* (New York: Harper & Row, 1960) for a discussion of "henotheism" (24–28). The term "patriarchy," which means literally "father-rule," is used more broadly here to indicate the unjust arrangement whereby females are devalued and subordinated to males. Thought systems as well as social arrangements can thus be "patriarchal." An extensive discussion of the usefulness of Niebuhr's thought for my understanding of George Eliot may be found in my "H. Richard Niebuhr's Ethics of Responsibility: A Resource for Literary Criticism" (Ph.D. diss., University of Chicago, 1982).

8. Ellen Ringler, "*Middlemarch*: A Feminist Perspective," *Studies in the Novel* 15 (1983): 55. One of those cited by Ringler as defending George Eliot's "feminism" is Kathleen Blake, who notes in "*Middlemarch* and the Woman Question" (*Nineteenth-Century Fiction* 31 [1976]: 285–312) that Rosamond deserves some sympathy. My own argument differs from Blake's (which concentrates on Dorothea rather than Lydgate), but I concur in her judgment that sympathy for Rosamond "depends less on our feeling that she is wronged than on our understanding that the wrong she does proceeds from her position as a woman" (302).

9. Ringler, *Middlemarch*, 59.

10. See, for example, U. C. Knoepflmacher, "Unveiling Men: Power and Masculinity in George Eliot's Fiction," in *Men by Women*, ed. Janet Todd (New York: Holmes & Meier, 1981), 130–46; and George Levine, "Repression and Vocation in George Eliot: A Review Essay," *Women and Literature* 7 (1979): 3–13. Levine attends briefly to Rosamond in this article and claims that a "social" model of interpretation allows one to recognize that "though she never becomes lovable, she is redeemed because she is understandable, and because the novel gives us evidence that had society been different and better, Rosamond would have been also" (10).

11. George Eliot, *Middlemarch* (1871–72; reprint, Harmondsworth: Penguin Books, 1965), 893. Subsequent references to *Middlemarch* are from this edition and are cited in parentheses in the text.

12. Ellen Moers, *Literary Women: The Great Writers* (1977; reprint, New York: Oxford University Press, 1985), 72. Earlier, Barbara Hardy had observed in *The Novels of George Eliot: A Study in Form* (New York: Oxford University Press, 1967) that in response to Dorothea's kindness Rosamond "performs her one unselfish act of confession and self-humiliation, but goes on to become Lydgate's 'basil plant'" (101). More recently, in an article that astutely discerns George Eliot's interest in questioning the gender stereotyping common in her day, U. C. Knoepflmacher describes Rosamond as "the executioner of the man who sarcastically accuses her of 'wonderfully' flourishing on a 'murdered man's brains'" (144). I agree that Lydgate's tone is sarcastic, but to my reading the judgment that Rosamond is Lydgate's executioner is problematic, echoing as it does the opinion of a character who remains blind to his own responsibility for his "misfortune."

13. George P. Levine has probed the philosophical roots of Eliot's interest in this problem in his illuminating essay "Determinism and Responsibility in the Works of George Eliot," *PMLA* 77 (1962): 268–79.

14. The terms "gender stereotyping" and "pedestalism" refer to attitudes and expectations that function to deny the full humanity of the female of the species. Dorothy L. Sayers captures the essence of both terms in the following ironic lines: "Women are not human... They are far above man to inspire him, far beneath him to corrupt him; they have feminine minds and feminine natures, but their mind is not one with their nature like the minds of men; they have no human mind and no human nature" (*Are Women Human?* [Grand Rapids, MI: William B. Eerdmans, 1971], 46). The dualism involved in stereotyping is reflected in Lydgate's perception of Rosamond as the basil plant that defeats his idealism (women as "corrupting influence") and of Dorothea as the exception to the norm (the exalted, more-than-human "saint").

15. George Eliot's use of the plural "natures" seems calculated to offset assumptions that "woman" has a special, easily defined "nature." Let me add that although for some purposes it is appropriate to distinguish the actual author from the implied author and narrator of a story, in view of the well-documented identification of George Eliot with the values of her fictional narrators, I shall not stress such distinctions here. This decision is reflected in my use of feminine pronouns to refer to the narrator, the gender of whom has been the object of some critical discussion.

16. Ironic passages such as the above are in my opinion appropriate expressions of the "healthy anger" Ringler (n. 8 above) finds lacking in *Middlemarch*. In view of the stereotypical assumptions about women's emotionalism, a feminist woman writer would not serve her purpose by simple ventilating rage. Irony and wit are some of the most important resources available to those who are oppressed and who hope to contribute to social change by changing attitudes.

17. We read, for example, in chapter 29 that "Dorothea had thought that she could have been patient with John Milton, but she had never imagined him behaving this way" (316).

18. The fact that Rosamond thinks of herself as intended for ornamental purposes is something that George Eliot also deplores. It is significant in this regard that the narrator's remark later in the same chapter that Rosamond "knew that she was a much more exquisite ornament to the drawing-room there [at Quallingham] than any daughter of the family" is followed by an observation about the Lydgate's inability to communicate with each other: "Between him and her indeed there was that total missing of each other's mental track, which is too evidently possible even between persons who are continually thinking of each other" (632).

19. Significantly, the narrator says of this conversation that "he gave himself up, for the first time in his life, to the exquisite sense of learning entirely on a generous sympathy, without any check of proud reserve" (p. 820).

7

IMAGINATIVE LITERATURE
AND THE RENEWAL OF MORAL THEOLOGY

With the skill at developing apt and sometimes playful metaphors that is manifest throughout this collection, Anne Patrick compares what we can learn from imaginative literature long after initially reading it to the effects of time-release medication. —HD

"When I was young there never was any question of right and wrong. We knew our catechism, and that was enough. We learned our creed and our duty. Every respectable church person had the same opinions."

The words above might have been uttered by any number of Catholics, especially in these decades since Pope Paul VI promulgated his 1968 encyclical *Humanae Vitae*, when ethical debates among us have received so much notice in the press. But actually this lament for the "good old days" when catechism knowledge settled every question of right and wrong, when believers all held the same "correct" opinion, does not date from the 1960s, nor was it voiced by a Roman Catholic. No, these words are a quotation from a fictitious Anglican woman named Mrs. Farebrother, a minor character in a famous novel about religion and social change in England nearly two centuries ago. The novel is George Eliot's masterpiece, *Middlemarch*, which is much studied in literature programs and has been successfully adapted for television and broad-

Adapted from the Paul E. McKeever Lecture given at St. John's University (Jamaica, NY) on October 21, 1997, and presented also as the McCarthy Lecture at the Washington Theological Union on November 9, 1997. Some of this material was presented on May 2, 1997 at Mt. St. Agnes Theological Center for Women, Baltimore, MD, and some of it is also discussed in my book, Liberating Conscience: Feminist Explorations in Moral Theology *(New York: Bloomsbury Academic, 1996).*

cast by PBS in a 1994 series.[1] George Eliot, whose own name was Mary Anne Evans, sought to write realistic fiction, and she knew that nostalgia for moral certainty might well be voiced by an Anglican as far back as 1830.

In my book *Liberating Conscience*, I quote Mrs. Farebrother to make three points: first, nostalgia for the good old days of moral certainty is by no means a recent phenomenon; second, Roman Catholics are by no means the only Christians who must deal with nostalgia for the simplicity of catechism or biblical answers to questions of right and wrong; and finally, contemporary ethical disputes among church people are best understood as part of the post-Enlightenment effort to balance new knowledge and changed historical circumstances with traditional religious authority.[2]

Here my interest in the nineteenth-century woman who misses the good old days when "every respectable church person had the same opinions" is slightly different. I am intrigued to notice that it was a *novelist* who got thousands of readers to think about this fact that longing for certitude and uniformity is not a brand-new thing. We can know this intellectually, of course, but when a character in a story takes such an idea into flesh-and-blood existence, the idea may engage us at the level of feeling too, and our own thought process goes deeper because we are also emotionally involved.

In the case of Mrs. Farebrother's remark, our first response may be simply one of amusement at her naiveté; but the scene may lodge in memory and take effect later, like a time-release medication. I have smiled on hearing Mrs. Farebrother put her longing for uniformity and certitude so baldly, but perhaps when I am least expecting it the time-release idea may surface, and make me wonder if I am being reasonable to expect every member of the church to agree with my position on, say, women's ordination, tubal ligation, or the use of plutonium in NASA's space program. Aha, the literary work invites me to think: maybe I am not quite so different from Mrs. Farebrother as I first supposed.

This example illustrates a truth voiced decades ago by the French literary critic, Denis de Rougement, who called art a "calculated trap for meditation."[3] Good novels and plays snag our attention and entice us to consider things more deeply than we might otherwise do. My thesis here is that because art can serve as a "calculated trap for meditation," serious literary artists have much to contribute to the renewal of Catholic moral theology. To demonstrate this claim I shall explore some ways in which artistically successful novels and plays can influence our doing of ethics.

Discussions of the Catholic moral scene in the popular media have tended to oversimplify our situation, depicting it as a stalemate in which conservatives and progressives go at each other with the boring monotony of a Punch and Judy show—although in view of the power differences involved, perhaps a better metaphor would come from heavyweight boxing. The Vatican knocks out Charles Curran, gets Leonardo Boff and Matthew Fox to withdraw from the ring, dismisses Ivone Gebara as a contender and sends her back to theological training camp, and is now defending its title against the Sri Lankan liberationist Tissa Balasuriya.[4]

I find this combat stereotype much too simple and prefer to think of the current tensions in light of Greek tragedy. I think *Commonweal* was right to say of the Balasuriya case that it will be *tragic* not only for Father Balasuryia, the author of a controversial book on *Mary and Human Liberation*, but also for the church at large, if the excommunication of a 72-year-old man who has been a priest for over forty years is allowed to stand without efforts to negotiate a compromise.[5] But what can tragedy teach us about these matters? How can novels and plays contribute to progress in the discipline of moral theology, and indeed, in our own moral lives?

To explore these questions I shall first define "moral theology" and describe three opinions about what its renewal requires: one from the Second Vatican Council, another from a British Jesuit named John Mahoney, and a third from my own research on conscience. Then I shall discuss several ways that imaginative literature can help in the general task of renewing moral theology, with some attention to the particular levels of academic moral theology, official church teaching, and personal conscience formation.

MORAL THEOLOGY: DEFINITION AND CALLS FOR RENEWAL

According to Sister of Mercy theologian Margaret A. Farley, *theology* is the effort of the Christian community to understand its faith, and *ethics*, or moral theology, is the effort of the Christian community to understand and articulate how this faith should be lived.[6] Two aspects of her definition stand out. First, ethics is the *community's* task, which means that everyone has a share in the work. It cannot be left entirely to the hierarchy or the professionally trained theologians, though these roles are distinct and important ones. And second, the idea that *effort* is required as the faithful seek to understand how we should live is crucial; moral theology is not a matter of merely conforming to rules or automatically applying principles to cases. It cannot, in other words, be done by computer, even with the most elegant Vatican software. Instead, Christian decision-making requires *discernment*, which is neither automatic nor unthinking. As the Dominican scholar Thomas O'Meara has observed, it is a mistake to think of the Bible and the pope as "answering machines" for our moral questions.[7] Instead, Christian ethics involves faith and reason working together at the task that Protestant theologian James M. Gustafson has described as to discern "what God is enabling and requiring us to be and to do."[8] In sum, then, moral theology is the branch of theology concerned with the practical implications of Christian faith for ideals, values, and behavior.

What is interesting for present purposes is that the Second Vatican Council singled out moral theology as especially in need of renewal. In the "Decree on Priestly Formation," in *Optatem Totius* (#16), the council declared: "Special attention needs to be given to the development of moral theology. Its scientific exposition should be more thoroughly nourished by scriptural teaching. It should show the nobility of the Christian vocation of the faithful, and their obligation to bring forth fruit in charity for the life of the world."[9]

This emphasis on fruitfulness, or practical benefit to the world, suggests that moral theology had failed to some degree—perhaps because its emphasis was too otherworldly, too preoccupied with the future state of believers' souls—to take sufficient notice of its effects on the earthly well-being of persons within and beyond the Catholic community. Today, decades after the council, this call for the renewal of moral theology still stands in need of fulfillment. Progress has been made, but the discipline is not yet sufficiently integrated with biblical spirituality, nor is it fully adequate to addressing the needs of our world.

Another way of setting the agenda for renewing moral theology has been given by the British Jesuit John Mahoney at the conclusion of his fine historical study from 1987, *The Making of Moral Theology*. Mahoney first traces how over a period of centuries moral theology developed into a discipline focused on helping confessors judge the gravity of sins. He then shows how teachings such as *Humanae Vitae* exacerbate the tendency toward legalism that went with the emphasis on helping confessors. Mahoney concludes by putting the need for moral theology's renewal in the following terms: Because Catholic moral theology has been concerned with proving to secular thinkers "that it is not irrational" and proving to other Christians "that it is not simply authoritarian," the discipline has been "in danger of forgetting that it is a branch of Christian theology," whose main concern must be with the mystery of God and our relationship with this ultimate mystery. As Mahoney explains, "The artistic medium in which God is fashioning and crafting...human creatures is the medium of their personal freedom; and the stuff, or material of moral theology is the sheer wonder of [human] being as it responds in freedom to the design of God."[10]

Now this is indeed a far cry from what students of the Baltimore Catechism thought moral theology was about, as may be seen by recalling two illustrations from the 1961 edition for children in the middle grades of elementary school. The first illustration, which was also sketched on countless blackboards across the nation, is designed to accompany a lesson on "Actual Sin." It involves three glass milk bottles. The first, under the heading "Original Sin," is an upside down bottle with explanatory notes: "We Inherit: No grace in soul; soul empty, as a milk bottle without milk." The other two bottles are under the heading "Actual Sins Two Kinds," and above the caption "We commit ourselves." On the left is the image of Mortal Sin, which is another inverted bottle and the description "soul empty again of grace," and on the right is the image of Venial Sin, a bottle standing upright, with images of "some spots in milk" to illustrate the fact that "grace stays in the soul."[11] This clear but reductive analogy conveys less of the mystery of sin and grace than would an example from interpersonal relationships, such as Jesus employed in the parable of the Prodigal Son (Lk 15:11–32), and it may well have inhibited religious development in persons who took it too literally for too long.

The illustration for Lesson 23 on "The Sacraments" is also interesting. It depicts the seven sacraments as buildings on a model railroad layout. The engine represents "our souls," and the ride begins at station #1, "Baptism." If the track were followed straight to its destination, "Heaven," the train would visit only stops #2, 3, and 5: "Confirmation," "Holy Eucharist," and "Extreme Unction." But the human condition includes a loop requiring station #4, "Penance," and two spurs branching off the main track and rejoining it just before the final station, each of which has a separate building. On the left is #6, "Holy Orders," and on the right is #7, "Matrimony." The underlying caption declares, "The seven sacraments make this way the safest road to heaven."[12] Again the Christian life seems to have more to do with things than with personal relationships, and the present life is reduced to something to "get through" for the sake of what lies beyond it. Instead of being invited to glimpse the depth and complexity of the mystery of our existence, youngsters were encouraged to imagine the Christian life in ways that made it seem material and mechanical.

Drawings like these may have served an appropriate pedagogical function for young catechism students, but they were etched too thoroughly on impressionable minds and have contributed to widespread misunderstandings of sin and grace. The image of the Christian life as a sacramental train ride, along with the famous "milk bottles of sin," makes Mahoney's point quite effectively: Moral theology needs to recover a sense of religious mystery about its task, since "It is the mystery of God which earths all theology and at the same time makes theological pluralism unavoidable."[13]

Indeed, a major problem of unrenewed moral theology has been the way it reduces the mystery of Christian living to a matter of staying on the tracks, a matter of obeying rules that earlier generations developed as they strove to live as faithful disciples in circumstances different from our own. For example, historical evidence suggests that castration was the issue when sterilization was originally condemned by church authorities, and yet today the magisterium insists that even medically indicated tubal ligations are out of the question for Catholics.[14] Given this inadequacy, the need today is twofold. First, we must recognize that the universal call to holiness, which was so rightly stressed by the Second Vatican Council, entails that all persons bear responsibility for discerning the moral obligations of our lives. Second, moral theology should provide leadership in helping Catholics become more confident and competent as ethical decision-makers.

These ideas are hardly new; classical teaching on conscience contains similar notions, but such teaching has not yet been integrated into the moral education of Catholics in a large-scale, practical way. Rather the message has been: Here is the behavior you must do or avoid under pain of serious sin; of course, you have a duty to obey your conscience, but if your conscience is a good one, it will virtually always agree with official church teaching. The net effect is either to advocate blind obedience or to provoke the opposite response of ethical intuitionism, neither of which does justice to the moral resources of individuals or the Catholic tradition. Blind obedience amounts to the abdication of personal responsibility, and we know from the trials of war criminals that "following orders" is never a sufficient approach to the moral life. But the opposite extreme of subjectivism and ethical intuitionism, which would replace moral reasoning with personal sincerity, is also an abuse of conscience. Simply to say "follow your conscience" is empty advice if there is not an adequate understanding

of relevant principles and values, or if there is insufficient analysis of
the likely consequences of a decision. After all, plenty of evil gets done
by folks who feel no compunction about their actions. An instance of
this phenomenon is seen in a 1997 interview in which the former
leader of the Khmer Rouge, Pol Pot, declared, "My conscience is
clear," despite the fact that most people regard him as responsible for
the "killing fields" in which a million Cambodians lost their lives during the 1970s.[15]

IMAGINATIVE LITERATURE AS RESOURCE FOR RENEWAL

How then can imaginative literature help us to remedy the problems
found at all three levels of moral theology: official church teaching, academic moral theology, and personal conscience formation? I would
suggest that there are several ways, four of which I shall discuss below.
These ways involve: (1) helping with the diagnosis, (2) setting an
agenda for scholarly research and reflection, (3) inviting less authoritarian modes of teaching and obedience, and (4) catalyzing insights about
our own moral situation.

Helping with the Diagnosis
The literary artist is like the canary in a coal mine; when the canary
keels over, the miners know there is something wrong with the atmosphere. The British novelist Graham Greene was so appealing to Catholics in the 1940s and 1950s because besides being an excellent writer, he
was on to something problematic about our tradition. Clearly Greene
loved the church—he was, after all, an adult convert—but his fiction
probed its weak points with penetrating accuracy. The authoritarian legalism that has plagued Catholic approaches to morality was soundly
criticized by one of his characters from *The Heart of the Matter* (1948), a
priest named Father Rank. At the end of this story about a man who
commits suicide because he cannot face the consequences of his adul-
terous behavior, Major Scobie's widow asks the priest whether her late
husband has been sent to hell for taking his own life. Father Rank responds to her question in a way that challenged readers to rethink the
moral calculus learned in catechism class: "The Church knows all the
rules. But it doesn't know what goes on in a single human heart."[16]
Now here was a British Catholic trying to restore a sense of mystery to
our moral tradition forty years ahead of John Mahoney, indeed, longer
than that, if we think about *The Power and the Glory* from 1940, another

Greene novel that shows the limits of oversimplified notions of morality and salvation.

Graham Greene was, of course, a very controversial writer in his
day, and Robert E. Lauder was right to remind readers of his column in
the *Long Island Catholic* that the controversy over the 1997 ABC television series *Nothing Sacred* bears some resemblance to arguments over
Greene's fictional clergymen that went on during the 1940s and 1950s.[17]
One need not agree fully with Father Rank's remark to appreciate the
fact that Greene has reason to let him utter it, or to see that his portrayal of Rank's frustration with what "the church" sometimes claims
to know is part of a diagnosis of a situation that must improve if we are
to be more respectful of the mystery of sin and grace.

Likewise, one need not approve of the way the pastor in the television series *Nothing Sacred*, Father Ray, declares a moratorium on hearing
sexual sins in confession, in order to appreciate that Ray is objecting to a
pastoral problem he faces on a regular basis.[18] This problem involves an
ecclesiastical climate that has insisted on conformity to sexual teaching
much more vehemently than teaching on certain other matters, especially matters of social justice, and at the same time has cut off reasoned
discussion of controversial questions in sexual ethics.

Setting an Agenda for Scholarly Research and Reflection
The diagnostic power of literature to show what is problematic about
the status quo, whether in the church or in the world, is surely an invitation to specialists in moral theology to address these inadequacies
that fiction brings to light. My own research has been inspired by many
imaginative writers, of whom I would single out the contemporary
Mexican author Carlos Fuentes for attention here. In his slim *Bil-
dungsroman* from 1959, *The Good Conscience*, Fuentes demonstrates how
Christian moral energy can be co-opted in the service of an unjust social structure. The novel depicts the development of a young man
whose family and class background stifles his early impulses toward
concern for others. We witness in this story how Jaime Ceballos is
transformed from a sensitive, idealistic child, who befriends a fugitive
labor organizer and a Marxist Indian youth, into a hardening egoist
who will follow in the footsteps of the hypocritical uncle whose values
he once despised. The novel demonstrates how reductive understandings of virtue are implicated in some of the most besetting problems of
Christianity today: injustice to women and the blindness of the middle
and upper classes to matters of social and economic justice. This text,
which I regularly teach in introductory courses in Christian ethics, has

set an agenda for much of my own work on matters of gender, virtue, and social justice.[19] Many other theologians and ethicists have also been inspired by works of literature—Stanley Hauerwas of Duke University comes immediately to mind in this regard—and I think it would be good for the field if the literary and cinematic roots of our investigations were shared more regularly in the specialized writings that we publish.[20] The Peruvian liberation theologian Gustavo Gutiérrez has set a good example in this respect, dedicating his groundbreaking *A Theology of Liberation* to the novelist José María Arguedas, whose works had helped catalyze the turn to the oppressed that Gutiérrez made after completing his studies in Europe. In *A Theology of Liberation* Gutiérrez quotes a scene from the Arguedas novel *Todas las sangres*, as illustrative of the point that "when justice does not exist, God is not known." In the same work he also refers to Luis Buñuel's film *Nazarin* as discrediting "a so-called charity which really has nothing to do with true love for men."[21] I have always found it interesting that the novelist Fuentes was likewise inspired by Buñuel's art. In fact, he dedicates *The Good Conscience* to Buñuel, "great artist of our time, great destroyer of easy consciences, and great creator of human hope."

Inviting Less Authoritarian Modes of Teaching and Obedience
Various scholars have noted that narrative has functioned from ancient times not only to articulate the values and virtues esteemed by a community but also to demonstrate that ideals of human goodness sometimes need correction, especially when they have been exaggerated to the point of diminishing returns.[22] The value of obedience to authority is a case in point. When it became known that this ideal was the defense employed by Nazi war criminals at Nuremberg—"I was only following orders"—society had to rethink whether obedience deserved quite the place it had enjoyed in the then prevalent paradigm of virtue. Thus it is not surprising that narratives satirizing military discipline, such as Joseph Heller's 1961 novel *Catch 22*, came to prominence in the postwar period, and helped to prepare an audience for the more systematic reflections on responsibility that were being published by theologians such as Bernard Häring and H. Richard Niebuhr.

This ability of narrative to help us think both critically and creatively about ethical dilemmas has been brought out very well by the classics scholar Martha Nussbaum in *The Fragility of Goodness* (1986).[23] Here Nussbaum shows that tragic drama can be a rich source for ethical reflection precisely because it touches the emotional as well as intellectual levels of human experience, and thus does better justice to the complexity of what is going on in a difficult situation. Her reading of Sophocles's *Antigone*, in fact, has provided clues for understanding the current conflict over Catholic moral teaching in a much richer way than the combat stereotype I criticized earlier in this article. With Nussbaum's help, I have come to see Vatican authoritarianism as similar to Creon's insistence in the tragic drama that his rebellious nephew Polyneices must be left unburied outside the walls of the city, and that his niece Antigone must be punished for violating this edict, even though she did so out of respect for her brother and the will of the gods.

My sympathies have tended to favor Antigone in Sophocles's drama, and analogously to favor Charles Curran, Bernard Häring, and the Sisters of Mercy in their controversies with Vatican absolutism on moral questions such as contraception and tubal ligation. Nussbaum, however, makes a good case for recognizing that Creon's concerns are not insignificant, although his perception of his duty as ruler leads him to act unwisely. Nevertheless, when one adds a feminist critique of patriarchal understandings of virtue to the analysis, what is clear is that the tragic action proves the futility of the ideals of authority, obedience, and responsibility that center in control and are governed by fear of losing control. Such an analysis further suggests that *listening*, giving ear to difference, is a crucial quality in a leader, who is more effective when acknowledging that full truth and goodness transcend anyone's control, no matter how great his or her responsibilities. One can interpret Creon's tragic flaw as related to a mistaken belief that his duty to preserve order makes it impossible to change the course he has decreed:

> If I allow disorder in my house
> I'd surely have to licence it abroad . . .
> The man the state has put in place must have
> obedient hearing to his least command
> when it is right, and even when it's not . . .
> There is no greater wrong than disobedience. (659–72, passim)[24]

When a responsible patriarch speaks with such conviction, it is difficult to raise an objection, even if the objector is his only son. But Creon's son Haemon is in a position to hear opinions that the powerful ruler has been shielded from facing, surrounded as he is by subordinates who fear his displeasure. And so Haemon musters the courage to state:

... the whole town is grieving for this girl [Antigone],
unjustly doomed, if ever woman was,
to die in shame for glorious action done...
This is the undercover speech in town. (693–95; 700)

Haemon goes on to suggest that wisdom would urge some flexibility in the matter:

And so the ship that will not slacken sail,
the sheet drawn tight, unyielding, overturns. (715–16)

But Creon remains unwilling to change his mind, and he orders Antigone walled up in a cave with just enough food to survive, but no hope of liberation. Later, when the prophet Teiresias declares that this course is unwise, Creon at first dismisses the advice, but is finally moved to reconsider when the prophet foretells that the Furies will seek vengeance against him. By the time Creon repents, however, the tragedy is beyond stopping. Antigone has hanged herself, Haemon soon falls on his own sword, and Creon's wife Eurydice also kills herself. Creon's only option at the work's conclusion is exile and unending sorrow.

This tragedy has rich implications for the present impasse between Vatican authority and revisionist moral theology, and indeed between the male hierarchy and women possessed of deep religious convictions of their dignity and moral responsibility. The fact that the play's action ends with the deaths of so many characters testifies to the loss entailed when positions once taken for good reasons become hardened into absolutes. Creon's form of ruling is too harsh and inflexible; his downfall reveals the limits of a patriarchal mindset that understands responsibility to require that total control be maintained over complex situations.[25]

Fortunately an alternative to the patriarchal mindset is available, one I call the egalitarian-feminist paradigm. In this model, the role of leader does not carry an impossible burden of omni-competence and full control. In this model, which seeks mutuality more than dominance, the roles are not defined so rigidly in terms of the superior commanding and the subject submitting, but rather both leader and follower practice the virtue of obedience in the sense of *listening* for all relevant clues to the truth and then pursuing as much good as seems reasonably attainable in the given circumstances. When leaders demonstrate their willingness to be influenced by aspects of truth beyond their original vantage, they gain the informed trust of their followers. Under such conditions, virtuous individuals are more likely to follow difficult requests for their cooperation, and even to sacrifice personal goods for shared objectives, precisely because they have reason to believe that such leaders have in fact gained a fuller picture of the situation than an individual can obtain.

Such a change of heart was impossible for the tragic figure Creon, who had come to believe that disaster would occur if even a quiet, unceremonious burial outside the city were provided for Polyneices. However, to apply the tragic wisdom to the case at hand, it is not too late for church authorities to put to rest past claims of possessing full and certain knowledge of God's will regarding all aspects of human sexuality. It is the absolutism and universality of magisterial claims about the meaning of sex and details of sexual behavior that are problematic, and if this sail can somehow be slackened, the Catholic approach to sexual ethics still has a great deal to teach women and men who are looking for wisdom on these matters.

Catalyzing Insights about Our Own Moral Situation
Whether we are hierarchical teachers, professional theologians, or ordinary layfolk, our powers of moral reasoning and self-assessment stand to gain from the time we spend caught in the "calculated trap for meditation" that literary art can represent.

I shall illustrate this last point with a brief discussion of a winner of the Pen/Faulkner Award, David Guterson's best-selling novel *Snow Falling on Cedars* (1994). This work takes us back to the 1940s and 1950s, and lets us experience the tense relations between Japanese-Americans and other citizens on an island off the coast of Washington during the Second World War and its aftermath. The effects of racism and war are especially evident in the situation of the main character, whose name is Ishmael Chambers. In contrast to the narrator of *Moby Dick*, this Ishmael confronts the mystery of evil not in a great white whale out at sea, but rather within his own family and community, indeed his own heart. The vision of Guterson's story presumes that nature is indifferent to humanity, but also suggests that human beings ought not to imitate this indifference. The story invites us to contemplate how often evil sets the context for our decisions, but love and hope can motivate a change of heart and inspire the appropriate action. "[A]ccident ruled every corner of the universe," Ishmael and the reader come to understand at the novel's end, "except the chambers of the human heart."[26] In this story Ishmael comes close to letting events take a course that might satisfy his desires but not his conscience, and readers too experience this pull toward a serious sin of omission because Ishmael's misfortunes, which include having lost an arm in battle, engage our sympathy and invite our participation in his way of reading the situation.

What happens to Ishmael in the end I will not reveal here, but I will say this story shows that contemporary fiction is occasionally capable of great revelatory power. Indeed, *Snow Falling on Cedars* reminded me of the biblical story in 2 Samuel, where the prophet Nathan sets a "calculated trap" for David's meditation, employing fiction to help David face his responsibility for having acted out of desire for Bathsheba to engineer her husband's death in battle. In the episode, Nathan tells David the story of a rich man who slaughters the only lamb of a poor man in order to feed a guest, instead of using one from his own ample flock. Upon hearing the story, David explodes in rage: "'the man who did this deserves to die! He must make fourfold restitution for the lamb, for doing such a thing and showing no compassion.' [And] then Nathan said to David, 'You are the man'" (12:5–7, Jerusalem Bible). Guterson does not use such straightforward language as Nathan's "You are the man," but the way he spins his yarn does show an alert reader how prone we all are to self-deception leading to injustice.

And thus, to sum matters up, I would submit that these various examples all show that literary artists are potential allies in the task of renewing Catholic moral theology. Tragedy can help us understand the significance of current struggles, and fiction in general has many ways of assisting in the process I have termed "liberating conscience." When this ideal is approached we are on the way to achieving the renewal called for by the Second Vatican Council. Persons will be achieving freedom from whatever inhibits a full response to the invitation to love God, neighbor, and self in ways that are recognizably good. Our deeds will in fact do what the Council asked: they will "bring forth fruit in charity for the life of the world."

Notes

1. George Eliot, *Middlemarch* (1871–72; Harmondsworth: Penguin, 1976), 199–200. The story is set in rural England just prior to the Reform Bill of 1832. The television adaptation was a BBC Masterpiece Theatre production, directed by Anthony Page and starring Juliet Aubrey.

2. Anne E. Patrick, *Liberating Conscience: Feminist Explorations in Catholic Moral Theology* (New York: Continuum, 1996), 19.

3. Quoted in George A. Panichas, *The Reverent Discipline* (Knoxville: University of Tennessee Press, 1974), 189.

4. Curran was dismissed from a tenured position at the Catholic University of America in 1986; Boff, who had received Vatican injunctions to refrain from

teaching theology, left the Franciscan Order and resigned the priesthood in 1992; Fox, also silenced for a period by the Vatican, and embroiled in a dispute over residency with the Dominicans, was dismissed by his order in 1993 and later joined the Episcopal Church, where he now functions as a priest; Gebara was silenced and ordered to undertake remedial studies in theology by the Vatican in 1995; and, Balasuriya received a decree of excommunication in January 1997, but has remained a member of the Oblates of Mary Immaculate.

5. See "Bad Karma," *Commonweal* (January 31, 1997), 5. Balasuriya's book, which was originally published by his pastoral research center in Colombo, Sri Lanka, in 1990, became generally available in this country only when Trinity Press International brought out a new edition late in 1997.

6. Margaret A. Farley, "New Patterns of Relationship: Beginnings of a Moral Revolution," *Theological Studies* 36 (1975): 629.

7. Thomas F. O'Meara, "Bible and Pope: The Search for Authority" (Tulsa: University of Tulsa Warren Center for Catholic Studies, 1988), 4–5.

8. James M. Gustafson, *Can Ethics Be Christian?* (Chicago: University of Chicago Press, 1975), 179.

9. Quoted here from Walter M. Abbott, ed., *The Documents of Vatican II* (New York: The America Press, 1966), 452.

10. John Mahoney, *The Making of Moral Theology: A Study of the Roman Catholic Tradition* (Oxford: Clarendon Press, 1987), 339–40.

11. Michael A. McGuire, *Baltimore Catechism No. 1*, New Revised Edition (New York: Benziger Brothers, Inc., 1961), 25.

12. Ibid., 84.

13. Mahoney, *The Making of Moral Theology*, 337.

14. For a lucid presentation of historical background and theological and moral issues concerning sterilization, see John P. Boyle, *The Sterilization Controversy: A New Crisis for the Catholic Hospital?* (New York: Paulist, 1977).

15. See Seth Mydans, "In an Interview, Pol Pot Declares His Conscience Is Clear," *The New York Times* (October 23, 1997), A-12.

16. Graham Greene, *The Heart of the Matter* (1948; rev. ed.; Harmondsworth: Penguin, 1971), 272.

17. Robert E. Lauder, "Differing Opinions," *Long Island Catholic* (September 17, 1997), 13.

18. The incident occurs in the first episode of the ABC Television series, which premiered in September 1997.

19. Carlos Fuentes, *The Good Conscience*, trans. Sam Hileman (New York: Noonday, 1961). For a fuller discussion of the ethical significance of this novel, see Anne E. Patrick, "Christian Ethics and *The Good Conscience*: Building a Course around a Novel," *The Annual of the Society of Christian Ethics* (Washington, DC: Georgetown University Press, 1988), 249–53.

20. See Stanley Hauerwas, *Vision and Virtue: Essays in Christian Ethical Reflection* (Notre Dame: Fides/Claretian, 1974) and *A Community of Character* (Notre Dame: University of Notre Dame Press, 1981).

21. Gustavo Gutiérrez, *A Theology of Liberation: History, Politics, and Salvation,*

trans. and ed. Sr. Caridad Inda and John Eagleson (Maryknoll, NY: Orbis Books, 1973), 195, 199–200.

22. See, for example, John D. Barbour, *Tragedy as a Critique of Virtue* (Chico, CA: Scholars Press, 1984).

23. Martha C. Nussbaum, *The Fragility of Goodness: Luck and Ethics in Greek Tragedy and Philosophy* (Cambridge: Cambridge University Press, 1986).

24. *Antigone*, trans. Elizabeth Wyckoff, in David Grene and Richard Latimore, eds., *Sophocles: I* (New York: Modern Library, 1954), lines 524–25. Subsequent references are to this edition.

25. For analysis of this mindset, see Sharon D. Welch, *A Feminist Ethic of Risk* (Minneapolis: Fortress, 1990).

26. David Guterson, *Snow Falling on Cedars* (1994; New York: Vintage, 1995), 460.

8

David Henry Hwang's *Golden Child* and the Ambiguities of Christian (and Post-Christian) Missions

This essay was written for a Festschrift for Anne's graduate advisor, Anthony Yu, at the University of Chicago. She once observed that she had not been told by her community until many years after completing her undergraduate degree that her academic work had been truly outstanding, lest the knowledge encourage pride. Certainly the K–12 teaching she undertook after her B.A. was valuable in many ways. But might she have pursued the type of career that was better suited to her own gifts had that evaluation of her exceptional academic abilities been shared with her immediately? Similarly, Charles Curran notes that assumptions about the unsuitability of moral theology for women delayed her entrance into that field. In any event, this essay and the others in this section do demonstrate how highly she valued her doctoral studies at Chicago and how much she profited from them. —HD

"I am becoming less interested in romanticizing the past...it's really the future that counts."
        —David Henry Hwang, interview October 25, 1993[1]

The ambiguities of Christian missionary activity in Asia, Africa, and the Americas are by now well known. What David Henry Hwang's *Golden Child*, a Tony Award nominee for best play in 1998, adds to the

Adapted from "David Henry Hwang's Golden Child *and the Ambiguities of Christian (and Post-Christian) Missions," in* Literature, Religion, and East/West Comparison: Essays in Honor of Anthony C. Yu, *ed. Eric Ziolkowski (University of Delaware Press, 2005).*

128

discussion is the personal perspective of the evangelized.[2] In contrast to such works as Peter Shaffer's *The Royal Hunt of the Sun*, a drama that probes the tensions of military and religious conquest in South America from the viewpoint of the Spanish conquistador Pizarro, or Barbara Kingsolver's *The Poisonwood Bible*, a fictional account of a Protestant missionary family laboring benightedly in Africa on the brink of anti-colonial uprisings, *Golden Child* brings Hwang's audience inside the world of a traditional Chinese family facing the possibility of conversion to Protestant Christianity in 1918.[3]

The patriarch's decision to be baptized means liberation from traditional footbinding for his daughter, the "golden child" of the work's title, but there is a tragic end for her mother and for another wife in the household that cannot continue to be polygamous. Hwang's play shows how the knotted lines of cultural and religious heritage continue to affect fourth-generation members of the family some decades after the golden child has emigrated to the United States. It also invites theological reflection on the ways religion and morality figure in complex cultural transactions.

Here I first locate *Golden Child* within the oeuvre of a playwright who has achieved remarkable stature in the American theatre since his youthful success with *F.O.B.* (1981), a play about tensions between an assimilated second-generation Chinese-American and a "fresh off the boat" acquaintance from China. I then probe *Golden Child*'s treatment of the agency of several characters whose lives are affected by Christian missionary efforts, with attention to the varying degrees of autonomy they enjoy. Finally, I consider how this play might enrich and extend discussions underway in two groups that are somewhat isolated from each other and from the wider public. These are the Christian theologians who probe the meaning of evangelization in an age of intercultural respect, and the feminists whose indictment of patriarchy sometimes misses the complexity of women's lives in foreign contexts.

What is so illuminating about *Golden Child*, I believe, is the way it gives voice on a contemporary American stage to the ambiguous experience of religious and social change, from the perspectives not only of those who choose or welcome it but also those who futilely resist it. By so giving voice to subjects who have too often been treated as passive objects of rescue by agents of superior insight, Hwang challenges his American audience to go beyond simply celebrating the Christian influence on China as entirely good, or condemning it as altogether bad. He also helps create a public that is better prepared to learn from the ambiguities of history, which is a step toward improving things in the future.

DAVID HENRY HWANG

Best known for his 1988 stage success *M. Butterfly*, which was released in a film version starring Jeremy Irons and John Lone in 1993, Hwang has produced more than a dozen plays. He has also written a number of film and television scripts, and librettos for musical works by Philip Glass and Bright Sheng.[4] Although the 1998 play *Golden Child* will be the focus here, since finishing that drama Hwang has gone on to complete various projects and launch others. He is co-author of the book for Elton John and Tim Rick's *Aida*, which earned four Tony awards in 2000. His play about the artist Paul Gauguin, *Savage in Paradise*, premiered in 2002 at the Chace Theater of the Trinity Repertory Company in Providence, Rhode Island, where Hwang was artist-in-residence. He rewrote the book for Rodgers and Hammerstein's 1958 stage musical *Flower Drum Song*. This revival enjoyed an extended run in Los Angeles in 2001 and was scheduled to open on Broadway in late 2002. A new musical play, *Largo*, had its world premiere during the 2002–2003 season of the Trinity Repertory Company, and Hwang went on to collaborate with composer Alexina Louie on *The Scarlet Princess*, an opera commissioned by the Canadian Opera Company.

In 1989 Douglas Street described Hwang as "the first widely acclaimed, Broadway-produced Asian-American dramatist to capture the imagination of the Asian-American communities on both coasts, the international Asian arts contingents, and the non-Asian theater-going public."[5] The accuracy of Street's assessment has been borne out in subsequent years. Widely acclaimed as a versatile and successful artist, Hwang was honored in his home city of Los Angeles in 1998 when the East West Players named their new stage the David Henry Hwang Theatre. Hwang's versatility is evident not only in the genres he employs, but also in his choice of themes, settings, characters, and theatrical techniques. Still, threaded through his multifaceted oeuvre are the recurring themes of identity, cultural exchange, and the problems of fundamentalist thinking.

Three of his works are strongly autobiographical in their exploration of these themes: *Family Devotions* (1981), *Rich Relations* (1986), and *Golden Child* (1996, revised 1998). Hwang grew up in the Los Angeles suburb of San Gabriel, the son of Henry Y. Hwang, who came from Shanghai in the 1940s to study business at the University of Southern California, and Dorothy Yu Huang Hwang, a native of Amoy raised in the Philippines. She met Hwang while studying at USC in pursuit of a career as a concert pianist, and after her marriage became a successful piano instructor, while Henry prospered as a banker. Their son David, born in 1957, and his two younger sisters were raised in an affluent, assimilationist, and strongly fundamentalist Christian home. David studied the violin from the age of seven, and attended integrated public schools and an exclusive preparatory school before enrolling at Stanford University, where he majored in English with the intention of eventually becoming a lawyer.

David became interested in the theater during his second year of college, and in the summer of 1977 he interned with East West Players of Los Angeles. He began his first play at a 1978 workshop in Claremont, and *F.O.B.* was staged in March 1979 at Stanford's Okada House, Hwang's dormitory. Soon after graduating that spring he learned that his play had been chosen for production at the 1979 National Playwrights Conference, and its subsequent production by Joseph Papp at the New York Shakespeare Festival in 1980 marked his arrival as a playwright with remarkable potential. Two new works were produced in 1981, *The Dance and the Railroad*, and the first of what can be called his religious autobiographical trilogy, *Family Devotions* (FD).

Family Devotions is a sort of spiritual farce, an absurdist drama that begins as a comedy and concludes tragically, with the deaths of the two fundamentalist elders whose family myth has come unraveled during a ritual gone awry. The action takes place in the sunroom and tennis court of a suburban Los Angeles home, and involves three generations of a Chinese immigrant family whose blended and still emerging identity is symbolized in the lacquer of young Chester's violin, which is strangely unhardened and impressionable. On the eve of Chester's departure to take a job with the Boston symphony, the family receives a visit from Di-gou, his great-uncle from the People's Republic of China. His grandmother (Popo) and her sister (Ama), both devout evangelicals, are hoping their brother will affirm the myth that has sustained their Christian piety through the upheavals of loss and cultural dislocation. During a ritual called "family devotions" they enjoin Di-gou to recount the story of their older sister's dramatically successful missionary journey after being infused with the Holy Spirit in China in her youth. The ritual gets underway at the end of Act One, in a room arranged like a church, complete with neon cross and pulpit, with family members singing from Handel's *Messiah*. Ama's opening prayer recalls the myth:

> When See-goh-poh, she hear your word—from missionary. Your spirit, it touch her heart, she accept you, she speak in tongue of fire…You continue, bless See-goh-poh. She become

agent of God, bring light to whole family, until we are convert, we become shining light for you all through Amoy.[6]

The ritual continues as Act Two begins, with the secularized younger members of the family arguing with each other as the elders lead the ritual. Popo reminds everyone that the biblical story of Jonah sustained her during a dangerous crossing from China to the Philippines: "So if God has plan for us, we live; if not . . . we die" (*FD*, 133). Bickering continues between the believers and the younger family members, with elements of comedy contributed especially by the husbands of Popo's and Ama's daughters, but things turn serious and eventually tragic after the older women pressure Di-gou to testify. He protests: "I want to take responsibility for my own life . . . How can you abandon China for this Western religion?" Ama replies, "It is not [Western]," but he counters, "There is no God!"

The sisters respond by tying Di-gou on a table in the ritual room with the intent of purging him of the "Communist demon." They insist that he should praise God for letting him escape China as a young man, and recount his journey with their miracle-working missionary sister, See-go-poh, "the trip which began your faith" (*FD*, 143). Di-gou protests that he does not remember, he was only a boy of eight, but after they hit him with an electrical cord and then start to strangle him, the younger members of the family intervene, and Chester calls the torture to a halt. Suddenly Di-gou rises, grabs his great-nephew, and speaks in tongues, and Chester is inspired to translate the astonishing story: See-goh-poh's "first evangelism tour" was not at all what it seemed, but rather an opportunity to give birth to a baby away from her family. Di-gou then presses his demythologized version home by asking Ama and Popo if they can name a single village where their sister preached, or give the name of one convert from her evangelism tour. "You do not remember. You do not know the past," he insists. "I was there! She was thrown out—thrown out on her evangelism tour when she tried to preach" (*FD*, 147). To their protests he hammers home the truth that subsequent "evangelism tours" were merely an excuse to visit her child. The family myth no longer serves, and Chester will be better off to follow his great uncle's advice: "The stories written on your face are the ones you must believe" (*FD*, 126). The old women hear this advice proclaimed again (*FD*, 148), and, in a turn of plot that strains credulity, both collapse and die onstage. Di-gou learns from this that "No one leaves America," and decides his only desire is "to drive an American car—very fast—down an American freeway" (*FD*, 149).

The play ends with young Chester silent about what has happened, although the spotlight reveals his face taking on a different shape.

Rich Relations presses home a similar indictment of fundamentalist Christianity, this time by displaying the corruption of a white American family, whose situation recapitulates some of Hwang's issues with suburban affluence and religious craziness without the complexities of an immigrant Chinese heritage. It is another "spiritual farce," with scenes that suggest a sort of "magic realism," as women seem to commit suicide by leaping from a balcony high above the rocks only to reappear intact in the next scene. Meanwhile the father (Hinson) and son (Keith), whose crimes range from drug dealing and money laundering to sexual misconduct with minors, interact with each other, the women, and a stage-full of electrical appliances.

Less dramatically successful than Hwang's other plays about families and Christianity, *Rich Relations* ends with the three females going out together for something to eat. They leave behind the corrupt father and son, who bend their ears to the ground in the hope of hearing a voice that "carries hope from beyond the grave," the hope of bringing "ourselves back from the dead."[7] Hwang had suffered a period of writer's block prior to completing *Rich Relations* in 1986, and he values the work for personal reasons despite its having been a critical and financial failure. He has described it as a "play about the possibility of resurrection," adding that, "it did indeed resurrect my own love for work and point the way toward the non-Asian characters that were to follow in such works as *M. Butterfly*."[8] He turned to other themes in the late 1980s, but by the mid-1990s, after his second marriage and the birth of a son, he once more set out to probe the religious issues of his past. In a 1998 interview with Nisha Berson, Hwang observed:

> You can trace an evolution in my attitude about [Christian fundamentalism] in these three family plays. *Family Devotions*, which I wrote at 23, is a very angry indictment of the Christian fundamentalist mindset. The family in that play has been corrupted by Christianity and has lost its true beliefs. In *Rich Relations* the younger character [Keith, a high school teacher guilty of taking sexual advantage of fourteen-year-olds] also has skeletons in his closet, so everyone's rotten. *Golden Child*, for better or worse, has a much more forgiving point of view, and I hope it's an anti-fundamentalist play in the largest sense —that is, against any belief system that casts things in black or white.[9]

Besides the more forgiving point of view, *Golden Child* also differs from Hwang's earlier plays on Christian themes by being set not in the contemporary suburbs of Los Angeles, but rather in 1918, in a village near Amoy on the southeast coast of China. Only brief opening and concluding scenes in present-day Manhattan frame the story, which mainly probes factors in Hwang's family history. He began the work that would become *Golden Child* when, at age ten, he interviewed his grandmother about her life story and turned this oral history into a ninety-page novel. Thirty years later he was in a position to transform this juvenile work into a successful drama:

> As in the play, my great-grandfather did convert to Christian-
> ity, at which point he unbound my grandmother's feet. The
> first and third of his wives died, and he was left with the one
> who was most ambitious. My grandmother's mother, his first
> wife, died of opium addiction. And my grandmother is, to this
> very day, very fundamentalist in her religious beliefs.[10]

The play represents a distilled and enhanced version of this story. It opens in the voice of an elderly grandmother, which quickly becomes that of the same woman as a girl of ten, still in China before her family emigrated to the Philippines and then the United States. This grand-mother/golden child (Eng Ahn, daughter of the First Wife) introduces the main plot, in which the three wives of the patriarch Eng Tieng-bin struggle with the changes entailed in his converting to Christianity in 1918.[11] She also provides the framing connection with the present at the play's beginning and conclusion, when she visits her grandson Andrew Kwong, and gives him advice.

"Andrew—you must be born again . . . Make money, not important; write successful book, not important. Only one thing important: you love Jesus" (*GC*, 5). This is what Ahn says as she intrudes into the Manhattan apartment of Andrew, a writer in his fifties troubled by the unplanned pregnancy of his third wife. Disturbing his sleep, she insists it is time to "cast out the demon of your anger," and "hear my story again—not with ear only, but also with spirit." Andrew protests that her tale of becoming a "religious fanatic" is "the last thing I need right now," but he cannot dismiss his ancestral ghost so easily (*GC*, 6). Suddenly his wife Elizabeth is transformed into Eling, the Third Wife of his great-grandfather, and the ghosts from 1918 take over the action. Ahn, the grandmother, slips a Chinese robe onto Andrew, and he becomes his great-grandfather, Tieng-Bin. Andrew will not only *hear* the story again; he will participate in it, and in this way come to understand why his ancestor forsook traditional Confucian practices for Christianity, and how his grandmother came to terms with cultural and personal loss by embracing the new religion so wholeheartedly.

A GRANDMOTHER'S TALE

Rey Chow begins her 1991 study, *Woman and Chinese Modernity: The Politics of Reading between East and West*, with these lines from G. C. Spivak: "Between patriarchy and imperialism, subject-constitution and object formation, the figure of the woman disappears, not into a pristine nothingness, but into a violent shuttling which is the displaced figuration of the 'Third World woman' caught between tradition and modernization."[12]

In *Golden Child* Hwang does not succeed entirely in restoring these "disappeared" women, nor in rescuing them from "violent shuttling," but he does give them names, voices, and memorable lines that guide reflection on the ambiguities of Christian and post-Christian missionary activities. Although Eng Tieng-Bin and his friend Reverend Anthony Baines have decisive roles in the plot, there are four strong female characters as well: Eng Sui-Yong, the First Wife, and her daughter, Eng Ahn (the Golden Child); Eng Luan, the Second Wife; and Eng Eling, the Third Wife. The playwright sees the polygamous situation as "a microcosm for all the competitiveness in the world," and is eager to avoid portraying these women merely as victims of men's actions. They are, after all, to some degree responsible for their lives, making choices within the limitations of their cultural situation. He describes their agency thus: "'These are the rules, this is the society I was born into, I'll try to play by the rules and get somewhere, to gather power.'"[13]

The stage set for *Golden Child* includes the living room of the family's main hall and three pavilions arranged in a semicircle, one for each wife. The action opens in the winter of 1918, with the wives arguing with each other as they prepare to welcome Tieng-Bin home after a three-year business trip to the Philippines. Young Ahn introduces the religious conflict when she adds a paper steamer ship to the offerings her mother is burning during prayers to her parents, and declares that the ancestors "want to be modern—like Papa." Siu-Yong responds scornfully that new things simply "have not had time to disappoint us," but Ahn has latched on to a possibility of great personal import: "Papa says, in the modern world they don't make girls wear bindings on their feet" (*GC*, 10).

The rivalry among the wives comes out as they welcome Tieng-Bin, vying to excel at the game of self-deprecation, since their culture values humility. As with *Family Devotions*, there are many humorous lines in this drama, which is basically serious and eventually tragic. Tensions build during the first act as the patriarch bestows gifts that displease his older wives (a cuckoo clock for Siu-Yong, who is in her forties, and a waffle iron for Luan, who is about ten years younger) and favor Eling, a woman in her early twenties. She receives a phonograph and recording of *La Traviata*, which Tieng-Bin describes as "the story of two lovers who only wish to be together—but their society makes this impossible" (*GC*, 18).

Ahn is caught between her father's openness to change and her mother's hostility toward Western influences, although there are indications she leans toward Tieng-Bin's position in her objections to Siu-Yong's use of opium and her own desire for unbound feet. Still, she is willing to go along with her mother's request that she spy on the sessions that Tieng-Bin and Luan will have when the missionary arrives. The first act culminates when Tieng-Bin orders Siu-Yong to unbind Ahn's feet. This is done offstage amid shrieks of pain, which her father endures while praying to his parents for forgiveness. The factors that will lead to tragedy are all in place as Reverend Anthony Baines arrives and the scene fades to black.

Act Two takes place in the spring of 1919. It opens with comic relief, much of which is supplied by Baines, a mainly ridiculous figure. He speaks the sort of broken English often scripted for stereotypical Chinese characters in American films, whereas the Eng family members all speak fluent English. The linguistic ineptitude symbolizes the broader cultural insensitivity that the missionary brings to his work. Nevertheless, Baines's halting speech expresses a notion that Tieng-Bin finds attractive, that of being an "individual"—standing alone, choosing one's own life, expressing what one thinks and feels—instead of always being conscious of "a whole web of obligation" and worrying how one's words will affect others (*GC*, 33).

Tieng-Bin wrestles with the idea of "one God/one wife," telling Baines that the ghosts maintain "'that the position of wives is fixed, like the bodies of the heavens'" (*GC*, 42). Yet the prospect of living only with his chosen love Eling is appealing enough to make him capitulate to Baines's declaration that the dead should no longer have power over him. When he visits the now pregnant Eling to discuss the plan to "pull down the family altars, live as though I had only one wife, even take you with me back to the Philippines," she raises objections based on concern for her parents and the First Wife. Tieng-Bin answers, "I thought you wanted to be modern," and her response states the central dilemma of the action: "I do. But does that mean I can no longer be Chinese?" (*GC*, 44–45).

When Eling defends her lack of interest in the religious discussions with Baines by revealing that Ahn has been participating only to spy for her mother, Tieng-Bin goes to confront Siu-Yong and finds her smoking opium, a practice dating from Luan's arrival as Second Wife. The ensuing argument leads to his smashing the picture of her parents and declaring that her behavior has led him to a decision. He will be baptized, take down the family altars, and require her to attend the lessons with Baines, since they "all need a fresh start, to begin a new life" (*GC*, 49). There follows a scene in which Ahn disrespectfully confronts the scheming Luan and predicts her downfall, but hears the retort, "Jesus...will save me and destroy your mother...Take my advice, Ahn—join us, forget your mother—and save yourself" (*GC*, 51).

These scenes of argument are followed by a scene of contrasting rituals, which are dramatized contrapuntally, the one a Christian ceremony of baptism and holy communion and the other a suicidal ingesting of opium by Siu-Yong. On one side of the stage Baines baptizes Tieng-Bin, who then receives the communion bread and wine, and on the other the First Wife swallows a ball of opium, answering Ahn's objections with, "Duty calls" (*GC*, 53). As Luan receives the Christian sacraments, Siu-Yong swallows a second ball, and then, following the baptism of Eling, a third dose. She loses consciousness while singing a macabre lullaby about filial devotion to Ahn. Whereas Luan has adopted Christianity without regret (she is the least traditional of the Chinese characters, praying only once, to forgive her father for selling her as a Second Wife and ask for power in compensation–*GC*, 11), Eling is ambivalent about a choice she regards as selfish and undutiful. She resolves the dilemma by willing her own death during a labor that results in the death of her child as well. The influence of Siu-Yong as ghost has convinced her that this sacrifice will be "the best thing for Husband" (*GC*, 58).

Tieng-Bin regards the tragic loss of these wives—the young one he loved and the older one he respected—as punishment for his having become an individual, and he is shocked to hear Ahn quote biblical platitudes that do nothing for his grief. When she says she will "tell great stories...about how you made us all born again," but will "not even remember" the name of "First Wife," he counters with newfound wisdom: "Ahn, your mother was from another time, that's all. I will always honor her name" (*GC*, 60), and the scene ends with Ahn telling her father that her gratitude to him will last beyond her death.

In the final scene the now elderly Ahn is back in present-day Manhattan visiting her grandson. When Andrew interprets her tale as a reason not to become a parent ("Your father tried so hard, but he only brought tragedy to himself and everyone around him"), she counters that Tieng-Bin's choices were well intentioned and led to some good effects: "He suffer to bring family into future. Where better life, I am able to live. I first girl in family to go school, choose own husband—and all the time worship Jesus." Finally Andrew understands that her enthusiasm for Christianity is not really a rejection of Chinese identity and Confucian ideals: "So—whenever you opened a Bible, or said a prayer to Jesus, you were actually making an offering... to your father. In spite of everything, you loved him so much," he declares, and Ahn confirms: "My father, Tieng-Bin—this one thing I will never forget: you see, he is the one... who take the binding from my feet" (*GC*, 61).

The play ends with Andrew newly able to relate to his ancestors, his wife Elizabeth, and their own anticipated "Golden Child." The visit from his ancestral ghost leaves him understanding that everyone has to struggle with the issue of "what to keep, and what to change," and hopeful that "Perhaps, if I do my best, in the imagination of my descendants, I may also one day be born again" (*GC*, 62). Andrew's insight is echoed in a brief essay Hwang wrote in 1996, "The Myth of Immutable Cultural Identity."[14] Without making direct reference to *Golden Child*, the piece serves as an explanation of why this play is so much more "forgiving" than Hwang's earlier attempts to come to terms with the Christian fundamentalism he had rejected so vehemently in college. He had earlier described *Family Devotions* (1981) as an autobiographical work opposed to "Western mythology": "I was raised as a born-again Christian, and the rejection of this Western mythology is, among other things, a casting off of the brainwashing white missionaries have consistently attempted to impose on 'heathen' Asian cultures."[15]

By the mid-nineties he had come to oppose with equal strength the sort of "cultural fundamentalism" that presumes that an "immutable cultural identity actually exists" somewhere, "separate from the corrupting influences of white America." Against this myth Hwang now maintains a complex theory of cultural fluidity. Since culture is "a living thing, born of ever-changing experience and therefore subject to continual reinterpretation," the task of searching for identity is coextensive with life itself.[16] A ghost-grandmother who carries a satchel marked "JESUS" and proclaims, "You forget—I am *Chinese* Christian. Best of East, best of West" (Eng Ahn, to Andrew Kwong, *GC*, 6), can be forgiven her pride, for her struggles have given her much wisdom to share with this grandson.

GOLDEN CHILD AND POSTCOLONIAL DISCUSSIONS
OF MISSIOLOGY AND FEMINISM

In a very appreciative review of *Golden Child* appearing in the Jesuit weekly *America*, Edward Mattimoe observes that the playwright "makes us wonder about all missionaries venturing into cultures not their own."[17] The important word in that sentence is "us," for Mattimoe writes about a general audience of theatergoers, whose backgrounds range over a spectrum of secular and religious positions. Although specialists would know that there is a large body of academic literature probing the ambiguities of Christian missions to China (and elsewhere), and a growing collection of postcolonial feminist writings, typical playgoers are not likely to have encountered these materials. Nor are they likely to have given much thought to the issues of cultural and religious imperialism, particularly as these have affected women. And yet, as James Reed demonstrates in *The Missionary Mind and American East Asian Policy, 1911–1915*, the mentality that characterized mainstream U.S. culture during the heyday of missionary activities had great impact on foreign policy through much of the twentieth century.[18] Today's heirs to the effects of the wars against Japan, North Korea, and North Vietnam can benefit from examining the mixed results of missionary efforts by Christians in the past. Hwang's play, which tells one representative story, cannot deal with all the complexities of this history, but it succeeds in causing "wonder," and it invites audiences to probe further into these matters.

Those who accept this invitation might be surprised to discover that much more was going on among Christians in Amoy (Xiamen), the port city directly west of Taiwan, than could possibly be shown on a stage featuring the Eng family home in a nearby village. Although Tieng-Bin grew interested in Christianity after meeting Rev. Baines on a voyage from the Philippines, British and American Presbyterians were long established in Amoy by the time of Hwang's story. Indeed, in 1864 a progressive mission agreement (the "Amoy plan") had been reached between the Reformed Church in America and the English Presbyterian Church, and the presbytery there (known as a *Tai-hoe*) was a forerunner of an independent Chinese church.[19] Nor were all missionaries as inept as Rev. Baines of Hwang's play. As early as 1890 a missionary conference in Shanghai had probed the extent to which Chinese Christians "should be required to abandon Native Customs," and although most missionaries opposed footbinding, concubinage, and "ancestor worship," there were minority positions on some issues.[20] Historian G.

Thompson Brown cites the 1906 case of Rev. Mark Grier, who with the support of some colleagues had baptized a man in Xuzhou without requiring him to break off relations with a second wife.[21] Because Baines is a stock character whose agency is not probed the way Hwang examines that of the Eng family members, we can only wonder how Baines felt about the results of his evangelical work. If we were to pursue the question more broadly, we would discover that many missionaries saw the ambiguous effects of their work, and some wanted to redefine their goals and emphasize a "social mission" over the winning of converts.[22] The "social mission" involved efforts to promote health and education, and to improve the situation of women. The results with respect to Chinese women have been analyzed by Kwok Pui-lan, a theologian from Hong Kong who now teaches at the Episcopal Divinity School in Massachusetts. With other postcolonial feminist theorists, Kwok recognizes that mission activity was closely linked with imperialism. "Missionaries were sent to win souls for Christ," she notes, "while bodies were colonized and foreign land violently confiscated," and sexual imagery employed to "romanticize" and justify the domination of a feminized foreign population.[23] Kwok is aware that concern for women's situation in places such as India or China often masked imperialist intentions, "helping to camouflage the brutality of colonialism by sugarcoating it as a form of social mission."[24] Nevertheless she recognizes that Christian missions contributed to the movement for women's rights in China, and notes that "[a]lthough a tiny minority in society, Christian women were the first group of Chinese women to organize themselves in order to publicly address women's oppression."[25] Despite being carriers of ethnocentrism, female missionaries, including doctors and educators, had catalyzed a sense of possibility among Chinese women. Kwok's overall assessment of their impact reminds one of Andrew Kwong's final understanding of his ancestors in *Golden Child*: "missionary women were neither saints nor villains but human beings caught up in an historical drama that was beyond their control and that produced results they had not intended."[26]

Kwok has recently complicated the discussion by showing that the residual effects of a colonialist mentality continue in the radical "post-Christian" feminist philosophy of Mary Daly, whose chapter on footbinding in the influential *Gyn/Ecology: The Metaethics of Radical Feminism* (1978) she criticizes on several counts. Daly's "colonialist mindset" is revealed in her portrayal of China as "unchanging and timeless," and in her failure to note variations in the practice of footbinding according to "region, class, and ethnicity." Daly cites no Chinese authors, and leaves Chinese women "invisible" and voiceless, even neglecting to mention the 1874 gathering in a church in Xiamen (Amoy) that resulted in the establishment of an anti-footbinding society. "The erasure of Chinese women's agency in their long struggle for freedom is troubling," Kwok insists, observing that "the post-Christian myth, when universalized, can be as dangerous as Christian imperialism in terms of its totalizing effect."[27] It is critical, she believes, for European and European-American feminists to "decolonize their minds and save themselves from the state of unknowing," before they can collaborate effectively with women of other backgrounds. This task, she adds, resembles "the unbinding of our feet" in that it is "indeed a long, long process."[28] David Henry Hwang's play *Golden Child*, which forsakes "totalizing myths" for the limits of a well-told story, could not possibly do full justice to the agency of any of the characters it brings to life so briefly on the stage. Although Ahn emphasizes her father's decision to unbind her feet, seeming to forget that her mother is the one who carried out the order, her own agency contributed notably to the event. Not only did she voice the desire for unbound feet more than once, she also cooperated in the spying operation at her mother's request, and this choice contributed to Tieng-Bin's decision to be baptized, with all the negative and positive consequences that ensued.

Hwang's audience is left with much to wonder about at the play's conclusion, and at the same time has some of Andrew Kwong's newfound sense of hope for the future. The pain of dealing with the ambiguities of one's heritage—whether familial, cultural, national, or religious—can be worth enduring if it contributes toward a freer stride in the direction of one's ideals. The playright's own recognition that "our identities as Asian/Pacifics cannot be separated from the other cultures which have also become part of our personal histories," deserves a reciprocal response from the European-Americans in the audience.[29] Our past is much more bound up with events in China and elsewhere than we might realize, had not *Golden Child* brought these matters so artfully to our attention.

Notes

1. Robert Cooperman, "Across the Boundaries of Cultural Identity: An Interview with David Henry Hwang," in *Staging Difference: Cultural Pluralism in American Theatre and Drama*, ed. Marc Maufort (New York: Peter Lang, 1995), 372–73.
2. David Henry Hwang, *Golden Child* (New York: Theatre Communications Group, 1998).

3. Peter Shaffer, *The Royal Hunt of the Sun* (New York: Samuel French, Inc., 1964); and Barbara Kingsolver, *The Poisonwood Bible* (New York: Harper Flamingo, 1998). Mark Twain and Herman Melville had brought issues concerning missionaries to public attention in the nineteenth century, and a Broadway adaptation of Somerset Maughm's novel *The Rain* sparked much discussion in the early 1920s.

4. For a recent discussion of Hwang's career, see Keith Lawrence and John Dye, "David Henry Hwang," in *Dictionary of Literary Biography*, vol. 212: *Twentieth-Century American Western Writers*, ed. Richard H. Cracroft, 2nd series (Farmington Hills, MI: The Gale Group, 1999), 133–42.

5. Douglas Street, *David Henry Hwang* (Boise, ID: Boise State Univ. Press, 1989), 46.

6. David Henry Hwang, *Family Devotions*, in *Trying to Find Chinatown: The Selected Plays* (New York: Theatre Communications Group, 2000), 129. Subsequent references to this play will be made parenthetically, as *FD*, and analogous internal citations will be employed for Hwang's other plays once they have been documented initially.

7. David Henry Hwang, *Rich Relations*, in *FOB and Other Plays* (New York: New American Library, 1990), 270–71.

8. David Henry Hwang, "Introduction," in ibid., xiii.

9. Quoted in Nisha Berson, "The Demon in David Henry Hwang," *American Theatre* 15 (April 1998), 16. This article, which includes an interview with Hwang, was published shortly before *Golden Child* opened on Broadway.

10. Ibid. Hwang elaborates further on his long relationship with the material in his introduction to the published version of the play, "Bringing up 'Child,'" (*GC*), v–ix.

11. Surnames are written first in East Asian contexts, and this convention is followed in the play. The great-grandson of Eng Tieng-Bin, however, follows the American convention: Andrew Kwong. (Names in the play differ from those in the oral history "novel" of Hwang's youth, and his mature imagination has altered many other details of the story as well).

12. Rey Chow, *Woman and Chinese Modernity: The Politics of Reading between East and West* (Minneapolis: University of Minnesota Press, 1991), v.

13. Hwang, quoted in Berson, "The Demon in David Henry Hwang," 18.

14. David Henry Hwang, "Foreword: The Myth of Immutable Cultural Identity," in Brian Nelson, ed., *Asian American Drama: 9 Plays from the Multiethnic Landscape* (New York: Applause, 1997), vii–viii.

15. Hwang, "Introduction," *FOB and Other Plays*, xii.

16. Hwang, "The Myth of Immutable Cultural Identity," in Nelson, vii–viii.

17. Edward J. Mattimoe, "Long Ago and Far Away," *America* (May 16, 1998), 23.

18. James Reed, *The Missionary Mind and American East Asian Policy, 1911–1915* (Cambridge: Harvard University Press, 1983). Reed argues that the notions of a "Christian China" and a wider "Christian civilization" were of great symbolic import in the U.S. during the early twentieth century, with "Christian

China" representing "American innocence reborn in East Asia" (34), to the detriment of U.S. relations with Japan.

19. G. Thompson Brown, *Earthen Vessels and Transcendent Power: American Presbyterians in China, 1837–1952* (Maryknoll, NY: Orbis Books, 1997), 122–23.

20. Ibid., 125.

21. Ibid., 144–45.

22. William R. Hutchison discusses various debates about mission policy in *Errand to the World: American Protestant Thought and Foreign Missions* (Chicago: University of Chicago Press, 1987). Of particular interest is the "Laymen's Report of 1932," in "Re-Thinking Mission," whose principal author (William E. Hocking) felt that the missionary's aim of "spiritual collaboration" should mean that Christians should not be hostile to other world faiths, "nor seek to displace them" (159). The "Report," which praised some outstanding missionaries while finding the majority "of limited outlook and capacity," sparked criticism, debate, and division (163). Hutchison observes that by 1980 about half of U.S. Protestants had broken with past approaches to mission (202). For more current Catholic and Protestant examples of progressive missiology, see Donal Dorr, *Mission in Today's World* (Maryknoll, NY: Orbis Books, 2000), and David J. Bosch, *Transforming Mission: Paradigm Shifts in Theology of Mission* (Maryknoll, NY: Orbis Books, 2000).

23. Kwok Pui-lan, *Introducing Asian Feminist Theology* (Cleveland: Pilgrim Press, 2000), 16–17.

24. Kwok Pui-lan, "Unbinding Our Feet: Saving Brown Women and Feminist Religious Discourse," in *Postcolonialism, Feminism, and Religious Discourse*, ed. Laura E. Donaldson and Kwok Pui–lan (New York: Routledge, 2002), 63.

25. Kwok Pui-lan, *Chinese Women and Christianity 1860–1927* (Atlanta: Scholars Press, 1992), 2.

26. Ibid., 22–23.

27. Kwok, "Unbinding Our Feet," 71–75.

28. Ibid., 79.

29. Hwang, "The Myth of Immutable Cultural Identity," viii.

III

THEOLOGICAL AND ETHICAL CONCERNS

9

VIRTUE, PROVIDENCE, AND THE ENDANGERED SELF

Religious Dimensions of the Abortion Debate

Anne Patrick analyzes the disagreement between a Catholic who adamantly opposes abortion and one who, like herself, considers the defense of choice consistent with Catholicism; she outlines their divergent positions in terms of the contrast between, on the one hand, a patriarchal model for virtue, which includes gendered distinctions, and, on the other, a feminist paradigm based on the "gender-integrated ideals" of love and justice. Each position, she demonstrates, involves a distinct set of principles. In defending the feminist paradigm, she demonstrates her characteristic commitments: a sharp analysis of language and symbols, careful distinctions, and a respect and understanding of divergent positions. Rather than rejecting older beliefs or simply parroting them, Anne reinterprets them in relation to contemporary developments—another achievement characteristic of her work. —HD

My interest in the symbolism of the abortion debate stems from a general concern for the well-being of women and girls and from a specific concern about the way Catholic energies and resources have been used in the last twenty years to fight what seems to be the wrong battle. To be more precise, I am troubled by the way Catholic voters have been manipulated into voting on a single issue—the antiabortion issue, manipulated into voting for candidates whose positions on many matters are quite opposed to Catholic principles of social justice.[1] The question I want to explore is why so many Catholics are vulnerable to this sort

Adapted from a chapter of the same title in Abortion and Catholicism: The American Debate, *ed. P. B. Jung and T. A. Shannon (New York: Crossroad, 1988), 172–80.*

of manipulation. My supposition is that certain religious symbols contribute to this vulnerability and that reinterpretation of some central religious beliefs is necessary if Catholics generally are to move to a stronger, more consistent position on public policy questions related to social justice.

The adversaries in the debate that interests me are neither women-hating rightists, eager to expand the address lists of potential contributors to political action committees for neoconservative candidates, nor are they faithless, irresponsible individualists without regard for the value of life in all its stages. Instead, I have in mind opponents with much more in common than these stereotypical extremes. I am concerned with a more central debate—a debate, let's say, between a Catholic woman who no longer accepts an absolute prohibition of abortion and another Catholic woman who continues to believe that directly intended abortion is always wrong. Both consider themselves feminists. The more "liberal" woman views the procedure of abortion negatively, but believes that in certain cases abortion is justified or at least tolerable, and that where public policy is concerned it is unwise and unjust to deny this option to women who conscientiously regard abortion as less harmful than other effects that would ensue from continuing a pregnancy. Her "conservative" adversary is not without concern for girls and women with problem pregnancies. Indeed, the "conservative" I have in mind is an actual woman who has demonstrated courage and conviction in defense of women's reproductive choice, exclusive of the choice to abort. I am thinking of a maternity nurse who lost her job in a Catholic hospital because she insisted that her patients should be given contraceptive information and prescriptions. Reproductive choice for women is clearly a high value for this opponent of abortion. Why does she balk at the point where pregnancy has occurred?

I believe the reason goes deeper than ethics, and that moral arguments alone will not change her mind. The remarks that follow are part of an effort to understand her position, which may depend upon religious symbols and metaphors that operate at levels not always conscious, but nonetheless are powerful and basic to the personality structure of many Catholics. Furthermore, I seek to understand how this woman's liberal opponent can also be devout, can see her "pro-choice" position as consonant with her deepest religious convictions as a Catholic.

VIRTUE

In the first place, to comprehend the intra-Catholic abortion debate, it helps to realize that there is currently a conflict between two different sets of ideals for character and virtue in the Catholic community. I believe the latter is gaining ascendancy in Catholic consciousness, and this accounts for the increasingly defensive articulations of the patriarchal paradigm by those in power who espouse it.[2]

A patriarchal model for virtue has long held sway in Roman Catholicism. Its shape has been affected by the otherworldly spirituality, the theological and social patterns of domination and subordination, the misogynism, and the body-rejecting dualism characteristic of Western culture. This model understands virtue to involve the control of passion by reason and the subordination of earthly values to "supernatural" ones. It articulates many ideals for character, but tends to assume that these are appropriately assigned greater emphasis according to one's gender and social status. All Christians should be kind, chaste, just, and humble, but women are expected to excel in charity and chastity, men are trained to think in terms of justice and rights, and subordinates of both sexes are exhorted to docility and meekness. This paradigm has come to function in a way that sees chastity as the pinnacle of perfection, absolutizing this virtue as defined by physicalist interpretations of "natural law." One of the features of this paradigm is the view that a lack of chastity in women deserves especially severe punishment, an attitude that both expresses and nourishes misogynism, with predictable results for the abortion debate.

In contrast to the anthropological dualism of the patriarchal paradigm, the feminist paradigm understands reason itself to be embodied, and women and men to be equal partners in the human community. Instead of *control*, the notion of *respect* for all created reality is basic to this model, which values the body and the humanity of women and promotes gender-integrated ideals for character. Rather than understanding power as *control over*, this paradigm operates with a sense of power as the *energy of proper relatedness*. Ideals of love and justice are not segregated into separate spheres of personal and social ethics, with responsibility for realizing them assigned according to gender; instead, love and justice are seen to be mutually reinforcing norms that should govern both sexes equally.

Perhaps because of the exaggerated attention given by advocates of the patriarchal paradigm to sexual purity, advocates of the feminist model tend not to focus on the virtue of chastity *per se*, though a reinterpretation of this virtue may be inferred from what they have written on love and justice, and also on particular sexual questions.[3] This paradigm sees sexuality as a concern of social justice as well as of personal virtue. It recognizes that the focal sign of religious devotion cannot be the directing of one's energy to controlling bodily impulses and other people, but rather must involve a stance of ongoing commitment to the wellbeing of oneself and others. This entails concern for building social relations of respect, equality, and mutuality.

Presently the feminist paradigm is capturing the imaginations of many believers, but the eclipse of the patriarchal paradigm is far from complete, and understanding its residual power is crucial to following the abortion debate. We need to ask, for one thing, why the virtue of chastity has been so absolutized. One reason, I believe, is because of obvious associations between sexual activity and the origins of life. There is a negative side to this, particularly the patriarchal preoccupation with paternity and progeny rights, but there is also a positive side. This has to do with the fact that the origin of life is intimately tied in with fundamental Christian myths and symbols concerning providence, creation, and salvation.

PROVIDENCE AND THE ENDANGERED SELF

"Providence" is the traditional symbol for affirming God's involvement in history. This doctrine is especially important in this context because what is at issue is not abortion, but rather *induced* abortion. We are aware that a very high percentage of concepti, embryos, and fetuses are spontaneously aborted, perhaps as many as 60 percent.[4] What is happening today is that new understandings of sexuality and reproduction, new medical technologies, and new appreciation of women's humanity have combined to raise new issues concerning human responsibility and the origin of life. We are faced with basic questions: What is it proper for human agents to do? How much is our responsibility? How much is God's? How one answers depends in part on one's style of faith and on how one understands traditional religious symbols such as the doctrine of providence. Furthermore, besides the issue of what it means to affirm that a loving God is involved in human history, which entails questions concerning the scope and limits of human freedom, the abortion debate also reflects the sense of peril that is felt on behalf of those perceived to be victims of unjust social policies regarding abortion. Two such "endangered selves" are thought by one side or the other to be at risk as the debate is usually

framed, but I believe that there is a third such "endangered self" involved in the controversy, and that attending to this third factor is essential if we are to reach a coherent and reasonable solution to the
controversy over public policy.[5]

The first endangered self is the "responsible self" of the woman
who is threatened with the lack of autonomy requisite for responsible
moral agency. It is important to realize that those who oppose strict antiabortion legislation are not in most instances supporting "choice" as
an absolute value nor arguing for extreme liberal individualism. They
are rather insisting that an appropriate degree of freedom is needed for
living responsibly as a human being in society, and pointing out that
women's well-being requires the ability to make moral choices about
using their reproductive powers.[6] They are aware that our culture has
been biased against women for millennia, and that our legal and moral
codes are only beginning to recognize women as fully human, responsible moral agents.[7] They lament the fact that women's moral wisdom
has largely been discounted by patriarchal religion, and are unwilling
to use coercion to add to the sufferings of existing persons for the sake
of bringing new lives into a world that is not justly ordered to their
nurturance. They correctly observe that it is inconsistent to allow persons to take mature human life under certain conditions while forbid-
ding them to take fetal life under any conditions. As a minimum, they
would remind fetal absolutists that their commitment to "life" is suspect if it stops at birth and is not equally and *effectively* concerned with
the sufferings of adult women and children.

The second endangered self is the "possible self" of the fetus. I am
convinced there is wisdom in respecting fetal life as a high value and
also in recognizing the wisdom of women's experience and of liturgical
and pastoral practice that senses increasing obligations of respect as
fetal life develops. As I look at today's [1988] intra-Catholic abortion
debate, however, I have to ask why the value of fetal life is currently
being absolutized by some participants in the debate. I was astounded
to read some time ago a headline over an editorial in the Jesuit weekly
America that declared, "Life, Not Choice, Is Absolute."[8] As a Catholic, I
have thought for some time that only God is absolute, and in view of
the fact that our tradition esteems martyrdom and endorses a just-war
theory, it cannot be the case that "life" is an absolute value. What the
trend toward absolutizing the value of fetal life suggests is that the
abortion debate touches a central religious nerve for many believers,
and this fact invites us to probe the way in which issues about the origin of life tie in with fundamental religious symbols, and particularly
with myths of creation.

This line of thought, then, leads us to recognize a third endangered self in the debate, one that is pivotal to any eventual resolution of the policy questions at issue. This is the "perplexed self" of the believer. The perplexed believer confronts a dilemma that can be put in these terms: If I tolerate human interference with the life process after conception, what will happen to my world of meaning and value?[9] A natural instinct to defend what is precious to oneself can lead to the belief that the safest policy is to be utterly passive in relation to the origins of life. But upon reflection some will acknowledge that the human task has always been to make decisions about natural processes and to accept responsibility for changing them when this seems to serve human welfare. To acknowledge this is by no means to resolve particular ethical questions, whether about in *in vitro* fertilization, abortion, or other matters, but neither is it to assume that an absolute prohibition of interference is certainly God's will in every case.[10] In my view, new understandings of sexuality and reproduction and new medical technologies not only raise new ethical questions but also challenge believers to be devout in a new way, to move from uncritical ways of relating to central religious symbols (providence, creation, salvation, and church) to a post-critical style of faith, a style the philosopher Paul Ricoeur describes as one of "second naïveté," which appreciates the truth of religious symbols without taking mythic language literally.[11] And in any case, it is clear that competing ways of being religious are very important to the moral and political debates on biomedical questions.

STYLES OF FAITH

In Jewish and Christian understanding, the doctrine of creation has supported the conviction that life is good and meaningful. The myth of the origins of the earth and of life in the Book of Genesis has been a powerful feature of Western religious sensibility, serving as a basis for a way of life that respects persons as created in God's image. So too the myth of the origin of individual life as the result of special divine creation has been very powerful, particularly for Catholics whose piety was shaped from an early age by memorizing the first question and answer from the Baltimore Catechism: "Who made you?" "God made me."

This seems important in view of what the anthropologist Clifford Geertz has observed concerning the way a religious perspective functions to sustain a world of meaning and an ethical way of life for the believers of any tradition. The religious perspective, he argues, involves cultural symbols that establish and reinforce a conviction that there is an unbreakable inner connection between the way things actually are and the way one ought to live.[12] Applying Geertz's anthropological insight to the situation in contemporary America, it seems to me that for some Catholics and Protestants, their meaning system depends on a literal interpretation of symbols of creation and providence. For such Christians, life would have no meaning if it were not the result of God's direct intervention.

This bedrock feature of religious sensibility cashes out in absolutist defenses of unborn life as well as in passionate espousal of creationist theories of the origin of species. We have here, in other words, another instance of the faith-versus-reason debate that has always been with us in one form or another. And from an insider's perspective, what faith provides is too valuable to be surrendered in favor of "mere reason." When the options are framed in terms of the security of fideism or literalistic, uncritical acceptance of religious myth and traditional religious authority, on the one hand, and the absurdity that results from corrosive critical reason, on the other, it is not hard to see why some people prefer the former. It is, after all, how they were brought up.

For Catholics, the myth of special individual creation ("Who made you?" "God made me") is joined with a strong doctrine of divine providence, whereby God's care is thought to involve conscious divine intervention in history: a great mystery in its workings, but one that provides meaning and support to a believer's life, particularly in times of hardship and suffering.

Furthermore, beyond doctrines of creation and providence, there is the Christian doctrine of salvation, which has been etched on the believer's consciousness through repeated hearings and visualizations of the Story of Jesus. Particularly relevant to our concerns is the myth of divine incarnation in the baby Jesus, the power of which is evident annually at the Christmas season. It is perhaps to belabor the obvious to point out that Catholics have long understood that Mary's *"fiat"*—her acceptance of *a pregnancy she did not plan*—was essential to "the divine plan of salvation." In Mary, providence was understood to have intervened in human history through a miraculous conception and pregnancy that made possible the salvation of the world.

In reviewing these symbols of creation, providence, and incarnation, and in attesting to their mythic power in Catholic consciousness, I am using the descriptive language of religious studies as an aid to understanding the religious sensibility that influences some strains of the abortion debate. Although the issue is usually framed in moral terms, my belief is that it carries tremendous religious weight at a deep, less than fully conscious level.

But are literalistic fideism and meaningless rationalism the only alternatives? Must the myths of creation, providence, and salvation be understood in these literalistic ways? Is it necessary for God to intervene directly in the processes of nature and history for God to be present to these processes? Most contemporary theologians answer no to these questions. This leads to another question: Why hasn't this scholarship been more widely popularized? Why have so many Catholics been encouraged to continue taking religious myths and symbols literally, allowed to remain at the stage of "primitive naïveté" faith, to use Ricoeur's phrase?

The answer to this question raises issues of ecclesiology and power, and would require an article of much greater length. Suffice it to say for the present that another myth of origin is relevant to this debate in addition to the myths of the origin of species and the origin of individual human life. This is the myth of the origin of the Catholic Church by biblical "blueprint," an image I borrow from New Testament scholar Raymond Brown.[13] This myth also requires critical scrutiny though I cannot undertake this here. What I would say by way of summing up is this. If we want to mobilize Catholic energies on behalf of justice for women then we need to be sure that believers are provided with the sort of religious education that will yield a new, more mature style of "second naïveté" faith. Such a faith will be capable of supporting a truly consistent "ethic of life," one that can be effective in a pluralistic culture because it is both realistic and willing, to negotiate in the pluralism of the political realm.

One resource for such a reeducation process is a small volume by theologian John Shea, *Stones of God*, which endeavors to popularize contemporary theological views on central Christian myths and symbols. Here Shea offers a new understanding of providence that is directly relevant to the debate about human involvement in prenatal biological processes. Instead of an "interventionist" understanding of providence, which sees God as a direct agent in human history a "disrupter of events," or "one of the cast," Shea advocates an interpretation of providence that supports a high level of human responsibility. Such a view understands God as a presence to all the cast, not a disrupter of events.[14] Building on Shea, I would add that rather than intervening directly in the workings of nature or history, this God invites us, through her Spirit of wisdom, to realize divine values of justice, truth, and love, as best we can under the conditions of finitude.

Such a view of providence not only recognizes the believer's need to trust in God but also appreciates the mutuality of a divine-human relationship in which the care of creation has been *entrusted* to us, which means that we have some responsibility for processes and events once assumed to be beyond our legitimate reach. Clearly many other religious symbols and doctrines are important to Catholics on both sides of the current debates about abortion. Sorting out the differing interpretations will, as in the case of providence, illumine some of the deep-seated causes of divergent views on abortion and related social policy, helping us to understand why generous and devout believers can see the issues as differently as they do.

Notes

1. A notable example of the problematic use of Catholic resources is a 1984 leaflet, published by the U.S. Catholic Conference, which was distributed in my rural Minnesota parish (and, I presume, in other Catholic churches around the country) on "Respect Life Sunday" in the final weeks of the presidential contest between Reagan-Bush and Mondale-Ferraro. This colorful and attractive pamphlet featured a picture of a man holding an infant and displayed prominently a quotation from Psalm 95, "Oh, that today you would hear his voice: harden not your hearts." The text began as a dialogue between God and a young couple: "'Hi,' he said. 'It's me, God. Got a minute?' 'Sure, God,' said the young couple in unison, 'for you we always have time. What's on your mind?'" The pamphlet proceeded to state that God was worried about how we were treating life and to imply that abortion is God's number one issue; indeed, it would be difficult for a reader not to draw the inference that one sure way to avoid "hardness of heart" would be to vote for a candidate who had a declared position against abortion.

Such "teaching" of course fails to communicate the truth about the ambiguities of abortion politics; and, in the context of the 1984 election, its distribution came close to partisan support of Reagan, especially in view of the National Conference of Catholic Bishops' decision to withhold any publicity on the then forthcoming economics pastoral until after the election. Later, U.S. Senator Patrick J. Leahy, a Catholic from Vermont, put the problem thus: "Today, the church is dangerously close to aiding single-issue groups—whether intentionally or not—in cutting down so much of what it has stood for in the past. If the right wing, through manipulation of single-issue politics, continues to defeat elected officials who support progressive steps, there will be no one left in government to shelter those broad values of compassion and justice the church has endorsed." See Leahy, "The Church We Love Is Being Used," *Conscience*, July/August 1987, 13.

2. My discussion of these competing models for virtue is also developed in the articles "Narrative and the Social Dynamics of Virtue," in *Changing Values and Virtues*, ed. Dietmar Mieth and Jacques Pohier (Edinburgh: T. & T. Clark, 1987), 69–80, and "Character and Community: Curran and a Church Coming of

Age," in *Vatican Authority and American Catholic Dissent: The Curran Case and Its Consequences*, ed. William W. May (New York: Crossroad, 1987), 127–43. The patriarchal paradigm reflects a sexist mentality and a social system that values males over females, is biased in favor of masculine authority, and is built on principles of domination and subordination. For an ethical analysis of "sexism," see Patricia B. Jung, "Give Her Justice," *America* 150 (April 14, 1984), 276–78.

Like Jung, I understand the concepts of "sexism" and "feminism" to be dialectically related, and thus use "egalitarian" and "feminist" interchangeably in discussing the newer model for virtue. In a sexist culture, one must be feminist in order to be egalitarian. By "feminist" I mean a position that involves (1) a solid conviction of the equality of women and men; and (2) a commitment to reform society, including religious society, so that the full equality of women is respected, which requires also reforming the thought systems that legitimate the present unjust social order. Both women and men can thus be "feminist," and within this broad category there is enormous variety in levels of commitment, degrees of explicitness of commitment, and, of course, opinions regarding specific problems and their solutions.

3. Works that reflect the values of the egalitarian paradigm include Margaret A. Farley, "New Patterns of Relationship," *Theological Studies* 36 (1975): 627–46, and *Personal Commitments* (San Francisco: Harper and Row, 1986); Beverly W. Harrison, *Making the Connections*, ed. Carol S. Robb (Boston: Beacon Press, 1985); and Joan Timmerman, *The Mardi Gras Syndrome* (New York: Crossroad, 1984).

4. Carol A. Tauer gives 56 percent as a "reasonable approximation" in "The Tradition of Probabilism and the Moral Status of the Early Embryo," *Theological Studies* 45 (March 1984): 3–33.

5. I am basing my discussion of "endangered selves" on a social theory of the self, such as that developed by the social psychologist George Herbert Mead. See *George Herbert Mead: Mind, Self, and Society*, ed. Charles W. Morris (Chicago: University of Chicago Press, 1984). Such a theory recognizes that one is constituted as a self in relationships. In other words, language, social interaction, and cultural myths and symbols are all very important in shaping the self.

6. Beverly W. Harrison stresses this point in *Our Right to Choose: Toward a New Ethic of Abortion* (Boston: Beacon Press, 1983).

7. In her 1984 presidential address to the Modern Language Association, Carolyn Heilbrun effectively illustrated the difference in what it can mean to be a self as a man or woman in a sexist culture by quoting fifteen words from two American poets. The first quote included thirteen words on a man's experience of selfhood, from Walt Whitman: "I celebrate myself and sing myself, and what I assume you shall assume." That left two words from a woman, Emily Dickinson: "I'm nobody." Assuming that Heilbrun's examples say something about this culture, we must ask: How can we reverse the effects of millennia of sexism? There are ambiguities, to be sure, but I believe we must begin by recognizing the moral competence of women. See Carolyn G. Heilbrun, "Presidential Address 1984," *PMLA* 100 (1985): 281–82.

8. *America* 153 (October 19, 1985), 229.

9. This is an important and deeply challenging question, and we find a parting of the ways when religious people attempt to address it. Many of the devout, whose faith often tends to be literalistic and uninfluenced by the various modern "critiques" of religion, will respond by enhancing the value of those minuscule human life forms that seem threatened by human agents to the point of absolutizing these life forms, though there is no evidence that embryos or early fetuses that spontaneously abort have become objects of parallel concern. Thus it may be that certain embryos and fetuses have come to function as symbols of the divine, besieged by modernity. What is more, they also may serve as symbols of the self—the fragile, imperiled self experiencing powerlessness in a hostile environment—and together these associations evoke the enormous energy of self-defense.

10. James E. Kraus expresses the difficulty involved in the case of abortion in the following terms: "[I]f it is a terrible thing to play God by terminating physical life, it is also a terrible thing, in another sense, to play God by imposing as a divine absolute a prohibition that may cause immense suffering both to individuals and to society." See Kraus, "Is Abortion Absolutely Prohibited?" in *Abortion: The Moral Issues*, ed. Edward Batchelor, Jr. (New York: Pilgrim Press, 1982), 109.

11. Ricoeur discusses this term in *Symbolism of Evil* (Boston: Beacon Press, 1967), 347–57.

12. See Clifford Geertz, *Islam Observed: Religious Development in Morocco and Indonesia* (Chicago: University of Chicago Press, 1971), 98.

13. See Raymond E. Brown, *Biblical Reflections on Crises Facing the Church* (New York: Paulist Press, 1975), 52–55.

14. See John Shea, *Stories of God* (Chicago: Thomas More Press, 1978), 89–116.

10

MARKERS, BARRIERS, AND FRONTIERS

Theology in the Borderlands

This essay both sustains and exemplifies Anne Patrick's recurrent assertion that the needs of the oppressed must be central to the mission of the church. As this book goes to press, national debates about curtailing immigration by reinforcing borders exemplify the continuing relevance of her work. These reflections also demonstrate her paradoxical but persuasive commitment to making relevant connections between the potentially opposed institutions of the academy and the church; she also insists on important distinctions between positive and negative concepts of borders. —HD

In *Borderlands/La Frontera: The New Mestiza*, the Chicana poet Gloria Anzaldúa provides powerful images of the borderland reality we confront as the College Theology Society, meeting in the beautiful but sundered metropolitan area of Tijuana/San Diego:

> I press my hand to the steel curtain—
> chainlink fence crowned with rolled barbed wire—
> rippling from the sea where Tijuana touches San Diego
> unrolling over mountains
> and plains
> and deserts,
> this "Tortilla Curtain" turning into *el río Grande*
> flowing down to the flatlands
> of the Magic Valley of South Texas
> its mouth emptying into the Gulf.

Adapted from a chapter by the same title in Theology: Expanding the Borders, *The Annual Publication of the College Theology Society, Vol. 43, ed. María Pilar Aquino and Roberto S. Goizueta (Mystic, CT: Twenty-Third Publications, 1998).*

1,950 mile-long open wound
    dividing a *pueblo*, a culture,
    running down the length of my body,
      staking fence rods in my flesh,
      splits me   splits me
        me raja me raja
This is my home
this thin edge of
    barbwire.

But the skin of the earth is seamless.
The sea cannot be fenced,
el mar does not stop at borders.[1]

The invitation to explore the theme, "Theology: Expanding the Borders," in the distinguished company of Carmelo Alvarez, Enrique Dussel, and Virgilio Elizondo, posed a question for me: What should I, a U.S. Anglo feminist theologian, add to this discussion? I whose cultural *mestizaje* is pale at best, invisible and imperialistic at worst, encompassing as it does, on my father's side, the complex ethnic and religious heritage of colonial Maryland and Virginia, and, on my mother's side, the Irish Catholicism of nineteenth-century immigrants to Minnesota. (The land these Irish immigrants came to in the 1870s had recently been confiscated by the U.S. government from the Dakota people, after an 1862 conflict the victors called "the Sioux uprising," although for the losers it was a desperate struggle against starvation.) I who further complicated this mix by joining the Sisters of the Holy Names, a religious community of women, originally known as *Les Soeurs des Saints Noms de Jésus et Marie*, women who learned more than a century ago that in some United States settings it was necessary to obscure their French Canadian heritage in order to succeed as educators. This group was founded in 1844 in Québec, the province whose conflicted status within Canada could be the subject of a quite different convention about "Expanding the Borders." All of this background has given me much greater knowledge of issues, language, and culture in the north than in the south of the borders of my native United States.

My first teaching assignment, as a music teacher at an academy for girls in Tampa, Florida, was a broadening experience in many ways, although in 1960, at age nineteen, I was not well prepared for theological reflection on just why so many young Latinas from abroad had been sent to boarding school in Florida, especially from Cuba. There we took a memorable day off from classes in October 1962 to plant an olive tree for peace on the day the Second Vatican Council opened, and there we huddled, students and teachers together in the basement, preparing for Russian bombs to fall. All of this I understand better now that I have completed my various college and university degrees on the slow track that workers with adult responsibilities know so well, and especially now that I have been able to continue this education by reading feminist and liberation theology in recent years.

But I have been south of the U.S. border only twice, for a total of just four weeks: first in 1975, as a representative of Sisters Uniting, an umbrella group of U.S. nuns, at the first International Women's Year Tribune in Mexico City, and again in 1991, when a Center of Concern conference on Liberation Theology and Catholic Social Teaching in Pétropolis, Brazil, gave me the opportunity to learn some things firsthand in base communities of the Parish of the Martyrs in a Sao Paulo *favela*, and also in the colonial capital of Salvador (which figured so prominently in Brazil's 400-year history of slavery), in a visit to my missionary cousin in the mountains of Ecuador (whose pastoral training came from summer courses with Gustavo Gutiérrez), and of course in the Pétropolis meetings themselves, where I learned much from Central and South American theologians, women and men.

From the 1975 women's conference I returned with a poster of Sor Juana Inés de la Cruz, which intrigued me because the Mexican feminists seemed so anti-clerical and yet had a white-robed nun on their conference poster. And so I read her story and some of her writings, and since then her image has presided over my office at Carleton College. Sor Juana was a seventeenth-century Mexican poet, who anticipated Mary Daly by three centuries in her willingness to critique dominant theology, and who predictably got into trouble for her efforts. In 1689 she sent a critique of a sermon by a contemporary Jesuit to her friend the bishop of Puebla. The bishop's reply, signed "Sor Filotea de la Cruz," prompted Sor Juana to defend her efforts with a magnificent essay, "*La Respuesta de la poetisa a la muy ilustre Sor Filotea de la Cruz*," or "The Poet's Answer to the Most Illustrious Sor Filotea of the Cross." In this famous "*Respuesta*," Sor Juana justified her position brilliantly, but she had nevertheless felt the sting of the bishop's accusation that for all their scholarly brilliance, her activities were worldly and unbefitting her spiritual vocation. She eventually reacted to this accusation (and to pressure from her confessor) by abandoning her literary and scholarly pursuits. She sold her library and musical and scientific instruments, and gave the proceeds to the poor. She devoted the last two years of her life to asceticism and died of an illness contracted while ministering to her sisters during an epidemic in 1695. It is, however, the image of Sor Juana in good health and surrounded by her books, which inspired the Mexican feminists of the 1970s and presides over my office today.[2]

From the 1971 visit to Brazil and Ecuador I returned with many images of natural and cultural beauty, as well as of poverty, injustice, and ecological devastation. As a result of this experience, I developed and have continued to teach courses for undergraduates on the ambiguities of five centuries of Christian influence in the Americas, as well as on theologies of liberation. I have also begun to study the Spanish language, a project I fervently wish were further along than it is.

It is the *mujerista* theologian Ada María Isasi-Díaz who has persuaded me to tell you these things about myself, for she makes a good case that all theologians need "to be aware of how our own social situation colors our analysis of the religion of our communities and colors the way we say what we say in our theological writings."[3] The point of such self-disclosure, she argues, is to substitute for unreal claims of "objectivity" the more realistic position of "responsible subjectivity," which includes self-disclosure in the doing of theology precisely so that what is said becomes "understandable to others not only out of their own experience but insofar as they have the ability to go beyond the limits of their experience and see how my experience, because it is part of the processes of living, relates to and intersects with their experience, no matter how different both experiences are."[4] Others besides Isasi-Díaz have also set a precedent for including an element of self-disclosure in their theological writings, whether in whole chapters the way Virgilio Elizondo has done in *Galilean Journey* and *The Future Is Mestizo*, and as Roberto Goizueta has done in *Caminemos con Jesús*, or else in brief asides or very fascinating footnotes, as Carmelo Alvarez and Enrique Dussel have tended to do.[5] I have been edified by their practice, which sets a good example for all theologians to expand our methodological borders across the artificial divide of supposed objectivity.

In what follows I shall first discuss some of the ambiguities latent in the metaphor that governs the theme, "Theology: Expanding the Borders." My purpose is to clarify certain aspects of the complex meaning of "borders." Then, in the final part of this chapter, I shall explore some of the borderlands where I judge theology will do well to deepen its commitment to the right sort of an expanded agenda, both by investing new energy in projects that are already underway and by venturing in new directions.

Markers, Barriers, and Frontiers

The idea of "expanding the borders" invites reflection on the several purposes that borders serve. Among the many dimensions of meaning the concept of "border" carries with it, there are three that warrant our attention: markers, barriers, and frontiers.

Markers. In the first place, borders serve the descriptive function of markers by establishing what is where, and what is whose. Although an excessive sense of personal or corporate ownership is problematic, the lack of any sense of boundaries on the part of an individual or a group is also problematic. It is true that what we usually think of as earth's boundaries are fictions; when the planet is viewed from space, what we see is not the mapmaker's patchwork of pink and green and yellow nations set against a background of blue seas, but rather a boundary-less blue-and-white marble with tan continents, fringed with green. Nevertheless, these cultural fictions of national boundaries, and other markers that distinguish individuals and groups, are important to us as historical beings.

Indeed, the whole discussion of "difference" so crucial to various movements for social justice is premised on the fact that difference can and should be discerned, and it is borders in the sense of "markers" that enable us to recognize and respect the differences that make us who we are as individuals and societies. It would be a mistake, even a form of theological imperialism, for theologians, and especially for Anglo theologians from the United States, to aspire to "expand the borders" in the sense of denying the importance of difference or pushing toward all-inclusive control of what is presently "foreign" or beyond our reach.

As Marquette University theologian M. Shawn Copeland observed in her 1994 address to this society, "Toward a Critical Christian Feminist Theology of Solidarity," the national temptations of this country have been twofold with respect to "difference": There is in the first place the racist pressure to absolutize one form of difference—skin color—and simultaneously obscure other differences, and in the second place there is the temptation to "dissolve" difference, as she says, "to ignore it or to meet it with sly or shame-faced side-long glances," as when a white feminist speaks of oppression under patriarchy as if her experience encompassed what women of other groups have suffered.[6]

Copeland's incisive analysis of the tasks required for building solidarity among feminists is relevant to the wider community of U.S. theologians whose aspirations toward justice are expressed in terms of "expanding the borders." Her analysis suggests a note of caution, which is appropriate because the "border metaphor" of difference, if applied uncritically, can lend itself to promoting both of the problems she discusses: the tendency to absolutize one marker of difference while ignoring others, and the counter-temptation to dissolve or ignore difference altogether. That is to say, because on the one hand border imagery involves the idea of a line that divides two-dimensional space, there is the danger that it may reinforce a problematic tendency to think of groups reductively in terms of binary oppositions, as happens, for example, in discussions that get stuck at the border between "white" persons and "persons of color." As Copeland has shown, this way of thinking obscures other important differences beyond racial ones, such as differences of ethnicity, religion, class, geography, history, and personal experience, on both sides of the privileged category of division, and it thereby legitimates social injustice. The dominant group ignores its own diversity for the sake of one absolutized point of similarity and proceeds from there to control its borders against inroads from those who do not share this absolutized characteristic. As Copeland argues:

> [D]ifferently similar Celtic-, Anglo-, European-American men and women in the United States . . . are rendered the same. On the other hand, the merely different in skin color—African, Latino, Chicano, Korean, Japanese, Chinese, American Indian men and women—are absolutized as the other and ruled out of authentic human participation in the various dimensions of life in the United States social order.[7]

Furthermore, the pitfalls of insufficiently differentiated thinking also become evident when we consider the increasingly widespread phenomenon of bi-racial and multi-racial identities. This fact is of course rendering the category of *mestizaje*, which is such a central contribution of Elizondo's work, an increasingly important category for ethical and theological reflection. Texts that deserve much wider study include his volume from 1988, *The Future Is Mestizo*, as well as the more recent anthology edited by Arturo J. Bañuelas, *Mestizo Christianity*.[8] Its contributors do not need to be reminded, although their readers may, that the category of *mestizaje* is well utilized only when the distinct features of what is found in the various mixtures are recognized and respected. In employing this concept, European-Americans should, in other words, try to avoid the second temptation Copeland identifies, namely dissolving or ignoring difference.

To put matters in the terminology of Enrique Dussel, instead of participating in the violent modern project of "eclipsing the other," the task for theology is to contribute to liberating projects that are welcoming of all "in their alterity, in the otherness which needs to be painstakingly guaranteed at every level."[9] What my discussion of "markers" is intended to do, in summary, is to argue that where the border as "marker" is concerned, theology's mandate should be less that of expansion and more that of complexification. However, the ideal of expansion does seem to apply well to theology's task regarding two other senses of "borders," namely its meanings as *barriers* and *frontiers*, and it is to these that I now turn.

Barriers. The lines that human beings draw to identify who they are and what is theirs have also served to keep those who are different from sharing in what is within the protected sphere controlled by groups in power. In reminding us that "The sea cannot be fenced, / *el mar* does not stop at borders," Anzaldúa is offering a means of respecting difference—borders as markers do exist—and also transcending it by an inclusivity of attention or consciousness. To put my own position directly: If the consciences of Christians on the north side of this barrier that divides San Diego from Tijuana were really attuned to the life situation of those to our south, the southern border of this nation would not be the "steel curtain" that it has become.

How to engage these consciences in a new ethical agenda is the task I undertook in my book on feminist moral theology, *Liberating Conscience*. There I argued that Christians are now poised at a third great turning point in our history; having already negotiated the "turn to the Gentiles" in the first century, and having survived the philosophical and scientific revolutions ushered in by the sixteenth-century "Copernican turn," we are now challenged to make the "turn to the oppressed."[10] This will require Christians, particularly those from wealthy and dominant groups in every nation, to press more deeply than ever before for answers to questions of human suffering and injustice, and, in light of the answers that emerge, to undergo a conversion of life much more radical than mere conformity to the bourgeois standards associated with the waning patriarchal paradigm of virtue.

Forces on all sides are inviting us to this conversion. Powerful works of fiction—from Joseph Conrad's *Nostromo* to Carlos Fuentes's *The Good Conscience* to Louise Erdrich's *Love Medicine*—have helped European-American Christians understand our ethical history and see the need to change patterns of domination and exploitation. Also very important is the critical historical work conducted by Dussel and others, which has uncovered the centuries of violence and oppression beneath present political and economic arrangements.[11] Other forces calling us to conversion include the witness of the many contemporary victims of violence, given voice by survivors such as Rigoberta Menchú of Guatemala and as well as by journalists and church workers.[12] The steady flow of liberation theology and more recently of Latin American and U.S. Latina feminist, *mujerista*, and ecofeminist writings are also among these forces. The title of María Pilar Aquino's important work, *Our Cry for Life*, states clearly what is at stake in these movements, and her text describes well the conversion of morals that is required: "To take life as the primary ethical criterion," she asserts, "leads to many particular tasks devoted to the eradication of structures and realities that deny the poor and oppressed the means to life and exclude women from their right and duty to be active protagonists" [in history].[13]

Recently I have been struck by the way nature itself has added its voice to the invitations to conversion already extended by liberation theologians, ecofeminists, church leaders, and various others since the 1960s. (Please note that I refuse to personify nature as an angry female, as a "mother" abandoning her usual nurturing ways). The floods that have devastated western Minnesota, eastern North Dakota, and southern Manitoba this spring have hammered home the lesson that the Red River of the North is no respecter of borders, although I did note that U.S. television seemed to lose interest in the story rather soon after the flood crest entered Canada. For weeks stretching into months, people from this ordinarily rich agricultural region experienced the nightmare of helplessness that is routine for so many human beings who live in the Caribbean islands and elsewhere south of our border with Mexico.

During the worst weeks of the flood, there was water on all sides, but none of it was safe for drinking, bathing, or doing the laundry. Surplus grain, stored in silos, absorbed this water, expanded and exploded through the roofs of these silos, and then scattered sodden and useless across miles of flooded fields. Thousands of families accustomed to comfortable homes and clean clothes were homeless and ill-clad for weeks on end, and found themselves exiled from the usual routines of work and school. Indeed, in April, before the leaves were even on the trees, entire school districts shut down for the year, and youngsters were told to go far from their homes if they wanted to attend classes in other districts. For Minnesotans, Dakotans, and Manitobans, a winter of eight major blizzards was followed by a spring of unprecedented disaster: flooding that happens only once in a century or five, something we turn to the federal government to remedy as fast as it can—

the same government we feel should always be lowering our taxes without cutting our programs of privilege. But no clean drinking water, no school, no safe home, no jobs—this constitutes life as usual for millions of Haitians, Brazilians, Mexicans, and other neighbors to the south, who are also in many cases under regular threat of direct violence from the military, from the police, from criminals they cannot move to gated suburbs to escape, and from family members who turn their anger and despair against the bodies most easily within reach.

I have wondered this spring whether the flood experience may not have its salutary dimensions as well as its tragic ones. If we could learn two things from this disaster—first to probe the way *human choices driven by greed* may be related to the extreme weather patterns and to the unprecedented behavior of our rivers, and second to *examine our own unusual deprivations in light of what life is ordinarily like for the world's poor*—if we could learn these things, then these floods will not have brought mere suffering, but suffering with redemptive possibilities for us and for those others who have reached much sooner than we the insight that Juan Luis Segundo identified as the starting point of liberation theology: "the world should not be the way it is."[14]

The barriers to opportunity for a life worthy of human dignity, which are symbolized in the steel "tortilla curtain" lamented by Anzaldúa, are blatant manifestations of what is wrong with the world. These barriers are what must be dismantled, what must be transcended, if the world is to become what God intended it to be. As Elizondo observes in his chapter "Beyond All Borders" from *Galilean Journey*, "True life and happiness is loving as God...loves, which means the rejection of any humanly made obstacles that limit our ability to love."[15]

It would be a mistake, of course, to limit our thoughts about borders as barriers too literally to the southern boundary of this country, however much this border has come to symbolize the violence and oppression we Christians of the United States are called to transcend. For the barriers to human dignity exist very much *within* and *beyond* the geographic limits of this country, and if the tortilla curtain were to become quite permeable tomorrow this would not by itself correct all the other injustices that are structured into our national life, and into our transnational economic systems and alliances of power.

There are, for instance, the barbed wire fences of illiteracy and generally inadequate education, which defend privileged citizens from competition in the job market by members of groups our "economy" (the faceless and nameless abstraction that absolves its beneficiaries of responsibility for its effects on other persons here and abroad) prefers to destine for work in undesirable, minimum wage jobs. There are also the walls preventing access to health care, amazingly solid in view of their motley bricks being shaped from paper made of boiled down drafts of exclusionary legislation, recycled insurance forms, strands of bureaucratic red tape, and the clay of human greed. And among the forces defending the obstacles to lives of dignity are surely this country's national devotion to an absurd view of liberty where guns and money are concerned, an absolutizing of "free choice" the pro-life movement has yet to question in any serious way, although guns in particular are a great impediment to education and a terrible hazard to health.

These are some of the barriers to human dignity that urgently need to disappear, reflective as they are of the borders that interest groups construct and defend with the idolatrous forms of faith analyzed so incisively by H. Richard Niebuhr decades ago in *Radical Monotheism and Western Culture*.[16] More recently the Costa Rican theologian Elsa Tamez has drawn on Latina experience and indigenous Mexican culture to add more concreteness and urgency to such analyses. In *Through Her Eyes: Women's Theology of Latin America*, Tamez sees the "god of the indigenous Mexican culture" as forming a "coalition with the God of the Bible...and calling us to forsake the false gods, especially the god of riches and the god who requires human sacrifice, and turn instead to the One who is Life-giver and Liberator of us all."[17] It is this One who calls for the dismantling of whatever barriers stand in the way of justice and solidarity among peoples, and indeed for a rethinking of neighbor-love to include nature and the earth itself.

Frontiers. The balance needed to respect difference, and at the same time to dismantle the unjust barriers that human groups are always putting up against the "others," which my discussion of the first two meanings of "borders" has been arguing we must achieve, this balance seems well expressed on the cover of a Brazilian Catholic monthly published in Sao Paulo. This magazine is called *Sem Fronteiras*, and its subtitle adds the balancing nuance I find so important: *A Igreja No Brasil Aberta ao Mundo*. The national marker of identity is retained, "the church of Brazil," but the posture is one of openness to the rest of the world. The Portuguese, *Sem Fronteiras*, which literally translates as "without borders," also connotes certain positive meanings that have long been associated with the word "frontier" in United States history, meanings which should not be forgotten entirely in our late-blooming repentance for the physical and cultural violence that characterized our national "expansion."

I am suggesting here that the "myth of the frontier," for all the evil it has legitimated, may still be put to some good use. Insofar as the frontier has symbolized the as-yet-unattained ideal, and insofar as its rigors have called for some still-useful virtues, I think we may well align a chastened form of frontier spirit with the ideal of "expanding the borders" proposed in this convention. What I have in mind here are such qualities as courage, hope for a better life, willingness to endure risk and hardship, and generosity among neighbors. All of these are qualities we can use today in the metaphorical borderlands that theology has reached on the cusp of a new millennium.

THEOLOGY IN THE BORDERLANDS

In this concluding section I shall discuss briefly two borderlands where theologians find ourselves today, and where the frontier virtues of courage, hope for a better life, willingness to endure risk and hardship, and generosity among neighbors may stand us in good stead. (These virtues, I hasten to add, are not unique to the pioneers of U.S. history, but are precisely what help today's refugees and immigrants to brave dangers on land and sea in order to get to a place that holds promise of a better life). I approach this topic as a moral theologian, interested in praxis as well as in character, so I will share an example or two of practical action or implementation.

In the first place, we are always in the *borderland between particular and general concerns*, and I see no way around the need to camp here forever. The local church and the local school district demand our involvement, and so do the national and international dimensions of the issues we encounter in these local settings.[18] Consider the matter of health care. The United States has great problems in this area, but the full extent of the issue is a global one, and this fact must somehow become more present to our attention. As James Hug has observed in a 1993 article on "Health Care: A Planetary Perspective," this country is home to less than five percent of the world's population, but it consumes 41 percent of the world's health resources.[19] For moral theology especially, such issues of global distributive justice must come more to the foreground, but all theologians have citizenship in the universal human community, and all of us can be more creative in expanding the borders of interest beyond national discussions of such questions.

There are many resources to support this creativity, and one I am particularly pleased to report on here is the new International Network of Societies for Catholic Theology, which was set up at a gathering at Sherbrooke University in Québec last summer, and which plans to use the Internet to foster sharing among Catholic theological societies worldwide. Among the groups represented at the founding meeting were societies from Brazil, Colombia, Chile, Argentina, Europe, the U.S. and Canada, and also the Ecumenical Association of African Theologians.[20] The Catholic Theological Society of America is making its computer resources available for this international project, which hopes to foster solidarity that will also have ecumenical and interfaith possibilities as the plan goes forward.

Another promising resource for expanding the borders of awareness among Christians is a calendar developed by a Vincentian priest from India who has served small rural parishes in Minnesota while preparing several fine volumes of inclusive language prayerbooks. Father Joseph Arackal has also designed an International Worship and Freedom Appointment Calendar, which seeks to increase understanding among the world's peoples by providing for the daily entries information not only about the liturgical significance and biblical readings for the day, but also about the nations commemorating their independence on that day. Arackal's hope is that users may record significant world events and significant personal moments in the blank space, and pray for the "special needs and concerns of the people celebrating freedom each day."[21] A list providing thumbnail descriptions of all the world's nations is given at the end of the booklet, indicating size, population, location, languages, and political status, especially in terms of independence. What I find so creative and valuable about this booklet is the way it connects the personal life of prayer and scripture reading with global political awareness.

A second borderland we are destined to inhabit for a long time is the one *between the church and the academy*. There are important reasons for theologians to affirm the academy and the freedom it gives us to do research without fear of reprisals, and there are reasons to press for academic freedom within church-sponsored institutions. But the longer I think about issues of *global* justice, the more I find myself becoming concerned with the positive theological task of supporting the church community and its leaders, and indeed of bringing their best teachings about social justice more to the foreground of discussions, and thereby fostering the development of this teaching in light of new economic, cultural, political, and ecological situations.

I confess to having been affected by some forceful words of Allan Figueroa Deck on these matters, particularly a 1995 article entitled "A

Pox on Both Your Houses: A View of Catholic Conservative-Liberal Polarities from the Hispanic Margins."[22] I am not suggesting that progressive theologians can or should change our stripes, but rather that we
may want to notice some cutting-edge issues where church leadership
and theologians can be well occupied together. Concerns about racism,
immigration, welfare and education policy—these are not matters
where theologians tend to dissent from the magisterium, but they are
nevertheless extremely challenging intellectual problems, for the issue
facing us is precisely how to win the informed consent of our Catholic
population to some fine but unfortunately obscure documents of our
bishops.

For people who are seeking to expand the borders, and for people
who are camping in borderlands, the quality we need above all is hope.
As this convention has been demonstrating so amply, theologians of
the United States have much to learn about hope, as about other matters, from beyond our borders. I have been struck, for example, by the
fact that women from the most ecologically devastated land on the
American continent, El Salvador, could declare of their situation in
1990: "The ecological problem is not an unsolvable problem. In order to
[remedy this problem] it is necessary to change the focus of development from an economic one focused on financial benefits to an ecological one focused on the survival of the country and the well-being of its
inhabitants."[23] "Hope," our colleague María Pilar Aquino reminds us,
"is realized in actions, attitudes, in everyday language, even in the
midst of great hardship and suffering. Neither women nor the poor of
the earth can give it up."[24] Nor, I would add, can we theologians, who
must continue to voice their claims for justice in the borderlands where
we live and work.

Notes

1. Gloria Anzaldúa, *Borderlands/La Frontera: The New Mestiza* (San Francisco:
Aunt Lute Books, 1987), 2–3.
2. This image, Miguel Cabrera's painting from 1750, "*Retrato de Sor Juana
Inés de la Cruz,*" is also on the cover of a recent critical edition and translation
by Electa Arenal and Amanda Powell: Sor Juana Inés de la Cruz, *The Answer/La
Respuesta, Including a Selection of Poems* (New York: The Feminist Press at the
City University of New York, 1994). In their "Preface" to this critical edition,
Arenal and Powell mention that Dorothy Schons, in a 1925 essay, "The First
Feminist in the New World," was the first to characterize *La Respuesta* as "a dec-
laration of the intellectual emancipation of women of the Americas" (vii).

For a contemporary theological interpretation of Sor Juana's contributions, see Pamela J. Kirk, *Sor Juana Inés de la Cruz: Religion, Art, and Feminism* (New York: Continuum, 1997).

3. Ada María Isasi-Díaz, *Mujerista Theology: A Theology for the Twenty-First Century* (Maryknoll, NY: Orbis Books, 1996), 76.

4. Ibid., 77.

5. See Virgilio Elizondo, *Galilean Journey: The Mexican American Promise* (Maryknoll, NY: Orbis Books, 1983) and *The Future Is Mestizo* (1988; New York: Crossroad, 1992); Roberto S. Goizueta, *Caminemos con Jesús: Toward A Hispanic/Latino Theology of Accompaniment* (Maryknoll, NY: Orbis Books, 1995); Carmelo E. Alvarez, "Theology from the Margins: A Caribbean Response," passim, and especially 2, n. 2; and, Enrique Dussel, *The Invention of the Americas: Eclipse of 'the Other' and the Myth of Modernity*, trans. Michael D. Barber (1992; New York: Continuum, 1995), 147, n. 17.

6. M. Shawn Copeland, "Toward a Critical Christian Feminist Theology of Solidarity," in *Women and Theology*, CTS annual vol. 40, ed. Mary Ann Hinsdale and Phyllis H. Kaminski (Maryknoll, NY: Orbis Books, 1995), 16.

7. Ibid.

8. Virgilio Elizondo, *The Future Is Mestizo*; Arturo J. Bañuelas, ed., *Mestizo Christianity: Theology from the Latino Perspective* (Maryknoll, NY: Orbis Books, 1995). See also Roberto S. Goizueta, ed., *We Are a People!: Initiatives in Hispanic American Theology* (Minneapolis: Fortress, 1992).

9. Dussel, *The Invention of the Americas*, 132.

10. Anne E. Patrick, *Liberating Conscience: Feminist Explorations in Moral Theology* (New York: Continuum, 1996), 70.

11. Enrique Dussel, *History of the Church in Latin America: Colonialism to Liberation, 1492–1979*, trans. Alan Neely (Grand Rapids, MI: Eerdmans, 1981); see also *1492–1992: The Voice of the Victims*, ed. Leonardo Boff and Virgil Elizondo (Philadelphia: Trinity Press International, 1990).

12. The experiences of Menchú, the 1992 Nobel Peace laureate, are described in her work, edited by Elisabeth Burgos-Debray, *I, Rigoberta Menchú: An Indian Woman in Guatemala*, trans. Ann Wright (New York: Verso, 1984). See also Penny Lernoux, *Cry of the People* (1980; New York: Penguin Books, 1982); Sheila Cassidy, *Good Friday People* (Maryknoll, NY: Orbis Books, 1991); and, Virgil Elizondo, ed., *Way of the Cross: The Passion of Christ in the Americas* (Maryknoll, NY: Orbis Books, 1992).

13. María Pilar Aquino, *Our Cry for Life: Feminist Theology from Latin America* (Maryknoll, NY: Orbis Books, 1993), 190.

14. Quoted in Robert McAfee Brown, *Gustavo Gutiérrez: An Introduction to Liberation Theology* (Maryknoll, NY: Orbis Books, 1990), 51.

15. Elizondo, *Galilean Journey*, 80.

16. H. Richard Niebuhr, *Radical Monotheism and Western Culture* (New York: Harper & Row, 1960).

17. Elsa Tamez, ed., "Introduction: The Power of the Naked," *Through Her Eyes: Women's Theology from Latin America* (Maryknoll, NY: Orbis Books, 1989), 13–14.

18. John Allen, for example, discusses the urgency of U.S. Catholics giving more attention to educational needs beyond the parochial and private school contexts in "Inequity in Funding of Public Education Raises Justice Issues," *National Catholic Reporter* (May 2, 1997), 3–6.

19. James E. Hug, "Health Care: A Planetary View," *America* (December 11, 1993), 8–12.

20. The founding of the International Network of Societies for Catholic Theology took place in conjunction with the August 1996 meeting of the Conference of Catholic Theological Institutions at Sherbrooke University in Québec. The International Network's headquarters are in Tübingen, Germany. The first elected president of the Network is Peter Hünermann (Tübingen); vice-presidents are Anne E. Patrick (Northfield, Minnesota) and Marcio Fabri dos Anjos (Sao Paulo, Brazil).

21. Joseph J. Arackal, V.C., *1993 International Worship and Freedom Appointment Calendar with Descriptions of the World's Nations* (Vermillion, MN: Patmos Publications).

22. Allan Figueroa Deck, "A Pox on Both Your Houses: A View of Catholic Conservative-Liberal Polarities from the Hispanic Margin," in *Being Right: Conservative Catholics in America*, ed. Mary Jo Weaver and R. Scott Appleby (Bloomington: Indiana University Press, 1995), 88–106.

23. *Unidad Ecologia Salvadorena*, quoted in Mercedes Canas, "In Us Life Grows: An Ecofeminist Point of View," in *Women Healing Earth: Third World Women on Ecology, Feminism, and Religion*, ed. Rosemary Radford Ruether (Maryknoll, NY: Orbis Books, 1996), 24.

24. Aquino, *Our Cry for Life*, 108.

11

FEMINIST THEOLOGY

When challenged to craft an overview of feminist theology for an en-
cyclopedia, Anne Patrick demonstrates here the gifts sustaining her
other work as well: a fidelity to extensive and thorough research and
the commitment to a fair-minded, balanced presentation of a range of
viewpoints that Charles Curran also honors in Anne's view of proph-
ecy. The essay reminds us how she set an example for other women to
actively engage with theology when that engagement was fraught and
controversial. —HD

Feminist theology examines the meaning and implications of Christian
faith from the perspective of a commitment to justice for females. An
intellectual development with profound spiritual, psychological, and
political implications, it shares with Christian theology in general the
classic aim of "faith seeking understanding," but is distinguished by
two additional features. The first is the assumption that standard theology has been skewed by longstanding sexism in the tradition. According to this analysis, both social arrangements (patriarchy) and
ideological biases (androcentrism) have privileged males and failed to
do justice to females; thus an intellectually and morally adequate theology will require significant correction of previous work in all theological disciplines. The second distinguishing feature of feminist theology
is a methodological commitment to emphasizing women's experience,
in all its complexity and diversity, while conducting the tasks of theological reflection. These tasks have involved three things: *critique* of
sexist interpretations and practices; *retrieval* of women's past contributions to ecclesial life and theological reflection; and, *construction* of
more just and accurate interpretations and practices.

Adapted from Anne E. Patrick, "Feminist Theology," in New Catholic Encyclopedia, *2nd ed., vol. 5 (Washington, DC: Catholic University of America Press, 2003).*

There are many definitions and types of feminism, and much controversy about the meanings and implications of the various types. Some definitions emphasize the participation of women as subjects of their own liberative process against the injustice of sexism, while others emphasize that human beings of both sexes are capable of recognizing and opposing this evil. These two types, which may be designated respectively as "woman-centered feminism" and "inclusive feminism," are different, but each captures true aspects of the movement and has useful practical applications. Feminism is understood here inclusively as a position that involves a solid conviction of the equality of women and men, and a commitment to reform society so that the full equality of women is respected, which requires also reforming the thought systems that legitimate the present unjust social order. Of course, those who espouse feminism differ widely in their analyses of injustice, levels of commitment to liberating action, degrees of explicitness of commitment, and opinions regarding specific problems and their solutions.

This essay will first sketch the main lines of the historical development of feminist theology, and then describe some of its substantive contributions to various fields or topics traditionally explored by theologians. Although the emphasis here is on U.S. Roman Catholicism, it is important to recognize that feminist theology has an inherently ecumenical dimension and has engaged the energies of many Catholic and Protestant (and some Orthodox) scholars throughout the world. It has an interfaith dimension as well, sharing concerns with analogous movements among feminist thinkers from Buddhist, Jewish, Muslim, and other traditions. From the first, Catholic women in the United States have played a leading role in the field's development, thanks to the insight and dedication of pioneering laywomen and nuns, and to the intellectual heritage of Catholic women's colleges. These institutions prepared a climate for the practice and reception of feminist theology by establishing a tradition of women's higher learning and leadership unparalleled elsewhere. The exclusion of women from the sacrament of Orders has also influenced some to pursue academic theology, since female leadership has been possible there whereas it has been ruled out in most ministerial settings because of male clerical privilege.

LAUNCHING A MOVEMENT: 1960–1975

Prior to the Second Vatican Council, theology had functioned mainly to educate future priests, who studied Latin texts in classes that were often isolated from wider social and intellectual currents. Some lay persons took courses in neoscholastic philosophy and theology in Catholic colleges and universities, and religious sisters and brothers read some works related to their vocation, but only the clergy had access to doctoral programs that would prepare them for research and teaching at advanced levels in the field. An early exception to this rule was the graduate program inaugurated at St. Mary's College in Indiana by Sister Mary Madeleva Wolff, CSC, in 1944, but only in the 1960s did wider access to theological studies become available in the United States. At that time a "second wave" of feminism was underway in this country, and papal and conciliar documents were beginning to affirm women's basic equality and political rights in ways that would have astonished those who decades earlier had campaigned for women's suffrage in the face of opposition from the hierarchy.

Several provisions of Vatican II's *Pastoral Constitution on the Church in the Modern World* (*Gaudium et Spes*) were particularly influential in inspiring Catholic women to look critically at their own tradition and undertake theological studies in view of advancing the reforms initiated by the council. The first was the recognition that because of the essential equality of all persons (*homines* in the original Latin, a term that includes females in a manner that "men" does not), "any kind of social or cultural discrimination in basic personal rights on the grounds of sex...must be curbed and eradicated as incompatible with God's design" (#29, Flannery translation, 1996). Furthermore, the council also affirmed a more dynamic, historically conscious understanding of God's will for humanity than had previously held sway, with all that this implies in terms of openness to the genuinely *new*:

> In each nation and social group there is a growing number of men and women who are conscious that they themselves are the architects and molders of their community's culture. All over the world the sense of autonomy and responsibility increases with effects of the greatest importance for the spiritual and moral maturity of humankind. (#55)

Although *GS* itself retains much of the androcentrism of its time, and hardly anticipates the effects its ideas would have on feminist readers, passages such as the above marked a significant change from previous thought and opened new vistas for progressive women and men.

Women were not specified in the crucial paragraph (62), which voices the hope that "more of the laity will receive adequate theological formation and that some among them will dedicate themselves professionally to these studies and contribute to their advancement," but the language, which does not rule out women's participation, was soon interpreted inclusively by various Catholic universities and seminaries. Moreover, by affirming intellectual freedom in theology, the final sentence of this paragraph states a principle that contributed both to male support of women's involvement in the discipline and also to the development of feminist positions by theologians: "But for the proper exercise of this role [of theologian], the faithful, both clerical and lay, should be accorded a lawful freedom of inquiry, of thought, and of expression, tempered by humility and courage in whatever branch of study they have specialized."

A number of Catholic women had anticipated this conciliar invitation and begun theological studies earlier in the United States or Europe, among whom Mary Daly, Elisabeth Schüssler Fiorenza, and Rosemary Radford Ruether have been particularly influential. Schüssler Fiorenza's *Der vergessene Partner*, a pioneering study of possibilities for women in ministry, was published in 1964, and Daly's highly influential *The Church and the Second Sex* appeared in 1968. Drawing on insights of feminist philosopher Simone de Beauvoir, Daly raised critical questions regarding Catholic doctrine and practice and offered some "modest proposals" for reform. Within several years Daly moved to a "postchristian" religious stance, and in 1973 she leveled a sustained critique of classical theology in *Beyond God the Father*.

Meanwhile many other Catholic women were moving through doctoral studies in various theological disciplines and beginning to publish early examples of feminist theology. These thinkers were influenced by biblical themes and traditional theology as well as by secular feminism and the works of "critical" and liberation theologians such as Jürgen Habermas, Gustavo Gutiérrez, and James Cone. By 1975, which had been declared International Women's Year by the United Nations, Ruether and Schüssler Fiorenza had published works that began to enlarge the feminist theological agenda by making connections with concerns about racism, anti-Semitism, colonialism, economic injustice, and ecological well-being.

The early phase in the U.S. feminist theological movement culminated in two historic events toward the end of 1975. First, in late November, over Thanksgiving weekend, some twelve hundred persons gathered in Detroit for the Women's Ordination Conference's national meeting, where for the first time a significant number of female theologians joined with male colleagues to probe a question of vital importance to the church (Gardiner 1976). After this historic meeting the WOC would sponsor a series of national events, including one to mark its twenty-fifth anniversary in Milwaukee in 2000, and would also help to plan an international conference on women's ordination, Women's Ordination Worldwide, held in Dublin, Ireland in 2001. Second, in December the Jesuit journal, *Theological Studies*, published a special issue on "Women: New Dimensions," which carried articles by women who would later contribute major works of feminist theology (reprinted in Burghardt 1977).

<h2 style="text-align:center">GAINING GROUND: 1975–1990</h2>

Organizational activities and feminist theological scholarship intensified in the second stage of the movement. North American and European women gained institutional power in colleges, universities, and seminaries, as well as organizations such as the American Academy of Religion, the Catholic Biblical Association, the Catholic Theological Society of America, the College Theology Society, the North American Academy of Liturgy, and the Society of Christian Ethics. Meanwhile women elsewhere began to claim a voice within the Ecumenical Association of Third World Theologians, which had been founded in 1976. During an EATWOT meeting in Geneva in 1983, attended also by some theologians from Europe and the United States, feminists established a Women's Commission to address the issues of sexism in male liberation theology and racism in the white women's movement. In 1986 the European Society of Women in Theological Research was established; it meets biennially and maintains a webpage at http://www.eswtr.org. Since 1993 ESWTR has published a yearbook of research and reviews; its first issue provides historical information on European feminist theology, including attention to the contributions of such leading scholars as Kari Børresen (Norway), Catharina Halkes (Netherlands), and Mary Grey (Britain).

Increasingly feminist theologians were contributing full-length books, several of which have now been widely studied and translated into many languages. In 1983 Ruether published the first "systematic" work of feminist theology, *Sexism and God-Talk*, which probed topics ranging from method to eschatology, and Schüssler Fiorenza published a feminist theological reconstruction of early Christianity, *In Memory of Her*. Both authors were among a number of feminist theologians who spoke at the first of three national "women-church" gatherings organized by progressive Catholic groups, which took place in Chicago that fall, to be followed by assemblies in Cincinnati (1987) and Albuquerque (1993). These gatherings were notable for efforts to provide program information in Spanish as well as English, and to offer simultaneous translation on a limited scale, a trend that has continued and expanded somewhat in a number of subsequent assemblies of religious feminists. The first bilingual work of feminist theology appeared in 1988, Ada María Isasi-Díaz and Yolanda Tarango's *Hispanic Women: Prophetic Voice in the Church.*

Meanwhile feminist theologians were being tenured in colleges and universities and elected to leadership in professional societies. Courses in women's history and feminist theology entered the curriculum, and in 1985 *The Journal of Feminist Studies in Religion* was launched, co-edited by Schüssler Fiorenza and Jewish scholar Judith Plaskow. That year Schüssler Fiorenza also co-edited, with Mary Collins, the first issue of what has become a regular series of issues of the international journal *Concilium* devoted to feminist theology. Subsequent volumes have been co-edited by Anne E. Carr, M. Shawn Copeland, and Mary John Mananzan, with articles from these journals collected in *The Power of Naming* (Schüssler Fiorenza 1996). Carr's volume *Transforming Grace: Christian Tradition and Women's Experience* probed doctrines of God and Christ as well as questions of theological method, women's ordination, and spirituality, and was a featured selection of the Catholic Book Club in 1988. In 1990 the establishment of a women's seminar in constructive theology as a regular part of the annual meeting of the Catholic Theological Society of America marked the solid gains achieved by feminist theologians in North America. Although still overwhelmingly a movement of white women, feminist theology had deepened its recognition of the interstructured nature of oppression, acknowledged the problem of false generalizations about women's experience, and enlarged the critique of patriarchy to include heterosexism as well as sexism, racism, classism, and mistreatment of the environment.

DEVELOPMENT AND DIVERSIFICATION: FEMINIST THEOLOGIES SINCE 1990

The last decade of the twentieth century saw the publication of many influential books and articles in feminist theology, often focused and constructive efforts to advance discussion in particular fields of theological inquiry. In a number of instances white women exhibited a more intense self-critique and greater attention to diversity within the movement, while theology published by women of color voiced concerns of cultural, racial, economic, and gender injustice with a new urgency and power. The need for this articulation is evident in the fact that nearly all of the influential women named above are white, heirs to systemic racial privilege that has been insufficiently scrutinized and remains far from remedied.

M. Shawn Copeland, the first African-American woman to give a plenary paper at a national meeting of theologians, set a new agenda in her address to the College Theology Society at its fortieth anniversary convention in 1994. "Mere rhetoric" of solidarity is insufficient, she argued; effective solidarity requires a deep-seated conversion, which involves different things for women from different social locations. Although white feminist theologians had acknowledged the links between racism, classism, and sexism for years, they had often written of "women" at a level of generality that glossed over significant differences, and had failed to attend to the voices of black, red, yellow, and brown women.

By the 1990s some theologians of color had developed particular designations for their writings in order to distinguish them from white feminist theology: womanist (African American), *mujerista* (Latina), and *minjung* (Korean). Other theologians of color retained the designation "feminist" and at the same time drew explicitly on their own heritages. The influence of the writings of both groups of women of color on the works of white feminists gives promise of a future when preoccupation with discussions of diversity will give way to sustained and effective collaboration on matters of concern to all. This hoped-for future of authentic solidarity will be anticipated here by designating feminist theologies in the plural in the rest of this essay, with the intention of explicitly including womanist, *mujerista*, white feminist, and other particular types of contributions under this plural category.

CONTRIBUTIONS OF FEMINIST THEOLOGIES TO THEOLOGICAL DISCIPLINES

By definition feminist theologies seek to overcome injustice, and thus there is an ethical dimension prominent in all of this work. Women theologians also have specialized training in other traditional fields of theological studies, and have made notable contributions to the following areas:

Theological Method
Ruether (1983), Carr (1988), Isasi-Díaz (1988, 1992), and Copeland (1996, 1998) are among those who deal extensively with questions of theological method, and they all regard attention to women's diverse experiences and the employment of sources beyond classical Christian texts as important for progress in the discipline. Isasi-Díaz is distinctive in

her efforts to bring the voices of U.S. Latinas from various cultural backgrounds directly into theological discussions, employing substantial quotations from these "grassroots" Christians in her writings. Concerning the norm for judging the adequacy of theological work, there has been some movement beyond a general insistence that good theology must promote women's human dignity to a more precise claim that good theology leads to the "flourishing of poor women of color in violent situations" (Johnson 1993). The overall task of Christian feminist theologies has been aptly described as that of correlating "the central and liberating themes of biblical and Christian tradition with the experience of women in the contemporary situation" (Carr 1988).

Biblical Studies, Hermeneutics, and History
Classical Christian texts are of crucial importance to scholars seeking justice for women in the tradition, and considerable work has been done to bring out the liberating potential buried beneath patriarchal records and interpretations of revelation. Whether this involves retrieving lost images and stories, probing possibilities of women's authorship and leadership, criticizing oppressive material, or reading between the lines to discover glimpses of equality in earlier societies, the project of feminist biblical criticism is both technically specialized and wide-ranging in its implications. Likewise, important historical work has been done to correct the record of women's activities, ideas, and influence in the centuries since biblical times, which casts new light on the development of doctrine as well as that of church law and practices. Scholars have made available newly interpreted writings of women from "patristic" and medieval times, and have invited reconsideration of the significance of female mystics and monastics, movements such as the Beguines, and various other expressions of female creativity and leadership (Schmitt and Kulzer 1996, Kirk 1998, Madigan 1998). They have likewise documented and probed the causes of misogyny and patriarchal efforts to control women—whether by doctrine, law, or violence—and challenged contemporary Christians to overcome these longstanding tendencies to sin. This critical revisionist history carries implications for all areas of Church doctrine and practice, and is particularly powerful when conducted by scholars who attend to the combined effects of racism, colonialism, and sexism.

Doctrine of God
At the heart of theology is the mystery of God, which transcends the human capacity for symbolizing and yet requires symbolic expression.

Because the symbol of God functions either to oppress or to liberate, feminist theologians have done extensive work to critique the unjust and idolatrous tendency to think that God is male. Strategies for calling attention to the problem, which is so engrained that most Christians require some reminder that all speech about God is analogous and incapable of conveying the Mystery, have included referring to the Deity as "God/ess" (Ruether 1983), "G*d" (Schüssler Fiorenza 1994), and "God...She" (Johnson 1993). Strategies for expanding the metaphors beyond the overused "Father" have involved personal images (for example, "Mother," "Lover," "Friend"), the biblical "Sophia" (Divine Wisdom), and other terms such as "Matrix," "Creator," "Liberator," and "Source of All Being," as well as such biblical images as "rock," "fountain," "midwife," and "coin seeker." Johnson's comprehensive study, *She Who Is* (1983), considers each person of the Trinity in light of the female-associated term "Sophia," and probes how these "dense symbols" convey Her relational, living, and compassionate nature.

Doctrine of Creation and Eschatology
Feminist theologies have stressed the goodness of creation and sought to overcome false dualisms that would value spirit at the expense of matter. They have also placed great emphasis on ecology. The central theme of Jesus' teaching, the Reign of God, has been understood as a reality affecting the present world, summoning and empowering human efforts to bring about a future of right relationships among all creatures of the earth. Various ways of overcoming patriarchal associations with traditional imagery of "Kingdom" have been suggested, including the *mujerista* neologism "Kin-dom" (Isasi-Díaz 1996). While characterized by a strong ecological and political emphasis, feminist eschatology also recognizes a transcendent, mysterious dimension to the ultimate future (Ruether 1992). Hope for divine healing of the broken bones of history's victims, especially poor women of color, should impel Christians to the praxis of solidarity in the here-and-now (Copeland 1998).

Theological Anthropology
A faulty understanding of human nature is basic to the racism and sexism that feminist theologies seek to overcome. Although mainstream modern theology has rejected classical notions that males from dominant groups enjoy a higher degree of rationality, and are thus created more closely in the "image of God" than females and subordinated males, vestiges of racism and misogyny continue to cause great harm. White feminists initially laid most stress on overcoming stereotypes

responsible for sexist attitudes and practices, such as the notions that women are "property," "temptresses," "irrational," of a different and lesser nature than men. Instead of blaming Eve for "original sin," they named patriarchy as a primordial sinful system, and argued about how best to articulate an anthropology that did justice to the equality of females and males while also respecting human embodiment and diversity of experience.

There has been widespread agreement that notions of "gender complementarity," which tend to idealize females while assigning them "special" roles, actually function to limit women to men's ideas of their worth and purpose and fail to respect their essential autonomy and dignity. Contributions by theologians of color have sharpened the critique in recent years, and led to further theorizing on the theological significance of difference and the complexity of women's experience (Graff 1995). *"La vida cotidiana"* ("everyday life") is a newly recognized resource for understanding and praxis (Isasi-Díaz 1996, Aquino 1998), and countering systemic violence against women and children must become the focal purpose of anthropological reflection (Copeland 1998).

Christology
The significance of Christ and the meaning of salvation have been addressed in various ways by feminist scholars. Recognizing that much previous Christology contributed to injustice to women, and yet disagreeing with Daly's view that male dominance and "Christolatry" are essential to the tradition, white theologians have emphasized the prophetic role taken by Jesus in his day (Schüssler Fiorenza 1994) and investigated the ways that gender and redemption have been related in Christian history (Ruether 1998). They have insisted that although the maleness of Jesus is a historical fact, this particularity is transcended in the identity of the Christ and has neither theological nor normative status (Schneiders 1986, Johnson 1992). Christologies by feminists of color have sought to liberate Jesus from the racism and imperialism of dominant theologies and stressed the identification of the historical Jesus with the poor and marginalized (Copeland 1996).

Ecclesiology, Mariology, and Sacraments
While criticizing the oppressive ways in which church structures have functioned, feminist theologians have maintained that Christianity began as a "discipleship of equals" (Schüssler Fiorenza 1983); since a "spirit-filled community" has long existed in tension with the patriarchal historical institution, the contemporary "women-church" movement should seek its ideals without being ultimately separatist (Ruether 1985).

Emphasis on an inclusive solidarity that affirms difference within the community as it struggles for justice (Isasi-Díaz 1993) is widely shared in feminist ecclesiologies. Work on embodiment and sacraments has deepened thought on marriage, ministry, eucharist, and worship, and kept the issue of women's ordination under discussion (Hilkert 1997, Byrne 1998, Ross 1998, Walton 2000). Feminist scholars have also developed new interpretations of Mary (Gebara & Bingemer 1989, Rodriguez 1994, Cunneen 1996) and the saints (Johnson 1998).

Ethics and Moral Theology
The implications of feminist theologies for the way Christians should live have been pondered in many works of feminist ethics, which are now influencing discussions of moral theology more generally (Curran et al. 1996). Among topics of particular concern have been agency (Isasi-Díaz 1993), commitment (Farley 1986), conscience and authority (Patrick 1996), ecology (Ruether 1992, Gebara 1999), economics and work (Andolsen 1989, 1998, Guider 1995), family (Cahill 2000), friendship (Hunt 1991), natural law (Traina 1999), power (Hinze 1995), sexuality and gender (Gudorf 1994, Cahill 1996, Jung 2001), and struggle and violence (Isasi-Díaz 1993, Mananzan 1996). Feminist theologians have brought their commitment to justice for females to many other topics in biomedical and social ethics, ranging from concerns about reproductive issues (Ryan 2001) to matters of war and peace (Cahill 1994).

Spirituality
Because all feminist theologies invite believers to a deep process of conversion, there has been considerable attention to topics in spirituality, which is a concept of wide appeal both within and beyond the churches today. Joann Conn has dealt with psychological aspects of spiritual growth (1989) and Shawn Madigan (1998) has gathered historically important spiritual writings by women. The lecture series sponsored by St. Mary's College in honor of Sister Madeleva Wolff has resulted in the publication of a new title in women's spirituality annually since 1985; recent overviews from African American, U.S. Latina, and white perspectives have been contributed by Hayes (1995), Rodriguez (1996), and Schneiders (2000).

That feminist theology as a discipline has come of age is now evident. There is a substantial number of scholarly books by recognized theologians, as well as many introductory texts designed for classroom use.

The Journal of Feminist Studies in Religion has been published in the United States since 1985, and *Feminist Theology* in Britain since 1992. The fact that a dictionary conveying the complexity of feminist theologies (Russell and Clarkson 1996) contains extensive entries under headings that include "African," "Asian," "European," "Latin American," "North American" "Pacific Island," and "South Asian" testifies to the global extent of this movement. The challenge now is for theologians from diverse backgrounds to carry forward their critical and constructive work, gain a wider hearing beyond the academic community, and develop an effective solidarity among themselves and among believers more generally, for the sake of building a just and ecologically responsible society.

Works Cited in This Chapter

B. Andolsen, *Daughters of Jefferson, Daughters of Bookblacks: Racism and American Feminism* (Macon, GA: Mercer University Press, 1986).

M. P. Aquino, *Our Cry for Life: Feminist Theology from Latin America* (Maryknoll, NY: Orbis Books, 1993); "Latin American Feminist Theology," *Journal of Feminist Studies in Religion* 14 (1998): 89–107.

W. Burghardt, ed., *Woman: New Dimensions* (New York: Paulist Press, 1977).

L. Byrne, *Woman at the Altar: The Ordination of Women in the Roman Catholic Church* (New York: Bloomsbury Academic, 1998).

L. S. Cahill, *Sex, Gender and Christian Ethics* (Cambridge, 1996); *Family: A Christian Social Perspective* (Minneapolis: Fortress Press, 2000).

D. L. Carmody, *Christian Feminist Theology* (New York: Oxford University Press, 1995).

A. E. Carr, *Transforming Grace: Christian Tradition and Women's Experience* (San Francisco: HarperSanFrancisco, 1988).

A. Clifford, *Introducing Feminist Theology* (Maryknoll, NY: Orbis Books, 2001).

R. Coll, *Christianity and Feminism in Conversation* (Mystic, CT: Twenty-Third Publications, 1994).

M. S. Copeland, "The New Anthropological Subject at the Heart of the Mystical Body of Christ," *Catholic Theological Society of America Proceedings* 53 (1998): 25–47; "Toward a Critical Christian Feminist Theology of Solidarity," in Mary Ann Hinsdale & Phyllis Kaminiski, eds., *Women and Theology* (Maryknoll, NY: Orbis Books, 1995), 3–38; "Theologies, Contemporary," in Letty M. Russell & J. Shannon Clarkson, eds., *Dictionary of Feminist Theologies* (Louisville: Westminster John Knox Press, 1996), 283–87.

C. Curran, M. Farley, and R. McCormick, eds., *Readings in Moral Theology No. 9: Feminist Ethics* (New York: Paulist Press, 1996).

M. Daly, *Beyond God the Father* (Boston: Beacon Press, 1973).

V. Fabella and M. A. Oduyoye, eds., *With Passion and Compassion: Third World Women Doing Theology* (Maryknoll, NY: Orbis Books, 1988).

V. Fabella and S. Park, eds., *We Dare to Dream: Doing Theology as Asian Women* (Maryknoll, NY: Orbis Books, 1990).

V. Fabella and R. S. Sugirtharajah, eds., *Dictionary of Third World Theologies* (Maryknoll, NY: Orbis Books, 2000).

M. Farley, *Personal Commitments: Beginning, Keeping, Changing* (San Francisco: HarperSanFrancisco, 1986).

E. S. Fiorenza, *In Memory of Her: A Feminist Theological Reconstruction of Christian Origins* (New York: Crossroad Publishing, 1983); *Discipleship of Equals: A Critical Feminist Ekklesialogy of Liberation* (New York: Crossroad Publishing, 1993); *Jesus: Miriam's Child, Sophia's Prophet* (New York: Crossroad Publishing, 1994); ed., *The Power of Naming: A* Concilium *Reader in Feminist Liberation Theology* (Maryknoll, NY: Orbis Books, 1996).

A. Flannery, ed., *Vatican Council II: Constitutions, Decrees, Declarations*, inclusive language edition (Northport, NY: Costello Publishing, 1996).

A. M. Gardiner, ed., *Women and Catholic Priesthood* (New York: pub. unknown, 1976).

I. Gebara and M. C. Bingemer, *Mary: Mother of God, Mother of the Poor* (Maryknoll, NY: Orbis Books, 1989).

I. Gebara, *Longing for Running Water: Ecofeminism and Liberation* (Minneapolis: Fortress Press, 1999).

A. Graff, ed., *In the Embrace of God: Feminist Approaches to Theological Anthropology* (Maryknoll, NY: Orbis Books, 1995).

C. Gudorf, *Body, Sex, and Pleasure: Reconstructing Christian Sexual Ethics* (Cleveland: Pilgrim Press, 1994).

M. Guider, *Daughters of Rahab* (Minneapolis: Fortress Press, 1995).

D. Hayes, *Hagar's Daughters: Womanist Ways of Being in the World* (New York: Paulist Press, 1995).

M. C. Hilkert, *Naming Grace: Preaching and the Sacramental Imagination* (New York: Bloomsbury Academic, 1997); *Speaking with Authority: Catherine of Siena and the Voices of Women Today* (New York: Paulist Press, 2001).

M. A. Hinsdale and P. Kaminiski, eds., *Women and Theology* (Maryknoll, NY: Orbis Books, 1995).

M. Hunt, *Fierce Tenderness: A Feminist Theology of Friendship*, rev. ed. (1991; Minneapolis: Augsburg Fortress, 2009).

A. M. Isasi-Díaz and Y. Tarango, *Hispanic Women: Prophetic Voice in the Church* (San Francisco: HarperSanFrancisco, 1988).

A. M. Isasi-Díaz , *En la Lucha: A Hispanic Women's Liberation Theology* (Minneapolis: Fortress Press, 1993); *Mujerista Theology: A Theology for the Twenty-First Century* (Maryknoll, NY: Orbis Books, 1996).

E. Johnson, *She Who Is: The Mystery of God in Feminist Theological Discourse* (New York, 1992); *Friends of God and Prophets* (New York: Bloomsbury Academic, 1998).

P. B. Jung, with J. A. Coray, eds., *Sexual Diversity and Catholicism* (Collegeville, MN: Liturgical, 2001).

U. King, ed., *Feminist Theology from the Third World* (Maryknoll, NY: Orbis Books, 1994).

C. LaCugna, ed., *Freeing Theology: The Essentials of Theology in Feminist Perspective* (San Francisco: HarperSanFrancisco, 1993).

M. J. Mananzan et al., eds., *Women Struggling against Violence: A Spirituality for Life* (Maryknoll, NY: Orbis Books, 1996).

A. E. Patrick, *Liberating Conscience: Feminist Explorations in Catholic Moral Theology* (New York: Bloomsbury Academic, 1996); "Feminist Ethics in the New Millennium," in F. Eigo, ed., *Ethical Dilemmas in the New Millennium*, vol. 1 (Villanova, PA: Villanova University Press, 2000).

J. Rodriguez, *Our Lady of Guadalupe* (Austin: University of Texas Press, 1994); *Stories We Live, Cuentos Que Vivimos: Hispanic Women's Spirituality* (New York: Paulist Press, 1996).

S. Ross, *Extravagant Affections: A Feminist Sacramental Theology* (New York: Bloomsbury Academic, 1998).

L. Russell and J. S. Clarkson, eds., *Dictionary of Feminist Theologies* (Louisville: Westminster John Knox Press, 1996).

R. R. Ruether, *Liberation Theology* (New York: Paulist Press, 1972); *Sexism and God-Talk: Toward a Feminist Theology* (Boston: Beacon Press, 1983); *Women-Church* (San Francisco: HarperSanFrancisco, 1985); *Gaia and God: An Ecofeminist Theology of Earth Healing* (San Francisco: HarperSanFrancisco, 1992); *Women and Redemption: A Theological History* (Minneapolis: Fortress Press, 1998).

S. Schneiders, *Women and the Word: The Gender of God in the New Testament and the Spirituality of Women* (New York: Paulist Press, 1986); *Beyond Patching: Faith and Feminism in the Catholic Church* (New York: Paulist Press, 1991); *With Oil in Their Lamps: Faith, Feminism, and the Future* (New York: Paulist Press, 2000).

J. Walton, *Feminist Liturgy: A Matter of Justice* (Collegeville, MN: Liturgical Press, 2000).

12

THEOLOGY'S PROPHETIC COMMITMENTS

Insights from Experience

This essay is significant for its analysis and celebration of the commitment of prophecy, which Anne Patrick interprets as both central to the theologian's calling and widely shared because it stems from baptism itself. Also significant, however, are the expressions of values and practices evident elsewhere in her writing and in her lifelong interpretation of her own calling. Thus she identifies a modest sense of human weakness as a prerequisite for speaking in a strong and at times unqualified voice. And she advocates the very approaches that this essay attributes to effective prophecy—"the balancing act of collaboration, courage, and prudence"—when writing on many other challenges as well. —HD

Last month someone sent me an old novel by Graham Greene from 1955 called *The Quiet American*. Some see *The Quiet American* as a prophetic work of fiction, because this story of the violence brought on by a high-minded American intelligence officer who helps out a "third force" in French Indo-China gave an early critical look at U.S. involvement in what would later become the Vietnam War. The 1950s were a time of militant anti-communism here and in Europe, and Greene's book about Indo-China was not well received. He was labeled a "pinko," if not a full-fledged supporter of communism, he had trouble getting a visa for the U.S., and he was denied the Nobel Prize in Literature, all because he published *The Quiet American*. In 1969, however, Greene received the Shakespeare Prize from the University of Hamburg, and his acceptance speech tells how he saw the writer's vocation. It is also a stunning indictment of Shakespeare, whom Greene faults for failing to

---

This essay is a slightly revised presentation given at the 2010 annual meeting of the Catholic Theological Society of America.

speak the truth about the injustices of his own day, particularly as they affected Catholics, and instead "receding from the dangerous present, the England of plots and persecutions, into the safer past."[1] "Of course he is the greatest of all poets," Greene admits, while lamenting the fact that Shakespeare stayed with the Establishment, and never took up the dangerous cause of Robert Southwell, a fellow poet who was tortured for three years and then executed for "so-called treason" in 1595.[2] Greene concluded his speech by comparing Shakespeare to Dietrich Bonhoeffer, and judging the German theologian the greater hero for his willingness to be hanged, as Southwell had been. "Perhaps the deepest tragedy Shakespeare lived," Greene declared, "was his own: the blind eye exchanged for the coat of arms, the prudent tongue for the friendships at Court and the great house at Stratford."[3]

These words have stayed with me for decades, and I think they have a bearing not just on the writer's vocation but on all Christians who share a prophetic calling. When we speak of "theology's prophetic commitments," after all, we are personifying the discipline, and I think it better to claim our own agency here and speak of the *theologian's* prophetic commitments. I also think we should locate the gift and call to prophecy in our baptismal commitment and not see it as part of a special professional role. I say this in part because I have apprehensions about a self-appointed guild of prophets, and also because I see problems in relegating the task of prophecy to groups that are excluded from other forms of power in the religious institution. After all, we have known in our day more than one example of prophetic speech by members of the hierarchy, including *The Challenge of Peace*[4] and Archbishop John Quinn's important book *The Reform of the Papacy*.[5]

The prophet is called to speak the truth to power, and to speak the truth in love. Among the things that theological training adds to this general call is an historically informed recognition that none of us knows for sure that we are speaking the full truth, much less voicing God's opinion when we offer ours; at the same time, however, we have the obligation to do our best, to share what we think is the case, especially when falsehoods and injustice seem to be carrying the day. When I confront this paradox I take comfort in a phrase that has lingered in memory from the religious investiture and vow ceremonies of my preVatican II youth. In these rituals the bishop would ask the superior if the candidates were worthy to receive the habit or make profession, and she would answer, "As far as human weakness can ascertain, your excellency, they are worthy." "As far as human weakness can ascertain," it seems to me, is the disclaimer we must at least make in prayer before we stand up to confront the powerful and the public with words that are *not* weakened with qualifications, and voice statements that might eventually be considered prophetic, and at the time make us nervous about whether we are putting our security, if not a coat of arms and house at Stratford, at risk.

Prophets have been the ones to announce that God is doing something new, and they have called for change—repentance—in light of what they judge to be God's values and God's concerns. Often they have condemned idolatry, and called for a turning from placing ultimate trust and loyalty in some finite reality to a renewed worship of the Divine Mystery. When Mary Ann Hinsdale proposed the convention theme she offered a model of one instance where theology's prophetic commitments were evident and effective, that of the *Kairos Document* in which South African theologians confessed that some forms of Christian theology had contributed to the injustice of apartheid. The South African theologians then proposed a new "prophetic theology" that "confronts the evils of the time and speaks out against them in no uncertain terms," carries a message of hope for the future, and is deeply spiritual, practical, and pastoral.[6] Three aspects of the production of this document suggest to me three commitments that we should continue to make as theologians who want to express God's gift of prophecy today.

In the first place, the *Kairos Document* came from the experience of those who ministered in the townships among those who suffered most under apartheid. Our own commitment should likewise be *rooted in the experiences and sufferings of those who lack voice in the systems of power*. The blindness and deafness that come with privilege need constant correction by attention to the marginalized.

Secondly, the *Kairos Document* was a collaborative effort, issuing in 1985 from a committee of more than thirty professional "theologians, ordinary Christians (lay theologians), and some church leaders."[7] It was then reviewed, critiqued, and revised in a process that involved thousands. During this year the theologian who served as "secretary and grammarian" for the committee moved to a distant city to avoid apprehension by government police. Everyone involved in the process took considerable risk, and the prudence of a principal collaborator was not due to lack of courage. Our own prophetic commitment should likewise *aspire to the effectiveness that is made more likely by the balancing act of collaboration, courage, and prudence*.

Thirdly, the document was written in as clear and simple a way as possible, so that it could be understood by ordinary Christians. When it published the revision in 1986 the committee voiced the hope that "this

edition will not be the end of the process of action and theological reflection on our situation" (vi), but rather will stimulate a continuing
cycle of action-reflection-action. I think this question of audience is
very challenging for academic theologians, and I believe a third commitment we should make is to *share our sense of truth more generously
with lay audiences.* We do this with our students, of course, but we could
do much more with our writing. The academy may not reward our
popular writing, but our Christian vocation seems to demand it. I
know I am edified by the theologians who have not hidden their light
in the safe groves of academe, and instead write op-ed pieces and accept invitations from parishes, interviews with the press, and popular
writing assignments that are often ill-timed in relation to the other responsibilities we carry.

Rather than expand this list of commitments, I'll conclude by men-
tioning two of many instances where I've been edified by theologians
who exemplify these three commitments: their work is rooted in the experiences of those who suffer at the margins; they strive to speak effectively by balancing collaboration, courage, and prudence; and, they
seek to communicate not just to the academy but also the wider public.
I lift up these two articles because I believe they are prophetic, they
bear on a current impasse that divides the U.S. Church, and perhaps by
reviewing them one or another of us will be inspired to contribute
something that will bring things to a new stage.

Though I could smile at the cartoon circulated in the wake of the
passage of the health care bill—it pictured a nun in habit with a basket-
ball labeled "health care bill" going up for a right-handed jump shot over
the arms of a bishop, all under the caption "March Madness—Nuns
Score Upset Win Over the Bishops"—though I could smile in March, my
amusement was over long before I saw the headline in May about Sister
Margaret McBride and Bishop Thomas Olmstead of Phoenix, "Nun Excommunicated For Allowing Abortion." The issues that divide Catholics—understandings of authority, sin, politics, grace, sexual and
medical ethics, women's role—these issues are many and difficult, but I
am hopeful that if theologians will bring our gifts to bear on interpreting our situation in new ways, God's Spirit will give us the language to
help heal the division in the church so that we may bear more credible
witness to the larger society, for the ultimate benefit of the poor and
marginalized here and abroad.

The first example I would mention is Margaret Farley's presidential address to the Catholic Theological Society of America in 2000,
"The Church in the Public Forum: Scandal or Prophetic Witness?" I

think Farley was right to insist that if the church as a whole is to "accomplish in the public forum what are its most serious aims—the awakening of all of us, and of our whole society, to the imperatives of justice and the respect and care of those among us who are wounded or ignored," then the church needs to "decenter abortion in [its] political agenda," and "revise [its] priorities for political action," among other things.[8] I cannot go into the details of her carefully reasoned argument here; I simply want to point out that ten years ago Farley took on a topic that was far from safe and comfortable, and called prophetically for a change of heart and strategy. In the light of continued scandal and "abortion trumps all" politics, I remain edified by her prescient remarks, and I think we would do well to revisit her address and consider what might be *done* to realize its hopes for a national Catholic influence that is effectively prophetic. Is it time for a committee of professional theologians, ordinary Christians, and church leaders to reflect together and offer "a theological comment on the political crisis in the United States," analogous to what was done a quarter-century ago in Johannesburg?

Besides Farley's presidential address, another resource for such a committee would be Cathleen Kaveny's insightful piece on "Intrinsic Evil and Political Responsibility," published in *America* for October 27, 2008, days before the last presidential election. In this courageous essay Kaveny asked whether the concept of intrinsic evil, which was prominent in the 2008 voting guide the bishops had prepared for U.S. Catholics, was a helpful one for voters. Her answer was largely negative, for reasons I cannot give fully, which included well-argued claims that "An intrinsically evil homicide is not always worse than every other wrongful homicide" (16) and "Preventing intrinsically evil acts is not always our top moral priority" (17).

What the piece also contributes is the very important insight that in *Gaudium et Spes* (27) and *Veritatis Splendor* the use of the term "intrinsic evil" has moved far beyond the technical use normally employed in Catholic action theory: it is "evocative, not analytical," and indeed it is an instance of "prophetic language." Kaveny believes that "the prophetic use of the term 'intrinsic evil' is meant to start an urgent discussion among people of good will about grave injustices in the world. It does not provide a detailed blueprint for action. Identifying infamies is one thing. Deciding upon a strategy to deal with them is something else again" (19).

Her analysis has helped me to grasp more fully how both sides of the divided church see themselves in prophetic roles. If we are ever to sort out the competing claims of would-be prophets on both sides of the "abortion trumps all" divide, do we not need the insights of courageous, prudent, and collaborative theologians, whose training gives us ways of protecting the ultimacy and mystery of the Divine from the recurrent human tendency to exalt our own values and categories in idolatrous ways?

Notes

1. Graham Greene, "The Virtue of Disloyalty," in *The Portable Graham Greene*, ed. Philip Stratford (New York: Viking, 1973), 606.

2. Ibid., 607–8.

3. Ibid., 610.

4. *The Challenge of Peace: God's Promise and Our Response. A Pastoral Letter on War and Peace* (Washington, DC: National Conference of Catholic Bishops, 1983).

5. John R. Quinn, *The Reform of the Papacy: The Costly Call to Christian Unity* (New York: Herder & Herder, 1999).

6. *The Kairos Document: Challenge to the Church*, rev. 2nd ed. (Grand Rapids, MI: Wm. B. Eerdmans, 1986), 18.

7. Ibid., Preface, vii.

8. Margaret A. Farley, "The Church in the Public Forum: Scandal or Prophetic Witness?" Presidential Address, *CTSA Proceedings* 55 (2000): 98–99.

13

CONSCIENCE AS THE CREATIVELY RESPONSIBLE SELF

In this excerpt from Women, Conscience, and the Creative Process, *Anne Patrick argues that conscience should involve not the passive replication of values imposed from outside the individual but rather a creative participation in formulating them. Her abiding commitment to replacing passivity with active engagement runs throughout her work on this and many other issues.* —HD

In the aftermath of World War II the term *responsibility* became prominent in Christian ethics, as thinkers such as Bernard Häring, Dietrich Bonhoeffer, and H. Richard Niebuhr sought to overcome the emphasis on duty and obedience that had dominated ethical reflection prior to the Nuremburg trials, when ex-Nazis tried to defend their atrocities on grounds of "following orders."[1] Niebuhr's book *The Responsible Self* is a profound philosophical essay on moral agency, which I still find an inspiring description of much that the experience of conscience involves.[2] Further research has convinced me, however, that we do well to distinguish two ways of being responsible, one that is more passive and the other more creative. The former involves fulfilling the commonly recognized duties of one's state in life, while the latter looks beyond the immediate obligations of commandments and social roles and seeks to contribute in new ways to the contexts of one's life, striving to accomplish good on a wider scale, and thus "bearing fruit for the life of the world."[3]

We might in fact interpret the story of Jesus and the rich young man who kept the commandments but could not risk leaving his goods to follow the imaginative teacher and healer to new endeavors (Mt 19)

This essay is adapted from Anne E. Patrick, Women, Conscience, and the Creative Process: 2009 Madeleva Lecture in Spirituality *(Mahwah, NJ: Paulist Press, 2011), 55–72.*

as voicing the desire of Jesus for disciples whose ethical ideals extend beyond conforming to law and social expectations, notwithstanding their importance. "If you wish to enter into life," Jesus tells the young man, "keep the commandments," and after having done that, "if you wish to be perfect, go, sell your possessions, and give the money to the poor, and you will have treasure in heaven; then come, follow me" (vv. 16–22). The gospel itself interprets this story as mainly concerning the danger of riches, and in subsequent centuries many Christians have interpreted the invitation to perfection as having to do with a vocation to the religious life with its vow of poverty. I believe, however, that this narrative can, in addition, be read as supporting an ethic that involves both appropriate conformity to law and duty and also a willingness to take appropriate risks and attempt new things that will make our love of neighbor a truly efficacious one.

Responsibility's passive dimension has been greatly stressed in Catholic literature, whereas there has been much less emphasis on creative responsibility, which involves the ability to think independently and to take risks for the sake of helping to improve life for oneself and one's neighbors. Both types of responsibility are needed, like the black and white keys on the piano. The problem is that socialization has equipped many of us too well for the one, and very poorly for the other. Women and men alike have received moral training that denies or minimizes the agent's role in recognizing obligations and in balancing obligations that conflict. Many women, however, face particular challenges insofar as the socialization of females has tended to foster passivity and stifle growth toward exercising power and original thinking.[4]

And yet we do have many instances of women who have exercised creative responsibility. Dorothy Day, cofounder with Peter Maurin of the Catholic Worker Movement, comes to mind, as does Mother Alfred Moes, OSF, a key figure in the founding of the Mayo Clinic. After a tornado had devastated the frontier town of Rochester, Minnesota in 1883, this community leader persuaded Dr. William Mayo to staff a hospital if she would build it. With the support of her religious community she could deliver on this promise, and she raised enough funds to open St. Mary's Hospital in 1889. In 1894 Dr. Mayo testified to the importance of her initiative, for he had at first been reluctant to change his medical practice. Speaking of the conversation that led to the hospital, he observed:

[T]he Mother Superior came down to my office and in the course of the visit she asked, "Doctor, do you not think a hospital in this city would be an excellent thing?" I answered,

"Mother Superior, this city is too small to support a hospital." I told her that the erection of a hospital was a difficult undertaking and required a great deal of money, and moreover we had no assurance of its success even after a great deal of time and money had been put into it. "Very well," she persisted, "but you just promise me to take charge of it and we will set that building before you at once. With our faith and hope and energy, it will succeed."[5]

There is a gospel parable that can encourage us to emulate such women as Mother Alfred Moes and to become more creatively responsible selves. This is the Parable of the Talents from Matthew's gospel (25:14–30). This story immediately precedes the narrative of the Last Judgment (25:31–46), in which Jesus rewards the faithful with the words, "I was hungry and you gave me food, I was thirsty and you gave me drink" (v. 35a). In the Parable of the Talents, three servants are given different sums of money as their master departs for a trip. The servant who received the least amount buried his money out of fear. The other two servants risked investing their talents, and their money doubled in value. In the end these creatively responsible servants are rewarded, while the timid, fearful servant does not fare so well. This fearful servant reminds me of someone who sees the moral life only as a matter of not breaking the rules. And we might interpret the difference between the two and the five talents as symbolizing the different levels of creative responsibility, what psychologist Mihaly Csikszentmihalyi distinguishes as everyday personal creativity, or creativity with a lowercase c, and eminent or culture-changing creativity, demarcated by an uppercase C.[6]

My grandmother, Stella Farrell Flynn, was probably closer to the lowercase form of creativity when she found a way to feed her eleven children during the Depression of the 1930s, and still had something for the unemployed men who came to their kitchen door hungry. Dorothy Day, on the other hand, is recognized as having made a lasting change in Catholic and urban culture, and Csikszentmihalyi would regard her as eminently creative. Like Dorothy Day and Mother Alfred Moes, Sister Madeleva[7] is another instance of eminent creativity, and her life also helps us appreciate the way creative responsibility is related to institutional and social life, or "domains" and "fields," as Csikszentmihalyi calls them.[8]

Madeleva's personal creativity showed itself in many ways—her poetry, her teaching, her correspondence, her essays, and her autobiographical writings, to mention a few. To my knowledge, however, she did not introduce lasting novelty into the domains of literature or pedagogy, so that we can say they will never be the same as a result of her efforts. But I think we can say that her creativity with respect to the Sister Formation Movement and the School of Sacred Theology at Saint Mary's College was of the eminent or culture-changing variety.

What she catalyzed with her efforts to ensure that teaching sisters received professional training before being sent into the classroom has had an enormous and lasting impact, not only on the religious congregations involved but on American Catholic culture as a whole. In her 1997 biography of Madeleva, Gail Porter Mandell stresses the importance of a panel she had organized for the National Catholic Education Association in 1949, which included groundbreaking papers by Madeleva and several others that were later published under the title *The Education of Sister Lucy*.[9] Three years later, Mandell notes, the first national gathering of U.S. religious took place in August 1952 at the University of Notre Dame, and this "formed the link between the ideas published in *The Education of Sister Lucy* and the actual Sister Formation program, established in 1954."[10]

Likewise the innovation of opening Saint Mary's School of Sacred Theology in 1943, which had resulted from Madeleva's interest in providing education for teachers of religion, was of the culture-changing variety. Today we tend to forget how dramatic a change it was when women first gained the credentials for teaching theology at the college and graduate levels, but it was the program started by Madeleva that first made it possible for non-clerics to earn graduate degrees in Catholic theology. According to the 1982 directory of the Catholic Theological Society of America, all the women members with Ph.D. degrees from the 1950s had studied at Saint Mary's College. Among them was Margaret Brennan, IHM, who earned her doctorate in 1953, and later, as leader of her congregation, systematically encouraged younger sisters, including Madeleva lecturers Sandra M. Schneiders, IHM, and Mary Ann Hinsdale, IHM, to pursue advanced studies in theology.[11]

Besides her work in community administration, which included service as president of the national Leadership Conference of Women Religious in 1972, Brennan taught numerous graduate students during twenty-five years as a professor of pastoral theology at Regis College of the University of Toronto.[12] Another eminent graduate of Saint Mary's School of Sacred Theology was Mary Anthony Wagner, OSB, who completed her Ph.D. in 1957 and taught theology at the College of St. Benedict and St. John's University in Minnesota for thirty-seven years. With Paschal Botz, OSB, she cofounded the Benedictine Institute of Sacred

Theology there for non-clerics and was associate dean for ten years. In 1974 this institute merged with the seminary at St. John's to become St. John's University School of Theology, and Wagner was its first dean, serving until 1978. She later edited the national publication *Sisters Today* from 1979 until its last issue in November 2000.

At the fortieth anniversary meeting of the College Theology Society in 1994, M. Shawn Copeland declared in a plenary address:

> By inserting women into the stream of academic theology, [Madeleva] laid the condition of the possibility of a distinctive theological contribution emerging from women's reflection on our particular human, religious, cultural, political, and economic experiences in light of the Word of God . . . Because of her labor, Roman Catholic women have been engaged in the study and practice of theology now for fifty years.[13]

In sum, the School of Sacred Theology at Saint Mary's College has had a profound effect on the discipline of Christian theology and arguably on global Christianity as well.

Both these influential efforts illustrate the social-institutional side of creativity. We might suppose that the School of Sacred Theology and the Sister Formation Movement were sudden inspirations that came from nowhere to Madeleva's convent room, perhaps as she was writing a poem or tying her shoelaces. But the process was more complex, as Mandell's biography makes clear, and it was much more *social* than the stereotype of the solitary creative genius suggests. In terms of the creative process, Madeleva had greatly desired to improve religious education and do better justice to the talents of women religious; she had done considerable preparatory work before coming up with her remarkably productive ideas; and the issues were incubating as she went about other tasks and talked with her friends. The insights may seem to have come suddenly, but they came to a well-prepared mind and to a moral agent who knew how to engage others in effecting change for the good.

With respect to the School of Sacred Theology, Mandell shows that Madeleva's creativity here depended very much on her social life and her involvement with the Holy Cross Sisters, the National Catholic Education Association (NCEA), and church leaders. By the early 1940s Madeleva had long deplored the quality of religious education in Catholic schools, but it took a remark by her friend Frank Sheed about the fact that nowhere in the country could a layperson do graduate studies in theology to give her the idea that something practical might be done about the problem. And when her requests to Catholic University, Notre Dame, Marquette, and other universities to admit non-clerics to their graduate theology programs were turned down, she mentioned this disappointment to Bishop Edwin O'Hara, the head of the bishops' committee on the Confraternity of Christian Doctrine, while he was visiting Saint Mary's, and it was *he* who suggested that she might start something on her own campus. Mandell reports:

> At the time [Madeleva] demurred, fearful of what she described as "presumption." At the next meeting of the NCEA, with all other possibilities exhausted, she responded to "a strange impulse outside [her] will." Rising, she announced: "I do not know how we will do it, but this summer [1943] we will offer at Saint Mary's a six weeks' graduate program in Theology... We will send you details in a fortnight."[14]

Madeleva's friends Frank Sheed and Edwin O'Hara had played key roles in this instance of her creativity, and she quickly enlisted others to help with implementing the idea of a School of Sacred Theology. Two Jesuits and a monsignor taught noncredit courses to eighteen sisters from various communities that first summer, and the school was formally established with doctoral- and master's-level programs in place the following year. Madeleva drew on her experience with this school in her contributions to *The Education of Sister Lucy*, arguing in "The Preparation of Teachers of Religion" that Catholic institutions were guilty of heresy if they thought that "any teacher wearing a religious habit can *de facto* teach religion," and asking why Catholic colleges and universities did not invest in theological studies the way they did in science:

> We have teachers who can make science and embalmed cats subjects for absorbing study. Will we, and when will we train teachers to make God and the science of theology the supreme subject in our curricula? We have millions of dollars for research in smashing the atom. Will we, and when will we devote our resources to the study of the Power that holds our atoms together?[15]

Saint Mary's School of Sacred Theology flourished for two decades, closing only when Madeleva's earlier goal of having university theology programs available to non-clerics had been achieved. During that time this small program prepared a generation of women theologians and has had an incalculable impact on the church.

Having mentioned some of the contributions of Margaret Brennan, IHM, and Mary Anthony Wagner, OSB, we have only to reel in the chain of causality represented by another graduate, this one from 1954, to reinforce this point about influence. I refer to the theologian-turned-philosopher Mary Daly, who helped launch the Christian feminist movement and its theoretical contributions to Christian theology. If Daly had not earned her doctorate at Saint Mary's College, would she have been motivated to seek further training in Europe so that her theological knowledge would be certified with the same pontifical degree that clerical theologians possessed? Indeed, if she had not studied Thomas Aquinas so assiduously at Saint Mary's College, would she have been able to hold her own as the only female in a sea of cassocked seminarians at the University of Fribourg in Switzerland? We may well wonder whether *The Church and the Second Sex* would have been written, and whether the discussion that ensued in Christian feminist theology would have been delayed or taken a different course.[16] The fact that Daly herself eventually rejected Catholicism and theology testifies to the ambiguous results of creativity, but does not deny either Daly's or Madeleva's participation in culture-changing creativity.

I would note that the quality that led Madeleva to seek new solutions to significant problems can be called the virtue of creativity, insofar as a virtue is a moral excellence, a strength of character that contributes to habitually good action in some respect. As a virtue, creativity involves the disposition to step back from a situation of difficulty, look at options imaginatively, and take reasonable risks for the sake of new and better possibilities. Creativity can, of course, be put to evil purposes, and in that case it is not virtuous.[17] And even when creativity is virtuous, its results will not be perfectly good, for under the conditions of finitude, human choices tend to have ambiguous results and unforeseen consequences.

Furthermore, not every moral dilemma calls for a "new" response; discernment is needed to ascertain whether conformity or creativity is called for in a given situation, and often conformity is needed. For instance, when the Vatican insisted in the early 1980s that the Sisters of Mercy halt discussions in their hospitals about whether some sterilizations could be allowed, the women leading the community realized that failure to do so would likely cause division in the congregation and ultimately result in harm to their ministry of health care. Although the Mercy leaders did not agree with the Vatican's reasoning, they obeyed its demand for the sake of what they judged to be the greater good under the difficult circumstances they faced.[18]

For all these reasons it may be better to speak of the virtue of creative responsibility than simply creativity, for "creative responsibility" conveys the element of prudence, discernment, and caring as well as imagination. But however we name the quality, the important thing is to cultivate it. And I think we improve the odds of fostering this virtue if we think of moral education in terms of developing creatively responsible selves, rather than as a matter of "forming" some abstraction called "conscience." The investment of talents, whether one or two or five, must happen with the awareness that one cannot fully predict the results of a deed undertaken in the hope of doing good. But the Parable of the Talents from Matthew's gospel makes clear that the willingness to take reasonable risks in responsibility before our Creator should characterize the person of faith.

The need for creative responsibility is evident in so many of the moral dilemmas we face on a daily basis. Take the case featured in the *Hastings Center Report* in late 2008, concerning a doctor and a nurse who seek to treat an immigrant woman from Sudan who tests positive for HIV. This woman, named Alna, speaks very little English and has mainly pointed at pictures to communicate with clinic workers, but she refuses to allow a translator into the room because she fears her HIV status will become known in the small immigrant community. Very likely Alna contracted the virus from her husband, and she is afraid of violence from him and separation from their children if her condition should become known. Yet the medical staff feels the obligation to treat Alna, and both doctor and nurse are frustrated by her unwillingness to admit an interpreter. The doctor puts the dilemma thus: "How can we treat her if we can't communicate with her, and how can we communicate with her without an interpreter? She needs HAART (highly active antiretroviral therapy), but for that to be effective, we need to help her understand how important it is to adhere to the prescription regimen to keep the viral load low. Without an interpreter, our hands are tied."[19]

When considered narrowly, this case might seem to be a matter of weighing the ethical principle of beneficence, and in particular the doctor's duty to care for a patient, against the principle of patient autonomy, and concluding either that Alna must be sent home untreated or else subjected to an interview in the presence of a Sudanese translator. But the ethicists who commented on the case for the *Report* took a much broader and more imaginative approach to the dilemma, one that invites the health care professionals to see the problem from Alna's perspective and assist her in providing for her own welfare within a context that is very different from their own. As commentator Christy Rentmeester put it, "Caring competently for Alna means more than just getting her the right prescriptions and monitoring her viral loads; it means making her feel confident that her caregivers understand what's at stake for her and partnering with her to figure out how to integrate new practices into her life with HIV."[20] On a practical level, commentator Dayle DeLancey suggests that this may mean spending some time with the translator when Alna is not there, and also seeking advice from "other local representatives of her culture" about how they might provide truly effective care for Alna.[21]

This case illustrates the need for creative responsibility because the imposition of a translator and even the "gold standard" of highly activated antiretroviral therapy may not be truly life-giving for Alna in her situation. There is at a minimum a need for a *new* approach to the problem, and this need calls on the creative imaginations of the moral agents involved. I would go so far as to say that it calls for them to exercise a *virtue* of creative responsibility, a virtue that includes the ability to take the problem apart, consider it from different angles, and look for a solution beyond the impasse originally presented.

Creative responsibility on a larger scale is called for in Daniel Finn's discussion of "morality in the marketplace" in the March 2009 issue of *U.S. Catholic*, especially in light of the economic crisis then affecting the global economy. In the current economy, Finn maintained, we cannot simply "legislate a just wage" in the United States, because in a global economy "to insist that everybody is paid $11.50 or $13.50 an hour may doom a corporation." Rather, he observed, "in a market economy, we have to find new ways to implement the values protected by the just wage doctrine."[22] Again, something *new* is needed, and thus creativity is required. Unfortunately, moral agents trained to think only in terms of conformity to principles are not well equipped for the imaginative work needed to preserve the values that the just wage doctrine served so well in the past, nor for that matter to address the new needs for justice that result from continual innovations in technologies and business practices around the world.

Finn's call for new approaches to economic justice reminds me of the story of Jacqueline Novogratz, an inspiring memoir in which Novogratz describes the influence of her first-grade teacher, Sister Mary Theophane.[23] Sister Mary had told her, "Regardless of what you become, remember always that to whom much is given, much is expected. God gave you many gifts and it is important that you use them for others as best you can," reinforcing values that Novogratz had learned at home, particularly about diligence and concern for others. Later in life, in seeking to contribute to a better situation for poor people she refused to be content with efforts that felt good subjectively but were not demonstrably effective in catalyzing real improvement. As she gained experience in international banking and microfinance work, she realized that business models that demanded results and accountability had something to offer philanthropists, and eventually she gathered the resources needed to put her ideas about "patient capitalism" to the test. In 2001 she launched the Acumen Fund, a world-changing philanthropic organization that by 2008 was managing more than $40 million in investments benefiting the poor in the developing world.

The story of Novogratz also illustrates an aspect of the creatively responsible self I have not mentioned yet, namely, tolerance for long-term involvement with a difficult problem or set of problems. Her creativity had been focused on effective assistance to poor persons for nearly two decades before the Acumen Fund was launched, and even its documented successes have not begun to complete her ambitious agenda. What sustains her in these long-term efforts is the vision of human interdependence she learned in childhood and has seen reinforced in exemplary lives she encountered since then. Quite simply, she is convinced that "we have only one world for all of us on earth, and the future really is ours to create, in a world we dare to imagine together."[24] And although the form of her commitment is very different from that of the saints depicted on the holy cards she received from Sister Mary Theophane in first grade, I believe those cards taught her to aspire to a life that was about much more than observing basic commandments and conforming to societal expectations.

The theologian Bernard Häring understood God to be seeking a creative response from human persons, and argued against moral formation that so emphasizes "literal obedience to static, inflexible norms" that well-intentioned persons "lack the power to see opportunities for doing good above and beyond the law."[25] By contrast, he pointed out, the Christian should learn from the lives of saints, whether canonized or not, that conscience is "the eye of love that discerned new paths toward the historical realization of the kingdom."[26] To be sure, the values of God's realm—love, justice, peace, truth—are never fully realized on Earth, but as baptized persons we are called to use our talents and especially our creativity in their pursuit. What problems of our religious and secular cultures call upon the creativity of each of us for solutions today? To what new paths, I wonder, is the eye of love inviting us?

Notes

1. Albert R. Jonsen describes this development in *Responsibility in Modern Religious Ethics* (Washington, DC: Corpus Books, 1968).

2. H. Richard Niebuhr, *The Responsible Self: An Essay in Christian Moral Philosophy* (New York: Harper & Row, 1963).

3. *Optatam Totius*, 16, "Decree on Priestly Formation," quoted here from Walter M. Abbott, ed., *The Documents of Vatican II* (New York: The America Press, 1966), 452.

4. I discuss this topic more fully in *Liberating Conscience: Explorations in Catholic Moral Theology* (New York: Bloomsbury Academic, 1997), 185–88.

5. See Ellen Whelan, OSF, *The Sisters' Story: Saint Mary's Hospital—Mayo Clinic 1839–1939* (Rochester, MN: Mayo Foundation for Medical Education and Research, 2002), 44. Whelan's chronicle adds that several sisters shared the reluctance initially voiced by Dr. Mayo. The July 1886 record of the sisters' executive council counted twenty-seven votes in favor and four against building the hospital (46).

6. See Mihaly Csikszentmihalyi, *Creativity: Flow and the Psychology of Discovery and Invention* (New York: HarperCollins, 1996).

7. Sister Mary Madeleva Wolff, CSC, an innovative educator of women and a poet and professor of literature, was president of St. Mary's College, Notre Dame, Indiana. The Madeleva Lectures in Spirituality are named in her honor.

8. Csikszentmihalyi, *Creativity*, 27–28.

9. *The Education of Sister Lucy* (Notre Dame, IN: Saint Mary's College, 1949). Madeleva's name is not given as editor, but she had invited the papers and written the opening and concluding essays: "The Education of Our Young Religious Teachers," in which the hypothetical Sister Lucy's educational needs are described (5–10), and "The Preparation of Teachers of Religion in College" (35–39).

10. Gail Porter Mandell, *Madeleva: A Biography* (Albany: State University of New York Press, 1997), 189. See also Karen Kennelly's recent history of the movement, *The Religious Formation Conference 1954–2004* (Silver Spring, MD: Religious Formation Conference, 2009).

11. Sandra M. Schneiders, in addition to being a prolific writer on biblical studies, spirituality, and religious life, has served as president of Society for the Study of Christian Spirituality and also the Catholic Biblical Association of America. Her Madeleva Lectures are *Women and the Word* (New York: Paulist Press, 1986) and *With Oil in Their Lamps: Faith, Feminism, and the Future* (New York: Paulist Press, 2000). Mary Ann Hinsdale was elected vice president of the Catholic Theological Society of America (CTSA) in 2008, with automatic succession to the presidency in 2010–11. Her Madeleva lecture, *Women Shaping Theology* (New York: Paulist Press, 2006), mentions (84) that the first two women members of the CTSA, who joined in 1965, were graduates of the doctoral program at Saint Mary's College: Cathleen M. Going (1956) and Elizabeth Farians (1958).

12. See Margaret R. Brennan, IHM, *What Was There for Me Once: A Memoir* (Toronto: Novalis, 2009), and Mary Ellen Sheehan, Mary Heather MacKinnon, and Moni McIntyre, eds., *Light Burdens, Heavy Blessings: Challenges of Church and Culture in the Post Vatican II Era: Essays in Honor of Margaret R. Brennan* (Quincy, IL: Franciscan Press, 2000).

13. M. Shawn Copeland, "Toward a Critical Christian Feminist Theology of Solidarity," in *Women and Theology*, ed. Mary Ann Hinsdale and Phyllis H. Kaminski (Maryknoll, NY: Orbis Books, 1995), 6.

14. Mandell, *Madeleva*, 185.

15. Madeleva, *The Education of Sister Lucy*, 39.

16. Daly's studies in Europe took place during the Second Vatican Council, and she was inspired by the energy for reform to publish *The Church and the Second Sex* (New York: Harper & Row, 1968). This hopeful, scholarly volume reviewed the history of sexism in the Catholic Church and offered some "modest proposals" for reform. It did not, however, win Daly tenure at Boston College, though that decision was eventually reversed in Daly's favor after student protesters took up her cause. By that time, however, Daly's patience as a Catholic reformer had been exhausted, and, like Martin Luther before her, she grew much more radical. Thus in October 1971, during a famous sermon in Harvard Memorial Chapel, she boldly declared Christianity and all patriarchal religions to be morally bankrupt, and urged her followers, women and men, to walk out of the chapel in a symbolic exodus from patriarchy. See Mary Daly, "The Women's Movement: An Exodus Community," *Religious Education* 67 (September–October 1972): 327–33; most of this sermon is reprinted in Elizabeth A. Clark and Herbert Richardson, eds., *Women and Religion: The Original Sourcebook of Women in Christian Thought*, rev. ed. (HarperSanFrancisco, 1996), 311–18. Two years later Daly published *Beyond God the Father: Toward a Philosophy of Women's Liberation* (Boston: Beacon, 1973), a theoretical rejection of Christian theology, whose arguments have since been countered in major works by feminist theologians, including Rosemary Radford Ruether, *Sexism and God Talk: Toward a Feminist Theology* (Boston: Beacon, 1983); Anne E. Carr, *Transforming Grace: Christian Tradition and Women's Experience* (New York: Harper & Row, 1988); and Elizabeth A. Johnson, *She Who Is: The Mystery of God in Feminist Theological Discourse* (New York: Continuum, 1992). Daly has provided autobiographical information in the "New Feminist Postchristian Introduction" to the 1975 edition of *The Church and the Second Sex* (New York: Harper & Row), and also in *Outercourse: The Be-Dazzling Voyage* (HarperSanFrancisco, 1992).

17. See, for example, the special issue of *Creativity Research Journal* 20:2 (2008) on "Malevolent Creativity."

18. I discuss this case more fully in *Liberating Conscience*, 45–48. Earlier, theologian Margaret A. Farley, a Sister of Mercy, offered an insightful analysis in "Power and Powerlessness: A Case in Point," *CTSA Proceedings* 37 (1982): 116–19, noting that the decision should continue to be reexamined and that the choice of the Sisters of Mercy to remain silent at the time was made in the hope "that theirs and other voices may ultimately prevail." She also acknowledged

that there was a danger in the "unfinished story" she had told, namely, "that the silence will grow, and that the power in the Church will be more and more isolated, especially from the experience of women" (119).

19. "Case Study: Trust, Translation, and HAART," with commentaries by Christy A. Rentmeester and Dayle B. DeLancey, *Hastings Center Report* 38 (November–December, 2008): 13.

20. Ibid., 14.

21. Ibid.

22. Daniel Finn, "Can This Market Be Saved?" *U.S. Catholic* (March 2009), 15.

23. See Jacqueline Novogratz, *The Blue Sweater: Bridging the Gap between Rich and Poor in an Interconnected World* (New York: Rodale, 2009).

24. Ibid., 254.

25. Bernard Häring, "Building a Creative Conscience," trans. Ingrid Knapp, *Commonweal* (August 11, 1989): 433.

26. Ibid., 435.

14
GOING AFTER A LIFE

The Myth and Mystery of Vocation

This extraordinary essay is very personal in its always implicit indications of how Anne Patrick found and developed her own spiritual vocation, and on the other very broad in its implications for entirely secular vocations as well as religious ones. While recognizing the roots of vocation in both myth and mystery, she also stresses our own responsibility for discernment. Her emphasis on how provisional and gradual the recognition of a vocation can be has many implications for policy within the church and in many other arenas of life. —HD

By the phrase "Going After a Life" I want to capture the desire we all feel to "make something of ourselves," to use our talents well, to make a difference for the better, and, at a minimum, "not to have lived in vain." The phrase is paradoxical, for we already *have* a life if we can bring such a feeling to consciousness, and yet we know there is a difference between merely living and "having a life" in the rich sense I mean it. Don't we know this from the rejoinder, "Get a life!"?

My thesis is that the classic idea of vocation is useful for this project of "Going After a Life" that makes a difference for the better, as long as we don't take the idea of calling too literally, or too passively. An author I admire, Andrea Lee, includes a teenage character named Sarah Phillips who longs for a signal as "unmistakeable as the blare of an automobile horn" to tell her what she should do at a turning point in her life.[1] Most of us can identify with Sarah's wish, though we are not surprised when things don't happen that way for her. Nor are we

---

Adapted from the Koch Lecture in Roman Catholic Studies at the College of St. Benedict, St. Joseph, Minnesota, given in March 2008. This lecture contributed to the fourth chapter of Patrick's book, Conscience and Calling *(2013).*

likely to get an unmistakable sign ourselves, much as we might wish for an automobile horn, or a fortune cookie with the formula for our future neatly printed on a slip of paper.

Instead I suggest that the traditional notion of vocation can guide our search for a life that we can affirm as uniquely positive and uniquely ours, if we are willing to confront the myth and mystery of vocation with discerning minds and generous hearts. My exploration has been inspired by many authors, and especially by Margaret Farley, RSM, a prominent moral theologian. Her early volume, *Personal Commitments*, probes the obligations we create for ourselves when we promise to love within a particular context, and asks whether our obligations may change as circumstances develop over time.[2] Although Farley doesn't focus directly on "vocation" as such, her reflections on personal commitments are a great resource for thinking in new ways about the concept. She provides a new metaphor for this idea of vocation, namely that of a "framework for love." I will come back to this idea of a framework for love later, but first I want to enlarge on the second part of my title, "The Myth and Mystery of Vocation." I believe "vocation" involves *both* myth and mystery. On the one hand, vocation involves a story-saturated symbol of tremendous power, which we can call a myth in the positive anthropological sense of that term. On the other hand, vocation also involves a mystery, and therefore eludes any attempts at full certainty about what we should be doing with our lives. So I will begin with the myth and mystery of vocation and then discuss this metaphor of vocation as a framework for love. Then I will give some examples of vocation as a "work in progress," and conclude with some practical suggestions.

THE MYTH OF VOCATION

Theologian John Shea describes religious myth as a story that does three things: it shapes consciousness, encourages attitudes, and suggests behaviors. He defines myth as "that story or formulation which establishes the world within which we live and out of which we act."[3] It is in this rich sense that one can speak of the myth of vocation. As Andrew Greeley stresses in *The Jesus Myth*, "There is nothing more real than [human] symbols and myths," understanding myths not as false ideas but rather in the sense of narratives that convey the fullest possible truth about the meaning of human existence.[4]

For Christians, the idea of particular callings in life is[5] grounded in many biblical accounts of God or Jesus summoning people to tasks and indeed to life-projects. The early chapters of Genesis establish a pattern whereby God speaks with human beings, and this metaphor of conversation between Creator and creature often extends to stories of a special divine summons. The story of the covenant with Abraham is a prime example, as is the episode we hear in the Easter Vigil about the prophet Samuel being roused several times from sleep by a call from God. Likewise the gospels portray Jesus calling fishermen to abandon their nets and become "fishers of men," summoning a tax-collector to abandon that work and become an apostle, and sending Mary Magdalene to tell the disciples the news of his resurrection.

From such narratives we get the concept of vocation, the idea that individuals have a life task we are destined to figure out and fulfill. A sense of vocation is very deeply etched into Western consciousness. Fundamentalists tend to speak of being called by God as if it were an actual summons, as if there were a "thing" called vocation out there somewhere to be experienced and known. Less literal Christians may not expect such clarity, but our imaginations have been deeply affected by stories of God calling individuals to tasks in life. Even secular persons speak of being called by the community, or by the times, or by one's deepest self, to undertake this or that life-project. And once a language of vocation is adopted, ethical judgments soon follow, particularly judgments about fidelity and infidelity. The good person is faithful to the demands of her calling, the good parent puts the welfare of the child above his own, the good artist is true to her vision.

THE MYSTERY OF VOCATION

The powerful myth that there is such a thing as a life-calling should be balanced by a counterweight, namely the recognition that the meaning and purpose of my life is ultimately a religious mystery, to be discerned gradually over the course of my existence. The biblical stories of callings and the subsequent literature of vocation are misleading if they are not interpreted in the context of the Mystery that created us and sustains us in being. Since God transcends our knowledge, and since the meaning and purpose of our lives is finally bound up in our relationship with God, there can be no complete answer to the question of our life-calling within the finite frame of our existence. What this means is not that the idea of vocation is worthless, but simply that our process of discernment must proceed with humility. The question of vocation amounts to the continual voicing of what James Gustafson has identified as the basic question of Christian ethics: "What is God enabling and requiring me to be and to do?"[5] Not just in this or that particular moment of my life, but for a significant portion of my life, and maybe even the "rest of my life."

Furthermore, although everyone's vocation is ultimately a religious mystery, there remains value in doing the hard work of ethical analysis about the matter. As Margaret Farley has said, "It is possible . . . to enter more deeply into the questions—to take a lantern, as it were, and walk into what may ultimately be a mystery to us, but which we do not deserve to call a mystery until we have entered it as far as we can go."[6]

THE DIMENSIONS OF VOCATION

So, having said a bit about the myth and the mystery of vocation, let me propose that we analyze an individual's vocation as a composite that involves three sorts of callings. First, everyone has a basic call to holiness. This is a succinct way of stating the biblical command to love God with our whole heart and soul and strength and our neighbor as ourselves (Mt 22:37–39). In the *Dogmatic Constitution on the Church*, the Second Vatican Council stated: "it is evident to everyone that all the faithful of Christ of whatever rank or status are called to the fullness of the Christian life and to the perfection of charity."[7] Second, beyond the fundamental call to holiness, there is the sense of being invited to focus love and creativity (and sexual energy) in a particular life-context. This is the meaning that vocation has had for many Catholics. We are accustomed to link the idea with the sacraments of matrimony and holy orders, or with a call to practice celibacy in community or individual life, speaking of these various states of life as things that God invites us to enter. Third, there is the matter of the many possible occupations that become vocations to the extent that they are seen as more than mere jobs. This third sort of calling, to productive secular activity, was emphasized especially by the reformers Luther and Calvin, who felt that the Roman Catholic stress on the clerical and vowed religious states had tended to obscure the baptismal vocation to holiness that belonged to all believers.

The distinction between a vocation in this occupational sense and a mere job depends on factors that are elusive but real. A given occupation fits somewhere on a continuum defined at one extreme in terms of economic utility ("What I do to earn a living") and at the other in terms of meaning and fit with one's unique capacities and inclinations ("The work I was born to accomplish"). Frederich Buechner's oft-cited characterization of vocation as "the place where your deep gladness meets the world's deep need" describes this very well.[8] This occupational sort of vocation goes beyond what we think of as a job or career to include our sense of being called to devote time and energy to various persons, projects, and causes. For example, to volunteer as a tutor, or get involved in protest or political action, can be an aspect of our vocation.

The three dimensions of vocation I have just outlined—the fundamental call to holiness, the call to a state of life such as marriage or the religious sisterhood, and the call to particular occupations, activities, or causes—are intimately connected with each other. Each concerns the love of God and neighbor, which is the fundamental obligation of everyone. The call to holiness is another way of stating the command to love God with one's whole heart, mind, soul, and strength, and one's neighbor as oneself. A vocation to a state of life such as marriage or celibacy establishes a focus and context for interpersonal love and sexual expression or abstinence. And a vocation to an occupation, cause, or project establishes the setting for labor suffused with love. The responses to these multiple callings can be separated out for purposes of analysis, and there are often conflicts over which demand takes precedence on a given day, but ultimately they are united in the will to love.

Having established the three basic dimensions of our callings and their common relationship to love, we still face many questions about this matter of vocation. What is it that lends such solidity to the idea of vocation? What gives it power and substance, the ability to demand countless deeds of fidelity over a lifetime? What is it that dissolves that substance and frees one from a formerly felt sense of obligation, or perhaps instead realigns that sense of obligation? I believe that the power of the concept of vocation depends on a process that combines the passive experiences of attraction and insight, and the active response of commitment. The passive side of the process involves the reception of a gift, known theologically as a grace, and the active side involves a series of decisions in response to this gift, including the choices to attend to what is attractive, to affirm the love that is evoked, and to promise future deeds of love. The power builds from the interaction of the passive and active aspects of the experience, sustained by a conviction that the ultimate source of the inclination is God, the Creator of one's life.

Because our vocations are complex, having several dimensions to them, and because ultimately they are part of the mystery of our relationship with God, we will not know for sure what our full vocation has been until our life is completed and we are at rest in God. But this side of eternity we can go forward with hope, embracing sometimes a strand of what seems to be our calling, and at other times perhaps a larger section. If we make these small and large choices with the sense that this step will allow for the love of neighbor to be linked with a grateful response to the gifts of God, we can be confident that there is something analogous between our situation and that of the biblical persons who have accepted a call. What is happening to me in this attraction, this sense that here indeed is the place where my own "deep gladness meets the world's great need," is like what those first disciples of Jesus experienced when they heard him say, "Come, follow me." And at the same time it is an altogether different experience, unique to my circumstances today.

So, to sum up, here's how I see the import of vocation as both myth and mystery. The myth of vocation structures our consciousness to be aware of possibilities for focusing our love and other talents, and it encourages us to take risks and let go of some possibilities for the sake of what seems most important, at least for now. And awareness of the ultimate mystery of our vocation frees us from the need to be absolutely certain about our choice of career and life context, and instead allows us to trust that if we have made a good effort to discern the dimensions of our call, God will bring us along in life to where we are meant to go.

FRAMEWORK FOR LOVE

I want to return to something that Margaret Farley has contributed to my thinking on vocation, namely the metaphor of a "framework for love." I like this metaphor because it helps us get beyond naïve expectations that a vocation is something out there, summoning us like an automobile horn. Derived from the human activity of building, the metaphor of a framework for love respects realities we might otherwise miss, especially the role that our own freedom plays in the sense of attraction of a calling. A framework is useful but provisional, and so are the settings in which human beings are meant to respond to God's love for us. The frameworks have moral weight, but they are not ultimately binding in themselves, because God alone is the proper object of an absolute love.[9] The metaphor of framework takes away the mystique of vocation and assigns human responsibility properly. Frameworks have been humanly built.

This metaphor also highlights the *active* dimension of our vocation, something recognized by other writers who seek to demystify the experience of vocation and acknowledge our role as co-creators of our own vocations. Douglas Schuurman, for example, has written that it is a "misconception" to think of vocation as providing a "blueprint" for life or an "unmistakable, miraculous call." Rather the "call" is mediated in "numerous and quiet ways," and is essentially a matter of employing "one's God-given gifts to be of use to the broader community."[10] Sandra Schneiders, who has written extensively about Catholic religious life, also wants to minimize miraculous interpretations of the imagery of call. Faith in God's guidance does not require that this call occur outside normal processes of attraction and influence. Far from being a thunderclap from the sky, for Schneiders the experience of vocation involves a

> convergence of interior factors such as attraction, talent, interest, experience, desires, ideals, and even realistic fears and awareness of personal limitations, with exterior factors such as people I admire, work that interests me, opportunity presenting itself, needs that move me, structures that facilitate exploration, invitation from another. This convergence is usually a rich mixture that is both confusing and exciting and leads a person to begin to explore what this might mean.[11]

VOCATION: A WORK IN PROGRESS

To put some flesh on the bones of my theory about vocation as myth, mystery, and a framework for love, let me share two stories about women I know who are discerning their vocations in ways I find interesting. Each has spoken publicly, and neither has completed her life, so the stories of their vocations are like our own, in that their vocations are not finally settled, but works in progress.

The first story is about a young woman named Elizabeth Robinson, who graduated from Carleton College with a religion major in 2001.[12] My colleagues and I had recognized her leadership abilities and appointed her to a position we give to two seniors each year, called Student Departmental Advisor. Elizabeth did a fine job, advising younger students, helping us hire a tenure track specialist in Islam, and designing a department t-shirt that proclaimed, "Carleton Religion Department: Synthesizing the finite and the infinite since 1955." She wrote a senior essay about the debate on the relative merits of religion and spirituality, and gave it the intriguing title, "No Monopoly on Kooks."

When it came time to graduate, Elizabeth did not have a clear sense of a career path to follow, but she was conscious that she had received much in life, including a good education, and so she decided to volunteer for a year with an organization called World-Teach. In 2002 she was assigned to a rural school in Namibia, a large country in southern Africa, just north of the Republic of South Africa and west of Botswana. Her assignment involved teaching English and math, and running the school's HIV-AIDS awareness and prevention club. She spent the year in very foreign surroundings, teaching young teens at a rural boarding school many hours' drive from the capital, in a largely desert country where about a quarter of the population was HIV positive. She took her meals with the nuns who ran the school, two Namibians and two Germans, and she entered into local life as much as possible.

After that first year she came home to the comforts of Connecticut for a visit, but she returned in early 2003 to spend another year at the school. In her work with the HIV-AIDS club, Elizabeth had been shocked to discover how much knowledge was lacking even among teachers, and she began to design creative educational materials and activities to be sure that the teens really understood the ABCs of HIV prevention. While the ABC program was somewhat controversial, such an integrated approach has proven the most effective way of preventing infections in Africa: A is for "abstinence," B for "be faithful," and C for "use a condom." Early on Elizabeth had realized that "just teaching English or math skills wasn't enough," since "these kids [weren't] going to put their English to use if they're dead" from AIDS. Having seen good results from her own teaching about prevention, she came back from Namibia at the end of 2003 with a sense of mission. She was determined to raise money that would allow her to publish a culturally sensitive HIV/AIDS resource guide for Namibian teachers, and to edit and distribute a prevention video that she and her partner at the time, Geoffrey Silver, had filmed with the students in her school.

Three years out of college Elizabeth found herself the CEO of a non-profit foundation called Sekolo Projects Inc. Sekolo means "school" in Setswana, the language spoken in the village where Elizabeth taught, and one of the thirteen languages spoken in Namibia. The mission of Sekolo Projects is to prevent new HIV infections in young people by providing and supporting education, physical care, and psychosocial support to those living with and affected by HIV. And this in a region where in 2002 one household in six was caring for an AIDS orphan, where the average life expectancy had dropped from seventy to forty-three years because of AIDS, and where half of new infections were among fifteen to twenty-four year olds. Since 2004, Elizabeth has traveled extensively on behalf of Sekolo Projects, training teachers and implementing her programs. With help from her parents and her Episcopal church in Connecticut, Robinson recruited a board of trustees that includes experts in education and disease prevention. By 2006 she had traveled to eleven of the country's thirteen regions, giving fifty-three workshops for nearly a thousand Namibian teachers. She has since gone on to establish a new organization, Sekolo Projects Namibia, with indigenous directors, and new programs that include support for orphans and vulnerable children, especially girls.

Elizabeth, I think we will agree, has accomplished much since she completed her religion major. She certainly "has a life," even though it doesn't fit the standard expectation of a young professional on a career track. She doesn't, for example, have a graduate degree, or even a mortgage. But she impresses me as living very fully into her vocation because she has listened with an open heart to what she experienced from living with and listening to others, and from listening to her own heart. And I believe she has discerned the call of God in this process—not a call that settles all the questions of her future, but rather one that says, for now, she should continue to use her talents for this cause of HIV prevention among a population devastated by the disease.

She reminds me in interesting ways of the young woman who founded my own religious congregation back in Quebec in 1844. Eulalie Durocher, now beatified and celebrated on October 6 as Blessed Marie Rose Durocher, was a young woman who saw a great need—in her case a need for basic education among the poor, especially girls—and who responded by gathering other women around her to teach them. In the nineteenth century the structures of canonical religious life were the most effective way for Eulalie Durocher to get this done, and in the twenty-first century Elizabeth Robinson has used the structures of a 501c charitable organization in the U.S. and its equivalent in Namibia. But in important respects they are similar: both were young women of faith who saw a need, responded to it wholeheartedly, and inspired others to come along and contribute to the mission.

Last January Elizabeth gave a talk on her work with Sekolo Projects at Carleton College, and the next day she came to my Christian ethics class for informal conversation. She had mentioned the loneliness she felt when she was a volunteer teacher in that rural boarding school, so far from home and the comforts of Western culture, and one of the students asked what had sustained her during that lonely time. Elizabeth's response was not what I expected: "Well," she said, "having chocolate now and then was a big help."

I'd been impressed by the fact that she had stayed at the rural school on weekends, whereas a volunteer who took her place in 2004 had a driver each weekend take her to the capital for a "Western" cultural fix. I was sure there was more than chocolate helping Elizabeth decide to share the simple life in the country with her students, lonely as she often felt, and I pressed her to say more about what had sustained her during her years of volunteer teaching. She later responded in more depth, describing something of the complex process of vocational discernment as it goes on in the midst of a busy life at age twenty-three or twenty-four.

> I attended Mass regularly with the kids, my teacher colleagues and the Sisters that I lived with. I found the singing enjoyable, but the entire service was in a language I couldn't understand, [and] it wasn't always a religious experience, or even nurturing to my faith. However, I enjoyed the community aspect of worship, and could participate in the community gatherings. [After a year in Namibia I went home for a visit, and] I recall that taking Communion at my home church over Christmas 2002 was a very moving experience [because as an Episcopalian] I had not received Communion for the entire year, as the Mokaleng church was Catholic. I had a small travel Bible with me, which I read occasionally, but didn't find great comfort in. Rather, the words I could remember from my years singing in the church choir, were a great source of comfort... Occasionally, in difficult and lonely times, I would think of my experience in Namibia in comparison to Jesus' time in the wilderness or desert—this was my desert. It was indeed a time of paring down and focusing on my core—who I was and what I needed in my life in order to experience fulfillment and in order to hear God's call. The whole experience made those things in my life that are "excess" or "extraneous" stand out vividly.

Elizabeth is not thirty yet, and her process of discerning the various dimensions of her vocation is by no means over. A vocation is always a "work in progress" while we are alive. Her example helps us to see the myth and mystery of this process, as well how our own activity helps to shape the frameworks within which our love can most effectively be expressed. Note particularly how she sees compatibility between experiencing her own fulfillment and hearing God's call. As she says of her desert time, "It was indeed a time of paring down and focusing on my core—who I was and what I needed in my life in order to experience fulfillment and in order to hear God's call."

My second example is someone further along in life. Patricia Fresen was born in South Africa to a family of European ancestry about 1940.[13] After graduating from high school she joined a congregation of Dominican sisters, and perhaps she thought at the time, or a few years later when she made her vows, that the question of her vocation was settled. For seventeen years she served as a teacher or school principal, all of them during the apartheid era. Black and white sisters lived together in her religious community, and this violation of an unjust law seemed right to the Dominicans, who answered to a higher law. The government turned a blind eye to their interracial living situation, but was not so tolerant when as a young principal, Fresen undertook to welcome black students to her school in the early 1970s. With help from Archbishop Denis Hurley and members of the African National Congress, she spent a year preparing parents, teachers, and students for what would be a notable violation of the apartheid laws. When a number of black students joined the white student body, Fresen was arrested and jailed overnight. She expected to be tortured, but was released with legal support from the archdiocese. During subsequent years, the school remained integrated.

Several years later, Fresen's religious superiors asked her to study theology in Rome, which she did for seven years in the 1980s. As she studied with Dominican and Jesuit seminarians her vocational question emerged in a new key: she felt a longing to become a priest. This was not a new desire on her part, but one she had "always suppressed . . . since it was unthinkable." Others in Rome, including two of her professors, had given qualified support to her longing: If ever women should be ordained, they said, she had the gifts that would make her a good priest. After these studies Fresen returned to South Africa and joined the staff of the national seminary in Pretoria, where for seven years she taught systematic theology, homiletics, and spirituality. Like a number of talented women, she taught preaching to seminarians, but could not preach herself. And keep in mind that her order, the Dominicans, uses the initials O.P., which stands for "Order of Preachers." "During these years at the seminary," she recalls, "I experienced much gender discrimination, but the desire to minister as a priest was growing stronger. People who knew me well confirmed their sense of my call to priesthood, but there was much fear about the consequences." But by then she had decided it was too late for her anyway; she felt too old to think of ordination for herself, and so she would devote her energies to preparing another generation for that possibility.

Meanwhile the apartheid era finally ended after a long struggle, and Nelson Mandela took office as president of the new South Africa in 1994. Soon after that, the nation's first Catholic university was founded in Johannesburg, and Fresen, by then a doctor of theology, accepted a position there in 1999. A year later I visited South Africa and was introduced to Fresen as a leader of the church in the Johannesburg area. We spoke of many things, especially racism, but somehow did not get around to the question of women's ordination. I recall being very impressed by her character and her faith, and when I later learned that she had been ordained a priest in 2003 in a ceremony not recognized by the Vatican, I knew this was not something Patricia Fresen would have done lightly. Indeed, she paid a high price for answering what she perceived as a call to violate a law of the Catholic Church in the hope that such action would contribute toward the eventual reform of church law and Catholic practice, much as breaking the laws of apartheid had led to a more just government in her country. Her ordination cost her both her teaching job at the Catholic university, and her membership in the Dominican congregation, to which she had belonged for forty-five years. When she spoke at Carleton College in 2006 she said that leaving the Dominicans was the hardest thing in her life, adding: "I will always be a Dominican in my heart."

My present interest is not so much the larger question of women's ordination in the Catholic Church, a reform movement that I have supported in print since 1972, but whose ultimate success or failure where Roman Catholicism is concerned we are not in a position to know. The jury is still out on whether in a century or two Fresen will be thought of as more like Catherine of Siena or Martin Luther, and my general understanding of the womenpriests movement[14] to which she is so deeply committed is expressed in something the first-century Jew Gamaliel said about the preaching of Peter, which we read in chapter 5 of the Acts of the Apostles: "For if this idea of theirs or its execution is of human origin, it will collapse; but if it is from God, you will never be able to put them down…" (5:38–39). Indeed, I think Fresen has been profoundly influenced by this chapter of Acts, and has developed her theology of prophetic obedience with the example of Peter himself in mind. When Peter and the others were called before the Council, the high priest declared: "'We expressly ordered you,' he said, 'to desist from teaching in that name; and what has happened? You have filled Jerusalem with your teaching…' Peter replied for himself and the apostles: 'We must obey God rather than men'" (5:27–29).

This is not the place to go into the details of her theology of prophetic obedience, which grounds the actions she has taken against apartheid and also in the womenpriests movement. What I want to focus on here is the way Fresen's story, very much a work-in-progress, captures some of the dynamics of the complex, lifelong process of vocational discernment. Her own desires played a large part in Fresen's experience of the call to priestly service, but her religious superiors had sent her to Rome where that desire was kindled, and she had also received affirmation from her students, professors, and colleagues. And, in 2002 she received an explicit invitation to priesthood from some European leaders of the womenpriests movement.

I should note something about the leadership of this movement. The names of the seven women first ordained on the Danube in 2002 are known, but we do not know the identity of the European bishop in good standing with Rome who subsequently, in 2003, ordained Christine Mayr-Lumetzberger and Gisela Foster as bishops so that apostolic succession can be publicly passed on in ceremonies of the movement. In 2005, the same bishop ordained Fresen a bishop. I think it is important to say that although Fresen had long desired to serve as a priest, and undertook this ministry with joy despite the price she paid, she was very clear that she was not called into clericalism, and she had no ambition to be a bishop. In fact, when one of the European male bishops asked her in 2004 if she would be willing to be ordained a bishop so that women's ordinations could continue, she turned him down. "I never wanted to be a bishop," she objected, and besides, it's enough to adjust to living in a new country and having a new ministry as coordinator of the formation program for the womenpriests movement.

Nonetheless, in a move that reminds me of the repetition of calls we get in such biblical stories as the one about Samuel, a year later this male bishop asked to meet with Fresen again. He said he didn't want to push her into anything, but only to consider his reasons for wanting to ordain her a bishop. These reasons included the fact that his own status as a bishop in good standing with Rome was somewhat precarious, the fact that most of the women in the movement were from North America, and none of the European women bishops were native speakers of English, and the facts of her age—you are not getting younger—and her doctorate in theology and experience teaching in a seminary. Fresen listened politely, but was swayed only when he offered his final reason: "Patricia, if we ordain you, it is not for you. It is for the people on whom you will lay hands. You will pass on the apostolic succession that was passed on to me. Please start thinking about this, and let us know if you are willing." At that point she declared, "I am ready." And so on January 2, 2005, this man ordained Fresen a bishop, in a ceremony where he openly wept as he anointed her with chrism. "That I have lived to see this day" was a sentiment Fresen had voiced when Nelson Mandela was sworn in as president of South Africa, and later when she learned that women had been ordained priests in Europe. It was evidently the male bishop's feeling in 2005 as well. Since then Fresen has been happy to ordain many women as priests and deacons, in various parts of the United States and Canada.

CONCLUSION

These two stories illustrate some of the main elements of my theory of vocation. The life-shaping myth that vocations exist has led both Elizabeth and Patricia to listen for the promptings of God's spirit in their own hearts, in what is happening around them, and in the words of others they respect. Each has accepted and even helped to construct certain frameworks within which to live out her call to love God and neighbor, and each sees her vocation as a work-in-progress, the full meaning of which is ultimately a mystery.

I end very briefly on a practical note. I have two suggestions for all who ponder their own vocations, at whatever stage of life. The first is to read biographies, to see the many ways that women and men have discerned, followed, and shaped their vocations. On the list of items for further exploration is one title to get you started, Robert Ellsberg's book about women saints, prophets, and witnesses for our time, *Blessed among All Women*.[15] The entries are very short, and if a reader has interest in a particular woman, Ellsberg provides additional resources.

The second suggestion involves what I call a "Four Step Process for Discernment." The shaping of our lives comes as a result of many decisions; when facing a particular question it can be helpful to employ a four-column technique. For example, if the question is the one Elizabeth Robinson faced in 2001—whether to volunteer for World Teach— Elizabeth could divide a page into four columns with the headings: pro World Teach, con World Teach, pro *not* World Teach, and con *not* World Teach. She would then fold the paper so that only one heading is visible, and prayerfully list all the reasons supporting that position. Then she would move to the second column, and so on. It might seem redundant to itemize the reasons *for* doing something and also the reasons *against not doing it*, along with those *in favor of not doing it* and *against doing it*, but different feelings and insights can come from posing the question in slightly different ways. The goal is not to come up with a mathematical proof that one decision is perfectly right, but rather to give ourselves time to attend to as many relevant considerations as possible and to be instructed by the patterns that take shape. At some point that you will detect, a provisional answer will be given, and you can proceed on that basis with a peaceful heart.

This method is a simple tool, but often simple things can help us at a level of spiritual depth. As the founder of the Catholic Worker movement Dorothy Day said at the conclusion of her own narrative of vocation, *The Long Loneliness*, "We have all known the long loneliness and we have learned that the only solution is love and that love comes with community. It all happened while we sat there talking, and it is still going on."[16] This has been going on since the beginning of Christianity, and it is still going on tonight and tomorrow in this conference.

Notes

1. See Andrea Lee, *Sarah Phillips* (New York: Penguin Books, 1984), 20.

2. Margaret A. Farley, *Personal Commitments: Beginning, Keeping, Changing* (San Francisco: Harper Row, 1986). This edition is used here but the book has since been reprinted by Orbis Books (2013).

3. John Shea, *Stories of God: An Unauthorized Biography* (Chicago: Thomas More Press, 1978), 52.

4. Andrew Greeley, *The Jesus Myth* (Garden City, NY: Doubleday & Company, 1971), 13. Greeley's prefatory Note begins with a defense of his title: "The word 'myth' is used in the title of this volume in a specific and definite sense. A myth is a symbolic story which demonstrates, in Alan Watts' words, 'the inner meaning of the universe and of human life.' To say that Jesus is a myth is not to say that he is a legend but that his life and message are an attempt to demonstrate 'the inner meaning of the universe and of human life.'" I concur with Greeley's judgment that there is great value in employing this term that is so "common among historians of religion, literary critics, and social scientists" and that Christians should overcome their fear of the word "myth" and appropriate it as a valuable tool for understanding their faith (12).

5. James M. Gustafson, *Can Ethics Be Christian?* (Chicago: University of Chicago Press, 1975), 179.

6. Farley, *Personal Commitments*, 11.

7. Vatican II, *Dogmatic Constitution on the Church* (Lumen Gentium), #32–39. All citations from the Second Vatican Council are from Walter M. Abbott, ed., *The Documents of Vatican II* (New York: America Press, 1966).

8. Frederick Buechner, *Wishful Thinking* (1993), 119. Cited here from Parker J. Palmer, *Let Your Life Speak: Listening for the Voice of Vocation* (San Francisco: Jossey-Bass, 2000).

9. Farley, *Personal Commitments*, 22, 84, 92, 99, and elsewhere. Subsequent references to this volume will be made parenthetically whenever possible.

10. Douglas J. Schuurman, *Vocation: Discerning Our Callings in Life* (Grand Rapids, MI: William B. Eerdmans, 2004), 127.

11. Sandra Schneiders, IHM, *Religious Life in a New Millennium: Locating Catholic Religious Life in a New Ecclesial and Cultural Context*, vol. 2, *Selling All* (New York: Paulist Press, 2001), 12–13.

12. Elizabeth Robinson has completed her work with Sekolo Projects and the foundations are now closed after distributing funds in Namibia. She has earned a Master's Degree in Development Studies and is currently completing a Mas-

ter's Degree in Public Health at New York University where she is also employed. She has a mortgage now and continues to ponder vocational questions.

13. Patricia Fresen continues some leadership with the Roman Catholic Women Priest Movement in Europe but mainly has been working in South Africa "for our model of priesthood, which is much more democratic, non-clericalist, inclusive and transparent than the traditional male model of priesthood." She lives in Stuttgart, and with Ida Raming leads a monthly Eucharist for a small community and assists when someone is sick or dying and wants a priest. Her main focus today is helping in South Africa.

14. Roman Catholic Womenpriests (RCWP) is an international initiative within the Roman Catholic Church. The mission of Roman Catholic Womenpriests North America is to spiritually prepare, ordain, and support women and men from all states of life, who are theologically qualified, who are committed to an inclusive model of church, and who are called by the Holy Spirit and their communities to minister within the Roman Catholic Church.

15. Robert Ellsberg, *Blessed among All Women: Women Saints, Prophets, and Witnesses for Our Time* (New York: Crossroad Publishing, 2005).

16. Dorothy Day, *The Long Loneliness* (1952; Harper San Francisco, 2006), 286.

15

GETTING READY FOR VOICE LESSONS

Toward a Catholic Feminist Ethics of Spirituality

Here Anne Patrick forcefully opposes the widely accepted contrast be-
tween religion and spirituality. Instead, she recommends both/and.
Suggesting connections between religion and spirituality, she dis-
cusses virtues that should be common to both—self-care, solidarity,
humility, and courage—stressing the need for balance and the cen-
trality of love. —HD

This is not an easy time to be a Catholic. It is an easy time to be
discouraged and to withdraw from the community fully or par-
tially, to exercise the option of "exit" in response to disillusionment with the institution. And it is a very easy time in which to
exercise an angry and resentful "voice." Both of these responses
are understandable. Neither is a particularly constructive option, consistent with our baptismal calling or with the long-
term good of the Christian community. Instead, I believe we
need to be developing a loyal voice, imagining and bringing
into being the church that God would have us live in, in this
place, in these times.

— Mary Jo Bane[1]

Just as human relationships are or ought to be governed by certain norms or ethical principles—in particular, norms of justice;
so also, institutional frameworks for commitment in human relationships ought to be subject to norms of justice. If they are

---

Adapted from a chapter of the same title in Feminist Catholic Theological Ethics:
Conversations in the World Church, *ed. Linda Hogan and A. E. Orobator (Mary-*
knoll, NY: Orbis Books, 2014), 258–68.

222

not, we challenge or forsake them, or we shrivel up within them.

—Margaret A. Farley[2]

These passages from eminent U.S. Roman Catholic thinkers frame the considerations I will raise here about the tendency to compare "religion" unfavorably with "spirituality," thereby justifying the relinquishment of church involvement. Social policy expert Mary Jo Bane, a professor at Harvard University's Kennedy School of Government, recognizes the appeal that withdrawal from Catholicism has for many Americans, but instead advocates developing a "loyal voice." Such a voice, she maintains, is "attentive to revelation and respectful of tradition but also confidently prophetic and visionary and as radical as the voice of the One who lives in the church forever."[3] Theological ethicist Margaret A. Farley, for decades a professor at Yale University Divinity School, wrote the words quoted above about the institution of marriage, but they are applicable as well to other institutional contexts in which Catholics discern what God is calling us to do, including the church itself. Farley summarizes the options well: challenging injustice in our institutions, leaving these institutions, or "shriveling up" within them.

In what follows I advocate developing an "ethics of spirituality," something that is preliminary to the construction of an "ethics of church participation," a project too large to begin here.[4] Such new foci for ethical reflection are, I believe, important for the well-being of Catholicism in the United States, and perhaps elsewhere as well. As a first step, I object to the tendency to oppose spirituality to religion, which may be contributing to the diminishment of one of the chief resources of our tradition, namely the idealistic and energetic young persons who were raised as Catholics but are easily disillusioned by the ineptitude, sins, and scandals that abound in our leaders, members, and structures. It cannot be a matter of indifference to theological ethics, especially in a world church, if the next generation of American Catholics lacks the loyal, prophetic voices that Bane advocates, or opts for leaving the church or shriveling up within it instead of calling Catholicism to live up to its ideals, as Farley's words suggest is preferable. Below, then, I describe the sociological context in which I object to the uncritical opposition of religion and spirituality. I then critique a popular articulation of this opposition, and argue that, instead of idealizing spirituality at the expense of religion, it is important to ask the same moral questions of both secular and religious forms of spirituality. Finally, I propose several qualities of character that both would do well to foster, and commend perspectives that value both religion and spirituality.

THE RISE OF THE "NONES" AND THE SPIRITUALITY-RELIGION DICHOTOMY

In the last half-century the shift of emphasis from an ethic of obedience to an ethic of responsibility has meant that contemporary Catholics are generally more willing to look critically at the institutional contexts of their lives than were believers of the mid-twentieth century, at least in the United States.[5] Indeed, many have been critical enough to leave the church entirely, so that by 2007 "former Catholics" comprised 10 percent of the U.S. population, outnumbering nearly all religious denominations, except the groups that still identified themselves as Catholic or Baptist. Nearly half of these former Catholics joined Protestant groups, a small number joined other religions, and about half claimed no religious affiliation.[6]

There is every indication that the trend toward disaffiliation will increase, as a 2012 study by the Pew Research Center has shown. In their report, "'Nones' on the Rise: One-in-Five Adults Have No Religious Affiliation," researchers found that 34 percent of Americans born during 1990–1994 checked "none" on a survey inquiring about religious affiliation, in contrast to only 5 percent of the generation born during 1913–1927. The 2012 survey also showed that for the first time in U.S. history Protestant Christians comprise less than half of the adult population, and while Catholics have remained "roughly steady" at about one-fourth of the population, an influx of immigrants from Latin America has masked the loss of many U.S.-born Catholics. Although the U.S. remains a "highly religious" country in comparison with European democracies, the recent survey indicates that it is becoming markedly less so, and Catholicism is rapidly losing members, especially younger ones. It is important to note that the decline in religious affiliation among Americans is happening mainly among *white* adults, while Americans of African and Hispanic-Latino descent are generally remaining religiously affiliated, though whether this will continue to be the case is uncertain.

The overall trend is clear. According to the 2012 study, the number of Americans who declare "none" when asked about their religious identity has risen to 46 million, nearly 20% of the adult population, compared to just over 15% in 2007, and "below 10% from the 1970s through the early 1990s." Current statistics for adults younger than thirty are even more striking, with one-third of them "religiously unaffiliated." Nevertheless, although they do not identify with a religion, "many of the country's 46 million unaffiliated adults are religious or spiritual in some way," with 68% saying they believe in God, 58% affirming feelings of "deep connection with nature and the earth," and 21% acknowledging they pray daily. Of particular interest here are the facts that 37% of the 46 million religiously unaffiliated Americans *"clas-sify themselves as 'spiritual' but not 'religious'"* and 74% *of them were raised in a religious tradition* (emphasis added).[7]

What factors allow, encourage, or justify this trend? Is it a trend that Catholic ethicists should be doing anything about? As interpreters of our moral tradition, should we merely observe or lament the loss, perhaps regarding it as inevitable given the state of church governance today, or should we be asking what can be done about it?

When I consider this trend toward disaffiliation of U.S. Catholics from the perspective of the world church I am deeply troubled. Despite its problems, institutional Catholicism has been a vessel of the gospel for our culture, and I do not see other institutions capable of challenging our racism, individualism, and consumerism, or calling us to love our different and distant neighbors as ourselves, with anything like the power that the church at its best can exert. Undoubtedly the reasons for the decline in Catholic affiliation are many and complex, but two factors are especially important for feminists, whether women or men. One involves the situation of injustice that Farley emphasizes, since church practice has not kept pace with the rhetoric of women's equal human dignity used in recent decades by popes and bishops. A second factor involves the anti-institutional bias that has been a recurrent theme in American culture, and is especially pronounced today. Catholics discerning what God is asking of them today conduct this discernment within a social context that regards both government and religion with considerably more skepticism than prevailed at the time of the Second Vatican Council. I believe this anti-institutional bias contributes to the uncritical preference for "spirituality" over "religion" among so many Americans.

SPIRITUALITY VS. RELIGION: A MISPLACED DEBATE

For years I have heard people say, "I don't belong to a religion, but I am into spirituality." Religion, they believe, is rigid and oppressive, while spirituality is altogether creative and liberating. Small wonder that they avoid identifying with an organized faith tradition, and instead affirm that spirituality is what keeps them going through life. They are happy to be independent of the ambiguous heritages that may have sustained their ancestors through poverty, war, disease, and dislocation, for something bright and free of flaws is available now.

For an extended articulation of this view one can turn to a volume by the popular writer Diarmuid O'Murchu, *Religion in Exile: A Spiritual*

Homecoming. The back-cover description is telling: "Following on his earlier work, *Reclaiming Spirituality*, Diarmuid O'Murchu continues to offer some penetrating and original insights into the changing and evolving spiritual awareness of our time, one that is rapidly outgrowing the time-honored but exhausted vision of formal religion."[8] There are indeed original insights in this book from 2000, but we also find strong echoes of Karl Marx, Mary Daly, and Matthew Fox, and far too little critical probing of their claims, especially those of Marx and Daly. O'Murchu declares, for example, that "While religion has aided the development of the human species," it has also "colluded with the patriarchal drive to exalt humanity over the rest of creation, thus breeding the ferocious anthropocentrism that reaps such havoc in our world today ...Religion in its essential essence is about alienation from the Earth and from the cosmos."[9]

Marx discerned that religion has functioned as an opiate, and that theological emphasis on the afterlife can lead to political passivity. But while religious beliefs have sometimes legitimated oppressive systems, and inhibited women and the poor from taking action to better their lives, religion has also inspired resistance and rebellion, a fact Marx failed to recognize.[10] Likewise, Daly deserves credit for having identified the patriarchal bias of world religions, starting with her own Roman Catholicism. The challenge Daly leveled in her groundbreaking book from 1973, *Beyond God the Father*, has inspired a generation of feminist scholars.[11] They are retrieving, re-imagining, and reconstructing religious thought and practice that respects women's full human dignity. Some do this work within their traditions, while others have walked away from the institutions that once nurtured their thirst for justice and for God. Finally, Matthew Fox has helped many readers see that too much stress on sin and redemption can skew the spiritual life by neglecting basic truths, such as the goodness of creation and the reality of divine incarnation.[12] Fox's own retrieval of a neglected heritage of creation-celebrating mysticism, epitomized in the brilliant works of Hildegard of Bingen, has added much to contemporary life. O'Murchu does well to look appreciatively at ideas from Marx, Daly, Fox, and others, but he goes too far when he endorses the outright rejection of institutional religion that Marx and Daly advocated.

The popular view that spirituality should supplant religion is also problematic for historical reasons. Historically, movements that define themselves as the opposite of institutional religion tend to institutionalize themselves and, although terminology may differ, functional resemblances to religion emerge. Individuals can live off the spiritual capital of their ancestors and their own youth for a while, but eventually there comes a need for shared stories and structures, and even for ritual and doctrine. This pendulum swing from a heavy emphasis on institutional participation to individual autonomy is just that: one doesn't strike a balance by foregoing organized religion altogether. Indeed, the happily unchurched may in time find themselves the aging parents or grand-parents of a new generation of devotees of a traditional faith, often a fundamentalist one, or of some new religious movement altogether.

What concerns me even more than the lessons from history are the moral implications of this trend. The belief that spirituality opposes or should supplant religion is elitist and dualistic, and it sometimes masks the unjust appropriation of cultural property of indigenous peoples.[13] Furthermore it is a naïve view of human nature and history. Would the Civil Rights Movement in this country have succeeded without the churches that provided the mimeographs, meeting spaces, and tele-phones, let alone the spiritual fire preached from the pulpits and alive in the people? What would have happened in South Africa if church leaders had not opposed apartheid policies and racist theology, as they did in the 1985 Kairos Document? Where would South Africa be today if religious radio had not preached the social gospel, if Regina Mundi Church had not provided a place for African National Congress mem-bers to gather in Soweto, and if black and white South Africans had been "into spirituality" instead of being involved in the churches?

Of course, organized religion can also be guilty of elitism, dualism, naïveté, and injustice, and Christianity was implicated in the evils of slavery and apartheid. My aim is to overcome the oppositional approach toward religion and spirituality, not simply to reverse the accusation that one is bad and the other good. My position is characteristically Catholic. Instead of accepting an *either/or* dichotomy I believe a *both/and* approach to the relationship between spirituality and religion is intellectually more adequate and morally more beneficial.[14] I am *not* saying that peo-ple who claim they are religious are better than those who avoid such statements in favor of saying they are "into spirituality." Nor am I say-ing the opposite. Rather I maintain that the cultural situation that fosters this way of describing things so that people feel they need to choose one or the other is problematic. Whose interests are served by opposing spirituality to religion? Who benefits when individuals sever ties with traditional communities of faith? Does it matter that often those who do this are affluent and well educated? Has "spirituality" become one more department in the aisles of today's supermarket of options for the liber-ally educated and affluent?

My conclusions are not as pessimistic as these critical questions might suggest, however, for I see promise in the fact that so many reli-giously unaffiliated Americans are willing to claim spirituality as a sig-nificant part of their identity. Perhaps this development reflects a new stage in the evolution of human religiosity, one that can benefit communities as well as individuals by promoting greater social justice and ecological responsibility. But for this to happen, such secular forms of spirituality need an ethic no less than do the traditional religious faiths. Both sorts of spirituality, the traditionally religious and the avowedly secular, should be asking the same moral questions. Does this spirituality build an inclusive community of justice and care? Does it offer hope to the poor and oppressed? Does it get at the truth of things? Does it promote the acquisition of virtue in its adherents, something that is not as easy as imagining oneself innocent, or wishing to be good?

TOWARD AN ETHICS OF SPIRITUALITY

As an initial step toward an ethics of spirituality, I will mention some qualities of character that both the avowedly religious and the avowedly secular forms of spirituality would do well to foster. I assume that all the virtues express and contribute to the perfection of love, and agree with Margaret Farley that justice must be the norm of love.[15] My list, which is by no means complete, describes qualities that contribute to a character capable of love that is just.

Self-care
Jesuit moral theologian James Keenan has proposed that self-care be considered a cardinal virtue.[16] In doing so, he resonates with a feminist scholar of religion, Valerie Saiving, who claimed in a ground-breaking 1960 article that the sins (and, by implication, the virtues) of women and men are affected by their differing social locations. Under patriarchy, the besetting temptations of women tend to involve not pride and self-aggrandizement but rather failure to have a centered self.[17] The appropriate correction is to recognize that cultivating proper self-esteem and caring for one's personal well being are essential aspects of fostering goodness, especially for those who have suffered from unjust power relationships. With regard to spirituality, self-care may entail, at times, a strategic withdrawal from religious systems or practices that are experienced as harmful, though it is a mistake to demonize these systems in the process.

Ideally such withdrawal would not be total or permanent. Even a feminist as critical of church patriarchy as Rosemary Radford Ruether argues against indefinite separation from the tradition and opposes the idea of separatism as an end in itself. Instead, she sees the independence of women from oppressive situations as a necessary stage on a journey toward a community of Christian women and men together engaged in liberation from patriarchy. Ruether is enough of a realist to know that a widely shared conversion from patriarchy is a long way off, and in *Women-Church* (1986) she recommends "neither leaving the church as a sectarian group nor continuing to fit into it on its terms." Instead she advocates "establishing bases for a feminist critical culture and celebrational community that have some autonomy from the established institutions."[18] She posits that historically the church is best understood as a dialectical interaction between two elements, namely the "historical institution" and the "spirit-filled community."[19]

In using this model it is important to recognize the presence of the Spirit in the larger historical institution, and not to assume that all truth and goodness reside with self-proclaimed prophetic feminists, much less that the latter are immune from error and sinfulness. Certainly the existing churches have a long way to go in the process of conversion from patriarchy, and self care vis-à-vis existing institutions represents both a necessary virtue and a great challenge to the traditionally religious. Self-care is also important for those whose spiritual affiliations involve less traditional groups. These groups are not immune from defects and oppressive ways simply because they define themselves as different from traditional religion.

Solidarity

All the virtues are related to the ideal of charity, and if self-care focuses on the quality of love for the self, solidarity is a way of characterizing the ideal relationship with one's neighbor. In *Mujerista Theology* (1996), the late theologian Ada María Isasi-Díaz argued that solidarity is the form that neighbor-love should take in our day. She saw it as a matter of effective, cohesive struggle governed by a shared understanding of issues.[20] But solidarity is much easier to talk about than to practice. In a 1994 address to the College Theology Society, African-American theologian M. Shawn Copeland cautioned that having common problems does not automatically lead to sisterhood. She said that Celtic-, Anglo-, and European-American feminists sometimes adopt the "rhetoric of solidarity," but nevertheless "consume the experiences and voices of the marginalized and oppressed, while, ever adroitly, dodging the penitential call to conversion—to authenticity in word and deed."[21] She advocated specific ways for white women and women of color to learn this virtue, and she enjoined all to be self-critical, honest, courageous, and willing to do the hard work of social analysis.

Courage

This virtue is essential to an ethic of "creative responsibility." Passive responsibility, embodied in duty, is important but secondary. Creative responsibility is distinguished by a willingness to think deeply and originally about the situations that confront us, and to take appropriate risks for the sake of promoting good and minimizing evil. The courage to take such risks comes from trust in God's power to act both in and beyond us, making up for what is lacking in our own efforts. Such courage also depends on the confidence that God's mercy is always there, supporting us and protecting us from the harms we fear, and especially from our own limitations.[22]

Humility
The root meaning of this term involves being "of the earth," that is, being constituted of the same elements that make up soil, rocks, and trees. This is easier to affirm in the abstract than in life, as the poem "I Know Women" by Christian feminist Mara Faulkner, OSB, suggests. Faulkner addresses a different problem, but one that has some bearing on the issue of seeking to disconnect spirituality from the flaws, or flesh, of religious institutions. She writes:

> I know women and even girls who want to leap out of the boat
> of their bodies—
> that leaky skin craft
> with its fragile ribs, its clumsy opaqueness
> whose every heavy movement is ambiguous and veiled.
>
> . . . .
>
> Women want to be pure mind, light
> Invisible as air
> free and beautiful like the idea of song
> that doesn't seem to need the pumping lungs
> the husky, muscled larynx
> the pink and flabby tongue.
>
> They can't believe that Jesus once set free
> would return to his body
>
> with cries of joy
> as to a long-lost friend.[23]

These lines suggest a continuing agenda for growth in the sort of humility that starts by affirming our physical bodies, and also accepts our creaturely need for structures to serve the social body.

CONCLUSION

Having commended the virtue of humility, I must acknowledge that my thinking about the relationship between religion and spirituality is ongoing. For me the complex picture is summed up by an image of two vast river systems, as well as many smaller streams, which can be distinguished although their waters mingle here and there. The first, and much larger system, represents the classical spiritual traditions we associate with institutional religion, be it Buddhist, Christian, Hindu, Islamic, or Jewish, each of which carries many subsystems within it. By contrast, the second principal system is detached from traditional religion, especially of the institutionally organized and creedally demanding variety. It is often linked with the love of nature, art, and beauty; with the concern for ecology, justice, and peace; and with the pursuit of physical and mental health, including recovery from the damage caused by aspects of institutional religion. It may be that both large systems are authentic responses to the Divine Spirit in history, as are the many smaller streams that represent indigenous or tribal forms of religion in this model. All of these "rivers" may be necessary in the human evolutionary process; certainly a God who loves biodiversity so much can handle religious diversity. Yet no spiritual system can hope to realize its humane ideals if its followers assume they are free from the limitations and evils that are part of being human.

Humility, being grounded in our finite, earthly condition, requires that we respect what is good in religious and secular traditions other than our own, as well as our own. It also requires that we acknowledge the problems of both institutional religion and secular spirituality, and not idealize one at the expense of the other. Were there space I would go on about a secular hero of mine, the nineteenth-century author Marian Evans who wrote fiction under the name of George Eliot. After a devout girlhood as an Evangelical Christian, she chose the secular stream of spirituality for herself, for reasons that still make sense. But unlike her contemporary Karl Marx, she knew that traditional religion had value, too, especially the Jewish tradition that most of her British contemporaries did not prize. Those who espouse secular spirituality today can learn much from her example.[24]

And all of us can learn from an earlier spiritual leader who received very mixed reviews in his day. Jesus managed to strike the right balance between religion and spirituality. As New Testament scholar Sandra Schneiders observes, "Jesus did not oppose his personal spirituality to his religious tradition but expressed his spirituality through his religious practice, even as he freely criticized the religious institution out of his own experience of union with God." She adds, "No one controlled Jesus' access to and relationship with God, but he was able to make his spirituality a resource for the reform of the tradition rather than an alternative to it."[25]

Building on Schneiders's insights, I conclude that the right relationship between religion and spirituality comes down to this matter of *balance*. Spirituality is a resource for religion, religion is a resource for spirituality, and ethics is needed to help each realize its potential for good. The virtues I have singled out for attention can be seen as paired counterweights that contribute to the equilibrium needed on both sides. Self-care and solidarity are mutually supportive and mutually correcting qualities, as indeed are courage and humility. The world can use more of them all. It is my hope that a balanced ethics of spirituality will encourage Catholics, especially the young, to develop the sort of "loyal voice" recommended by Mary Jo Bane, one that helps transform the church into the community "that God would have us live in."

Notes

1. Mary Jo Bane, "Voice and Loyalty in the Church," in Steven J. Pope, ed., *Common Calling: The Laity and Governance of the Catholic Church* (Washington, DC: Georgetown University Press, 2004), 181.

2. Margaret A. Farley, *Just Love: A Framework for Christian Sexual Ethics* (New York: Continuum, 2006), 260.

3. Ibid.

4. Preliminary work toward an ethics of church participation is found in Anne E. Patrick, *Conscience and Calling: Ethical Reflections on Catholic Women's Church Vocations* (London: T & T Clark/Bloomsbury, 2013).

5. See Albert R. Jonsen, *Responsibility in Modern Religious Ethics* (Washington, DC: Corpus Books, 1968) for discussion of the post-World War II shift of emphasis from "obedience" to "responsibility" among Protestant and Catholic thinkers.

6. Pew Forum on Religion & Public Life, "U.S. Religious Landscape Survey," February 25, 2007. According to the survey, "While nearly one-in-three Americans (31%) were raised in the Catholic faith, today fewer than one-in-four (24%) describe themselves as Catholics. These losses would have been even more pronounced were it not for the offsetting impact of immigration...Approximately one-third of the survey respondents who say they were raised Catholic no longer describe themselves as Catholic. This means that roughly 10% of all Americans are former Catholics." Quoted here from http://religions.

pewforum.org/reports?sid=ST2008022501236 (accessed Dec. 31, 2012). In an article commenting on this study, Thomas J. Reese, SJ, noted that if these ex-Catholics "were a separate denomination, they would be the third largest denomination in the United States, after Catholics and Baptists." See Reese, "The Hidden Exodus: Catholics Becoming Protestants," *National Catholic Reporter* (April 15, 2011), 1.

7. Pew Forum on Religion & Public Life, "'Nones' on the Rise: One-in-Five Adults Have No Religious Affiliation," October 9, 2012; available at http://pewforum.org/uploadedFiles/Topics/Religious_Affiliation/Unaffiliated/NonesOnTheRise-full.pdf (accessed Nov. 27, 2012).

8. Diarmuid O'Murchu, *Religion in Exile: A Spiritual Homecoming* (New York: Crossroad Publishing Company, 2000). O'Murchu is a social psychologist and member of the Sacred Heart Missionary Order who has worked as a counselor in London, who travels internationally to give workshops on adult faith formation, and who has recently published books that include *In the Beginning Was the Spirit* (2012), *Jesus in the Power of Poetry* (2009), and *Consecrated Religious Life* (2005). I infer from his website (accessed Dec. 20, 2012) that his 2000 polemic against religion is not his full position on the subject. Indeed, *Religion in Exile* is not listed among his books "currently in print" at http://www.diarmuid13.com/the-cosmic-walk/the-cosmic-walk-1/home-1. Nevertheless, *Religion in Exile* remains available at Amazon.com (accessed Dec. 20, 2012), with the description: "...O'Murchu offers penetrating and original insights into the changing spiritual awareness of our time. He believes that we are rapidly out-growing the time honored but exhausted vision of formal religion."

9. O'Murchu, *Religion in Exile*, 66.

10. For a solid presentation and critique of Marx's position, see Daniel L. Pals, *Eight Theories of Religion*, 2nd ed. (New York: Oxford University Press, 2006), 118–48.

11. Mary Daly, *Beyond God the Father* (Boston: Beacon Press, 1973).

12. See, for example, Matthew Fox, *Original Blessing* (Santa Fe, NM: Bear & Co., 1983), and *Creation Spirituality* (San Francisco: HarperSanFrancisco, 1991).

13. See Ronald L. Grimes, "Forum: American Spirituality," *Religion and American Culture* 9 (1999): 145–52. Grimes paraphrases the observation of a Native American colleague thus: "Every time...I hear a white person use the term 'spirituality' rather than 'religion,' I worry, because I know that person is in the process of packaging for export the very practices I grew up with and continue to revere" (150).

14. Eminent among various others who take this position is Sandra M. Schneiders, who probes the relationship between spirituality and religion in many writings, including, "Religion vs. Spirituality: A Contemporary Conundrum," *Spiritus* 3 (2003): 163–85.

15. Margaret A. Farley, "New Patterns of Relationship: Beginnings of a Moral Revolution," *Theological Studies* 36 (1975): 627–46.

16. James F. Keenan, SJ, "Proposing Cardinal Virtues," *Theological Studies* 56 (1995): 726–28.

17. Valerie Saiving, "The Human Situation: A Feminine View," *Journal of Religion* 40 (1960): 100–12.

18. Rosemary Radford Ruether, *Women-Church: Theology & Practice of Feminist Liturgical Communities* (San Francisco: Harper & Row, 1986), 62.

19. Ibid., 11.

20. Ada María Isasi-Díaz, *Mujerista Theology* (Maryknoll, NY: Orbis Books, 1996), 86–104.

21. M. Shawn Copeland, "Toward a Critical Christian Feminist Theology of Solidarity," in Mary Ann Hinsdale and Phyllis H. Kaminski, eds., *Women and Theology* (Maryknoll, NY: Orbis Books, 1995), 3.

22. See Anne E. Patrick, *Women, Conscience, and the Creative Process* (New York: Paulist Press, 2011), 67–72.

23. Mara Faulkner, OSB, "I Know Women," *Hedgebrook Journal* (August 2000), 6. Used with permission of the poet.

24. See Bernard J. Paris, *Experiments in Life: George Eliot's Quest for Values* (Detroit: Wayne State University Press, 1965), and also George Eliot's final novel, which is concerned with Jewish identity and traditions, *Daniel Deronda* (1876).

25. Sandra M. Schneiders, *With Oil in Their Lamps: Faith, Feminism, and the Future* (New York: Paulist Press, 2000), 101.

16

PROPHECY AND
CONTEMPORARY CONSECRATED LIFE

Raising Some Ethical Questions

This essay argues that the idealistic approach to prophecy of the National Assembly of Women Religious (subsequently renamed the National Assembly of Religious Women) contributed to its decline. Anne Patrick traces the conceptions of the prophetic voice developed by Sandra M. Schneiders and Michael H. Crosby, concluding that prophecy should be seen not as an alternative to supporting and building religious institutions but rather as a necessary companion to critiquing them. —HD

The phrase "the embodiment of love," used to describe contemporary consecrated life and ecclesial movements, suggests the quality of idealism I associate also with recent emphasis on the prophetic nature of active, or ministerial religious life. As an ethicist I am interested in asking what qualities, activities, and practices can help today's religious to realize the ideals of embodying love and acting prophetically.

This essay builds on research I completed for the volume *Conscience and Calling: Ethical Reflections on Catholic Women's Church Vocations.*[1] In the third chapter of that work, "A Ministry of Justice," I looked at the history of a very idealistic organization of U.S. Catholic sisters, the National Assembly of Women Religious, which aspired to a prophetic role in relation to church and society. Some of the conclusions I reached from asking why that organization lasted only twenty-five years, from 1970 to 1995, have led me to see the usefulness of raising

Adapted from a chapter of the same title in God Has Begun a Great Work in Us, *ed. Shannon Schrein and Jason King. College Theology Society Annual Volume 60 (Maryknoll, NY: Orbis Books, 2015), 56–65.*

ethical questions about the emphasis on prophecy found in contemporary works on religious life.

My discussion will proceed in three stages. I will first summarize some findings about the National Assembly of Women Religious, or NAWR, which expanded its membership in 1978 to include women not in vowed communities, and for that reason changed its name to the National Assembly of Religious Women (NARW). Then I will give a brief description of the emphasis on prophecy in recent works by two scholars I greatly admire, Sandra M. Schneiders, IHM, and Michael H. Crosby, OFM Cap. I have learned far more from them about religious life and prophecy than I can begin to do justice to here. Finally, in light of all this, I will pose some ethical questions for consideration.

Findings from NAWR/NARW's History

U.S. sisters founded the National Assembly of Women Religious in 1970 with a twin commitment to ministry and social justice. Its early publications helped spread the word about creative developments in individualized ministries for justice that took place after the Second Vatican Council. NAWR's membership peaked five years later, when it had about one hundred sisters' councils and senates as group members, and some five thousand nuns as individual grassroots members. The expansion of membership to other laywomen (and change of name in 1978) did not increase overall numbers, however, and by 1980 there were only twenty-three group memberships and fourteen hundred individuals. Fifteen years later, the decline in membership and turnover in leadership led to a financial crisis, and NARW disbanded in 1995, although its influence has continued through three organizations, two of which it helped to found: the Women's Ordination Conference and NETWORK, the Catholic social justice lobby now famous for "Nuns on the Bus." Its influence also carried over into the Leadership Conference of Women Religious, especially as sisters who had been grassroots members of NAWR/NARW were elected to office in their religious communities and brought their commitment to a "ministry of justice" to LCWR.

Why did NAWR/NARW last just twenty-five years? It seems to me that idealism, including the ideal of prophecy, was a contributing factor in its decline. NAWR members tended not to theorize about prophecy, or to analyze the relationship of the prophetic vocation to the more general call to Christian discipleship. They simply felt responsible for denouncing injustice where they perceived it, and for working to improve unjust situations in light of what they understood to be

God's values. The organization's power came from the way talented and dedicated women were able to articulate a mission that flowed directly from the Christian gospel, which they expressed in terms of commitment to "a ministry of justice."

Once assembled, however, the idealists found it hard to choose among ways of focusing their efforts and structuring their membership. Aspirations to prophecy, articulated explicitly as such in the group's 1981 assembly, aimed at such a perfection of justice that the journey itself became difficult for some members to sustain over time. Trying to be prophetic can sometimes result in a moralism that brings discouragement and disunity. Also, the conciliar spirit of openness, and especially the value of inclusivity, led NAWR/NARW to invite increasingly diverse women into its ranks and governing board, and for a time led to ambiguity about its Catholic identity. Such changes contributed to the erosion of the original membership base. Although the ultimate reason for the group's demise was lack of funds, its collapse seems attributable, at least in part, to the increasing weight of its own idealism.

Even a brief life, of course, can do much good, and not only in terms of NAWR/NARW's influence on the Women's Ordination Conference, NETWORK, and LCWR. I also admire the virtues of its members, who were motivated by zeal for God's reign, and hunger and thirst for justice. With time and experience many of these generous idealists also gained a new sense of humility and patience as they came to grips with the organization's and their own limitations. This appreciation of finitude did not diminish their zeal, but it did prove an asset for subsequent efforts to speak and act prophetically. As NAWR/NARW's short history was drawing to a close, women religious were starting other organizations and movements with more focused agendas, such as the Intercommunity Peace and Justice Center in Seattle and the national "Sisters of Earth" network.[2] What the earlier activists of NAWR/NARW have in common with the peace and justice leaders and the "green sisters" of today is the sense of being called to dedicate their lives wholeheartedly to the values of God's realm, and thus to act prophetically and influence history for the well-being of all God's creatures.

PROPHECY IN RECENT DISCUSSIONS OF RELIGIOUS LIFE

I now turn to some works by scholars who have contributed richly to our understanding of prophecy in relation to religious life. In her 2012 book *Prophets in Their Own Country*, Sandra M. Schneiders, IHM, articulates the ideal of prophecy in terms of the evolution of a "new form of

Religious Life." She writes: "Religious Life...is a charismatic lifeform, called into existence by the Holy Spirit, to live corporately the prophetic charism in the Church."[3] All three volumes of her trilogy on *Religious Life in the New Millennium* emphasize this calling to prophecy. In volume 1, *Finding the Treasure* (2000), she associates this prophetic vocation with "contemplative immediacy to God and social marginality" and stresses the connection between consecrated celibacy and prophecy: "For the Religious, celibate solitude has as its primary purpose the fostering of contemplation..., [which] involves participation in the divine perspective from which prophecy arises."[4] In a chapter subtitled "Prophets in Their Own Country" she astutely observes that the "the arena in which the prophetic power and institutional challenge of Religious Life has been most evident" of late "is surely the encounter between the Church and feminism," an observation confirmed in recent years by the Apostolic Visitation of U.S. sisterhoods and the Doctrinal Assessment of the Leadership Conference of Women Religious.[5] In volume 2, *Selling All* (2001), Schneiders describes religious life as "ideally, a primary prophetic witness in the Church to the kind of community Jesus intended."[6] Finally, in the recently published volume 3, *Buying the Field* (2013), she speaks of religious communities as "prophecy embodied," and argues that the witness of such vowed communities is a gift to both the Church and the world.[7]

In developing a renewed theology of the vows, Schneiders especially links the vow of obedience with prophecy, suggesting that this vow should now be understood as "a prophetic commitment to moving our world away from the politics of Satan's kingdom toward the politics of the Reign of God."[8] Instead of a politics of domination by the powerful over their subordinates, this new form of religious life seeks to incarnate "the discipleship of equals that the Gospel proposes and the collegial form of government that the early Church developed and that Vatican II reaffirmed."[9] She goes on to declare that "A vibrant theology of prophetic obedience might be the most urgent contribution Religious Life has to offer in our seriously dysfunctional Church and society, which swing between the anarchy of unrestrained individualism and the repression of totalitarian power structures."[10]

Prophetic obedience rejects patriarchal, military, and monarchical models of community, and presumes the radical equality of all members, who together seek to discern God's will. The task of obedience remains the "appropriate response to genuine authority," which always involves listening and "serious engagement," and usually requires "cooperation and compliance," but this involves an act of conscience, not of blind submission.[11] She draws a sharp distinction between the obedience that ordained clergy owe to the hierarchy and the religious vow of obedience, which "is made only to God according to the Constitutions of the Order."[12] In imitation of the prophetic obedience of Jesus, religious aspire to "total obedience to God lived freely in the service of God's people."[13]

While Schneiders was completing her trilogy, Michael H. Crosby, OFM Cap, published in 2005 a book that poses the question: *Can Religious Life Be Prophetic?* Crosby accepts the prophetic ideal for religious, but wonders if it has been coopted by Pope John Paul II's insistence that the "'prophetic stimulus'" of religious life "can be 'guaranteed' only when it functions in 'full harmony with the Church's Magisterium and discipline,'" and by other such instances of hierarchical control.[14] Crosby further wonders if religious claiming a prophetic role need a "reality check" insofar as "few if any religious congregations [are] *publicly* and *regularly* challenging the abuse of patriarchal power," and while some religious may "act very prophetically," often they are "isolated from and even rejected by the wider membership" of their communities.[15]

Crosby believes that besides a fuller understanding of biblical prophecy, which he offers in chapters on Isaiah, Jeremiah, and Ezekiel, vowed religious need "something institutional that *constitutes and sustains ourselves in the prophetic tradition.*"[16] Without describing exactly what this would involve, he notes that "we need regular and ongoing support if we are to be prophetic," and he draws on the examples of St. Francis and St. Clare to develop several principles to bear in mind when "non-assent" and "non-submission" seem called for with respect to positions of church officials.[17] For example, he observes that "When dissent is deemed necessary, our approach should be respectful and courteous as we continually request dialogue about our differences," something we have lately seen exemplified in statements by LCWR.[18]

SOME ETHICAL QUESTIONS

After reflecting on the insights of Schneiders and Crosby about the prophetic dimension of active religious life, I think it is important to continue the conversation from the perspective of ethics. The questions that guide my approach to ethics are basic ones. With H. Richard Niebuhr, I believe a first question about any situation must be "What is going on?" if we are to fit our response to events into what we perceive as God's design for us and other creatures.[19] A second question builds on this: In light of what is going on, with James Gustafson I then ask, "What is God enabling and requiring *us* to be and to do?"[20] For now, let the "us" in this question be Catholic women like myself, who happen to be feminist members of LCWR religious congregations. By "feminist" I mean someone who believes in the equal dignity and worth of women and men, and who seeks to reform structures and thought systems so that this equality is fully respected.

What is going on?[21] I feel it is important to observe that the dramas of our congregations' lives are playing out in a much larger world historical context today. Three "signs of our times" from recent headlines tell us much about this situation: the kidnapping of hundreds of Nigerian schoolgirls by Boko Haram in April 2014; the visit of Pope Francis to the Middle East in May 2014; and, scientific reports on climate change and the irreversible melting of the ice surrounding Antarctica. The kidnapping incident is a reminder that females are at special risk in the power struggles of the world so loved by God. Pope Francis's efforts in the Middle East to strengthen ecumenical and interreligious relations, to promote a peaceful resolution of the Palestinian-Israeli conflict, and to encourage the dwindling population of Christians who face violence and persecution, show a creative minister using all the symbolic capital he can muster for the sake of this world that God so loves. And if, as rumor has it, his first encyclical turns out to be about the environment, will this not be further evidence of some blending of the roles of priest and prophet?

At the very least I am reminded that Max Weber's typology of religious roles such as "priest" and "prophet" is an idealized abstraction, and things are more complicated in reality. This brings me to some further questions for American feminist nuns like myself. What is the best way to balance our idealism with institutional realism? Is it really true, as Schneiders has observed, that "Jesus, in prophetic word and work, not in institution maintenance, is the model of ministry for Religious"?[22] Or is there a need for something like "institution maintenance," or better, "institution building and renewal" within groups aspiring to prophecy? My experience with NAWR/NARW has inclined me to think that there is, and the sociologists Mary Johnson, SNDdeN, Patricia Wittberg, SC, and Mary Gautier suggest as much in their 2014 study, *New Generations of Catholic Sisters.* They observe: "Prophetic words that are not undergirded by strong and life-giving structures with clear boundaries will exist only on the pages of documents. But structures that are not enveloped in the flesh of rich values, charisms, and visions will be like skeletons, just piles of dry bones."[23] Is it possible that some women religious who aspire to prophecy are also called beyond critique to tasks of institutional creation and construction, tasks we might refer to as "founding" and "re-founding"? If the call to prophecy is now understood to be extended to groups as well as individuals, what models of organization, decision-making, and leadership are needed to balance the norms of charity and justice, and to foster the welfare of the group and its members? How should ministerial religious discern which situations call for corporate prophetic action, and which for supporting, or for challenging, individual members who feel called to prophecy?

Perhaps all of this will seem easier when the goal of full equality for women in the Roman Catholic Church is realized, and all ministries are open to baptized females. But we are living before this reform, which is desired so passionately by many, and feared with equal intensity by others. In this meanwhile, then, are there virtues that are especially needed by feminist women religious aspiring to prophecy? Three such qualities come to mind, the first of which is humility. By humility I do not mean a false sense of unworthiness, much less internalized oppression on sexist or other grounds. Rather I mean being grounded in the knowledge of our human sinfulness and finitude, with the accompanying recognition that salvation is God's gift, and not the result of our actions. When we experience criticism it is natural to go on the defensive, and especially to claim the moral high ground against those we regard as oppressors. The criticism may in fact be unjust and misguided, and humility does not rule out answering it with the fullest truth we can articulate. I am not advocating "mea culpa" as the default response to criticism, but I think we can all learn from the example of Pope Francis, who has publicly voiced his sense of identity as "a sinner" and who asked everyone to pray for him before he began his papal ministry.

At a minimum it seems wise to acknowledge that when serious matters are at issue for religious people, more than one side may feel called to prophecy. I also wonder whether humility might encourage feminists to be more discriminating in our critique of something called "hierarchy," for it seems to me that the term does not *necessarily* presume domination over subordinates by those who judge themselves as ontologically superior, but can simply denote an administrative system with clear lines of accountability. How to design more instances of the latter requires a virtue I have called "creative responsibility," which involves the disposition to step back from a situation of difficulty, look at options imaginatively, and take reasonable risks for the sake of new and better possibilities.[24] Creative responsibility requires a third virtue, which also helps to keep humility in balance, namely the virtue of courage.

Prophets are called to speak their sense of truth to power, and to speak it in love. There are risks involved in doing this, and courage is needed to face the suffering and loss that may come from taking such risks. Because living a prophetic vocation requires strength from beyond ourselves, perhaps courage is a virtue more to be prayed for than cultivated, and certainly community support will be needed to nurture this virtue when it is given. How to structure these communities for the future seems a very pressing task for today. Many of the women who entered active congregations before Vatican II experienced ten or fifteen years of a monastic form of apostolic life, which provided spiritual disciplines and common experiences that have sustained us through decades of change and many prophetic positions. Younger women, from various age cohorts, may have different expectations and needs regarding community and prayer life than our generation did. How should we respond when the prophets among them voice these needs?

Ideals such as "the embodiment of love" and "prophecy embodied" are worth striving for, and are the work of a lifetime. I have raised here more questions than I can answer, in the hope that considering them will contribute to vibrant and truly prophetic expressions of religious life.

Notes

1. Anne E. Patrick, *Conscience and Calling: Ethical Reflections on Catholic Women's Church Vocations* (New York: Bloomsbury Academic, 2013). In the discussion of NAWR/NARW that follows I draw from this work (85–105). My research on the organization's history was originally done for a Lilly Endowment funded project on mapping American Catholicism, led by Mary Jo Weaver and R. Scott Appleby, and an earlier version of this chapter was published in Weaver's edited work, *What's Left: Liberal American Catholics* (Bloomington: Indiana University Press, 1999), 176–87.

2. The involvement of women religious in earth ministries is richly described in Sarah M. Taylor, *Green Sisters: A Spiritual Ecology* (Cambridge: Harvard University Press, 2007).

3. Sandra M. Schneiders, *Prophets in Their Own Country: Women Religious Bearing Witness to the Gospel in a Troubled Church* (Maryknoll, NY: Orbis Books, 2011), 100.

4. Sandra M. Schneiders, *Finding the Treasure: Locating Catholic Religious Life in a New Ecclesial and Cultural Context*, vol. 1 of *Religious Life in a New Millennium* (New York: Paulist Press, 2000), 137, 139.

5. Ibid., 350. For analysis of the Vatican investigations of U.S. sisters and LCWR, see Schneiders, *Prophets in Their Own Country*; and, Patrick, *Conscience and Calling*, 1–17 and 147–54.

6. Sandra M. Schneiders, *Selling All: Commitment, Consecrated Celibacy, and Community in Catholic Religious Life*, vol. 2 of *Religious Life in a New Millennium* (New York: Paulist Press, 2001), 245.

7. Sandra M. Schneiders, *Buying the Field: Religious Life in Mission to the World*, vol. 3 of *Religious Life in a New Millennium* (New York: Paulist Press, 2013), 256.

8. Ibid., 364.

9. Ibid., 422.

10. Ibid., 424.

11. Ibid., 591.

12. Ibid., 500.

13. Ibid., 471.

14. Michael H. Crosby, *Can Religious Life Be Prophetic?* (New York: Crossroad Publishing Company, 2005), 12.

15. Ibid., 18, 17.

16. Ibid., 20.

17. Ibid., 82.

18. Ibid., 171.

19. H. Richard Niebuhr, *The Responsible Self: An Essay in Christian Moral Philosophy* (New York: Harper & Row, 1963), 60.

20. James M. Gustafson, *Can Ethics Be Christian?* (Chicago: University of Chicago Press, 1975), 179.

21. For an extended analysis of contemporary religious life by two very astute participant-observers, see the essays by IHM sister Sandra M. Schneiders and Redemptorist Archbishop Joseph W. Tobin in Schneiders's *Prophets in Their Own Country*.

22. Schneiders, *Prophets in Their Own Country*, 92. In raising this question I have been influenced by a traditional understanding of the varieties of spiritual gifts (see 1 Cor. 12), as well as by William C. Spohn's study, *Go and Do Likewise: Jesus and Ethics* (New York: Continuum, 1999), which emphasizes the need for Christians to use imagination and analogical reasoning as they strive to follow the example of Jesus. As Spohn observes, "Jesus did not come teaching... a uniform way of life to be replicated in every generation. Rather his words, encounters, and life story set patterns that can be flexibly but faithfully extended to new circumstances. These patterns lead us to envision analogous ways of acting that are partly the same and partly different" (49). I would point out here that the *imitatio Christi* motif has been a powerful one for all who feel called to discipleship, and that of the three roles traditionally associated with Christ (prophet, priest, and king), the role of prophet has been accessible to Catholic women in ways that priesthood and religious authority have not.

23. Mary Johnson, Patricia Wittberg, and Mary L. Gautier, *New Generations of Catholic Sisters: The Challenge of Diversity* (New York: Oxford University Press, 2014), 59.

24. Anne E. Patrick, *Women, Conscience, and the Creative Process* (New York: Paulist Press, 2011), 55–72.

IV

THE STATUS OF WOMEN

17

A CONSERVATIVE CASE
FOR THE ORDINATION OF WOMEN

The ordination of women is paradoxically but powerfully supported through values associated with conservatism: the significance of the sacraments, the recognition of God's calling, and a respect, qualified but still essential, for church authority. Demonstrating that the decline in numbers of women religious significantly exceeds the decline in the number of priests, Anne Patrick attributes the difference in part to the church's reluctance to respond to changes in the status of women. —HD

One thing that intrigues me about the current discussion of women's ordination is how seldom either advocates or opponents give evidence of understanding that the proposal to ordain women reflects a rather conservative theological orientation.

Perhaps I am taking a "progressive" view of conservatism but I am inclined to agree with John Gardner's claim that "in a world buffeted by change, faced daily with new threats to its safety, the only way to conserve is by innovating. The only stability possible is stability in motion." What I would like to suggest in this article is that certain values are in tension in the Catholic community today—namely the value of woman as a person, the value of sacraments, and the value of church order—and that this situation has the potential to lead either to new growth or the loss of much that has enriched the Catholic traditions.

What has led to this tension? I suspect that what we are experiencing is the result of the gradual acceptance of woman as a fully-endowed human being, equal to man in dignity and worth. We tend to forget

Adapted from an essay in New Catholic World, *vol. 218, no. 1305 (May–June 1975): 108–11.*

that for centuries eminent doctors of the church and brilliant theologians have taught a doctrine of a fundamental inequality between the sexes, and not to realize that the affirmation of woman's essential value is relatively recent for our religious culture. What we are experiencing now is the lag between understanding and practice.

In an era when the best theologians described woman as "the devil's gateway" (Tertullian) or a "misbegotten man" (St. Thomas Aquinas), it made sense to exclude women from sacramental ministry and hierarchical leadership. The problem today stems from the fact that church practice has not kept pace with statements such as the following from the Second Vatican Council document *Gaudium et Spes* (n. 29):

> Since all men possess a rational soul and are created in God's likeness, since they have the same nature and origin, have been redeemed by Christ, and enjoy the same divine calling and destiny, the basic equality of all must receive increasingly greater recognition. True, all men are not alike from the point of view of varying physical power and the diversity of intellectual and moral resources. Nevertheless, with respect to the fundamental rights of the person, every type of discrimination, whether social or cultural, whether based on sex, race, color, social condition, language, or religion, is to be overcome as contrary to God's intent. For in truth it is to be regretted that the fundamental personal rights are not yet being universally honored.

But how has the new acceptance of woman's value as a person placed the traditional values of sacraments and church order in jeopardy? Clearly this development of a new tension has been a subtle process, but I think that some relationship between a new appreciation of woman and the erosion of appreciation for sacraments and church order can be demonstrated if one examines the current pastoral situation.

It is a fact that more and more women, generally but not always members of religious congregations, are involved in areas of ministry that until quite recently were reserved for ordained priests. It is not uncommon these days to hear of women who are hospital chaplains, campus ministers, and even "associate pastors," "assistants," or members of pastoral teams in Catholic parishes. In view of the tremendous needs for general pastoral care and for the sort of evangelization that takes place in educational programs, counseling situations, and cooperative efforts for social justice, one has to affirm the fact that the talents of women are now available for this sort of pastoral ministry.

To me it represents progress when a woman describes her ministerial situation as one in which she is esteemed as a colleague by the priests with whom she works, and reports that her professional judgment is respected. But despite this very positive development, the fact that she often sums up her situation by declaring "I do everything that the priests do except sacraments" gives me pause. For this to be the case in one or two situations may be of small account, but as instances multiply, more and more will be forced to ask, consciously or otherwise, "What's wrong? Is it that this dedicated capable person is not worthy to administer the sacraments? Or could it be that the sacraments are not worth her time?"

To phrase the problem this baldly may seem an exaggeration, but I believe it is a fair enough description of the tension in values we are currently experiencing. Changing to an egalitarianism between the sexes without opening all ministries and sacraments to women seems to be a contribution directly to the secularizing tendencies that are already making enough inroads of their own.

I do not mean to imply by this that cultic or sacramental functions are the only important ones for ministry. Indeed, preaching, teaching, prophecy, hospitality, pastoral care, administration, and other services are also essential for the community. Nor do I mean to suggest that popular understandings of sacramental theology are entirely adequate. But the sacraments remain important in our tradition, and it would seem that the ordination of women at this juncture has the advantage of underscoring the value the church attaches to the sacramental ministry in general at the same time that this change would make the experience and talents of so many dedicated women available for full ministry within the church.

No one of us, male or female, can claim to be worthy of our Christian vocation, and it strikes me that a return to the traditional emphasis on God's freedom to call whom God wills is needed if we are to resolve the tensions between the value of women and that of sacraments in favor of both. The early church faced this question in another form in dealing with the issue of whether or not to accept Gentiles into the community. Certainly the cultural difficulties experienced by Jewish Christians in coming to accept Gentiles who did not follow the Mosaic law were greater than those Catholics today will have in accepting women as priests.

Another value with a long history in our tradition is that of church order and respect for authority. This history has its dark side, of course, but nonetheless Catholics have affirmed church order as important to the well-being of the community, indeed, as divinely established. I can sympathize with the frustrations of women who believe the importance of the ministerial activities denied them and who feel that ecclesiastical prescriptions are in many cases depriving God's people of sacramental celebrations of God's presence and forgiveness. But it nevertheless jars my traditional Catholic sensibility to hear a woman campus minister exclaim, "Who needs a bishop to tell me what I can or cannot do?" Nobody, of course, needs an autocratic bishop, but anarchy does not seem helpful either. And yet, in situations like this, it seems as if more and more of the faithful are reluctantly opting to ignore structures and prescriptions that appear to them to contradict the elementary ideals of social justice which the church so strongly (and with good reason) articulates to the secular world.

I find it ironic that so many regard the movement for the ordination of women as a rebellious enterprise, apparently failing to note that the very world ordination bespeaks a valuing of *order*, though hopefully an order that will be more just than the present one.

Many creative and beautiful things are going on in ministry today, and it hardly makes sense to leave them on the periphery of the church's structure. Mary B. Lynch, who heads the U.S. Section of the International Association of Women Aspiring to Presbyteral Ministry (the European branch is led by 79-year-old Dominican Sister Valentine Buisseret), has stated in regard to women's ordination that "service and leadership within the authoritative church will be increasingly affirmed with clarification of roles as they are really practiced today."

Catholics with a sense of tradition will probably be glad to learn that it was to the U.S. bishops that a group calling itself the Ordination Conference Taskforce first appealed for spiritual, moral, and financial support in their efforts to organize a national meeting for next fall on the theme "Women in Future Priesthood Now: A Call to Action." The taskforce, comprising representatives of seven Roman Catholic seminaries, eight national Catholic organizations, and eleven congregations of women religious, seeks not to undermine church order, but rather to convene persons who are committed to making the talents of women fully available for ministerial service in the Roman Catholic Church and to inform the church about women preparing for a new expression of full priesthood. Although many Catholics may be surprised to learn that women are enrolled in some seminaries now, the news should be encouraging to those who have come to value not only church order and sacraments, but women as well. It is symbolic, I believe, that the taskforce has chosen to use the National Center for Church Vocations (305 N. Michigan Ave., Detroit, MI 48226) as its mailing address. For it seems to me that the very word conservative applies literally to the movement for women's ordination in the sense of conservation of the personnel.

It is well known that the church in the United States has sustained a substantial loss of priestly and religious personnel in the last decade. Interestingly enough, although losses from religious communities of women are much greater than the drop in clergy, the official church leaders have yet to demonstrate, in a significant way, that they are concerned over this. Our national bishops' conference allocated half a million dollars for a recent study of the American priesthood, but the National Sisters Vocation Conference has received only about $4,000, largely in contributions from individual bishops and vicars for religious, to fund studies regarding women religious. And yet the statistics concerning sisters are, at the very least, unsettling to those who appreciate the value of full-time, dedicated church personnel. The following chart is based on figures from the *Official Catholic Directory*:

	Priests	Sisters
1954	45,451	154,055
1964	57,328	180,015
1974	56,712	139,963

Of course, many of the over 40,000 former sisters continue to be active in lay ministries, but the fact that they have left the traditional structures certainly warrants the attention of the institution's leaders, especially since a great number of the sisters who remain are close to retirement age, or have already retired. Nor are future projections encouraging. According to Msgr. Andrew McGowan, who heads the National Conference of Diocesan Vocation Directors, seminary enrollment is down 55 percent since 1965, and enrollment in the sisterhoods has dropped 81 percent (*Commonweal*, Dec. 20, 1974).

Until these data are studied scientifically, one can only suggest possible reasons for the discrepancy between the drop in numbers of clergy and of women religious, but I suspect that an important factor is that church structures have not adapted to the new status of women. In the March/April 1972 issue of this magazine, Sister Annette Walters, one of the leaders of the Sister Formation Movement, described the situation thus:

Sisters were and still are "minors" in Church law, subordinate to men at all levels of Church structure. The *Official Catholic*

Directory has listed in full the names of all priests in the U.S., down to the youngest recruit from the seminary. It has referred to Sisters anonymously, however, as "20 Sisters of St. Joseph" or "8 Sisters of Notre Dame." The men were "persons," the Sisters were "personnel"—interchangeable, nameless and faceless. Even in the areas of their greatest competence Sisters could only with difficulty take part in the decision-making that affected their lives and work.

Many have recognized that an institution perpetuating this sort of discrimination will find it increasingly difficult to attract young women to its religious structures, especially since "affirmative action" policies are now so widely publicized by governmental and secular service agencies, not to mention private industry. Can the church afford this loss of personnel? Among those who think not are the members of a committee of the Catholic Theological Society of America, who reported to the U.S. bishops in 1971 that

today the Church is faced with the changed role of women both within the world and within the Church. It behooves the Church as it did St. Paul to be sensitive to its social milieu. It is the privilege of the Church to have within its community not only men with spiritual and professional qualifications but also women who have proved their competence in various fields and are eager to share their talents with others in the Church. Indeed, the question is being asked whether the Catholic Church can afford to deny admission to this ministry to one half its membership. Secular society employs its talented women. In the Greek Orthodox Church the ordination of women as deaconesses has continued to the present day. Other churches have already extended the diaconate and other ministries. For the most part the free churches place no restriction on the ministry of women. The Catholic Church must be open to the Holy Spirit in this field as it is elsewhere, for many women experience a desire to serve in capacities of spiritual leadership and sacramental service not available to them in the present structures and institutions of the Church.

It should be pointed out that for some Catholic women the sense of call to spiritual leadership and sacramental service is strong enough to lead them to pursue theological studies in seminaries of other denominations. The fact that financial aid for women is virtually non-existent in Roman Catholic seminaries has something to do with this, but some of these women are preparing to be ordained for service in Protestant churches, and a few are actually serving Protestant congregations now.

Although it would be a mistake to assume that admitting women to sacramental orders will of itself eliminate the vocation crisis, I am convinced that this reform will at least contribute toward improving the situation. The principal reason for this is that ordination will mean the full acceptance of women into the sacramental life of the church, and this symbolic gesture of welcome is bound to touch the hearts of women who, thanks to the women's movement, are growing increasingly conscious of their dignity as persons. Paradoxical as it may seem, by changing one non-doctrinal aspect of the tradition, the church stands to gain in many vital ways. On the other hand, the effects of not including women in the full sacramental and hierarchical ministries of the Catholic community are bound to be negative for the institutional church. Bishop Carrol T. Dozier of Memphis states the problem forthrightly in his recent pastoral letter:

> "Woman: Intrepid and Loving": Twentieth-century woman cannot be expected to treasure those institutions that have limited her freedom, growth, and opportunity in life. In faith, she has remained faithful to the Church. But we must share the pained presence of those who seek to relate more maturely in love and service to the whole people of God. Let us hear, then, those voices that vocalize woman's determination to assert her equality and profess her competence. Heedless institutions must inevitably pay the costs of indifference.

At this juncture I can only hope that the institution will respond to the challenge facing it, that it will hear the voice of the Spirit inviting the Catholic community to grow to a state of maturity where the gifts of all are equally respected. The stakes involved are too substantial for the church to attempt to avoid this issue. At the 1971 synod of bishops, Patriarch Maximos Hakim V of Antioch reminded the church leaders of an important truth: "Once women announced the good news to Peter. If we listen to them again today, women may have something to tell us."

18

THE AMBIGUITY OF POWER

In defining ways women can seek power responsibly, avoiding both its self-serving misuse and its submergence in dutiful passivity, Anne Patrick draws on a range of fields, including sociology, philosophy, and psychology. Here as elsewhere she demonstrates the broad interdisciplinary interests that enriched her work. Her emphasis on the responsible use of power can also gloss the reply she gave a friend who asked if she had considered leaving her community at a time when many other women religious who shared her ethical values and concerns about some actions by the church hierarchy were doing so. She cited one factor central to her decision to remain a woman religious: she could influence the ethical and theological issues with which she was so deeply and passionately engaged more effectively as a member of her community than as a lay person. —HD

To live by faith means to accept one's own power, always partial and finite, always power-in-relation, but nonetheless real … The opposite of faith is despair, hopelessness, acquiescence to one's powerlessness, and refusal to act as a responsible agent in moral struggle.

— Beverly Wildung Harrison[1]

Do women want power? How eager are we for leadership roles, for positions of authority? How willing are we to use the power of influence by speaking out, by writing for publication, by direct and sustained confrontation with others?

Women are, at best, ambivalent about power, and there are good reasons for this. For one thing, power is ambiguous. We can distinguish

Adapted from a chapter of the same title in Walking in Two Worlds: Women's Spiritual Paths, *ed. Kay Vander Vort, Joan Timmerman, and Eleanor Lincoln (St. Cloud, MN: North Star Press, 1992).*

the negative power of coercion from the positive power of energy, possibility, and influence. We can visualize, on the one hand, the power of Simon Legree with the whip and, on the other, the power of the battery that brings a car to life in fifteen degrees below zero or the power in a friendship that energizes us in ways we had not imagined possible.

Contemporary theologians have probed these ambiguities. Carter Heyward wants to leave behind views of power based on competitiveness (where power is something that either one or the other party has but never both at once) in favor of a power of mutual relationship.[2] Bernard Loomer contrasts "unilateral power," which produces effects without mutuality in the process, and "relational power," or the "capacity both to influence others and to be influenced by others"; in other words, the "capacity to sustain a mutually internal relationship."[3]

Although such distinctions are useful, they can be misleading if we expect that under the conditions of finitude the good type of power will be one hundred percent realizable whenever we wish it. This unrealistic expectation can paralyze us with an idealism that refuses to act in imperfect situations, thereby removing us from politics, the "art of compromise." This matter of perfectionism is related to a second reason why we are ambivalent about power; this has to do with our socialization as females. Since girlhood we have been schooled in precisely those traits of character that make it difficult for claim our power.

Valerie Saiving recognized this problem as early as 1960. She argued that traditional notions of sin and virtue reflect experiences typical of males who enjoy power in society.[4] For such men, pride has rightly been identified as a most harmful inclination, with temptation to sensual indulgence at the expense of others also a recurrent danger. Thus, exhortations to cultivate humility and self-sacrifice are appropriate for them. But to universalize this analysis, and especially to apply it to women, whose social location is ordinarily quite different, exacerbate the moral problems most women face. Given the disparate social experiences of the two sexes, the *temptations* of women are different from those of men. Instead of pride being the greatest danger, for most women the chief temptation has been the opposite—to fail to have a centered self, to yield up responsibility for identity and actions to other persons and environmental factors. Whereas men of privilege are tempted to *abuse their power,* women (and men of oppressed groups) tend to *abdicate their possibilities for using power properly* for the sake of approval and security. What women in patriarchal society need are not exhortations to humility and self-sacrifice, but encouragement to value ourselves and our possibilities. We need to risk criticism and even failure for the sake of accomplishing things that are good and reasonably attainable. We also need new models for virtue and new stories involving what I call the "pretty good" use of power, in contrast to the unattainable "perfectly good" use of power—in other words, stories where women act when, while some of the evidence is unavailable, they are willing to undertake a reasonable risk of losing a present good for the sake of a greater good that is likely to come.

This moral growth entails moving from a style of being responsible that is predominantly passive to one that includes creativity and risk-taking. Passive responsibility involves being dutiful and living up to the demands of our roles. Creative responsibility looks beyond the predefined role descriptions of the "good Catholic laywoman" or the "good sister" and sees a myriad of possibilities for action, indeed a world in need of transformation. Creative responsibility involves being conscientious in promoting good through a realistic appraisal of the likely consequences of a decision. It requires a willingness to act without an absolute assurance of being right. Instead of relying entirely on others' formulas for behavior, we can do our own interpreting of what is happening and our own analysis of how our actions might contribute to the betterment of life for ourselves and our neighbors. This by no means rules out benefiting from the wisdom of others, but it does rule out abdicating our judgment to other authorities. We risk being mistaken and criticized, but the rewards are high: an enhanced self-esteem and a sense of being a full adult participant in life rather than a minor who is only marginally involved in shaping self.

Both types of responsibility have their usefulness, like the white and black keys on a piano. The problem is that our socialization has equipped us too well for the one and very poorly for the other. Women and men alike have been damaged by forms of moral training that minimize the agent's role in interpreting obligations and balancing those that are in conflict. Women, however, face special problems as the result of our socialization that typically fosters passivity and stifles growth toward exercising power and creative responsibility.

This socialization sometimes sets women on a tragic, misguided quest for innocence, which confuses goodness with not taking action in ambiguous circumstances. Playing into this dynamic is a spirituality that lacks trust in God's daily forgiveness and in God's supportive presence in our process of making choices in situations where innocence is hardly possible, given the ambiguities of life situations. Jesus seems to have known about such ambiguities. Why else would he have stressed the need for daily forgiveness in the prayer he taught his disciples? But in subsequent centuries of ecclesiastical management of divine forgiveness the ready accessibility of forgiveness has been forgotten by many Catholics. What we need above all is a sense of God's enabling power and presence, along with a reconstituted vision of what authentic moral responsibility requires.

The theological argument I have sketched draws on insights from other fields, including sociology, philosophy, and psychology. I shall discuss some findings from these disciplines on women's socialization and the use of power.

In her 1983 volume, *The Political Integration of Women*, sociologist Virginia Sapiro describes her efforts to discover why, more than sixty years after women gained the vote in this country, we are still quite marginal to political life. For her research, Sapiro administered questionnaires to school girls and to adult women and compared the results. The striking difference was that the girls felt very knowledgeable and self-confident about politics and their potential for affecting the world. But the women had lost this sense of capability and power. Why? The hypothesis that provided the best answer to this question was that the responsibilities associated with women's adult roles contribute directly to the political marginality of women. Sapiro identifies "privatization" as a key culprit in this regressive process. Privatization involves the mindset that women are intended to center our lives on traditionally "feminine" concerns, mainly domestic and nurturing ones, with the result that we are perceived, and we see ourselves, as not really capable of effective action on broader matters.

Clearly Sapiro is talking about passive responsibility when she says such things as, "adult norms become internalized in a desire to be a 'good parent,' 'good wife,' 'good worker,' or 'good citizen.' Adult responsibility means knowing what is expected of one and fulfilling that expectation."[5] She finds that efforts to conform to the ideals associated with "feminine" roles—efforts to be docile, passive, supportive of men—result in low self-esteem and low estimates of women's power. These efforts keep us from being full participants in our democratic society. In short, the orientations fostered by being a "responsible" woman in the passive sense "form a clear picture of the acquiescent member of a political community."[6] And so women wait. We wait for a liturgy that nourishes our spirits; we wait for a meaningful work situation or supportive living environment; we wait for justice in the church and in the world.

The image of waiting is also prominent in Madonna Kolbenschlag's 1979 book, *Kiss Sleeping Beauty Goodbye*, which examines several fairy tales as "parables" of women's socialization and shows how cultural myths can dwarf our spiritual and ethical capacities.[7] In a chapter called "Sleeping Beauty at Seventeen," Kolbenschlag describes how young women are conditioned to wait for that magic kiss that will awaken them to existence. In this state of waiting, they allow their own spiritual powers to atrophy. Typical of this attitude of waiting is what Kolbenschlag calls "the desire to live for another." She writes:

> This role will school [the young woman] in self-forgetfulness, service and sacrifice, in nurturing rather than initiating behaviors. Above all, it will teach her to "sleep"—to wait, forever if necessary, for the expected other who will make her life meaningful and fulfilled. She will give up everything when the expected one comes, even the right of creating her own self. Whether it is a husband, a religion or a revolution, she is ready to live outside of herself, to abdicate responsibility for herself in favor of something or someone else.[8]

Women who have been drugged by our cultural myths, Kolbenschlag says, will seek fulfillment through others and, while waiting for this vicarious fulfillment, will regard themselves as persons "that things happen to, not as [persons] who make them happen."[9] ·

Carol Gilligan makes a similar point in her study of psychological theory and women's development, *In a Different Voice*. She speaks of the perceived conflict between "selfishness" and "responsibility" that leads in many instances to the "mysterious disappearance of the female self in adolescence," when an underground world is mapped out and "kept secret because it is branded by others as selfish and wrong."[10] Influenced by cultural pressures to epitomize "the morality of self-sacrifice," a woman may live and suffer under the mistaken assumption that "she is responsible for the actions of others while others are responsible for the choices she makes."[11] Such women will usually be very responsible in the passive sense. They will pour vast amounts of energy into conforming to others' expectations, but in a deeper sense they remain morally asleep.

The poignancy of this situation for any woman is expressed by the character Monica in *The Three Marias: New Portuguese Letters*: "In the end, what difference can my absence from this world make to you, if all I gave you was my absence from myself..."[12] All in all, Kolbenschlag's investigation of feminine myths and models leads to a finding remarkably similar to that of Virginia Sapiro: "The passivity and privatization of women in our society are the most serious obstacles to their own autonomy and personal growth, and also to the transformation and re-demption of the entire social structure."[13]

This research leaves us with the obvious question. How are we going to overcome this socialization to passivity that keeps us from really claiming our power? To begin to address this question, let me suggest three factors that are required for our moral empowerment: (1) we need to understand and accept these ambiguities involved in responsible action in a world where few choices are without risks or negative consequences; (2) we need a support system that both challenges and nurtures us; and (3) we need models of self-critical decision-making in which the ambiguities of power are taken into account.

As an example of such a model, consider the following case, which Yale theologian Margaret Farley analyzed in 1982 at the convention of the Catholic Theological Society of America. In a talk entitled, "Power and Powerlessness: A Case in Point," Farley described the then recent conflict between the Vatican and the Religious Sisters of Mercy of the Union over the issue of tubal ligation. Note the clear reasoning that went into the decision of the leaders of the community to submit to a Vatican directive to withdraw a letter they had sent to hospital administrators inviting dialogue on whether tubal ligations should be available in Mercy hospitals.

> The decision to forego a public position of dissent was not made because of a new belief in the teaching of the magisterium (on the issue of tubal ligation) or out of religious obedience to a disciplinary command. This does not mean that the Sisters of Mercy accept no fundamental authority in the Church, or that they see themselves in regard to their life and ministry as only autonomous agents in the Church, not subject to the Church and its legitimate authority in an important sense. It does mean that in this case they could not find the teaching of the magisterium persuasive and, in fact, interpreted the demands of the magisterium as an attempt to use juridical power to settle a question of truth. Perhaps even more importantly, they perceived the demand for continuation of a policy which they were convinced was unjustly injurious to other persons (patients in their hospitals) as contradictory to the overall obligation of the Sisters of Mercy (in fidelity and obedience to God and the Church) to carry on a ministry of healing. In other words, without special further justification, these specific demands by church officials entailed doing evil.[14]

Why then did these women decline to take a public position in opposition to the magisterium? After attending to three competing values
—community, ministry, and truth—they judged that in this instance silence and submission were necessary to preserve the religious community and its ministry. And so they accepted the evil entailed in "material
cooperation" with a problematic Vatican directive and hoped that their
decision would lead ultimately to greater good for the Church.

Farley describes the decision in terms of a relatively adequate
choice that must continue to be scrutinized:

> The decision of the Sisters of Mercy must still be reviewed and
> critiqued by those within the Community and without. The an-
> swer to the question, "Why did this group of women agree to
> be silenced?" seems ... to be this: "In order that theirs and
> other voices may ultimately prevail." The danger, of course, is
> that the silence will grow, and that power in the church will be
> more and more isolated, especially from the experience of
> women. But this story is unfinished.[15]

These words show that the fact that knowledge is limited need not
paralyze our powers of judgment, but rather can allow for decisions to
be made in trust and hope, with a conscience consoled by the assurance
that God's mercy will compensate for the ambiguity entailed. It is too
soon to know whether the community leaders' choice was better than
the alternative in terms of its effects, but I find the decision-making
process a model in terms of the awareness the women brought to the
process and their willingness to tolerate the ambiguities that seemed
necessary to endure.

The task I see ahead, then, involves continually challenging ourselves to be responsible in modes that include ourselves among those
deserving of our care and that refuse to relinquish the task of discerning our obligations and acting according to what we judge God is asking of us. To move thus to the level of creative responsibility will
inevitably lead to clashes with patriarchal authority, for to leave behind
passive responsibility is to stop living up to the Victorian ideal of
women as "angels in the house." Sad to say, those who judge by patriarchal stereotypes have only one other category in which to put women
who are not angels, namely that of monsters. Thus we should not be
surprised when our judiciously thought-through decisions evoke responses all out of proportion to what we have said or done. The response is not to the words or deeds themselves so much as to a
monstrous image of female insubordination. Women are not supposed

to be assertive or autonomous or powerful, and those who do not be-have like Snow White will inevitably be linked with the Wicked Witch of the West.

As long as *we* have other categories for interpreting ourselves be-sides angels and monsters, this aspect of existence under patriarchy need not trouble us unduly. But being aware of the stereotypes that we face is part of what is necessary for a realistic assessment of the likely consequences of what we decide to say and do.

I conclude with another positive model, an example of a woman acting with power under ambiguous circumstances in Washington, DC, that city of politics and power. I have in mind Sr. Theresa Kane's deci-sion to respond to repeated refusals for private conversations with Pope John Paul II by using the occasion of a formal welcome to convey a message she deemed urgent for him to hear. After greeting the pontiff at the beginning of a prayer service at the National Shrine of the Im-maculate Conception in October 1979, Kane, then the president of the Leadership Conference of Women Religious, went on to say:

> I call upon you to listen with compassion and to hear the call of women who comprise half of humankind... The church in its struggle to be faithful to its call for reverence and dignity for all persons must respond by providing the possibility of women as persons being included in all ministries of our church.[16]

Kane's action was unexpected and controversial, but it epitomized creative responsibility in the way it balanced conflicting values within limited circumstances. She had the duty to express welcome and re-spect; she had the obligation to represent the injustices experienced by those who had chosen her as leader. Both concerns found their way into the course she finally elected, and, to my mind, she succeeded in "speaking the truth in love," providing a new image of what goodness for a Catholic woman can mean, of what the responsible use of power in ambiguous circumstances can look like.

Notes

1. Beverly Wildung Harrison, *Our Right to Choose* (Boston: Beacon Press, 1983), 92–93.
2. Carter Heyward, *Our Passion for Justice: Images of Power, Sexuality, and Lib-eration* (New York: Pilgrim Press, 1984), 116.

3. Bernard Loomer, "Two Kinds of Power," *Criterion* 15 (Winter 1976): 20, 23.

4. Valerie Saiving, 'The Human Situation: A Feminine View," in *Womanspirit Rising*, ed. Carol Christ and Judith Plaskow (New York: Harper and Row, 1979), 25–42.

5. Virginia Sapiro, *The Political Integration of Women: Roles, Socialization, and Politics* (Urbana: University of Illinois Press, 1983), 47.

6. Ibid., 106.

7. Madonna Kolbenschlag, *Kiss Sleeping Beauty Goodbye: Breaking the Spell of Feminine Myths and Models* (New York: Bantam Books, 1981), 3.

8. Ibid., 10.

9. Ibid., 12.

10. Carol Gilligan, *In a Different Voice: Psychological Theory and Women's Development* (Cambridge: Harvard University Press, 1982), 51.

11. Ibid., 82.

12. As quoted in Kolbenschlag, *Kiss Sleeping Beauty Goodbye*, 27.

13. Sapiro, *The Political Integration of Women*, 78.

14. Margaret Farley, "Power and Powerlessness: A Case in Point," *Proceedings of the Catholic Theological Society of America* 37 (1982): 117.

15. Ibid., 119.

16. Theresa Kane, quoted in *The Washington Post*, 8 October 1979, A–25.

19

"WHAT IN GOD'S EYE [S]HE IS"

Prospects for Women in Tomorrow's Church

This was one of Anne Patrick's last major lectures. In its engagement with literature, it exemplifies the approaches of the second section of this volume; in its anatomy of the three roles available to women—the mystical, ministerial, and prophetic—it dovetails with discussions of those roles throughout this volume; in its analysis of how change can occur within the church, it demonstrates Patrick's shrewdness and sensitivity. Like other essays in this volume, it also demonstrates the extraordinary amalgam of bravery and judiciousness with which Anne Patrick repeatedly addressed problems central to the church during the half-century between her final vows and her death. —HD

In going to Gerard Manley Hopkins for the title of my lecture, and giving attention to his poem, "As Kingfishers Catch Fire," I'm trying to repay a debt I've owed to Hopkins for nearly forty years, ever since I was a graduate student at the University of Chicago. Nearby was a Jesuit house of studies called Hopkins Hall, and for me Hopkins Hall came to symbolize the friendship and hospitality offered by Chicago Jesuits in the seventies, men who not only supported the idea of women's gaining a voice in the church, but who also offered practical help as we broke new ground as women studying theology.

So when Father Fitzgibbons invited me to take part in this program under the theme of "Inflaming the Religious Imagination: Like Shining from Shook Foil," it felt right to search for another line from Hopkins to crystallize the thoughts I would share with you at Marquette. As you

Adapted from the Marquette University Catholic Intellectual Tradition Lecture of the same title, Marquette University, Milwaukee, April 6, 2011.

savor the poem, I think you'll see why I chose "As Kingfishers Catch Fire" to launch an inquiry into "Prospects for Women in Tomorrow's Church." Hopkins wrote "Kingfishers" in March or April of 1877, when he was thirty-three years old and studying theology in northern Wales. Later that year he would fail his final exam but still go on to ordination, and eventually to fame as a poet. It gives us all hope!

With Hopkins guiding my efforts, I've proposed an alliterative outline for tonight's talk, since Jesuits love outlines and poets love alliteration: (1) The Poem, (2) The Problem, and (3) The Prospects.

THE POEM

I don't claim to understand everything in this poem, but I find it helps to know that a kingfisher's crown and wings are electric blue, while its breast is orange. The image of kingfishers "catching fire," then, is a way of saying how they look when they take flight, when the orange feathers soar above us like flames. And the image is perfect for Hopkins's point, namely, that what the birds do is what they are. So let's enjoy the poem:

As Kingfishers Catch Fire, Dragonflies Draw Flame

As kingfishers catch fire, dragonflies dráw fláme;
As tumbled over rim in roundy wells
Stones ring; like each tucked string tells, each hung bell's
Bow swung finds tongue to fling out broad its name;
Each mortal thing does one thing and the same:
Deals out that being indoors each one dwells;
Selves—goes itself, *myself* it speaks and spells,
Crying *Whát I dó is me: for that I came.*

Í say móre: the just man justices;
Kéeps gráce: thát keeps all his goings graces;
Acts in God's eye what in God's eye he is—
Chríst—for Christ plays in ten thousand places,
Lovely in limbs, and lovely in eyes not his
To the Father through the features of men's faces.
                              —Gerard Manley Hopkins, SJ

How literally shall we take Hopkins? Is God actually a Father? Is Christ "lovely" to God only in male limbs and eyes and faces? Or does the claim "*Whát I dó is me*" invite a less literal interpretation of the second stanza altogether? If so, we can affirm God's fatherhood as one image of Divine Reality, without denying that God can also be imaged as a mother, or, in a wonderfully mixed biblical metaphor from Deuteronomy 32:18, as the Rock who gave us birth. Or indeed, as Hildegard of Bingen loved to image God, as the greening power that surprises us with new life each spring.

And with respect to humanity, can we understand Hopkins to be using the literary device of synechdoche, the substitution of the part for the whole, in what he says about men? This would mean that the just woman also "justices," "keeps grace," and "Acts in God's eye what in God's eye [s]he is—Christ"? Hopkins may, in fact, have assumed that women are included when he speaks of "men," for in his day even female authors commonly wrote in what we call "the generic masculine" to describe humanity. Indeed, liturgical language still does this, as Catholics know from the line of the Nicene Creed that refers to the incarnation, undertaken "for us men and for our salvation." Women have been baptized from the dawn of Christianity, and no one has questioned whether God intends our salvation. There are, however, disputes about the extent to which women can image Christ. And this is the problem we must face.

THE PROBLEM

Women are told we can and should *imitate* Christ, practicing the virtues and promoting the values of God's realm; but for now, at least, we are considered by official Catholicism as incapable of acting *in persona Christi*, of taking on Christ's role of community leader and celebrant of the sacraments. There's a difference of opinion, in short, on whether or not women are capable of being ordained priests, deacons, and bishops. And in adapting Hopkins's line to the feminine, "what in God's eye [s]he is," I want to call attention to the centrality of this theological issue of the meaning of women's humanity for any view of what we can look forward to in tomorrow's church.

What in God's eye is women's nature? In raising the question I must admit that we can never answer this fully, for who can know the mind of God but God? Indeed, to speak of God's mind or God's eye is anthropomorphic, instances of the analogical language that tells us *something* about the Divine but can never be adequate to Her Reality. In using the feminine pronoun here I want to underscore the fact that it is just as true—and just as untrue—to speak of Her Divine Reality as it is to speak of His Divine Reality, for God transcends gender entirely, though when our pronouns and images are overwhelmingly masculine we may tend to forget this (see Catechism, 239). On this point I'm struck by the words of a girl named Sylvia, who long ago contributed a prayer to Art Linkletter's book, *Children's Letters to God*. Sylvia got right to the point: "Dear God, Are boys better than girls? I know you are one, but try to be fair."[1] Let's hope Sylvia eventually got to study theology at Marquette and read Elizabeth Johnson's *She Who Is*, or in some other way came to learn that God is not male, nor does God intend gender injustice for human beings.

Not many years before Sylvia wrote her letter to God, the bishops at the Second Vatican Council had things to say about human nature and justice, and the documents they published hold such contradictions; I would suggest anachronistically that a close encounter with Elizabeth Johnson's writings would also have done them good. The Council's Pastoral Constitution on the Church in the Modern World (*Gaudium et Spes*) contains a strong passage against discrimination: "With respect to the fundamental rights of the person, every type of discrimination, whether social or cultural, whether based on sex, race, color, social condition, language, or religion, is to be overcome and eradicated as contrary to God's intent" (29). This principle, however, is undercut by subsequent emphasis on the preservation of the "domestic role of women" (52) and by the qualification "in accordance with their own nature," attached to the passage recommending that women assume "their full proper role" in cultural life (60). Underlying this qualification is the assumption that woman's nature is well defined and limited.

Although the bishops had affirmed the equal human dignity of women and men, and shown some approval of the women's movement for social and legal equality, their message to women at the close of the council indicates that past attitudes still held sway. Even the existence of a special message to women is telling, since there was no similar message addressed simply to "men," although there were messages addressed to "rulers," "men of thought and science," "artists," and "workers." This arrangement of categories implies that women were thought of primarily in sexual roles, while men were seen in terms of diverse vocational contributions. The message to women begins, "And now it is to you that we address ourselves, women of all states—girls, wives, mothers, and widows, to you also, consecrated virgins and women living alone—you constitute half of the immense human family."

The message goes on to mention that "the vocation of woman" is in the present era "being achieved in its fullness," a statement whose tone of assurance that the bishops already know what this vocation is stands in marked contrast to what is said in the message to workers ("very loved sons"): "The Church is ever seeking to understand you better." Here, in sum, we have a conundrum that continues to permeate official Catholic thought: the nature and meaning of human existence is a religious mystery, illuminated by the light of Christ, but never fully knowable to finite minds (*GS* 10); yet somehow the nature of woman is clear, and her role subordinate.

If we fast forward to more recent documents, including the Catechism of the Catholic Church, we find this conundrum persists. The Catechism states that "equality and difference are willed by God," and interprets this to mean that gender difference renders some human beings capable of receiving seven sacraments, while others can receive only six. And all decision-making power is currently in hands consecrated by that seventh sacrament. To Sylvia and many of her brothers and sisters this seems unfair. They name it an instance of injustice, specifically sexism, a sin that has both personal and institutional forms. Not all Catholics, however, agree with Sylvia on this point, for they find what the Catechism says persuasive:

> "Only a baptized man (*vir*) validly receives sacred ordination." The Lord Jesus chose men (*viri*) to form the college of the twelve apostles, and the apostles did the same when they chose collaborators to succeed them in their ministry. The college of bishops, with whom the priests are united in the priesthood, makes the college of the twelve an ever-present and ever-active reality until Christ's return. The Church recognizes herself to be bound by this choice made by the Lord himself. For this reason the ordination of women is not possible. (Catechism 1577, quoting CIC canon 1024)

Sylvia and her friends, however, cannot agree with the Catechism here. They notice that it is the privileged males who render this judgment, and the Catechism seems to ignore the historical fact that ordination as we understand it today did not take place in the early church, as well as the fact that in ancient Christianity deaconesses held positions equivalent to those of deacons. And when liturgical rites for deacons did evolve, so did rites for deaconesses. A rite from the eighth century, called "Prayer for the Ordination of a Deaconess," in fact, is contained in the Vatican Library's Codex Barberini (gr. 336), and it reads as follows:

> The candidate to be ordained deaconess is presented to the bishop...As she bows her head the bishop imposes his hand

...praying: "Holy and almighty God, who by the birth of thine only begotten Son of a virgin hath sanctified womankind, and hath poured forth the grace and coming of the Holy Spirit not only on men but also on women, now therefore look upon this thy handmaid, and call her into the work of thy service, and send the abundant gift of thy Spirit upon her. Amen."

The bishop imposes his hand on the head of the ordained, praying: "Supreme Lord, who dost not reject women consecrating themselves to fitting service in thy holy temples, but admittest them into the order of thy ministers, even upon this thy handmaid, wishing to consecrate herself to thee and to carry out the grace of thy ministry, pour forth the grace of thy Holy Spirit, as thou admitted Phoebe to the work of thy chosen ministry..."

Phoebe is the first-century woman whom Paul called "*diakonos* of the church at Cenchreae" in his letter to the Romans, chapter 16:1 (*NJB*). I confess that I did not discover this prayer for ordaining a woman in the Vatican Library myself, but rather in the pages of *Commonweal* last January [2010]. We may reasonably suppose that it will not show up soon in *Our Sunday Visitor*.[2]

There are many issues being debated where justice for women is concerned, and I focus on the question of ordination because sacraments are so central to our tradition. Forty years ago I had two experiences that influenced me on this matter. The first was an attempted suicide by a high school student, who was rescued at the last minute by someone who smelled gas escaping from the science lab. After this girl was taken from the emergency room to a psychiatric hospital, I learned that because she'd been so badly abused by her stepfather she could only be treated by female therapists. I wondered: What does that mean for her Catholicism? So many prayers to God as father, having to confess her sins to a man, how could she benefit from the sacraments?

Later that year—1971—I had the opportunity to address a small committee of bishops on women's roles in the church. I made the best argument I could in favor of women's ordination, and was dumfounded when all four of them said, "I agree with you; our problem is we don't have the votes." There went my stereotype of bishops! These four were a minority in the Bishops' Conference, and even if all the American bishops should favor women's ordination, this would not mean a change in church policy. That became clear during the 1980s, when the Vatican stymied our bishops' efforts to develop a pastoral letter on Women's Concerns following their prophetic letters on nuclear weapons

and the U.S. economy. After four drafts and significant Vatican intervention, they were unable to reach a consensus, and so they quietly published the last draft as a committee report. Later, they confessed in a
reflection called "Strengthening the Bonds of Peace," that "sexism, defined as 'unjust discrimination based on sex,' is still present in some
members of the church," and pledged to work against it in teaching and
practice.[3] The issue here is whether or not sacramental discrimination is
unjust, and the bishops are not of one mind on this point, though for the
sake of Catholic unity none has expressed a dissenting view publicly
since Pope John Paul II declared the question settled in 1994. I think we
can say today that we have some *Commonweal* bishops, but many more
who lean toward *Our Sunday Visitor*.

There is also a great divide within the U.S. laity where views on
women's ordination are concerned. To cite sociologist William V. D'Antonio and his colleagues, on the whole American "Catholics have
greatly increased their support for having women priests since the earliest survey in 1974." Their 2005 survey found that 54 percent of American Catholics "thought it would be a good thing if 'married women
were allowed to be ordained as priests,' and 61 percent thought it
would be a good thing if celibate women were allowed to be ordained
as priests." On the other hand, the same study found that even in 2005,
29 percent of American Catholics would strongly oppose such a change,
for they regard "a celibate male clergy" as "essential" to the Church.[4] Of
course, in Jesus' day I'm sure a survey of Jews would have found a
much higher percentage who held that worship at the Temple in
Jerusalem was "essential" to their tradition, though this proved not to
be the case when Rabbinic Judaism developed after the Romans destroyed the Temple.

But back to Catholicism and the issue of women's ordination. In
2005 there were about 64 million U.S. Catholics,[5] and while more than
half of us were open to change on this question, some 19 million vehemently opposed change. That's a lot of people, and the stakes are high.
Add to this the fact that papal authority, both in its teaching and its ap-
pointments of bishops, strongly supports this view. And on top of this
the fact that the entire U.S. Catholic population is only about 6 percent
of the global membership of the church, and although there are support-
ers of women's ordination on every continent, this is not a priority issue
in the developing world.[6] Thus I think we must admit that even restoring the diaconate to women is unlikely for the immediate future. I won't
go as far as the reporter John Allen does in his book *Future Church*,[7]
where he predicts that there will be no change on the question of
women's ordination in this century, but I doubt we will see change in

the next twenty-five years. And David Gibson, another journalist, may be right in thinking that the "unparalleled import" of this momentous change "is such that the church should be of one mind, or as close to an accord as possible, before making such a transformation."[8] Meanwhile, where justice for women is concerned, the world church can act on matters where there is much greater agreement against sexism—matters such as female infanticide, genital mutilation, human trafficking, and the privileging of boys when it comes to food, medicine, and schooling.

When I look at the large picture, then, I conclude that sacramental sexism may be with our tradition for some time. What then are the prospects for women who seek to "Act in God's eye what in God's eye" they are, namely, Christ? What are the prospects for the women on every continent who want to respond to the call of their Creator with all their gifts of mind and heart, including gifts of spiritual leadership and insight? Indeed, what are the prospects for the women and men throughout the world who agree with the North American majority that excluding women from sacramental leadership is unjust? We seem to have reached an impasse.

THE PROSPECTS

When the road to progress seems so definitively blocked, we are in need of the inflamed religious imagination that the theme of this mission week at Marquette calls to mind. In characterizing this religious imagination as "like shining from shook foil," the mission week planners drew on another Hopkins poem, "God's Grandeur," a poem that exudes an amazing confidence that the messed-up world of sexism, racism, economic injustice, heterosexism, and environmental damage is not left to its own devices: "Because," in the words of the poet, "the Holy Ghost over the bent / World broods with warm breast and with ah! bright wings."

The Holy Ghost of Hopkins's poem is the same Spirit that Jesus promised would transform his followers after his death, and that Christians have continued to experience to this day in the mystery we name Pentecost. If we receive such gifts of the Spirit, what then will our inflamed imaginations see? Will the prospects for women in tomorrow's church turn out to be more than meets the eyes of John Allen and other journalists, and will these prospects give us grounds for hope in a time of impasse? The word "prospects" connotes vistas, the long and wide view of a scene, perhaps gained by climbing to a high vantage point. "Prospects" also connotes treasure, something valuable that ends up in the miner's pan after a day of bending over a bone-chilling stream to wash off the junk that obscures a nugget of gold. So what vistas open up when our religious imaginations are inflamed with the mystical vision of Hopkins? What nuggets of treasure might we discover if we try to look at the scene with "God's eye" and to "act in God's eye" what in God's eye we are?

Hopkins meant the word "act" in the sense of acting a role in a play. So let's say that women really have been assigned the role of Christ. How can we learn to act our part well? Contemplating the Jesus of the gospels is something we'll need to do, and likewise it helps to look at the lives of holy women and men closer to our time, to see how their interpretation of the role of Christ might inspire our own. This "acting" assignment is more one of improvisation than of rehearsing a prepared script, for the scene and characters around us are changing as we move through history.

The world and the church are not the same today as they were fifty, or even ten years ago. But some things do not change, and one of these is God's faithfulness and care for all her people, especially those who are poor and disadvantaged. And so today [in April 2011], can the eyes of faith give us a clear enough vision of the current scene that Catholic women can improvise with confidence about our role of acting in God's eye as Christ? All that Jesus said about the *basileia*, the word translated as "kingdom" or "reign" of God, still applies. God *is* acting in history to bring to full realization the values of her realm, and much of that activity is hidden from sight. And marvelously, we are part of that activity.

One of my favorite *basileia* sayings is from the gospels of Matthew and Luke, about the yeast hidden in dough, which gradually leavens the whole loaf (Mt 13:33, Lk 13:21). This image reminds me of the stage of the creative process called incubation. After someone has studied a problem or worked intensely on a creative project for a while, there usually needs to be some "down time," when the mind is not consciously at work on the solution, before the answer presents itself. You may have experienced this when working on a term paper or a math problem. You've struggled for hours with all your brain power, to no avail. So you do your laundry, play Frisbee, or go to bed, and suddenly the right idea surprises you, a gift from the subconscious mind that had been working below the surface of awareness while you were sleeping or otherwise away from the problem. I think this idea of "incubation" also applies to the way reforms take place in church history. Efforts by reformers are important to the process, but in God's providence they do not usually lead to immediate results. The leavening process may take a long time.

Years ago I heard the communications expert Kathleen Hall Jamieson remark that papal teaching does change, but only after there has been a period of papal silence on a question. Pope John Paul II's efforts to settle questions of sexual ethics once and for all in his 1993 encyclical *Veritatis Splendor*, and his 1994 attempt to forbid discussion of women's ordination, may have opened such a period of papal silence on some of the most controversial matters of our day. How long it will be until there is change remains to be seen, and perhaps there will never be change. But history offers many examples of what was once thought to be the "last word" proving not to have been final after all.

In the meanwhile, besides contemplating Jesus and his view of God's action in history, women can take inspiration from others who have experienced injustice from the church and yet remained faithful to the spirit of the gospel, which paradoxically they learned about in this flawed institution. An outstanding example is the witness of African-American Catholics, who have demonstrated an "uncommon faithfulness" during centuries of injustice far more damaging to body and spirit than the sexism that excludes twenty-first century women from ordination. As former Marquette professor Shawn Copeland reminds us in the book *Uncommon Faithfulness*, the Catholic Church has a "blemished" record on slavery and very few Catholics were abolitionists.[9] Nor did an unequivocal condemnation of slavery come from Rome until Vatican II.[10]

Moreover, the racism that had sustained slavery did not end with the Emancipation Proclamation or Civil Rights legislation, but has shown itself in countless ways down to the present, as works such as Father Bryan Massingale's book on *Racial Justice and the Catholic Church* make clear.[11] Although white Catholics no longer discourage minority religious vocations so flagrantly, or relegate persons of color to the back of the communion line, we have not yet examined in the depth necessary for real change the ways that white privilege makes our lives unfairly easier than those of our brothers and sisters of color. When I think about the patience and holiness that Black and Latino Catholics especially have shown despite racism in church members and structures, I find sources of inspiration and suggestions for strategies for all Catholic women who long for an end to institutionalized sexism. The lives of two saintly African Americans come to mind here, Henriette Delille and Augustus Tolton, Catholics who showed great faith and creativity in dealing with obstacles to what each felt God was asking of them.

Henriette Delille was a free woman of color in nineteenth-century New Orleans, who was destined to follow her mother into the system of sexual slavery known there as *plaçage*, and end up as the concubine of a wealthy white man. Instead, Delille's love for God and neighbor led her to found a society of black women that eventually became the Sisters of the Holy Family, a group of vowed religious dedicated to the works of mercy among their own people. By her choice of this "countercultural life," Delille confronted the "congealed evil" of her own society, and, in Copeland's words, "reconceived, redefined, and reconsecrated the colonized and abused bodies of black women." Professor Copeland's Madeleva Lecture on *The Subversive Power of Love* analyzes Delille's accomplishments and offers inspiration for women today who may be discouraged about the barriers to their own hopes and dreams.[12]

Augustus Tolton was baptized as an infant slave in 1854, and later his parents escaped slavery though his father died in the Union Army during the Civil War. A priest befriended the family and encouraged Augustus to pursue a priestly calling, but no seminary in this country would accept this black man. So Tolton went to Rome and studied at the College of the Propogation of the Faith, and was ordained in 1886 for his home diocese of Quincy, Illinois. But a white priest made ministry impossible there, so Tolton moved to Chicago, and served eleven years in the black community there before dying from heat stroke when he was forty-three.[13] Like Henriette Delille, he is now being considered for sainthood. Both Delille and Tolton dealt with impasse by making a way out of "no way," and their lives are instructive for Catholic women today who seek to "act in God's eye what in God's eye they are—Christ."

To "act in God's eye" in our circumstances, we need a plural strategy, one that respects different gifts and callings. There are many roles requiring wisdom and improvisational skill, and I will discuss four: a mystical role, a ministerial role, a leadership role, and a prophetic role. A woman may of course play more than one of these roles.

The *mystical role* involves dedicating time and energy to the experience of God's presence, power, and love—in other words, to prayer. The focus here is on the reality of divine love, which Copeland's book demonstrates has an amazingly subversive power. There have never been sexist barriers to mysticism in our tradition, and women mystics such as Catherine of Siena have at times had great influence on church leaders. Besides such famous mystics, there have always been women of deep prayer in our parishes and communities, and these visionaries help us to see not only our own situation but the suffering of a world that yearns for God's peace, justice, and reconciliation.

I believe that a crucial role for North American women mystics today, especially those privileged by race, class, and education, is to keep the injustice we suffer in perspective, by expanding our vision to encompass *all* those God loves. As one such mystic, Carmelite Sister Constance Fitzgerald, has observed, "privileged women's experience of social or ecclesial marginalization" pales in comparison with "women's experience of chattel slavery or sexual and physical abuse." And, I would add, it pales in comparison with the agony of seeing one's child die for want of clean water or basic health care, or because of senseless violence. In light of all this, today's Catholic women—especially those of us who are well-fed, educated, and white—we can allow our dreams of full equality in canon law to be deferred for a time, and focus more attention on the injustices experienced by racial minorities and the poor in this country, and indeed, by economically poor women throughout the world.

The *ministerial role* is available to women today to an extent that would have amazed our foremothers. Before Vatican II the role of "lay ecclesial minister" did not exist, but by 2005 there were 31,000 of them in the United States, and 80 percent of these were women.[14] When I went to Alaska sixteen years ago, a woman functioned as pastor in all of the small town parishes I visited, with a priest flying in for the sacraments a couple of times a month. The fact that women are providing most of the pastoral care in Catholic parishes, hospitals, and schools is contributing to future change in an organic way, for these women ministers *are* experienced as representing Christ by those they help, so when ordination finally becomes possible the people will have been prepared for this change. Admittedly the role is subordinate to male authority, and women who work for the church do not always enjoy the job security, an adequate pay scale, and the working conditions they deserve. However, the rewards of pastoral service are many, and women "acting in God's eye" in officially sanctioned ministerial roles are laying the groundwork for a future Church that will, in God's time, fully repent of sexism.

Although sacramental leadership is not now an officially sanctioned possibility, other leadership roles are open to women in the Church, and those who "act in God's eye as Christ" as leaders are also helping to prepare for the eventual full equality of women in Catholicism. John Allen notes that "At the most senior levels in dioceses, 26.8 percent of executive positions are held by women," and if the positions of bishop and vicar general are removed from the equation, the figure rises to 39 percent.[15] Women have been serving as chancellors and personnel directors at the diocesan level, and at the national level have had major responsibilities at the Bishops' Conference and other Catholic organizations. Canon lawyer and Sister of Mercy Sharon Euart was associate general secretary of the Bishops' Conference for thirteen years, and Sharon Daly was a vice-president of Catholic Charities USA for a dozen years. Dolores Lecky headed the Bishops' Secretariat for Family, Laity, Women, and Youth for twenty years, and Mercy Sister Mary Ann Walsh is currently Director of Media Relations for the bishops. Sister Carol Keehan, DC, is president of the Catholic Health Association, and was named "2010 Person of the Year" by the *National Catholic Reporter* for her leadership in helping to bring "health care coverage within the reach on an additional 32 million Americans."[16] The Vatican does not yet have a woman leading an agency, but in 2004 Pope John Paul II named Mary Ann Glendon head of the Pontifical Academy for Social Sciences, a significant "first."[17]

Finally, the *prophetic role* involves the willingness to risk security and other goods in order to voice one's convictions about what God wants in a situation. The task of a prophet is to speak the truth to power, and to speak the truth in love. If one's sense of truth is critical of current church policy, the role may not be compatible with church employment, and this can be a difficulty for women who feel called to ministry. The Roman Catholic Women Priests movement sees itself as a prophetic group called to "push the envelope" on what its members regard as a fundamental question of justice for all the baptized. I have been especially impressed by the story of one of their leaders, Patricia Fresen, a white South African whom I met in Johannesburg a decade ago.

During the apartheid era Fresen had been arrested for integrating the Catholic school of which she was principal. Later her Dominican religious community sent her to study theology in Rome, where two priest-professors told her that if ever women should be ordained, she had the gifts that would make for a good priest. Fresen then returned to South Africa and taught theology at the national seminary in Pretoria, and then at the Catholic university in Johannesburg. When I spoke with her in 2000 we discussed many things, including racism, but never got around to the topic of women's ordination. I recall being edified by her character and faith, and when I later learned that she had been ordained a priest in a 2003 ceremony that Rome regards as wrong and invalid, I knew she would not have done this lightly. Indeed, she has paid a high price for answering what she perceived as a call to violate a law of the Catholic Church in the hope that such action would contribute toward eventual reform, much as breaking the laws of apartheid had led to a more just government in her country. Actions she views as prophetic have cost her a teaching job and her membership in the Dominicans after forty-five years, and she has also been formally excommunicated. However, she still claims to be loyal to the

Catholic Church, and she has the support of two or three bishops in Europe, who to avoid schism do not voice this publicly.

The jury is still out on whether in a century or two Fresen will be thought of as more like the Dominican Catherine of Siena or the Augustinian Martin Luther, but she and her colleagues are unquestionably serious about reform. I believe that the words of the first-century Jew Gamaliel concerning the preaching of Peter are relevant to their situation; as we read in the Acts of the Apostles: "For if this idea of theirs or its execution is of human origin, it will collapse; but if it is from God, you will never be able to put them down" (Acts 5:38–39). When it comes to prophecy, it seems to me, there are two things to keep in mind: whether it is true or false is not always evident right away, but only in God's time, and in any case the role of prophet is not for the faint of heart.

Where is God in this complex scene, which includes other agents and roles than those I've described, the women who improvise as mystics, ministers, leaders, and prophets? It takes an inflamed religious imagination to discern this divine activity, as Jesus did in his many sayings about the reign of God on earth, and it takes an inflamed religious imagination to be patient while the wheat and tares grow up together until the harvest. Such an inflamed imagination is evident in some words often attributed to the martyred archbishop of San Salvador, Oscar Romero, but which were actually written by the late bishop of Saginaw, Kenneth Untener:

> It helps now and then to step back and take the long view. The reign of God is not only beyond our efforts. It is beyond our vision. We accomplish in our lifetime only a tiny fraction of the magnificent enterprise that is God's work. Nothing we do is complete, which is another way of saying the reign of God always lies beyond us . . . We cannot do everything but there is a sense of liberation in realizing that because this enables us to do something and to do it well. It may be incomplete but it is a beginning, a step along the way, an opportunity for God's grace to enter and do the rest.[18]

And so we come full circle to the poem with which we started. Hopkins shared with the mystic Teresa of Avila the conviction that, "Ours are the eyes through which the compassion of Christ looks out upon the world. Ours are the feet with which [Christ] goes about doing good. Ours are the hands with which [Christ] blesses the people."[19] That is the reality that we need to remember. And we can also take encouragement from our poem's opening line, "As kingfishers catch fire," for this image captures the fact that when it is God's time, change happens with a beauty and suddenness that takes our breath away.

Notes

1. Quoted in Casey Miller and Kate Swift, *Words and Women* (New York: Anchor Books, 1976).

2. Damian Barry Smith, "Fitting Service," January 28, 2011, 3, in letter from Joseph J. Koechler, February 25, 2011, 2.

3. Strengthening the Bonds of Peace: A Pastoral Reflection on Women in the Church and in Society (Washington, DC: United States Catholic Conference, Inc., 1995).

4. William V. D'Antonio, James D. Davidson, Dean R. Hoge, and Mary L. Gautier, *American Catholics Today: New Realities of Their Faith and Their Church* (Lanham, MD: Rowman & Littlefield, 2007), 77, 26.

5. Ibid., 55.

6. John Allen, *The Future Church: How Ten Trends Are Revolutionizing the Catholic Church* (New York: Image Books, 2012).

7. Ibid.

8. James Gibson, *The Coming Catholic Church: How the Faithful Are Shaping a New American Catholicism* (New York: Harper One, 20004), 71.

9. M. Shawn Copeland, ed., *Uncommon Faithfulness: The Black Catholic Experience* (Maryknoll, NY: Orbis Books, 2009), 1.

10. John T. Noonan, Jr., *A Church That Can and Cannot Change: The Development of Catholic Moral Teaching* (South Bend, IN: University of Notre Dame Press, 2005), 120.

11. Bryan N. Massingale, *Racial Justice and the Catholic Church* (Maryknoll, NY: Orbis Books, 2010).

12. M. Shawn Copeland, *The Subversive Power of Love: The Vision of Henriette Delille*, The Madeleva Lecture Series (Mahwah, NJ: Paulist Press, 2011), 61, 52.

13. *National Catholic Reporter* online December 3, 2010.

14. Allen, *The Future Church*, 195.

15. Ibid., 196.

16. *National Catholic Reporter*, January 7, 2011.

17. Allen, *The Future Church*, 198.

18. Quoted by Thomas Gumbleton in a homily for March 28, 2004.

19. Quote from Teresa of Avila by Camille D'Arienzo, RSM, "A Sisters' History," *America* (February 7, 2011), 27.

20

THE VATICAN, FEMINISM, AND U.S. WOMEN RELIGIOUS

This essay examines the apostolic visitation of non-cloistered U.S. women's congregations, initiated by Pope John Paul as what was widely seen as an attack on women religious. Anne Patrick stresses the need to determine whether central attitudes to gender are human constructs or divinely ordained principles and the need to respect divergent opinions. Here, as in other essays, she affirms that a hierarchical system is not necessarily oppressive or patriarchal. —HD

Twice in recent months Catholics have breathed a sigh of relief when press conferences in Rome announced the friendly settlement of difficulties between Vatican officials and American women religious. On December 16, 2014 the Apostolic Visitation of non-cloistered U.S. women's congregations that began in 2009 came officially to a close with gracious statements from representatives of the Vatican's congregation for religious, the Leadership Conference of Women Religious (LCWR), the Council of Major Superiors of Women Religious (CMSWR), and the American sister who had been the official Visitator, Mother Mary Clare Millea, ASCJ.[1] And on April 15, 2015, in a report issued jointly by officers of LCWR and the bishops who had been mandated to investigate the group's doctrinal orthodoxy, both sides agreed that the mandate had been accomplished and their conversations had "borne much fruit." The report adds:

> The very fact of such substantive dialogue between bishops and religious has been a blessing to be appreciated and further

---

This article is based on "Tensions Over 'Feminism': U.S. Women Religious, and the Contested Reception of Vatican II," a presentation on May 22, 2015 at Georgetown University for the Ninth Ecclesiological Investigations Network International Conference, "Vatican II—Remembering the Future."

encouraged. The commitment of LCWR leadership to its crucial role in service to the mission and membership of the Conference will continue to guide and strengthen LCWR's witness
to the great vocation of Religious Life, to its sure foundation in
Christ, and to ecclesial communion.[2]

These words were affirmed by Archbishop Peter Sartain and Bish-
ops Leonard Blair and Thomas Paprocki, and by LCWR officers Sharon
Holland, IHM, Marcia Allen, CSJ, Carol Zinn, SSJ, and Joan Marie
Steadman, CSC.

In an essay for the volume *Power of Sisterhood: Women Religious Tell
the Story of the Apostolic Visitation*, Dominican sister Patricia Walter
aptly describes the Apostolic Visitation as part of "the contentious
process of receiving the Second Vatican Council," and this is true of the
Doctrinal Investigation of LCWR as well.[3] In my book, *Conscience and
Calling: Ethical Reflections on Catholic Women's Church Vocations*, I observe that the two groups of officers of non-cloistered U.S. women's
communities, LCWR and CMSWR, give evidence of being influenced
by different conciliar documents.[4]

Both groups of women religious studied all the major documents
of Vatican II more assiduously than did most Catholics, and integrated
these teachings into their processes of renewal. Over time it became
apparent that the larger group, representing about 80 percent of U.S.
sisters, has been especially influenced by *Gaudium et Spes*, with its emphasis on mission to eradicate injustice, while the CMSWR communities have stressed *Perfectae Caritatis* and undertaken their renewal with
greater concern for preserving some monastic aspects of religious life
and a distinctive habit, and with following an agenda set by the hierarchy. In distinguishing these two groups of sisters, it is important to
recognize that there is diversity within both organizations, and that although their visions for radical discipleship may differ, sisters from
both sorts of communities have much in common. As theologian
Christine Firer Hinze notes in an online article for *America*, June 18,
2012:

> [B]oth LCWR and CMSWR communities serve the gospel at
> contemporary frontiers, living lives of passionate love in and
> from the heart of the church. Both articulate and practice the
> basic elements of consecrated life (vows of poverty, chastity
> and obedience; life in community, and mission) in light of
> prayerful discernment of the needs of the church and the signs
> of the times.[5]

That said, Hinze adds that the CMSWR communities tend to understand gender, sexual difference, and men and women's vocations in a way that is much closer to Pope John Paul II's emphasis on gender complementarity than do LCWR communities. Indeed, it seems clear that those responsible for initiating the Apostolic Visitation and the Doctrinal Investigation were more comfortable with understanding women's nature and role as special and limited, and with concerns that feminism, at least in its "radical" form, has harmed women's religious life in the United States. (Officials who complained about "radical feminism" did not define what this means, or explain how it differs from the sort of feminism they might approve).

There are many definitions and types of feminism, and feminists differ widely in their analyses of injustice, levels of commitment to liberating action, degrees of explicitness of commitment, and opinions about specific problems and their solutions. I have defined the term "feminist" broadly to indicate a position that involves a solid conviction of the equality of women and men, and a commitment to reform society so that the full equality of women is respected, which also requires reforming the thought systems that legitimate the present unjust social order.[6]

Both aspects of this definition are important. Certainly affirmations of women's equality show progress in a tradition that taught for centuries, thanks to Aristotle, that females were a lesser form of humanity than males. Affirmations of women's equal human dignity achieve little, however, if they are not accompanied by efforts to remedy the twin injustices of sexism, namely patriarchy and androcentrism. Patriarchy literally means "father rule." As an ethical term it designates social patterns of domination and subordination, especially (but not exclusively) those flowing from attitudes that do not respect the full humanity of females. Such attitudes, which revolve around the experiences of males, are termed androcentric.

Androcentric attitudes include not only viewing women as inferior to men, but also seeing them as so essentially different from men that their roles must be circumscribed, or "special." Sometimes in the latter case women are thought to be superior in specified ways, but when thus placed on a pedestal they are deprived of rights and opportunities that ought to be recognized. When Cardinal James Gibbons opposed women's suffrage in an interview for the *New York Globe* on June 22, 1911, he exemplified this "essentialist" thinking: "Why should a woman lower herself to sordid politics?...When a woman enters the political arena, she goes outside the sphere for which she was intended."

Certainly Pope John Paul II did not oppose women's suffrage, but his teaching on gender roles and his emphasis on a special "genius" of women betray a type of androcentrism that is increasingly seen as problematic. Many of Pope Francis's statements about women are also tinged by this essentialist understanding of human nature, which sees women as complementary to men in ways that effectively limit women's contributions.[7] There are of course women who share such an understanding of women's nature, but the problems in this position quickly become evident if we imagine a situation in which all sacramental and decision-making power in the church were in the hands of women. If such an imaginary female prelate were to call for an infusion of "the masculine genius" into this woman-dominated structure, would that not seem condescending?

Although Pope Francis gives evidence of androcentric thinking, I believe his commitment to initiating processes of reform that allow for the voicing of divergent views is promising where justice for women is concerned. Clearly he recognizes that women should have greater influence in the church, and his actions in washing the feet of young women on Holy Thursday and allowing the investigations of U.S. women religious to be ended without imposing strict new controls on women's communities and their officers give reason for hope. In an article on "Women in the Church in the Age of Francis" for *A Matter of Spirit* (Summer 2015) I discuss these matters more fully. Here I will conclude by listing several issues that deserve prayer and reflection now that the official investigations of U.S. women religious and LCWR have ended in a friendly way:

1. Is the gender-based imbalance of power in Catholicism that made the Apostolic Visitation and Doctrinal Investigation possible in the first place a human construct subject to reform, or a divinely established order to be maintained despite cultural change? This is the fundamental theological issue at the heart of the recent controversy.

2. How should we address the sociological reality of the dramatic decline of younger Catholics' involvement in the church, and the historic shift, noted by Patricia Wittberg, SC, in "A Lost Generation?" in *America* (February 20, 2012), to a situation where fewer young Catholic women are interested in religious vocations than young men?

3. How much change in opportunities for women is optimal in the global church, and how can it best be introduced?

4. How can the diversity of perspectives (on feminism and other topics) be accommodated in a spirit of charity and unity?

5. How can feminists come to appreciate that hierarchy is not necessarily patriarchal, or based on claims of ontological superiority, but can be simply a way of arranging for administration and accountability in a large, complex institution?

Notes

1. See Dan Stockman, Joshua J. McElwee, and Dawn Cherie Araujo, "Visitation ends with praise for US sisters," *National Catholic Reporter* (January 2–15, 2015), 1, 6–7.

2. http://www.scribd.com/doc/262046698/Vatican-announcement-on-end-of-LCWR-mandate.

3. Patricia Walter, "Situating the Apostolic Visitation in Historical and Theological Context," in *Power of Sisterhood: Women Religious Tell the Story of the Apostolic Visitation*, ed. Margaret Cain McCarthy and Mary Ann Zollmann (Lanham, MD: University Press of America, 2014), 24.

4. Anne E. Patrick, *Conscience and Calling: Ethical Reflections on Catholic Women's Church Vocations* (New York: Bloomsbury, 2013), 4–5.

5. Christine Firer Hinze, "At Cross Currents? The Vatican, U.S. sisters and the LCWR," June 18, 2012; http://americamagazine.org/content/article.cjm?article_id=134567 (accessed June 23, 2012).

6. Anne E. Patrick, *Liberating Conscience: Feminist Explorations in Liberation Theology* (New York: Bloomsbury Academic, 1997), 7–8.

7. See Anne E. Patrick, "Women in the Church in the Age of Francis," *A Matter of Spirit* (Summer 2015), www.ipjc.org/journal/AMOSSummer15.pdf. Michael G. Lawler and Todd Salzman provide a valuable comparison of these two popes' positions in "Pope Francis brings nuance to notion of complementarity," May 29, 2015, http://ncronline.org/news/theology/pope-francis-brings-nuance-notion-complementarity (accessed August 27, 2015).

21

THE GIFT OF PAPAL SILENCE

In this response to the papal synod of 2013, Anne Patrick expresses her insight that Pope Francis was not only encouraging change but also doing so in a wide range of ways, from direct and forceful statements in certain circumstances to carefully considered silence in this case. Especially acute was the analysis she expressed elsewhere very early in his papacy about his predilection for carefully preparing the ground for future change, a position that was to be confirmed by many of his subsequent actions. —HD

In the months since his election in March 2013, Pope Francis has been more than generous with his words. There have been addresses, homilies, conversations, phone calls, interviews with the press, and, among other writings, a lengthy apostolic exhortation on "The Joy of the Gospel" (*Evangelii Gaudium*), released last November. At the same time, the pope has been silent, or very reticent on certain questions.

These days Catholics are wondering whether the discussions at the special Synod of Bishops that met in Rome, October 5–19, 2015, will lead to any changes in teaching or pastoral practice concerning marriage and the family, and whether women will ever be eligible for ordination and decision-making roles in the church. As they ponder these questions, they may find it helpful to be reminded of something that communications expert Kathleen Hall Jamieson said at the time of Saint John Paul II's visit to the United States in 1987. In response to a newscaster's question, "Does papal teaching ever change?" Jamieson declared: "Yes, papal teaching does change. But only after there has been a period of papal silence on the question."

In preparing for the recent synod, Pope Francis showed strong leadership in planning for the process of the meeting, but did not disclose

Published online; Anne E. Patrick, "The Gift of Papal Silence," NCR Online Global Sisters Report *(April 14, 2015); www.globalsistersreport.org/node/23291.*

his desires regarding specific results. Using a model he experienced as a member of the Latin American Conference of Bishops (CELAM), the pope invited 174 members of the hierarchy, and 54 nonvoting observers and experts, to discuss "the pastoral challenges of the family in the context of evangelization." He expected their discussions to result in a report that could profitably be considered by dioceses around the world in preparation for a follow-up synod next year, after which he would release a papal "apostolic exhortation" on these matters.

A preliminary report issued midway during the synod expressed a remarkable new tone of openness, and the final report maintained this tone to a lesser extent and gave evidence of disagreements among the bishops on various questions. Highlighting his esteem for a transparent process, Pope Francis called for publication of the entire report, including the record of how many synod members approved or disagreed with each paragraph. Included in the final report are three paragraphs concerning gay people and the availability of sacraments to divorced and remarried Catholics, which had not received the two-thirds majority support awarded the rest of the document. This effectively leaves the topics on the table for further consideration in the years ahead.

At the close of the synod the pope exhorted synod members in general terms to go out and find the "lost sheep" it is their duty to feed, while steering a middle course between excessive rigor and "false mercy." Significantly, Pope Francis has not said what specific changes in church teaching or practice he would like to see recommended by the 2015 synod. Rather he trusts that the Holy Spirit will guide the extended process of discussion and reflection, and that any needed adjustments to church teaching and practice will eventually emerge from this process. Very likely he also hopes that his example and his general emphasis on pastoral mercy will influence the process, but at this point he is neither emphasizing official doctrine nor calling for change in Catholic teachings and pastoral practices regarding marriage and family life. He will, of course, have an important opportunity to voice his position in the apostolic exhortation that is expected to come after the 2015 synod.

Many Catholics would like to have seen women have a stronger voice in the synod, and regret that only a small number of married women and one woman religious were invited, with voting reserved to members of the hierarchy. It represents progress that some 25 women were able to participate in the synod as observers or experts, but all of the 183 prelates who voted were male.

Although Pope Francis stated in *Evangelii Gaudium* that "demands that the legitimate rights of women be respected, based on the firm conviction that men and women are equal in dignity, present the church with profound and challenging questions that cannot lightly be evaded," he has not judged this to be the time for confronting these questions or for finding a "possible role of women in decision-making in different areas of the church's life." All of those voting at the synod were ordained, and, as Catholics know well, women are ineligible for ordination to the priesthood or episcopacy. Pope John Paul II forbade discussion of women's ordination to the priesthood, and Pope Benedict XVI reinforced his predecessor's teachings and approved severe penalties for those involved in "attempted ordinations" of women.

Nevertheless, many Catholics worldwide, and especially in Europe and North America, have voiced a readiness for women's ordination. The organization Women's Ordination Worldwide, in fact, is planning a meeting for September 18–20, 2015 in Philadelphia, shortly before Pope Francis is expected to come to the United States. Under the theme, "Gender, Gospel, and Global Justice," participants will "explore the interconnection between the exclusion of women from leadership roles in the Catholic Church and the global impact the Church has on women and girls." Clearly the question is not going away.

In assessing the first year of this papacy, Vatican expert Thomas Reese, SJ, noted in the *National Catholic Reporter* (March 14, 2014) that because of his overwhelming emphasis on compassion, love, and concern for the poor, Pope Francis has "rebranded Catholicism and the papacy," and changed the impression that the church is mainly concerned with opposing abortion, gay marriage, and birth control. Reese indicated that Pope Francis has undertaken promising steps toward reforming the Vatican bureaucracy, but suffers the limitations of coming from a culture "that is patriarchal and paternalistic."

In some of his remarks, Pope Francis may have been attempting to overcome these limitations, as when he gave an informal press conference during a flight from Brazil to Rome in July 2013. At that time he observed, "The role of women doesn't end just with being a mother and with housework...we don't yet have a truly deep theology of women in the church. We talk about whether they can do this or that...but we don't have a deep theology of women in the church." He went on to state: "On the ordination of women, the church has spoken and said no. John Paul II, in a definitive formulation, said that door is closed."

In declaring that "we don't have a deep theology of women in the church," Pope Francis spoke rightly of the official church literature, which has not yet incorporated the excellent theology that members of the church have published since the 1970s. The People of God already have access to some very deep theology of women in the writings of Elizabeth Johnson, Margaret Farley, Rosemary Radford Ruether, and many others, and one can hope that eventually their insights will be claimed by the official tradition. It seems significant that the pope stressed in a September 2013 interview for *America* that "The image of the church I like is that of the holy, faithful people of God," and also said that "We should not...think...that 'thinking with the church' means only thinking with the hierarchy."

Pope Francis sees reform as a long process that requires "dialogue among the people and the bishops and the pope" with the assistance of God's Spirit, and he has stated that today's challenge is "to think about the specific place of women also in those places where the authority of the church is exercised..." Still, on the plane from Brazil, and in subsequent remarks, Pope Francis has reminded us that Pope John Paul II said "no" to the question of ordaining women priests and bishops, though he did not address the question of diaconate. This "papal no" may remind some Catholics of the passage from the Gospel of Mark (7:24–30), in which Jesus said "no" to the Greek woman from Syria who requested a cure for her child. We have Mark's report that when she argued with Jesus, he changed his position, and told her that as a reward for what she had pointed out, the demon had left her daughter. The question of priestly ordination for women may not be as settled as some believe. After all, Pope Francis only said "the door is closed." He did not say it is nailed shut and sealed for all eternity.

In his first extensive papal document, *Evangelii Gaudium*, the pope elaborates a similar position, seeking to enhance the status of women in the church without opening the possibility of ordination. He describes his aim with a musical metaphor: he wants to transpose all church activity "into a missionary key," a tonality that speaks to the challenges of today. Catholic feminists are likely to hear more than he meant to say when Pope Francis declared, "No to an economy of exclusion," and "No to the inequality that spawns violence." The pope may have been speaking of the economically marginalized when he wrote, in paragraph 59, "When a society...is willing to leave a part of itself on the fringes, no political programs or resources spent on law enforcement or surveillance systems can indefinitely guarantee tranquility." Some Catholics, however, will hear different overtones in such words, perhaps thinking of the ineffectiveness of visitations to communities of sisters, and public rebukes to their leaders.

Women are discussed more directly in a section about laypeople headed "Other Ecclesial Challenges." Paragraphs 103 and 104 deal directly with women, and they suggest that Francis shares the "complementarity" anthropology of his predecessors, viewing women as essentially different from men, and gifted with particular qualities, though he qualifies this position somewhat. "The church acknowledges the indispensable contribution that women make to society through the sensitivity, intuition and other distinctive skill sets that they, more than men, tend to possess." He acknowledges that "many women share pastoral responsibilities with priests," and says "we need to create still broader opportunities for a more incisive female presence in the church."

We can see what feminist scholars regard as "essentialism" when he quotes the Pontifical Council for Justice and Peace in paragraph 103: "Because 'the feminine genius is needed in all expressions in the life of society, the presence of women must also be guaranteed in the workplace,' and in the various other settings where important decisions are made, both in the church and in social structures." He goes on in paragraph 104 to say, "Demands that the legitimate rights of women be respected, based on the firm conviction that men and women are equal in dignity, present the church with profound and challenging questions that cannot be lightly evaded," and immediately adds, "The reservation of the priesthood to males, as a sign of Christ the Spouse who gives himself in the Eucharist, is not a question open to discussion, but it can prove especially divisive if sacramental power is too closely identified with power in general." Priesthood, he insists, is "always a service to God's people." He recognizes that "This presents a great challenge for pastors and theologians, who are in a position to recognize more fully what this entails with regard to the possible role of women in decision-making in different areas of the church's life."

Although the anthropology and position on ordination in this section are disappointing to many, Pope Francis allows for the possibility that views of women's nature and roles can develop, after further reflection involving others in the church. Indeed, it is very important that he concludes this section on ecclesial challenges by stating in paragraph 108, "I have not sought to offer a complete diagnosis, but I invite communities to complete and enrich these perspectives on the basis of their awareness of the challenges facing them and their neighbors." He advocates listening to the elderly, who have "memory and experience" and to the young, who "represent new directions for humanity and open us up to the future, lest we cling to a nostalgia for structures and customs that are no longer life-giving in today's world."

The tone of this paragraph is very different from that found in the writings of Popes John Paul II and Benedict XVI. To some extent such remarks undermine the earlier assertion that the door is closed on women's ordination, as does the pope's discussion of preaching as "a mother's conversation" in paragraph 139. If preaching is a maternal activity, should we not at least expect to see women deacons?

But on this question and on specific policies concerning marriage and family life, Pope Francis has been offering the kind of silence that Kathleen Hall Jamieson found to have been necessary before there can be change in papal teaching. Significantly, in saying "the door is closed" on the question of ordaining women, Pope Francis is not repeating the arguments of his predecessors. *He* is not going to discuss this matter, much less change the practice during his papacy. But he may be laying the groundwork for future change by setting in motion consultative processes toward other reforms that will challenge the clericalism and careerism that have blighted ordained ministry in the past.

Pope Francis recognizes that women should have a more prominent role in the church, but does not yet grasp, or does not feel it is the time to deal with, what many Catholics regard as a very problematic fact—namely, the fact that sacramental sex discrimination undermines claims to recognize the full human dignity of women. Those concerned about justice for women and girls in the church have reason to be hopeful that things will change for the better, but the process in a global church will require more time than many would like. The gospel image of yeast hidden in dough, which gradually leavens the whole loaf (Mt 13:33, Lk 13:21), may well apply to the way reforms take place in church history. Efforts by reformers are important to the process, but in God's providence they do not usually lead to immediate results. The leavening process takes a while. Pope Francis says something to this effect toward the end of *Evangelii Gaudium*, when he recommends in paragraph 223 that we be "concerned about initiating processes rather than possessing spaces." "What we need," he says, "is to give priority to actions which generate new processes in society and engage other persons and groups who can develop them to the point where they bear fruit in significant historical events. Without anxiety, but with clear convictions and tenacity."

How long it will be until the process bears fruit remains to be seen, and perhaps there will never be the sort of sacramental equality that many of us advocate. But history offers many examples of what was once thought to be the "last word" proving not to have been final after all. And there is reason to hope that the tone Pope Francis is setting, the processes he is starting, and the restrictions he has imposed on his own speech, will contribute much to the reforms we need. Maybe the silence of this pope will prove to have been a gift after all.

V

POSTLUDE

22

ON BEING UNFINISHED

(De Imperfectione)

Visitors to my office at Carleton College often notice the books shelved high on the walls. "So many books," they say. "Have you read them all?" "By no means," I confess, "but they come in handy."

There's not much room for art on these walls, but between the windows on the south wall I've hung my authentic globalized Indian blanket, which is to say a 10 x 20 inch Navajo pattern in black, white, and turquoise that was woven in a factory in India for sale to tourists in Colorado. And below that, in a 9-inch square frame, is the image I want to describe today.

This is a watercolor by the Navajo artist Harrison Begay, entitled "Navajo Weavers."[1] When I first saw it twenty years ago at the Philbrook Museum in Tulsa, I was enchanted. I liked the painting so much I bought two small copies in the museum shop. I had one framed for my office and affixed the other with clear contact paper to a folder I've carried in my briefcase ever since.

Begay has depicted two Navajo weavers, a woman and a girl seated on a light green rug before a loom made from rough tree branches. Wearing red dresses, their black hair neatly tied at the back, they are shown in profile at work on a rug that is not quite halfway finished. The rug has angular patterns that will feature central diamonds of red, gray, white, and black, encasing one another in progressively larger sizes. At this stage, however, we see only part of each diamond, and it looks like only one of them will fit on the rug when it is done. When will it be done? In about 180 hours, I'd guess, since it takes about 350 hours to weave a small rug this way.

Adapted from a commencement address (the Honors Convocation) given at Carleton College, Northfield, Minnesota, on May 29, 2009.

What arrested me about this painting, and what captures me still, is how the artist shows beauty in a project not even halfway completed. Our eyes tell us that the painting is already beautiful, and the rug will be beautiful, but I think what Harrison Begay wants us to appreciate is that the weaving process itself is beautiful, even at an early stage. The painting expresses the Navajo spiritual ideal of *hozho nasha*, of walking in beauty, indeed, of working in beauty—that is, doing our tasks in a balanced way, in harmony with the created universe.

Seeing beauty in the incomplete, however, is not something our academic culture encourages, as we all know when our papers are not finished and a deadline looms large. From admonitions in childhood to "finish your peas and carrots" and "finish your homework," we get the impression that we'll be more acceptable and better off, maybe even happier, when we finish whatever it is we are doing. But I'm not so sure this impression is right. The overemphasis on being finished can sap a lot of the joy out of life, for most of the time when we have a work-in-progress, by definition we haven't finished what we are working on.

The "Navajo Weavers" painting reminds me of the paradox of the creative life. Most of the time we are not finished with what we are doing, and I think we would do well to get comfortable with our unique creative process and celebrate the beauty in what is not quite here but on its way-into-being. At the same time we need to devote ourselves to this process in view of the goal of completing, in timely fashion, the tasks we've set for ourselves. What I take from the Begay painting, which draws our eyes to the beauty in what is underway, is the certainty that I'm much better off focusing on the row where I'm weaving than I am looking up at the plain gray warp and lamenting the fact that I haven't finished the rug yet.

I believe we are all creatively gifted, though we exercise our creativity in different ways. I've long agreed with the educator E. Paul Torrance who wrote, "Creative abilities are inherited to the extent that a person inherits his sense organs, a peripheral nervous system, and a brain."[2] I've also appreciated what psychologist Donald MacKinnon learned from his study of "highly effective individuals" at Berkeley decades ago. MacKinnon refers to something he calls the "briefcase syndrome of creativity":

One of the most striking observations we have made [in our study of highly effective individuals] is that the creative person seldom fits the layman's stereotype of him. In our experience, he is not the emotionally unstable, sloppy, loose-jointed Bo-

hemian … [of popular imagination. Instead] we discover ourselves using such adjectives as deliberate, reserved, industri-
ous, and thorough to describe truly original and creative persons
… The truly creative individual has an image of himself as a responsible person and a sense of destiny about himself as a
human being.[3]

MacKinnon's words catalyzed for me years ago the sense that creativity and ethics are linked through this notion of responsibility. I
think his final sentence characterizes most of the Carleton students I've
taught. To repeat, paraphrasing for the sake of inclusivity: "The truly
creative individual has an image of [herself] as a responsible person
and a sense of destiny about [herself] as a human being."[4]

This year I have been doing research on creativity and the moral
life, and in particular four topics I've been learning about: imperfection, creativity, flow, and attention. Continuing with Begay's theme of
diamonds, let's imagine a softball field, and I am coaching at the bases.
On first base I'll talk about the Latin title of this presentation, *"De Imperfectione."* As an honors convocation address, I wanted to offer something in the classical tradition of Cicero "On Friendship," or Longinus
"On the Sublime." I came up with "On Being Unfinished," and with
help from a colleague, I found that this translates pretty well as *"De Imperfectione,"* a phrase connoting an essential quality of the creative life,
namely acceptance of the imperfection of our best efforts.

Legend has it that in some spiritual traditions rug makers deliberately weave a mistake into their rugs as testimony to the fact that only
the divine is perfect. We may not want to go that far with our own projects, but as we approach them it is important to turn down the critical
speaker of our internal stereo system. The internal critic, by the way,
only gets stronger with education, and so the further we advance the
more crucial it becomes to keep our internal critic quiet when we are
starting to work out our ideas. The time for critiquing and revising our
work is after it is well underway, not when we are just beginning. In
order to get to first base with our senior projects or our novel, we must
quiet the internal critic and make a start—even before we feel we are
ready to begin. We shouldn't let the elusive quest for a home run make
us freeze up at the plate. Whether we get to first base with a solid hit,
or a bunt, or a walk or being hit by a pitch, the point is to get there—to
get the project started and trust that the teammates of our creative abilities will find a way to bring us home.

By now you should be on second base, and I turn to creativity. You
can learn much about your own creativity by reading about the lives of

eminently creative people. A good place to start is Mihalyi Csikszentmihalyi's 1996 book on creativity and the psychology of discovery and
invention. Csikszentmihalyi and his University of Chicago research
team interviewed ninety-one individuals, including the novelists Na-
dine Gordimer and Naguib Mafouz, the founder of Citizens for Clean
Air Hazel Henderson, the historian John Hope Franklin, the discoverer
of a vaccine against polio Jonas Salk, the poets May Sarton and Denise
Levertov, and the Nobel-prizewinning scientists Linus Pauling and
Rosalyn Yalow. Among the things he learned was that these highly successful persons from diverse fields shared some characteristics. Prominent among them was the fact that they tended to take on large and
long-term projects, and were motivated to persevere in their usually
unfinished work by the "quality of the experience they felt when they
were involved with the activity."[5] Csikszentmihalyi has described this
experience in an earlier book, called *Flow*, and as you advance to third
base I'll describe this concept.

"Flow" is the psychological state we experience when our talents
are fully engaged and our attention entirely focused on the activity at
hand. We may know it when reading, solving a puzzle, playing tennis,
composing a letter or a painting. The theory of flow assumes that the
mind's natural state is chaotic and unfocused, and thus we are easily
bored, anxious, or depressed. To understand "flow," picture a two-dimensional grid where a base line represents a situation that presents no
challenges to our abilities, and where as a result we feel bored. Then
imagine a vertical line representing challenges that exceed our abilities—the five-page paper due in ten minutes, for example—and here the
feeling is one of anxiety. Now imagine a diagonal line that slopes up
from the corner where the base and the vertical line meet. Along that diagonal, where our talents are fully engaged but not unreasonably taxed,
is the experience of flow. "[I]n flow it is clear what has to be done, and
our skills are potentially adequate to the challenges."[6] We are so involved in the activity that we lose track of everything else, including
time. We are "in the moment," and it is a pleasurable experience.

As our talents develop, we will seek greater challenges that enhance
the pleasure of discovery and novelty in the activities that give us the
experience of flow. We will want an intermediate tennis league, or a Su-
doku puzzle with three stars, or to compose an opera. We will crave
with all our hearts a way to halt the spread of AIDS, or to reduce the in-
cidence of gun violence, or to improve the U.S. health care system.

Finally, as you head for home plate, a word on attention. Attention
is a limited commodity, and in order to experience "flow," one needs to
focus. It is necessary to discipline our creative desires as well as to kin-

dle them. We cannot work on everything at once. As Csikszentmihalyi has observed, "our nervous system cannot handle more than a limited amount of information in consciousness at the same time, and we cannot attend to more than a few things at a time."[7] Multi-tasking has its limits, and three Carleton students were on to something last year when they tried fasting from computers for a month, freeing their minds from the attention-grabbing powers of Facebook, You-Tube, and e-mail. We may not be able to disconnect ourselves from computers and cell phones for more than a brief period, but I believe we are wise to set some boundaries, and protect our powers of concentration so that we can attend to what is of central importance. Practices such as meditation, Sabbath observance, or running can enhance our ability to focus and attend.

Part of the beauty we see in "Navajo Weavers" comes from the fact that there is just one loom calling for attention. I hope Navajo painter Harrison Begay and I have encouraged you to enjoy the process a bit more. I congratulate the seniors who are completing college, and are well equipped now to continue learning and take joy in creative projects all your lives. I also congratulate the students being honored today for outstanding work, and I hope you have experienced a good measure of beauty in the process of compiling the writing portfolios, entering the contests, and conducting the research that led to your awards. Whether or not your name is on this year's program of honors, I honor all who have taken courses and undertaken projects with great potential for learning, whatever the effect on their G.P.A.

Last week I asked several graduating students about their senior projects and particularly whether they had enjoyed the process of working on them. Five out of five of those surveyed answered that yes, it had been an enjoyable process. This is a large and long project, but it is intended to be a satisfying one, one that will teach you about your own process of working as well as about the content you have selected. So as you set up your loom and get the threads ready to weave, know that there is beauty in the process as well as in what you will produce. May you work in beauty—to enjoy the process of working with what is incomplete and imperfect until it is time to let it go—as you weave your own texts or textiles, or whatever project you undertake.

Notes

1. Harrison Begay, "Navajo Weavers," Watercolor, 1948. Philbrook Museum of Art, Tulsa, Oklahoma.

2. E. Paul Torrance, "Nurture of Creative Talents," in *Explorations in Creativity*, ed. Ross L. Mooney and Taher A. Razik (New York: Harper & Row, 1967), 185.

3. Donald W. MacKinnon, "The Highly Effective Individual," in *Explorations in Creativity*, ed. Ross L. Mooney and Taher A. Razik (New York: Harper & Row, 1967), 65.

4. Ibid., 65.

5. Mihaly Csikszentmihalyi, *Creativity: Flow and the Psychology of Discovery and Invention* (New York: HarperCollins, 1996), 110.

6. Mihaly Csikszentmihalyi, *Flow: The Psychology of Optimal Experience* (New York: Harper & Row, 1996), 112.

7. Ibid., 426.

23

A Homily
in the Context of Anointing

With frankness and grace in more than one sense of that second term,
Anne Patrick explains that she interprets the Bible "not as literal
statements of how things actually are between God and her creatures,
but as limited human records of how our forebears experienced the
Mystery at the heart of creation." This telling example of her process
of interpretation and reinterpretation recalls her reply to a secular
friend who asked what she believed about the afterlife: "I am sure that
in some sense our spirit remains." —HD

All you who are thirsty, come to the water!
You who have no money, come, receive grain and eat;
Come, without paying and without cost, drink wine and milk!
Why spend your money for what is not bread;
Your wages for what fails to satisfy? (Isaiah 55:1–2a)

Come to me, all you who labor and are burdened, and I will
give you rest. Take my yoke upon you and learn from me, for I
am meek and humble of heart; and you will find rest for your-
selves. For my yoke is easy and my burden light. (Mt 11:28–30)

Thank you for coming to pray with and for me today! There's nothing
like illness to make us aware how *interdependent* we are; I know that
your kindness and support will be a great help to me as I adjust to having cancer and face the treatments ahead. What am I dealing with?
Why did I ask Father Jon for this ritual?

Suddenly last month, after decades of fine health, I got a whole new
agenda. I have a rare form of breast cancer, one that doesn't show up in

---

Held November 12, 2002, at Carleton College Chapel, Northfield, Minnesota.

the breast but instead has taken up residence in my lymph system and now has its eye on some upscale housing in my vital organs. To protect these places I plan to start chemotherapy very soon. Already, with wonderful help from colleagues, I have scaled back my work, though I still hope to teach one course in winter and spring terms, and believe this will be good for my health. I'm counting on students to help me in many ways—but working to the best of your abilities, by visiting me in the office, by inviting me to a meal now and then, by walking or skiing with me in the arboretum, and by keeping me in your prayers.

As soon as I got the diagnosis, I knew it was time to ask for the Sacrament of the Sick. In the last couple of weeks I've been blessed, anointed, and prayed over in Minneapolis, St. Paul, Maryland, and now here. I'm grateful to Father Jon, Theresa Engel, and the readers from the Newman Club, Chaplain Carolyn Fure-Slocum and the chapel associates, Larry Archbold, and to all of you for coming.

This is an occasion for me to draw strength for whatever lies ahead, and to reflect theologically on a problem that occupies us all, namely the mystery of suffering. Not just the suffering caused by my cancer, but also that brought on by last month's plane crash, yesterday's tornadoes, and alas, what seems likely to be tomorrow's war. All of this is beyond my ability to grasp, even the small piece of illness that has turned my life around.

My case of cancer is rife with mystery. I don't know why these cells have gone haywire, the doctors don't know why either, and they can't even find the cancer's primary location. And although we start treatment with great hope for improvement, we don't really know what will result from medical efforts. So where is God for me in all of this?

Well, the time has come to confess—that I read the Bible and other things from my tradition very selectively. I view these texts not as literal statements of how things actually are between God and her creatures, but as limited human records of how our forebears experienced the Mystery at the heart of existence.

I think sometimes those forebears got it wrong, particularly when they assumed that Divine Power intervenes directly in natural and historical processes. I disagree vehemently with those who think that tornadoes, plane crashes, HIV, and other packages of trouble are sent to us by God for some reason that we'll understand sooner or later. I just don't think that way. I don't think God intervenes in history in any such fashion. Instead, I think the things that cause suffering result from a mix of determinate and indeterminate factors in nature, which include but are not limited to that reality we treasure so much at Carleton College, which goes by the name of "human freedom."

So, if God isn't responsible for the packages of trouble, where is God in these events? What I find most true in the biblical record of people's experience of God, imperfect and limited though it may be, is the conviction that God is the one who wants our wellbeing, our deliverance from evil. God's care for me in this illness is already evident in the ways medical technicians try to ease my fears of needles and noisy machines, and in the kindness of doctors and nurses trying to restore me to health. And God's care is richly seen in the ways the people around me have shown their love and support.

I must also confess that I am by no means the first one to read the tradition selectively. Today's readings from scripture themselves were *selected* because they affirm the truest thing we know, namely that the Mystery into which we ultimately fall will give us what we need—relief from hunger and thirst, whether literal or metaphorical, and rest from our anxiety and troubles.

Handel did some wonderful things with these words from Isaiah 55, to my mind even better than he did with that word "hallelujah." "Come unto me, all you who labor... and you shall find rest unto your souls."

How to respond well to adversity is the challenge I now face, and I hope with your help to do so creatively. I could do a lot worse than some Franciscan sisters did after a tornado devastated their frontier town in 1883. These women rolled up their ample brown sleeves and said, let's build a hospital and ask a family of physicians we know to staff it. Yes, a Catholic nun's response to evil is a part of the causal chain resulting in the Mayo Clinic. And those Rochester Franciscan sisters have a little gift for you today, the prayer traditionally associated with their founder, St. Francis, but maybe the real author is St. Clare or some other woman. I wouldn't be surprised.

What matters more than authorship is that this prayer knows something about causality. It knows that God's peace, God's healing, or any of the goodness we attribute to Divine Power needs human instruments.

So what? So what if our traditions aren't yet all they should be. The closing hymn for this service is a case in point. I heard it very selectively in church the Sunday after the [Paul] Wellstone campaign ended so tragically. I mainly remembered the tune ("What Wondrous Love Is This") and a few of the lines, and I asked Chaplain Carolyn if we could end with it today. I leave it to you to guess which lines I would rephrase if I had time, and which lines I would leave intact. And I thank you with all my heart for coming to sing and pray with me today!

[*Anne E. Patrick died on July 21, 2016 in Silver Spring, Maryland.*]

What Wondrous Love

1 What wondrous love is this, O my soul, O my soul!
What wondrous love is this, O my soul!
What wondrous love is this that caused the Lord of bliss
to bear the dreadful curse for my soul, for my soul,
to bear the dreadful curse for my soul?

2 When I was sinking down, sinking down, sinking down,
when I was sinking down, sinking down;
when I was sinking down beneath God's righteous frown,
Christ laid aside his crown for my soul, for my soul,
Christ laid aside his crown for my soul.

3 To God and to the Lamb, I will sing, I will sing,
to God and to the Lamb, I will sing;
to God and to the Lamb who is the great I AM—
while millions join the theme, I will sing, I will sing;
while millions join the theme, I will sing.

4 And when from death I'm free, I'll sing on, I'll sing on,
and when from death I'm free, I'll sing on;
and when from death I'm free, I'll sing and joyful be,
and through eternity, I'll sing on, I'll sing on,
and through eternity I'll sing on.

*

INDEX